The Vatican
Its History—Its Treasures

Published by
Letters and Arts Publishing Co.
New York

FOREWORD

The need of a standard work on the Vatican, as the great centre of ancient and modern culture, suggested the idea of the present volume.

The first step of the Editors, when they entered upon their task over two years ago, was to secure for each division of their subject the writer who was peculiarly fitted above all others to do it full justice. Their next care was to arrange with these authors for the illustration of all those important features of the Vatican which arouse the interest and admiration of visitors to Rome. A large proportion of the photographs used were taken specially for the present work with the permission of the Vatican authorities, and not a few are of objects never before photographed.

The large number and inherent value of these illustrations give a unique interest to the present volume. The names of the contributing authors are a sufficient guarantee as to the value of the text.

Having entrusted the printing of this book to The De Vinne Press—a household synonym for artistic work—the Editors hope to have satisfied the most exacting expectation of beautiful book-making.

October, 1914.

CONTRIBUTING AUTHORS

—

COMMENDATORE CORRADO RICCI
Director-General of the Department of Antiquities and Fine Arts under
the Italian Government, formerly Director of the Brera in Milan.

COMMENDATORE ORAZIO MARUCCHI
Archæologist of the Sacred Palaces, Director of the Vatican Egyptian Museum and
of the Lateran Christian Museum, Professor of Christian Archæology
at the University of Rome and at the Istituto di Propaganda.

MONSIGNOR PAUL MARIA BAUMGARTEN, J.U.D., S.T.D.
Member of the Prussian Historical Institute at Rome, Domestic Prelate to the Pope.

DR. FEDERICO HERMANIN DE REICHENFELD
Director of the National Gallery, Rome.

DR. ALESSANDRO DELLA SETA
Professor of the Royal University of Genoa.

DR. LEANDRO OZZOLA
Inspector of the Royal Gallery of Ancient Art and of the
National Cabinet of Prints at Rome.

DR. ANTONIO MUÑOZ
Royal Inspector of Roman Monuments, Professor of the History of Medieval and
Modern Art at the University of Rome.

COMMENDATORE LUIGI CAVENAGHI
Director of the Vatican Picture Gallery, Artistic Director of the Vatican Museums,
Member of the Roman Superior Council of Fine Arts, Member of the
Ambrosian Academy of Fine Arts, Academic Councillor
of the Royal Academy of the Brera.

BARON RODOLFO KANZLER
Director of the Vatican Christian Museum.

COMMENDATORE BARTOLOMEO NOGARA
Director of the Gregorian Etruscan and Profane Museums, Member of the
Archæological Commission of Rome.

DR. UGO MONNERET DE VILLARD
Professor of the Polytechnic of Milan.

COMMENDATORE CAMILLO SERAFINI
Director of the Vatican and Capitoline Numismatic Collections, Fellow of the
Pontifical Academy of Archæology.

PROFESSOR SALVATORE NOBILI
Director of the Vatican Mosaic Factory.

—

Editors

ERNESTO BEGNI, J.D.   JAMES C. GREY, Ph.D., B.C.L.

THOMAS J. KENNEDY, B.A.

CONTENTS

—

Part I

HISTORY AND GENERAL DESCRIPTION OF THE VATICAN PALACES AND GARDENS

Part II

THE STATE APARTMENTS AND CHAPELS

Part III

THE VATICAN MUSEUMS AND COLLECTIONS AND THE MOSAIC FACTORY

CONTENTS

PART IV

LIST OF ILLUSTRATIONS

THE LOGGIE OF RAPHAEL

PAGE

Door leading to the Loggie (Sixteenth Century) 168
Loggia of Raphael 169
The First Toil of Man (Raphael and Pupils) 170
Lot and His Family Leaving Sodom (Raphael and Pupils) 171
Another Loggia 172
Isaac and Rebecca (Raphael and Pupils) 173
Jacob and Rachel (Raphael and Pupils) 174
Portion of a Loggia 175
Moses saved from the Nile (Raphael and Pupils) 176
Candelabra in the Loggia decorated by Mantovani 177
Detail of the Ornaments in the Pilasters (Raphael and Pupils) . . 177
Decorations showing the Arms of Gregory XIII over a Door in the Loggie 177
Candelabra (Mascherini, Sermoneta and Nogari) 177
Moses Presenting the Law to the People (Raphael and Pupils) . . 178
David and Bathsheba (Raphael and Pupils) 179
Door showing the Arms of Clement VII (Sixteenth Century) 180
Solomon and the Queen of Sheba (Raphael and Pupils) 181
Door showing the Arms of Gregory XIII (Sixteenth Century) 182
The Adoration of the Magi (Raphael and Pupils) 183

THE NEW PICTURE GALLERY

One of the Halls in the Old Picture Gallery 190
The Ceiling of a Hall in the Old Picture Gallery (L. B. Alberti) . . 191
The Hall of the Trecento or Primitives 192
The Hall of the Trecento 193
The Hall of the Quattrocento, or Melozzo Hall 194
The Madonna and Child, with Saints and Angels (Fra Angelico) . . 195
Episodes from the Life of St. Nicholas of Bari (Fra Angelico) . . . 196
The Miracles of St. Vincent Ferrer (Francesco del Cossa) . . . 197
The Miracles of St. Vincent Ferrer (Francesco del Cossa) . . . 198
The Miracles of St. Vincent Ferrer (Francesco del Cossa) 199

THE NEW PICTURE GALLERY—Continued

PAGE

The Miracles of St. Vincent Ferrer (Francesco del Cossa) . . . 200
St. Jerome (Leonardo da Vinci) . . 201
Portrait of Francesco Sforza (Bernardino de' Conti) 201
Head of St. Jerome (Leonardo da Vinci) 202
Pope Sixtus IV and Il Platina (Melozzo da Forlì) 203
Details from Pope Sixtus IV and Il Platina (Melozzo da Forlì) . . 204
The Hall of the School of Umbria and the Marches 205
Madonna and Child (Francescuccio Ghissi) 206
The Camerino Triptych (Niccolò Alunno) 206
The Madonna della Spineta, or the Adoration of the Magi (Lo Spagna) 207
The Coronation of the Virgin (Pinturicchio) 207
The Virgin of the Rota (Antoniazzo Romano) 208
The Madonna Enthroned with Saints (Perugino) 209
The Coronation of the Virgin (Raphael) 210
The Madonna of Monteluce (designed by Raphael and painted by Giulio Romano and Penni) 210
The Annunciation (Raphael) . . . 211
The Adoration of the Magi (Raphael) 212
The Presentation in the Temple (Raphael) 213
The Madonna of Foligno (Raphael) . 214
Detail from the Transfiguration (Raphael) 215
The Transfiguration (Raphael) . . 217
Madonna and Child (Carlo Crivelli) . 218
Pieta (Carlo Crivelli) 219
The Madonna of St. Nicholas dei Frari (Titian) 220
St. George Slaying the Dragon (Paris Bordone) 220
Mary Magdalen Anointing the Dead Christ (Montagna) 222
The Deposition (Caravaggio) . . . 222
Detail from the Last Communion of St. Jerome (Domenichino) . . . 223
The Last Communion of St. Jerome (Domenichino) 224
The Martyrdom of St. Laurence (Ribera) 225
St. Margaret of Cortona (Il Guercino) 226
A Rest during the Flight into Egypt (Baroccio) 226

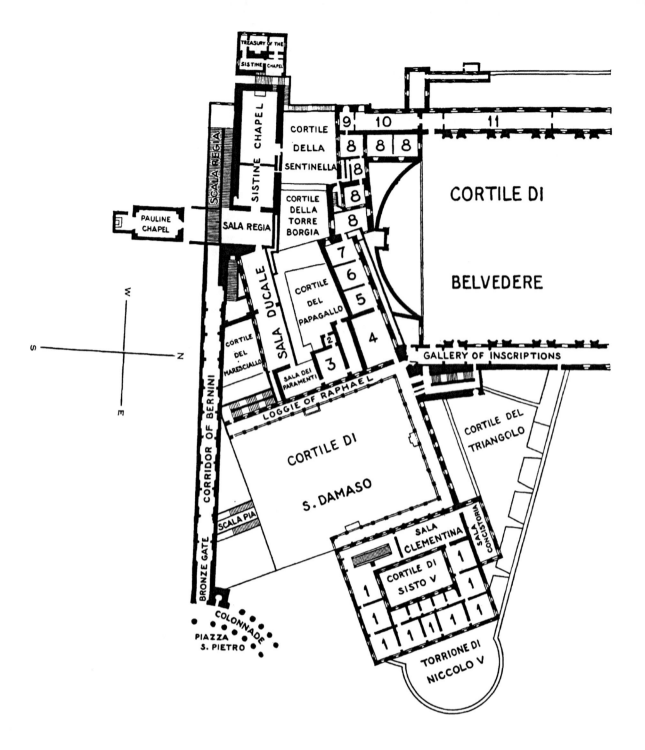

1 . Papal Apartments. .

2 . Chapel of Nicholas V.

3 . Sala dello Spogliatoio.

4–7 . (*Lower floor.*)   Appartamento Borgia.

4–7 . (*Upper floor.*)   Stanze of Raphael.

8 . Torre Borgia (including portion of the Appartamento Borgia).

9 . Chapel of Pius V.

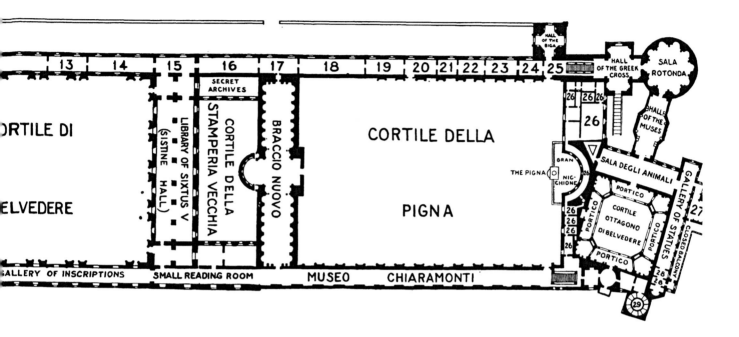

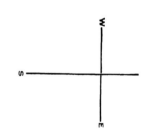

10–14 . (*Ground floor.*)   New Picture Gallery.

10–25 . (*First floor.*)   Halls of the Library, including the Christian Museum (11) (Cf. pp. 470–473).

10–25 . (*Second floor.*)   Gallery of Geographical Charts, Gallery of Tapestries, Gallery of the Candelabra.

26 . (*Lower floor.*)   Egyptian Museum.

26 . (*Upper floor.*)   Gregorian Etruscan Museum.

27 . Cabinet of the Masks.

28 . Hall of the Busts.

29 . Scala Bramante.

    The Mosaic Factory is situated under the Gallery of Inscriptions.

    The Numismatic Collection adjoins the Appartamento Borgia.

NOTE.—These plans are intended only to show the general location of the most important portions of the Vatican Palaces. Inasmuch as the arrangement of the rooms differs greatly on the different floors, more than approximate exactness could not be attained here.

PART ONE

—

HISTORY AND GENERAL DESCRIPTION OF THE VATICAN PALACES AND GARDENS

HISTORY AND GENERAL DESCRIPTION
OF THE VATICAN PALACES

SCIENTIFIC excavations always awaken a special and wide-spread interest, when the spade of the digger reaches the ruins of a royal palace or a lordly mansion, and begins to bring to the light the long-forgotten treasures of the past. Schliemann's achievements in this direction, to quote but a single example, held the whole world of culture breathless, and supplied so much information concerning the earliest periods of civilization that much time was needed for the scientific appraisal and proper coördination of his discoveries.

Why do such excavations especially arouse our interest? Doubtless the reason is simply that in the palaces of the great the civilization of a period is, as it were, focussed. Whatever valuable apparatus of a scientific, cultural, social, or material kind the men of an age possess, will naturally be represented by their choicest specimens in the mansions of the mighty and the wealthy, in the castles of the nobility, in the palace of the king. It is therefore not remarkable that archæologists engaged in extensive excavations rejoice beyond measure when they are so fortunate as to discover a handsome castle or the palace of a vanished dynasty.

And what holds good for relics long buried in the earth, holds also good, *mutatis mutandis,* for the royal palaces which remain standing to-day. We need only turn over the pages of the guides of the sixteenth century and their successors down to the modern Baedeker and Murray to be convinced of this fact, for we there find that, almost without exception, the seats of the rulers throughout the entire world of pagan and Christian civilization are described in detail as centres of special interest for pilgrims and travellers; and the older such palaces are, the further their history extends back into the past, the richer and more perfect, as a rule, is their equipment.

That so ancient a dynasty as that of the Popes—who, with a few exceptions, always resided in Rome—needed from the very beginning a large palace for the accommodation of the ecclesiastical court, for the reception of distinguished guests, and for other requirements, is seen from the fact that, at the same time as he removed the shackles of the Church, Constantine the Great assigned such a palace to its Pope. This was the Palace of the Laterani, an old Roman family; and from the name of this family the papal residence was briefly named the Lateran. In the course of the centuries this palace became so equipped with works of art of every kind that Dante declared there was no more beautiful residence on earth.

But when the Popes left Rome for a long interval in the fourteenth century, their palace fell into decay and suffered considerable damage from fire; and after the return of the Papacy to Rome, subsequent to the Council of Constance (1417), the Lateran never recovered its position as the centre of ecclesiastical life. The Popes went first to S. Maria in Trastevere, then to S. Maria Maggiore (the Quirinal), and finally to the Vatican. Since then the last-named palace has remained, practically without interruption, the residence of the Popes. This does not mean that they dwelt there uninterruptedly, especially during the sultry months of the year. Nor does it mean that attempts were not made to transfer elsewhere the chief papal residence permanently—for example, under Paul II, who had destined for this purpose the Palazzo di Venezia, which he erected. Nor, finally, does it mean that occasionally the Vatican did not remain unoccupied for long intervals. Still it is perfectly correct to say that, since the fifteenth century, the world has been accustomed to associate the term Vatican with the chief residence of the Popes.

All other papal palaces, whether in Rome, Viterbo, Perugia, Anagni, Avignon, Castel Gandolfo, or elsewhere, yield the palm to the Vatican without a protest.

While situated in a distant corner of Rome, the Lateran residence lay within the city walls and belonged to the city. The spot, however, where Christ's first Vicegerent on earth was martyred and buried lay outside the city, on the right bank of the Tiber. Over the grave of St. Peter Constantine the Great erected his glorious basilica. On this hallowed spot assembled crowds of pilgrims from all lands, and here the Popes repeatedly held the most glorious ecclesiastical functions. As most of the great feasts began on the Vigil—that is, on the afternoon preceding—the Pope had on such occasions to spend the night at St. Peter's with his whole retinue. Hence arose the urgent necessity of erecting in the vicinity a larger residence for the Pope. Again, in the course of time many princes and kings had to be received and lodged by the Pope near St. Peter's. Thus, under the force of circumstances, the originally modest residence developed into a great palace immediately adjacent to the Basilica Constantini. The Pope only did what the

General View of the Vatican Palaces and Gardens

Christian nations in Europe did in these early centuries for their subjects visiting Rome. In a small circle around St. Peter's arose pilgrim-houses for the Anglo-Saxons, the Germans, Oriental pilgrims, and so on. The grave of the Prince of the Apostles was thus surrounded by a number of more or less pretentious buildings, of which all served indirectly to show veneration to St. Peter. And all lay outside the city walls. It was a settlement of a peculiar kind which was there established. Without any orderly arrangement of streets, houses, numberless churches, and cemeteries were spread in an artistic group over the plain at the foot of Mount Vatican.

This settlement, however, was exposed to every hostile invasion. The Saracens on one occasion sacked the Basilica and all the adjacent buildings so thoroughly that Leo IV (847–855) determined to surround the Vatican Hill with walls. Of these a small portion, with two powerful towers, may be still seen in the Vatican Gardens. The settlement thus became a portion of the city, although as yet the municipal administration of Rome exercised no authority over the Vatican district. It was, indeed, not until the sixteenth century that the separate papal administration of the Leonine City (as the district was named, after Leo IV) was merged in the general administration of the City of Rome.

ARCHITECTURAL HISTORY.—Neglecting the maze of conjectures concerning the origin of the first dwelling of the Popes near St. Peter's, we meet the certain information that Pope Symmachus (498–514) built a palace immediately adjacent to the Basilica, on the left and right. What further buildings were erected there in the following centuries is not known. Under the Popes from Eugene III to Innocent III, inclusive (1145–1216), fairly extensive buildings grew up around St. Peter's, so that between the Portico of St. Peter and the Vatican Hill a very beautiful palace had arisen.

Pope Nicholas III (1277–1280) conceived magnificent plans for covering the Vatican Hill with buildings. He began the erection of a very extensive palace there, and this was brought to approximate completion by his immediate successors. By extensive purchases of land through his Apostolic Chamber (that is, the Papal Ministry of Finance), Nicholas assured to the Popes the undisturbed possession of the Vatican Hill and the surrounding property. The present Vatican Gardens represent a large portion of Nicholas's purchase.

In so far as the investigations into the history of the building of the old Apostolic Palace beside St. Peter's extend, and in so far as this history may be deduced from the masonry, we may state that the buildings erected by Nicholas and his successors occupied approximately the site where the western, southern, and eastern boundaries of the Cortile del Papagallo are now situated, and communicated with the buildings which lie around the Cortile del Maresciallo.

In 1305—a few years after the completion of this new palace, which stood high on the Vatican Hill and dominated the Basilica—the Archbishop of Bordeaux was elected Pope and took the title of Clement V. Instead of proceeding directly to the Curia and Sacred College at Perugia, he summoned them to meet him in southern France. If he

Part of the Piazza di S. Pietro, showing the Vatican Palace

ever seriously entertained the thought of going to Rome, he never put this plan into execution. For, after wandering irresolutely for a time in southern France, he finally settled in Avignon. Thus began the Avignon Exile of the Papacy, which lasted until the beginning of the great Western Schism in 1378, when the Anti-Pope Clement VII of Avignon opposed the rightful Pope (Urban VI) in Rome. The schism was finally settled by the election of Martin V at the Council of Constance in 1417, after which the Roman Pope (Martin V) was accepted by the whole Catholic world as the only and rightful successor of Peter. Another schism was indeed later caused by the Anti-Pope Felix V (1439–1449), whose name is closely associated with the Council of Basle, but it exercised no appreciable effect on the general peace of the Church.

The departure of the Popes from Rome to Avignon (1305) left the Eternal City desolate. Churches, streets, and palaces fell into decay; internal feuds caused grievous bloodshed; impoverished Rome sank away into insignificance. The general fate of the city was shared by the buildings around St. Peter's. The roofs leaked; the rains beat in through the windows; those who desired to pilfer building material from the edifices did so without interference.

The chief residence of the Popes had hitherto been the Lateran Palace, but a fierce fire had, as already remarked, almost completely gutted it. And thus it came to pass that the Popes of the fifteenth century adopted as their chief residence the Vatican Palace, which was gradually undergoing a complete restoration.

Where the visitor beholds to-day with wondering admiration the Loggie of Raphael, the state rooms of the Appartamento Borgia, and the Stanze of Raphael, Nicholas V (1447–1455) undertook to build an extension to the existing buildings. At the end of the same century Alexander VI (1492–1503) erected a strong tower immediately adjacent (the Torre Borgia), which, being now deprived of its militant crown, conveys no longer the impression of a tower.

The south side of the old palace was beautified by Pius II (1458–1464) and Paul II (1464–1471), while Innocent VIII undertook such a fundamental renovation of the first palace, adjacent to the Portico of St. Peter, that he might be said to have practically rebuilt it. Consequently, this portion of the Vatican buildings has been since known as the Palazzo di Innocenzo VIII. For purposes of defence, Pope Nicholas V erected at the foot of the Vatican Hill, in the direction of S. Angelo, a powerful bastion whose mighty walls awaken even to-day the astonishment of every visitor. It was named Il Torrione di Niccolò V.

All these buildings were confined to the eastern and southern sides of the Vatican Hill, and thus lay in the immediate vicinity of St. Peter's. The only exception was a summer-house, which Innocent VIII erected at a distance of about seven hundred metres to the north of the palace in the Gardens. How Clement XIV (1769–1774) and Pius VI (1775–1799) transformed this Casino d'Innocenzo VIII, with its glorious ceilings and other princely decorations, into one of the most important portions of the Vatican Museum of Statuary, will be discussed below.

Pope Sixtus IV (1471–1484), the gifted founder of the Palatine Library, erected on the ground floor in the northern wing of the buildings enclosing the Cortile del Papagallo the state rooms for his collection of books.

To this fairly uniform group of buildings Julius II (1503–1513) added a long gallery at right angles. It begins near the Loggie and extends to the Casino of Innocent VIII. This contains to-day the Galleria Lapidaria or Corridoio delle Iscrizioni (Gallery of Inscriptions) and the Museo Chiaramonti (a section of the Sculpture Gallery). Parallel to the above and beginning from the Borgia Tower, Pius IV (1559–1565) built a similar long and narrow row of buildings in which are accommodated to-day the Vatican Pinacoteca (Picture Gallery), a

Cortile di Belvedere

large portion of the Library and of the Museum, and also the Secret Archives. As a kind of connecting link between the ends of these parallel buildings, the same Pontiff erected the monumental Loggia known as Il Gran Nicchione (the Great Niche).

Where the above-mentioned row of buildings meets the Borgia Tower, Pius V (1566–1572) established three chapels, one over the other, and all the buildings to the north are to be credited to the same Pope.

The building connecting the palace and the Torrione di Niccolò V owes its origin to Pius V and his successor, Gregory XIII. The power-

Cortile di S. Damaso

Scala Pia

Scala Nobile

ful block, in which the Popes themselves had long lived and still live, runs at right angles to this connecting building and to the Torrione, and covers the last spurs of the Vatican Hill in the direction of S. Angelo. It was begun by the great Sixtus V (1585–1590), but was only completed under Clement VIII (1592–1605). Extending along the southern slopes of the hill towards the Piazza di S. Pietro, Julius III (1550–1555) erected some low buildings upon mighty, almost cyclopean substructures. These buildings were not quite completed until the reign of Pius IX (1846–1878).

Bronze Gate

Sixtus V erected a transverse building joining in the middle the two wings which run to the Gran Nicchione. In this building he established the new library, and the mighty court was now divided into two parts. The upper half of this court was further divided by a transverse wing, known as the Braccio Nuovo, in which Pius VII (1800–1823) placed a number of choice treasures of the Sculpture Gallery. All the other buildings about the Gran Nicchione devoted to the Museum were either built or rebuilt under Pius VI and Pius VII (1775–1823). A very small wing, arched over the passage leading to the Museum and containing valuable antiquities, was built by Paul V (1605–1621).

The quarters of the Swiss Guard and the gendarmes lie in front of the Torrione, and date from the nineteenth century. Other smaller scattered groups of buildings may be here passed over, inasmuch as they are without importance in the architectural history of the palace. Leo XIII (1878–1903) erected on the top of the hill in the Vatican Gardens a summer-house of modest dimensions, which now serves as the Vatican Observatory. Finally, Pius X has erected a large building near the Palace of Sixtus V for the clerks and servants of the Vatican. Of the last we shall speak further below.

PAPAL APARTMENTS.—Visitors crossing the bridge of S. Angelo and hurrying through the Borgo Nuovo to St. Peter's, see to the right a mighty, but rather unsightly palace towering high above the Colon-

Section of the Ceiling, Sala Concistoria

Sala Concistoria

nades of the Piazza di S. Pietro. To the left of the palace lies a courtyard surrounded on three sides by Loggie, which were formerly open, but are now enclosed by glass windows. The palace is that of Sixtus V. The north side of the open court is bounded by the row of buildings erected by Pius V and Gregory XIII, while the buildings on the west were built by Nicholas V.

The Decano

The Pope dwells on the second and third stories of the Palace of Sixtus V, and his Secretary of State occupies the first floor. Visitors invited to a private audience enter the palace through the Bronze Gate (Portone di Bronzo), the portal at the beginning of the right colonnade, and are directed up a staircase by the non-commissioned officer or sergeant-major of the Swiss Guard posted there. This abnormally broad flight, with its massive granite steps and marble balustrade, was erected by Pius IX to provide the Vatican Palace with a monumental stairway, and is consequently known as the Scala Pia. A door on the second landing leads to the office of the Sub-Prefect of the Apostolic Palaces, while the door on the third and last landing leads to the offices of the High Chamberlain of His Holiness, the Maestro di Camera.

A few steps further on we reach the Cortile di S. Damaso (Court of St. Damasus). Two papal gendarmes guard the entrance, and direct visitors to any part of the palace. This Cortile di S. Damaso is the open court which we see from the Piazza di S. Pietro, and now fills us with wonder and admiration, its quiet majesty being disturbed only by the automobiles awaiting some ambassadors and envoys who are visiting the Cardinal Secretary of State.

Our way now leads us diagonally across the courtyard to a somewhat unsightly tower before which two gendarmes are on guard. After a careful scrutiny of our invitation to the audience, we are admitted and ascend a few steps to meet some sentries of the Swiss Guard, who are stationed at the Scala Nobile (Noble Staircase) with halberd on arm. This staircase is lighted by two stained glass windows, restored by the late Prince Regent Leopold of Bavaria after those donated by King Louis had been destroyed by the shock of a powder explosion in the neighborhood. Over the staircase itself, the steps of which are of white marble, arches a coffered roof, while the walls are lined with yellow artificial marble. On the first landing are seen the doors leading to the chambers of the Cardinal Secretary of State; one of the Swiss Guards is stationed here also, and directs us to the next landing. Having reached this landing, we are confronted by a glass door through which we see an immensely high and almost square hall—the Sala

Sala Clementina

Clementina (Clementine Hall), named after its founder, Pope Clement VIII Aldobrandini (1592–1605). Should the visitor be unaware of the family from which this Pope sprang, the arched roof covered with frescoes, in which the arms of the Aldobrandini appear in every possible combination, quickly informs him. A picket of Swiss Guards stand on sentry at the end of the hall, and present arms while the Maestro di Camera goes to wait on His Holiness. The impression made on the visitor by this wonderful hall, with its great architectural beauty, is deep and lasting. It is the magnificent antechamber to the reception rooms of the Holy Father, and, on account of its size, is often used for the reception of pilgrims.

Behind the Sala Clementina is the Sala Concistoria (Consistorial

Hall), a long but narrow room hung with red damask. The richly coffered roof gleams with a lustre of gold. In the background rises a throne, richly caparisoned but exercising not an entirely pleasing effect; this was presented to Pius X by the Catholics of Venice. From the Sala Clementina we proceed to the Anticamera Bassa, where servants in dark red uniforms assist the visitors to remove their overcoats and wraps. The head servant in black dress-coat, who is called the Decano, takes our invitation, leads us through a series of apartments to the Throne Room, and there leaves us to await our turn. The first of the well-lighted rooms through which we pass is known as the Sala dei Gendarmi, because here on solemn occasions two gendarmes in full uniform with high busbies keep guard. The second apartment traversed is a corner room, and is therefore known as the Sala del Cantone; it is also called the Sala della Guardia Palatina, because a division of the Palatine Guard render honorary service here on festivals. In the third room—a room of moderate size—hang three Gobelins; as the lilies conspicuous in the coat of arms decorating these tapestries might suggest, they were presented to the Pope by Louis XV. The fourth room is narrow, and in this members of the Noble Guard are stationed.

The door in the background leads to one of the private chapels of the Holy Father, who sometimes administers Easter Communion there to the prelates on Maundy Thursday. The floor of the Throne Room, in which we now find ourselves, is entirely covered by a thick carpet manufactured specially for this hall. The carpet is a present from Spain and is of great value. The arms of Leo XIII show that it dates from his pontificate. The walls are hung with red damask. On the longitudinal walls are seen a pair of monumental marble consoles with valuable French chimney clocks from the time of Louis XVI. Two huge windows admit a light softened by white silk curtains and green silk draperies; these windows command a delightful view of S. Angelo, the Pincio, and the city between. The new Palace of Justice, with its steep roof and its obtrusive ornamentation, is a disturbing element in the picture. Opposite the windows stands the plain throne, surmounted by a canopy.

We have just had time to examine carefully our surroundings, and to allow the glorious simplicity and pure restfulness characterizing the decorations of all the rooms traversed to make their impression, when we hear the voice of the Chamberlain in waiting summoning us to follow him. We first enter another corner room, the Anticamera Segreta (Privy Antechamber), which is occupied by the immediate personal attendants of the Pope. The yellow tint of the old and very valuable

Throne Room

Privy Antechamber

Gobelin carpet which covers the floor is in complete harmony with the quiet but refined decorations. The little table in the corner indicates that some official is regularly stationed there. This Privy Antechamber separates the general reception rooms from those which are used for the various grades of private audience. At the end of this suite lies the large library used by the Holy Father both as a working room and for receptions. We are next led through two small rooms

Sala del Tronetto

whose atmosphere is one of supreme restfulness. A smaller room is then reached, known as the Sala del Tronetto from the plain throne it contains.

We now stand before a door hung with red draperies. The Chamberlain in waiting knocks, genuflects, and then announces us. At a sign from the Chamberlain we enter, make the prescribed triple reverence, and see fixed on us the kindly eyes of an aged, gray-haired man clothed in white. Standing, he greets us, motions us to take our places near his writing-table, and quickly dispels our embarrassment with his kind and reassuring words.

Three large windows light the lofty and broad room, which serves as the private library of the Pope. A number of book-cases line the walls; a mahogany table of gigantic dimensions runs through the middle of the room, and is littered with books, documents, presents of all

Private Library of the Pope

kinds, a few vases, and other objects. A row of valuable oil paintings, representing wild animals, hangs over the book-cases. Three busts resting on magnificent marble pillars complete the furnishings. On the writing-table ticks a valuable clock, and a number of small presents from all lands fill every space on the table left unoccupied by books and documents. A second door leads from the hall to a vestibule, and thence a stairway leads to the third story. After work is done in the evening, or when meal-time comes, the Pope ascends by this stairway to the living-rooms which he occupies with his two private secretaries. On this upper floor are the bedrooms, the dining-room, the sitting-room, rooms for the servants, the kitchen, and the other rooms pertaining to housekeeping. All these rooms are furnished with great simplicity, and the houses of many well-to-do burgesses possess much more costly furniture than the private apartments of the Pope.

From time immemorial it was customary for the Pope to take his meals alone. Only when (before 1870) he was on summer holidays (for example, at Castel Gandolfo) or on a journey was he accustomed to dine with the high court officers and specially invited guests. Leo XIII observed this rule strictly, but Pius X, who is very sociable as compared with his more reserved predecessors, could not sentence himself to loneliness at meal-time. After the first few days of his pontificate, he invited his two private secretaries to join him at meals, just as he had done as Patriarch of Venice. He went even further, and when occasionally he consecrated a bishop he invited the new prelate and his nearest of kin to lunch. He also frequently invited to breakfast illustrious guests to whom he had administered Holy Communion during his Mass. The traditional isolation of the Pope has thus to a great extent ceased since the coronation of Pius X, and in this respect ceremonial has been greatly modified, at least for the present pontificate.

Writing-table of Pope Pius X

SOUTHERN AND EASTERN SECTIONS.—Suppose we have received the black-bordered invitation which entitles us to attend the Solemn Requiem in the Sistine Chapel, celebrated each year for the happy repose of the predecessor of the reigning Pontiff. As our invitation informs us, the entrance is through the Bronze Gate, below on the Piazza di S. Pietro. Thence we proceed along the long corridor which leads to St. Peter's, but is also the immediate approach to the Scala Regia (Royal Staircase). This was built by Bernini under Alexander VII (1655–1667), and, owing to a very remarkable arrangement of the pillars supporting the vault, which project further from the wall below than above on the staircase, a very imposing perspective effect is gained.

At the end of this architecturally striking portion of the staircase we turn to the right and ascend a broad flight of steps to an extraordinarily high door which admits us to the Sala Regia (Royal Hall). This hall has seven doors. Besides that by which we entered, a door in the small wall to the right leads to the Pauline Chapel (Cappella Paolina), the parochial church of the Vatican parish. On the opposite wall the first door leads to the huge Aula, situated over the Portico of St. Peter; the middle door gives access to the Cortile del Maresciallo over a servants' staircase; a huge door in the left corner leads from the Sala Regia to the Sala Ducale. To the left of the door by which we enter is the sixth door, leading to the Sistine Chapel. The seventh door, to the right as we enter, leads to a servants' room.

The present writer has seen this celebrated chapel when it was prepared for the exequies of Leo XIII, for the celebration of great feasts, for the Conclave (when all the canopied seats for the electors lined the walls), for Secret Consistories, and for many other events now registered in the annals of Church history.

On the present occasion, the Cardinal Deacon celebrates the Requiem, and the Pope assists on the throne. In the quadrangle behind the latter are seated the cardinals, ranged according to their rank and seniority. Behind the cardinals are stationed the archbishops, bishops, the colleges of prelates, the generals of the religious orders, the judges of the Papal Courts, and many other high officials. In the rear portion of the chapel, behind marble barriers, are assembled the Roman aristocracy, the diplomats accredited to the Holy See, and other invited persons from every land. In the Sistine Chapel is held the Conclave for the election of a new Pope.

Scala Regia

The Sacristan, or Pastor of the Vatican and the Apostolic Palaces, who is always a titular bishop, exercises his office in the above-mentioned Pauline Chapel, and has the spiritual care of the many hundred residents of the palace.

Public Consistories are usually held in the Sala Regia, while the Sala Ducale is especially suitable for the reception of bodies of pilgrims. From the Sala Ducale a door leads to the Sala dei Paramenti, in which the Pope ordinarily assumes the pontifical vestments when he undertakes some function in any of the above-mentioned halls. The assembled cardinals await the Pope in the neighboring room, the Sala dello Spogliatoio, in which also the prelates take their places. These halls receive their light from the Loggie of Giovanni da Udine, of which more will be said below. The walls of these rooms, access to which is denied the general public, are covered with red damask, and are also adorned with some Gobelins richly ornamented with life-sized figures. After the Holy Father has administered Holy Communion to the spiritual portion of his family on Maundy Thursday, the communicants are by his orders here entertained at breakfast. The Majordomo, or in his absence the Maestro di Camera, does the honors on such occasions.

We are here on the second story of the palace, and, if we step out from the Sala dei Paramenti to the Loggie situated before it, we can look down on the Cortile di S. Damaso. The bay windows protect the paintings of the Loggie, which are the work of the great master Giovanni da Udine. The sketches for the paintings and stucco decorations of these once open halls were made by Raphael himself, as is suggested by the marble bust of the master at the head of the hall. Leaf- and tendril-work border the airy architectonic lines, and the effect is enlivened by animals of every kind, while the groining of the vaults presents a picture instinct with gaiety and joyous coloring. A few small earthenware figures of great artistic value adorn the sparely ornamented walls. Among these is a particularly striking figure of Leo XIII in full papal vestments. The other portions of the Loggie on this story are furnished in essentially simpler fashion, and offer nothing of special artistic note.

Near the Loggie of Giovanni da Udine lies the Appartamento Borgia, which receives special treatment elsewhere. Passing the door leading to this Appartamento and ascending a few steps, we reach the Gallery of Inscriptions, an extremely long corridor in which about six thousand inscriptions are shown. This collection was begun under Clement XIV (1769–1774), continued under Pius VI (1775–1799), and completed under Pius VII (1800–1823). Gaetano Marini, the famous scholar, who has been named the second founder of Latin epigraphy, here applied his great diligence and marvellous learning to the systematic arrangement of the inscriptions, the Christian being inserted in the left wall and the pagan in the right. Marini's magnificent work awakens the astonishment of every visitor, and is of incalculable value to the student.

At the end of the Gallery of Inscriptions we see on the left a huge door on which is written: Bibliotheca Vaticana. Until recently this was the main entrance to the reading-room of the Library. How things are now arranged will be dealt with later. Adjoining the Gallery of Inscriptions is that portion of the Sculpture Gallery which is known as the Museo Chiaramonti.

As already mentioned, the Holy Father has his reception rooms on

Section of the Ceiling of the Sala Regia

Section of a Wall in the Sala Regia

Sala Regia

the second floor. If the visitor on entering the Sala Clementina, instead of proceeding to the papal apartments on the right, passes through the opposite door on the left, he arrives at the Loggie of the second floor. Straight before him lie the Stanze of Raphael, and at the entrance thereto, immediately to the left, the Loggie of Raphael. The works of art collected in these comparatively small rooms through the royal liberality of the Renaissance Popes, enjoy a universal celebrity, and are described by expert pens in special chapters of this book.

NORTHERN AND WESTERN SECTIONS.—Should we proceed around St. Peter's to visit the Vatican Collections, we pass through an arched door and encounter a very long wing of the palace, in the middle of which arises a powerful quadrilateral tower. This whole long row of buildings, erected by Pius IV, is devoted exclusively to art and science. Right before us we see the entrance to the Vatican Picture Gallery. It is situated on the ground floor, and the fire-proof arches receive their light from the east. Further on, also on the ground floor, lie a number of the rooms devoted to the Vatican Secret Archives. The full length of this wing on the first floor is occupied by the state rooms of the Vatican Library, to which the two huge halls in the cross-building built by Sixtus V and large rooms in the opposite longitudinal wing also belong. On the second story are special portions of the Museum, the Gallery containing the renowned tapestries of Raphael, and the Gallery of Geographical Charts—sections of the Vatican Collections which will be treated fully elsewhere. The buildings of the northern wing, grouped around the Gran Nicchione, are devoted entirely to the Museums of Antiquities and Sculpture. By referring to the plans of the palace, the reader can easily identify the numerous divisions of the palace mentioned in the preceding sections. They represent practically all the really noteworthy portions of a mighty palace which possesses a deep interest for everybody.

COURTS OF THE VATICAN.—The reader is now requested to return to the Cortile di S. Damaso to undertake, under the writer's guidance, a round of the various courtyards. A passage on the right of the Cortile di S. Damaso leads into the inner court of the Palace of Sixtus V, known as the Cortile di Sisto V. An entrance, recently reopened, leads over some steps and passages to the Cortile del Triangolo, a three-cornered court situated exactly behind the Cortile di S. Damaso but on a much lower level. Passing along the outside wall of this court, we reach the Cortile di Belvedere. A short halt here will repay the visitor. In the middle of this mighty courtyard, which the Swiss Guards formerly used as an exercising-ground, murmurs a magnificent fountain, in the basin of which ducks of numerous fancy breeds disport themselves. Every side

Section of the Ceiling, Sala Ducale

Sala Ducale

of the court is flanked by lofty buildings. From this point the Picture Gallery may be seen on the lofty first floor of the opposite side, the entrance being on the ground floor. Beneath the powerful arches which support the Picture Gallery and the other collections mentioned above runs a steep carriage-drive. The Library of Sixtus V abuts on the one narrow side of the court in the right corner, and the other longitudinal side accommodates the Gallery of Inscriptions. The second short side protrudes in a sharp curve below, and here the Appartamento Borgia and the Stanze of Raphael greet us with their small windows. It is a glorious view

Medieval Gate leading to the Cortile del Papagallo

for visitors who can slowly drink in its beauties and realize that they are here surrounded by the most precious treasures of science and of art. In one corner rises defiantly the Torre dei Quattro Venti (Tower of the Four Winds), in which the scholars engaged by Gregory XIII (1572–1585), under Lilius, Clavius, and Chaconius, worked out their famous reform of the calendar. Great festivals were once celebrated in this court, and even in our days festivities are occasionally held here in the presence of the Holy Father.

Let us now ascend the above-mentioned covered drive, in the middle of which begins the subterranean passage, constructed specially for Pius X, which leads under the Picture Gallery and the adjoining carriageway to the Vatican Gardens. We thus reach the Cortile della Sentinella, so called because a sentry of the Swiss Guard here guards the entrance. We can now behold the massive substructure of the Sistine Chapel, which mounts high into the air beside St. Peter's. A plain portal inserted in the buttresses of the building gives access to the Cortile della Torre Borgia (Court of the Borgia Tower), which was mentioned above. A few steps more and we reach the Cortile del Papagallo (the Parrot's Court). An old story is associated with this strange name. The first parrots were brought to southern Italy after the discovery of the Canary Islands. As it was then customary for the rulers of every land to offer novelties as a present to the Pope, these birds were sent

Cortile della Pigna, showing the Braccio Nuovo

to the Vatican. On their arrival they were housed in a separate hall, and were assigned a special attendant. All expenses incurred in connection with them may be found detailed in the papal account-books. Later all the papal palaces in Italy, and even that in Avignon, possessed a Sala dei Papagalli (Parrots' Hall). As in the Vatican the hall lay in one of the wings enclosing the court, the name was extended from the hall to the court.

The ground floor, on the northern side of this court, contains the old library of Sixtus IV. Passing now through a passage on the right, we see facing us the roof of the Colonnade of St. Peter's. This serves as the southern boundary of the Cortile del Maresciallo (the Marshal's Court), which we now enter. When a Conclave is being held in the Vatican for the election of a new Pope, the hereditary Marshal of the Conclave, Prince Chigi, is stationed here to protect the Conclave from outside interference. A covered passage brings us back to the Cortile di S. Damaso.

The Cortile della Stamperia is accessible only through the vestibule of the Torre dei Quattro Venti or through the Vatican Library. It owes its name to the fact that the Vatican Press once occupied rooms on this court which are now incorporated in the Vatican Library.

The last court to call for mention is the Cortile della Pigna. As already stated, this and the last-mentioned courts once formed with the Cortile di Belvedere a single gigantic court, which was then divided into three parts by Sixtus V (Library of Sixtus V) and Pius VII (Braccio Nuovo). The Cortile di Belvedere is very low-lying; the Cortile della Stamperia is several metres higher, while the Cortile della Pigna lies on a level with the first floor.

General View of the Cortile della Pigna

In the Gran Nicchione (Great Niche), which forms the extraordinarily impressive boundary of this third court, stands a huge bronze pine-cone (*pigna*), dating from very early times. This has given its name to the court. In the middle of this court, which the gardener's skill has greatly enhanced, rises a high column of precious marble, on the pinnacle of which a figure of St. Peter stands. This was erected in commemoration of the Vatican Council of 1870. Around the foot of the walls lie a large number of antiquities, which can claim no place in the Museum itself, but which are nevertheless well worth attention. The buildings surrounding the court belong almost exclusively to the great Museum, the principal works of art being preserved in the buildings behind the Gran Nicchione and in the Braccio Nuovo, which lies opposite.

A view of all the above-mentioned courts may be secured by ascend-

Bas-relief with Warriors, Cortile della Pigna

ing to the Cupola of St. Peter's. From there we see far below us the
mighty ashlars of the different palaces; the smaller courts yawn beneath us like pits, while the larger in their majestic repose bring into
sharp prominence the lines of the surrounding buildings. It is a remarkable view for those who meditate that in this palace, peacefully
reposing at their feet, have been enacted during a long succession of
centuries an endless chain of the important scenes of religious and
secular history. This palace, erected by the very side of the grave of
the Prince of the Apostles, has been for almost five centuries the chief
abode of the Papacy. For forty-three years indeed it has also been the
prison of the Popes, who lost practically all their possessions in the
year 1870, and who now possess but this palace and this tiny handful
of earth. From our present position we can survey the Vatican Gardens, the only refuge of the white-haired Pope when he wishes to
walk in the open air. If fortune favor us, and the day be clear, we
may see His Holiness taking his half-hour's outing along the broad
path in the Gardens. For a short while the carriage halts in the full
sunlight at the top of the Gardens near the Leonine Wall, and then the
Pope takes a short walk with his attendant.

ENTRANCES TO THE VATICAN.—The guarding of all the entrances to

Apotheosis of Antoninus and Faustina—Bas-relief,
Cortile della Pigna

the palace from the city is entrusted to the Swiss Guard. Four gates are under their protection. The main entrance, or Bronze Gate, under the Colonnades on the Piazza di S. Pietro, is known to every Roman and every visitor. Here is stationed the strongest guard, under the command of one of their chief officers, especially during the afternoon. At the approach of all dignitaries, archbishops, bishops, and prelates, when these are recognizable as such by their dress, and at the approach of all officers of the Vatican military or police corps, the picket fall into line at the summons of the sentry. If the visitor does not wear his official dress, but is personally known to the sentry, the latter alone gives the prescribed salute. On solemn occasions, such as the high ecclesiastical feasts, the banner of the Swiss Guards is here suspended, and the sentry wears parade uniform. This gate is closed at night, and all persons then seeking admission, unless they dwell in the Vatican or are personally known to the sentry, must establish their identity fully. They are then admitted through a very small door in one of the wings of the portal. During the night the sentries wear undress uniform and the appropriate cape. The second entrance is through the Portal of Alexander VI, in the middle of and behind the Colonnades.

It is immediately adjacent to the quarters of the Swiss Guard. The use of this door by strangers is prohibited, unless they are going to the canteen of the Swiss Guard or wish to visit some one in the vicinity. The third entrance is from the street to the Vatican Press and the dispensary, both of which are situated in the immediate neighborhood of the Torrione di Niccolò V. Through this door passes the brisk business traffic with the dispensary and printing offices. It serves as the general family entrance to the new building which has been erected by Pius X for the Vatican employes and their families. Behind St. Peter's, at the foot of the Sistine Chapel, is the fourth entrance, situated on the

The Pigna

public road leading to the Vatican Collections. The guarding of this entrance is especially important, since all cars and automobiles proceeding to the Cortile di S. Damaso enter this way. The guards must possess an excellent memory for persons so as to give the appropriate salute to each cardinal, ambassador, envoy, and prelate as he passes.

EXTERIOR OF THE VATICAN PALACES.—Persons who make a complete tour of the Vatican, and view the exterior of the palace from the various courts, are in a certain sense disappointed. If we leave out of consideration certain individual features and several poetical corners, and regard the palace as a whole, we receive the impression of vastness, solidity, and magnificence, but for architectural beauties we seek in

vain. The Popes, who all contributed their share to the erection of
this mass of buildings, devoted re-
markably little attention to the
external appearance of the palace.
The Cortile di S. Damaso, the main
wall of the Cortile della Pigna, and
a few other portions of the palace
do indeed possess architectural
charm. But, taking the palace as
a whole and passing over perhaps the buildings of Sixtus V,
we see only buildings erected for
a definite purpose and walls
constructed only in the plainest
way.

That only very few visitors are
conscious of this fact may be simply explained, because visitors as
a class desire chiefly to become

Tower of the Four Winds

acquainted with the treasures of the interior, and are usually quite
content with a leisurely survey of the Palace of Sixtus V and the Cortile
di S. Damaso from the Piazza di S. Pietro. The picture which thus presents itself to the gaze of the visitor is so intimately associated with the
front of St. Peter's owing to the aspiring bare gable of the Sistine
Chapel, that the eye loses, as it were, all details in the grandeur of the
picture as a whole.

The quiet court lying at the foot of the Palace of Sixtus V and
bounded on the right by the Torrione di Niccolò V and on the left by
the wall which connects the palace with the Castle of S. Angelo, is accessible only to very few. In this quiet retreat some huge elms wave softly
in the breeze. The garden behind the Museum, with its glorious view
and ancient associations, is known only to the elect. How many of the
thousands who hurry from the Museum to the Appartamento Borgia
pause to admire the view from the window of the Gallery of Inscriptions obliquely across the Cortile di Belvedere towards the Torre dei
Quattro Venti? It is of a rare beauty, and it recalls the times of Gregory XIII, when there in the tower above Christianity recovered its correct chronology. Of such charming views there are many, and they all
deserve a visit.

If, on the other hand, we proceed around St. Peter's to the Museum,
we have on our right a bare interminable wall whose monotony is

broken only by large windows. The carriage-road leading from the Cortile di S. Damaso assumes a forbidding if impressive air when we look up at the walls of the narrow courts. A few traces of earlier frescoes remaining in the Cortile del Papagallo show that in times long vanished the decoration of the external walls of the palace was begun. If we now proceed from the Vatican Press to the Cortile di Belvedere, we see facing us a great wall several hundred metres long, whose surface seems scarcely broken by a few windows. Even the extraordinary inscription, formed of huge letters of cut marble, can give no life to this wall. All this, however, does not alter the fact that the general impression made by the Vatican Palace, viewed either from a distance or close at hand, is deep and lasting.

THE RULER OF THE VATICAN.—In his mode of life Pius X is extraordinarily, in fact astonishingly simple. Life could scarcely be simpler in the home of a burgess in moderate circumstances. In so far as the doctors allow him, he adheres in his diet to Venetian cooking, to which he has been accustomed all his life. He partakes of his chief meal in the middle of the day, and afterwards rests for a little while. His bedroom, sitting-room, and dining-room are rather cold in appearance. The Pope insists on one of his private secretaries sleeping in the next room, with only the wall between, so that at any moment he may have within reach the consolations of religion.

Of the numerous rooms on the third story occupied by the Pope, only one half are fitted for occupancy. The remainder are provided with shelves and presses and are used by the Pope as store-rooms. In the latter the Pope keeps, for example, all the vestments for poor or needy churches that are presented to him, so that he may always have those objects at hand when he requires them. Two of the sisters of the Holy Father live in the Palazzo Rusticucci, situated in the immediate vicinity of the Colonnades of St. Peter's. Together with a younger sister recently deceased, these kept house for the Pope while he was Bishop of Mantua and Patriarch of Venice. When he became Pope, Pius X brought his sisters to Rome and assigned to them a simple but comfortable residence and a modest but sufficient pension. On Thursdays and Sundays the sisters are admitted into his presence for an hour's conversation. When he was seriously ill they naturally spent a long period daily either in the Antechamber or in his sick-room.

For several hundred years it has been customary for the Popes to raise their relatives to the rank of Roman princes or to grant them other distinctions. Leo XIII, for instance, raised his family to the rank of counts, although they had previously been simple country squires. Pius X completely ignored this custom, and left his relatives in the

Tunnel leading to the Vatican Gardens

Exit of Tunnel

very simple and modest circle in which they were born. He rightly believes that men whose lives have been spent cultivating their fields with their own hands cannot easily mix, and have no desire to mix, in fashionable circles. When individual members of his family come to attend great festivities at Rome, a special platform near the throne or the altar is assigned to them and his sisters. In his intercourse with his relatives, his private secretary, or Venetian pilgrims, Pius X prefers to use his native Venetian dialect. From his pronunciation of Italian one can readily deduce that he comes of Venetian stock.

In manner Pius X is very sympathetic and unaffected. Despite the

Private Chapel of Pope Pius X

exalted position of his host, the visitor feels quickly at ease, however agitated or nervous he may have been when he entered the presence of the Holy Father. With his paternal kindness he unites an iron will which refuses to be diverted from its goal when, after constant prayer and ripe consideration, he has decided on a definite course of action.

Besides the pontifical garments and liturgical vestments in general, the distinctive dress of the Pope consists of a white soutane of fine woolen material with double sleeves and cape. The cuffs are of white moire silk, and a broad cincture of the same material with gold tassels encircles his waist. A white skull-cap completes the distinctive papal dress. Outside the palace the Pope wears a red hat with gold string and tassels and a red mantle with a very narrow gold border. The large hood of red velvet lined with a narrow strip of swanskin, called the *camauro* (the ancient *camelaucum*), is never used by Pius X, although Leo XIII wore it fairly frequently. This head-dress is seen in numerous pictures of the Renaissance Popes.

ADVICE TO VISITORS.—In the summer months the Vatican Palace is almost deserted. Strangers are very few, while in the Collections and Galleries, the Loggie and Stanze, the Appartamento and Chapels only isolated visitors may be seen. The staff of the Antechamber is reduced to a minimum. The heads of the legations are all on vacation, and what little diplomatic business there is is discharged by the younger agents. For two months the Secretary of State lives in the country in the neighborhood of Rome, but comes at regular intervals to the city to attend to pressing affairs.

But when the winter months arrive the stream of strangers begins to flood the palace. Towards Easter a visitor to the Museums may be almost said to take his life in his hands. There the crowds push and pull one another; the air is filled with the most banal opinions of the artistic treasures; the dust rises in clouds, and one wonders what brings so many thousands of people to view the works of art, for enjoyment of them is absolutely out of the question. The mercenary drone of the guides mingles with the loud conversation of the crowd, suggesting to the listener the murmur and buzzing of a gigantic hive. The hunt for an invitation to an audience reaches its climax as Palm Sunday draws near, since the Antechamber is closed and no audiences are granted in Holy Week. Every imaginable reason is made to do service in the hope of securing this privilege, and the patience and endurance of the Maestro di Camera are put to a hard test. As the result of extended experience, the writer may offer one suggestion to intending visitors: Never visit Rome at Easter, if you wish to enjoy properly and peacefully the works of art in the city and especially those of the Vatican Palace. The writer remembers well the time when admission to the Vatican Collections was free, as was admission to most of the State Museums in Rome. When, however, the reasonable regulation of charging a lira to visitors was introduced for the State Museums, this example was followed by the Curia. The budget of the Holy See was thereby relieved of no insignificant burden, since, owing to the extraordinary number of visitors, a sufficient sum is realized annually to pay for the administration and proper maintenance of the Museums. As entrance to the Museums is free on Sundays, the crowds of visitors on that day are naturally uncomfortably large.

But whether it is winter or summer; whether the business to be done is much or little; whether the Vatican Palace is overflooded with visitors of every nation and tongue, or seems to rest in contemplation under the August sun; whether his highest advisers or his humblest servants enjoy some relaxation and the fresh breezes of the country or sea, there is little or no variation in the general life of the Pope, the supreme lord of all. He may not go forth, however greatly he himself, and more especially his physicians, may desire it. He must remain where he is; for him there now remains but one change, and that will come when he is borne forth in his coffin from the Vatican Palace, which during his life as Pope he may never leave. When he is then solemnly carried to the Throne Room, when all the impressive ceremonies are enacted about his corpse, when his last earthly dwelling, the small wooden house, has received his remains, then, amid the solemn lamentations for the dead, the Pope will at last leave his palace to find a temporary resting-place near the choir chapel in St. Peter's, within sight of the grave of the Prince of the Apostles, the first of his line. There still lie the remains of Leo XIII, since the authorities do not dare to run the risk of carrying them through the streets of Rome to their final and long-prepared resting-place in the Lateran.

THE VATICAN GARDENS

THE Vatican Gardens lie to the west of the palace, between it and the walls of the ancient Leonine City. They are irregular in shape and of an extensive area. Important traces of the old Leonine Wall still remain; there is, for instance, at the highest point of the Gardens a battlemented circular tower of the usual medieval character (Torre Leonina). Fortifications of this nature were built under Leo IV between 848 and 852, when the Saracens, who held the Tyrrhenian Sea and terrorized the seacoast, made frequent incursions into the Papal States, laying waste the country up to the very gates of Rome. Thus originated the Leonine City, which included not only St. Peter's but the entire Borgo. The old walls were often demolished—especially in 1084, when Robert Guiscard drove the Emperor, Henry IV, from Rome, and again in 1379, when the Roman people seized the Castel S. Angelo. A notable enlargement took place during the sixteenth century, under various Popes from Julius II to Pius IV, when the fortifications were completely rebuilt and extended under the best military advice, but the old wall remained even after Michelangelo had rebuilt the bastion of the Belvedere, and served as a boundary for the Vatican Gardens. It was about this time that the Vatican Gardens began, and the print published by Falda in his work on Roman gardens shows them as they existed in 1683. By comparing the print with the present gardens we see that the changes that have taken place are very slight.

While the Vatican Gardens do not compare in beauty with the gardens of many Roman villas (for instance, with those of the Villa Falconieri or of the Villa d'Este at Tivoli), they are a very good example of Italian landscape art in the sixteenth century. Two main alleys at right angles divide them into four sections, which are subdivided by many minor walks, and buildings of various shapes have been set up in different parts of the gardens. Near the above-mentioned Torre Leonina stands the Casino of Leo XIII; both of these buildings, as well as a second tower of the old fortifications, are now occupied by the Vatican Observatory. Not far distant may be seen a copy of the Lourdes Basilica, and a little below a copy of the Lourdes Grotto, set up

in 1905 as a gift of the Catholics of France. These very modern con-
structions have little artistic merit.

The Casino of Pope Pius is undoubtedly the most important building in the gardens, and deserves special attention. Giovanni Pietro
Caraffa, who succeeded Marcellus II and took the name of Paul IV, began the "fabbrica del boschetto" ("building in the wood"), or "Boscareggio," a small house in the Vatican Gardens beyond the broad Belvedere alley. It had a fountain, as we learn from a letter written in 1558

Corner of the Vatican Gardens and Cupola of St. Peter's

by an envoy of the Signory of Florence, and a print by Marius Kartarus,
dated 1574, showing the Belvedere Garden. In the papal registers for
1560 there appears a payment to a stone-cutter, Domenico Rosselli, for
work done on the new papal building.

In December, 1559, the Milanese Gian Angelo Medici became Pope,
and took the name of Pius IV. In the words of the Venetian ambassador, "he was very fond of building, spent liberally, took great
pleasure in hearing his work praised, and was wont to say that the
Medici House was a house of builders." In 1560 work on the Casino
was renewed with vigor, and among the papal bills we find payments

to the architects Pirro Ligorio and
Salustio Peruzzi, to the superintendent Bernardino Manfredi, to
the foreman mason Francesco da
Como, and to a host of stone-cut-
ters, carpenters, and plasterers.
Rocco da Montefiascone worked
at the stucco work of the façade
and the vault of the portico.
Nicolo Bresciano had charge of
the marble pavement. Battista da
Frasino worked on the roof within.
Among other artists at work were
the sculptor Tommaso del Bosco
of Montepulciano, Giovanni di S.
Agata, who made the marble basin
in the middle of the piazza, and
Jacobo da Casignola and Bene-
detto Schella, who took part in the
decorations. The first of the paint-

The Torre Leonina

ers came in 1561. This was Pietro Venale. Then came Giovanni da
Cherso Veneziano. Santi di Tito (or Santi del Borgo), Pier Antonio
Alciati da Como, Federico Zuccaro da S. Angelo in Vadis, Pierleone da
Giulio, Genga da Urbino, and, greatest of all, Federico Barocci da
Urbino, who appears to have worked at the Casino from November,
1561, till June, 1563. Much of the work was still unfinished when Pius
IV died and was succeeded by the Ghisleri Pope, St. Pius V, whose coat
of arms may be seen in many parts of the Casino, as are also the arms
of the Castagna Pope, Urban VII, and the Barberini Pope, Urban VIII.
Under Pope Clement XI Albani the work was redone, and additions
were made by Benedict XIII, Clement XIII, and Leo XII.

Chief credit for this exquisite building belongs to Pirro Ligorio, the
architect, a man who has a sorry record in other ways. Ligorio was
not satisfied to be an architect, but dabbled in archæology, the history
of ancient monuments, and particularly in epigraphy. In this last
field he is famous as a bold forger. He was born in Naples: Lanciani
gives the year as 1527, while Hülsen says 1510. At any rate, we find
him in Rome in 1542 doing some fresco work on the palace of the
Archbishop of Benevento, Francesco della Rovere. Between 1549 and
1555 he was in the service of Cardinal Ippolito da Ferrara as an antiquarian with a salary of seven scudi sixty-three baiocchi a month.
Under Paul IV he became official architect of the Papal Court at a

Grotto of Lourdes

The Chalet and Torre Leonina

salary of twenty-five golden scudi
a month. He held this post also
under Pius IV in association with
Salustio Peruzzi, son of the famous
Baldassarre.   From this period
dates his work in the Cortile di
Belvedere, the Gran Nicchione, and
the Casino of Pope Pius. In 1566
he made a design for the tomb of
Pope Paul IV, which is adorned by
a statue of Giacomo Casignola,
now in S. Maria sopra Minerva. In
1567 he was at Tivoli in the service
of the d'Estes, working on their
magnificent gardens, which are
among the most beautiful ever
planned.   Afterwards he accompanied Duke Alfonso d'Este to
Ferrara, where he resided until
his death in October, 1583.

The Casino of Leo XIII

Ligorio was not a great architect, and his work in the Vatican Gardens is said to be a copy from the antique. In 1766 Venuti wrote: "This
Casino is a copy from the antique made by Pirro Ligorio, a Neapolitan
antiquarian and architect.   The original stood near the Lake of
Gabinio, and was built by the Romans so that they might enjoy the
pleasant view of the waters. Ligorio copied its plan, and as recently
as sixty years ago the ruins of the original were still to be seen." There
is probably some exaggeration here. The Casino does not differ considerably from many other summer houses built at the close of the
Renaissance period, the chief of which are Caprarola and the Villa of
Pope Julius. These were all light and gracious but not over-pretentious
structures, and very pleasant places to spend a day in.

The interior plan consists of a somewhat elongated oval courtyard.
Arched entrances reached by steps lie at the ends; on one side is a
Loggia overlooking a fountain, while on the other is the vestibule
proper of the Casino. A simple balustrade runs round the courtyard;
behind this balustrade, on each side of the Casino, is a wall with decorative arches. The arched entrances form two rectangular rooms
adorned with niches. The walls are covered with graceful multicolored mosaics in classic style, and the barrelled vaulting is covered with
stucco work. In the centre of the courtyard stands a fountain, at either
end of which is a boy riding a dolphin.

The two most important architectural features are the façades of the Loggia and the Casino, which are symmetrical, and have on the ground floor the same architectural arrangements—a Doric portico with four columns, flanked by heavy masonry. The Loggia has no upper floor, but consists of a single hall and terminates on each side in an apse. In front, above the ground floor, runs a great stucco frieze, and above this a triangular tympanum. The Casino, on the other hand, has two upper floors separated by Greek cornices. The façade also is

Reception Room in the Casino of Leo XIII

over-decorated with stuccos, alto-reliefs, and statues in niches. The interior of the Casino proper is very simple. Beyond the vestibule lie two rooms, one leading into the other. On one side of the second room is a small hall, and on the other a staircase which leads both to the story above and to the basement. The upper floor is laid out in the same manner. This simple architectural plan lends itself to the sumptuous pictorial decoration. The stucco work by Rocco, the gilding by Venale, and the paintings by Zuccaro are in the Loggetta. The two rooms on the ground floor were decorated by Barocci, Genga, and their pupils. Above the staircase are paintings by Santi di Tito, who also decorated one of the rooms above; the other room of the upper floor was done by Zucchero and Giovanni da Cherso.

Barocci's work enjoys a great celebrity to-day, and calls for particular notice. Barocci was born in 1526 at Urbino, and there painted his earliest works: St. Margaret in the Confraternity Chapel of the Corpus Domini, and the Martyrdom of St. Sebastian and St. Cecilia in the Cathedral. According to Bellori, his biographer, he fell early under the influence of Correggio, and from him learned that "smoky man-

The Sala Rotonda in the Torre Leonina

ner" which is one of the chief characteristics of his paintings. In 1561 he was at work on the Boscareggio with Federico Zuccaro. In 1569 he painted one of his masterpieces, the Descent from the Cross, at Perugia; and in later years he produced the Madonna di S. Simone and the Louvre Madonna.

It is difficult to describe in detail the paintings in the first room, where Barocci did so much, and the arabesques and the figures which compose them. Besides the Boys and the Virtues grouped in the corners, which are well executed, the Holy Family in the central panel is noteworthy, as also are the surrounding paintings representing the

Baptism of Christ, the Meeting with the Samaritan Woman, and the Woman taken in Adultery. In the second room the central medallion of the Annunciation is also the work of Barocci. The staircase decorations have in the middle the arms of Pius IV, and around these are grouped four medallions with figures and four views: the whole is the

Bed-room of Leo XIII adjoining the Torre Leonina

work of Santi di Tito. The views introduced in the decorations are: one of the Casino itself, one of Monte Cavallo, one of the Via Flaminia, and one of the Gran Nicchione.

The paintings in the following room are also by Santi di Tito. The central medallion shows Jesus in the Garden of Gethsemane, and the four paintings on the four walls are the Way to Calvary (on the north wall), the Last Supper (on the south), the Ascension (on the west), and Christ appearing to a Monk (on the east). In the corners, among other decorations, are some very beautiful female figures. The gallery is decorated with arabesques, like those executed by Giovanni da Udine in the Vatican Loggie.

Besides the main garden there are other smaller ones within the precincts of the Vatican. One of these is known as the Pigna Garden, and was formerly part of the old Cortile di Belvedere. An important

Courtyard of the Casino of Pius IV

feature of this garden is the Gran Nicchione built by Bramante; in front of this is set up the bronze pine-cone which has given its name to the Cortile. Its preservation is due to Pope Symmachus, who set it up as an ornament in the middle of the quadri-porticus in front of old St. Peter's. Here it was seen by Dante, who refers to it in Canto xxi of his "Inferno":

"La faccia sua mi parea lunga e grossa
Come la pina di San Pietro a Roma."

When St. Peter's was rebuilt, the gigantic pine-cone was brought to the garden near the Palace of Innocent VIII in the Belvedere, and there it remained until it was erected near the Nicchione in the seventeenth century. It is the work of Publius Cincius Salvius Libertus, and rests on a capital, on which is represented the coronation and acclamation of a victorious prize-fighter.

The Vatican Palaces were joined together by Bramante in the days of Julius II. "That Pontiff had an idea," says Vasari, "to make use of the space between the Belvedere and the Palace." The small valley lying between the buildings of the old palace was to be formed into a rectangular court, flanked by two long corridors through which one

Loggia or Caffeaos opposite the Casino of Pius IV

could proceed from the palace to the Belvedere. The work was begun in 1503, and Vasari gives us a description of the Cortile, the Nicchione, the fountains, the stairs, and the strange inscriptions with which the famous architect decorated the buildings. Besides the pine-cone, of which we have just spoken, this garden is decorated with various other antiquities. It is sufficient to state here that the work on the Pigna Garden was brought to a close by Pirro Ligorio, the architect who had charge of the Casino of Pope Pius. The Cortile has a rather mean appearance to-day, but formerly it was an imposing place, as is shown by the above-mentioned print of Falda. (Cf. p. 28.)

The second Vatican Cortile of note from an artistic point of view is the Octagonal Court, so called from its shape. An octagonal peristyle on antique columns was erected for Clement XIV by the architect Michelangelo Simonetti, and in it were gathered many copies of antiques. Inscriptions and bas-reliefs were placed on the walls, and outside the porticoes in the open air many ancient sarcophagi are covered by the clinging ivy. In the centre is a small fountain, and on the four shorter sides of the octagon are four little rooms in which are contained the more precious objects of art.

The Casino of Pius IV

Famous in history were the old Roman gardens, the Horti Agrippinæ, along the Via Cornelia, which contained a portico and a circus known as the Gaianus, after its builder. All that remains of it is the obelisk which formerly adorned the circus, but is now in front of St. Peter's. Traces of these gardens were found when St. Peter's was being rebuilt, and both then and on other occasions many pagan and Christian tombs were discovered along the line of the old Via Cornelia to the north of the Horti Agrippinæ. A large part of these old gardens was enclosed within the wall erected by Leo IV to protect the Leonine City against the invasions of the Saracens. The length of the wall was about three thousand metres, and its height varied from fifteen to twenty-two. Two inscriptions on the arch of the Via di Porta Angelica give us some information concerning the troops that defended Rome in those days. There were three gateways and two postern doors in the wall of the Leonine City. The first was St. Peter's Gate, which opened on the Elio Bridge under the bastion of Castel S. Angelo; the second was the Postern of S. Angelo, which agreed more or less with the modern Porta Castello; the third was the Porta Sancti Peregrini, which coincided with the Porta Angelica; the fourth was the Porta in Turrione, which coincided with the Porta Cavalleggeri; finally, there was the Postern of the Saxons, which Antonio da Sangallo changed into the monumental Porta di Santo Spirito.

When Antonio da Sangallo, under Paul III, extended and rebuilt the precinct of Rome near the Vatican, the Vatican Gardens took their present shape and area. They date from an era of prosperity in the Roman Court—a happy epoch when art flourished, and when everywhere in Italy gardens were being made that were to be models for all lands. And, though to-day they are more often passed over and forgotten by visitors, they still bear traces of their former beauty and greatness.

PART TWO

—

THE STATE APARTMENTS AND CHAPELS

THE CHAPEL OF NICHOLAS V

IN the year 1445, Fra Angelico, already famous, was called to Rome. His delightful artistic creations in the Convent of St. Dominic at Fiesole had been followed by the frescoed visions with which he adorned the walls of the Convent of St. Mark, Florence, and his success there, as Vasari says, had won him fame throughout all Italy. But Vasari is mistaken when he tells us that to Nicholas V belongs the credit of having called Fra Angelico to Rome, and he is likewise mistaken when he says that the Pope offered the artist the archbishopric of Florence, which was modestly refused. It was Eugene IV who called Fra Angelico to Rome to paint the Sacrament Chapel, which was pulled down later by Pope Paul III and redecorated by Michelangelo. According to Vasari, Fra Angelico painted in the Sacrament Chapel a few scenes from the life of Christ, into which he introduced portraits of many famous contemporaries. A year after the coming of the painter to Rome, Pope Eugene died, but his successor, Nicholas V, equally appreciative of Angelico's work, called on him to decorate the private oratory which he used as a workroom and study, and which is now known as the Cappella Nicolina. When Fra Angelico went to Rome, he did not go alone. With him went Benozzo Gozzoli, who had helped him at St. Mark's in Florence, and who accompanied him in 1447 to Orvieto, where they painted the Chapel of St. Brigit in the Cathedral, in accordance with an agreement with Messer Enrico Monaldeschi, Lord of Orvieto. It was after September 28, 1447, that Angelico undertook the decoration of the Chapel of Nicholas V, and, in spite of all that the people of Orvieto could do, the painter refused to leave Rome again and return to their city. Why, we do not know. In the registers of the Vatican Treasury, which have been carefully investigated by Müntz, there is a record of all payments made to the artist up to 1449. On January 10, 1450, we find Angelico prior of his convent at Florence; and in 1452 the head of the Commune of Prato called on Archbishop Antonino to use his influence to persuade the artist to undertake the decoration of the principal chapel in their cathedral. Fra Angelico refused, and the work was carried out by Fra Filippo Lippi. It is prob-

The Ceiling of the Chapel of Nicholas V
(Fra Angelico)

able that Fra Angelico did some work in Rome after 1449, but the
records make no mention of it.

In the Chapel of Nicholas V Fra Angelico has painted the Calling,
the Apostolate, and the Martyrdom of St. Stephen and of St. Laurence. The chapel, as Venturi tells us, is painted to resemble a
room decorated for a feast-day. Garlands of laurel leaves and red flowers divide the ceiling into four sections, separate the different scenes
in the lives of the saints, and serve as the frame for the two arcades
which lie respectively above the window and the door. In the vaultings
above the door and the window are Sts. Ambrose and Augustine, and
Gregory and Leo respectively; on the pilasters beside the door and the
window are Sts. Thomas Aquinas and Bonaventure, Chrysostom and
Athanasius. On the roof, in a starry blue sky, are the Evangelists,
enthroned on clouds, and on the walls the stories of Sts. Stephen and
Laurence are told in two parallel series of paintings, the series dealing
with St. Stephen being above and that dealing with St. Laurence below.

In the first picture St. Stephen is ordained priest. The interior of a
church is shown; St. Peter, to the left, is standing on the altar steps, in
a green robe with a yellow cape, handing the chalice and paten to St.
Stephen, who kneels before him. Behind the Saint, six persons assist

St. Thomas Aquinas
(Fra Angelico)

St. Bonaventure
(Fra Angelico)

The Ordination of St. Stephen　　　　St. Stephen Distributes Alms
(Fra Angelico)

The Sermon of St. Stephen   St. Stephen Disputes with the Judges
(Fra Angelico)

at the scene. The whole has neither the solemnity of Giotto nor the force of Masaccio, but it expresses an ardent spirit of brotherly love and deep religious fervor.

In the second scene the Saint is distributing alms. He is standing in a gray robe and yellow mantle, and is giving a coin to a woman who extends her hand. Beside him stands a deacon, and before him are seen some beggars and other persons against a background showing a dim Oriental landscape.

The third picture contains two distinct events. To the left, the Saint is seen preaching on a public square to a group of women seated on the ground, while the picture to the right shows him disputing with the judges in the synagogue. The two events are kept distinct in the picture by means of intervening architectural features, a plan employed by Angelico in the Brancacci Chapel and in a fresco at St. Mark's where Christ is shown in the Garden.

The last scene in the history of the Protomartyr shows his death: he has been dragged outside Jerusalem, and is being stoned by two false witnesses in the presence of a crowd of curious onlookers.

Beautiful as are these scenes, they are not quite so well balanced or constructed as the scenes from the life of St. Laurence in the panels below.

In the first the Saint is ordained Deacon.   In the centre aisle of a large basilica, Pope Nicholas V is represented as Sixtus II, wearing the tiara and a blue dalmatic.   He is seated surrounded by priests, and is giving the chalice to Laurence.   The heads in this painting are marvellously executed, and seem to be portraits of earnest, deeply religious men.

In the second picture the Pope is entrusting to Laurence the treasures of the Church for distribution in alms.   The scene is laid in the court-yard of a palace.   The Pope comes from a large door and blesses Lau-

St. Stephen Dragged out of Jerusalem   St. Stephen Stoned to Death
(Fra Angelico)

rence, who is kneeling before him, while servants bear the treasures in trays.   One of the Pope's companions turns suddenly in surprise at the noise of the soldiery who are trying to break in the door of the Pope's dwelling.   The whole scene is graphic and thrills with life.

In the third scene Laurence is shown distributing the treasures to the poor.   Through an open door you see a spacious basilica with three naves; on the door-step stands Laurence in gorgeous priestly robes, holding a purse in his hands from which he is in the act of giving alms. Around him are grouped the afflicted in the most natural of poses: a blind man taps the ground with his stick; an old man with a long beard bends over to hold out his hand; a mother clasps her babe to her bosom, and a lame man leans on his crutch.   The faces of all are lighted up with joy at sight of the Saint's charity.

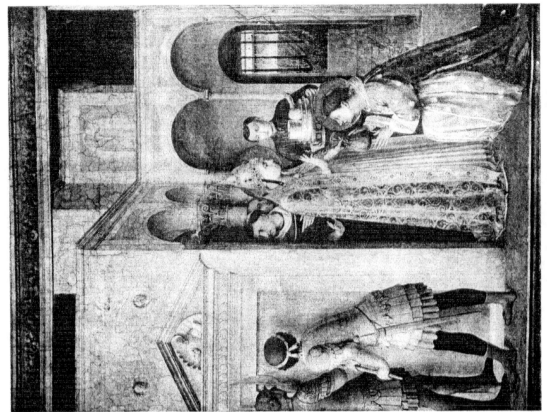

St. Laurence Entrusted with the Treasures of the Church
(Fra Angelico)

St. Laurence Ordained Deacon
(Fra Angelico)

In the next scene the Saint is dragged before the Emperor. Decius, clad in a rich robe, sits on his throne; at his feet are the instruments of torture, to which he points imperiously. Laurence is held by a soldier, while a crowd of frightened people listen to the sentence. The background shows an architectural design behind which rise the tops of exotic trees. The study of ancient art is very marked in this scene. In the architecture we discern beautiful Classical motives—leaf-work, capitals, and friezes in the architraves. The architectural detail is correct in every way, the soldiers' armor is just as accurately drawn, and the bust of Decius seems to have been copied from an ancient statue.

St. Laurence Distributes the Treasures
among the Poor
(Fra Angelico)

A breath of the greatness that was Rome pervades the whole work.

The last scene depicts the Saint's martyrdom. Behind the window bars of his prison we see Laurence consoling his jailer, while on a terrace without the Emperor and his retinue assist at the execution. In the foreground the executioners are lighting the fire under the grate on which the Saint is stretched, and three assistants laugh at his torture. Venturi was right when he considered this picture the most powerful in the chapel. He points out that the artist, to bring out his figures, heightened his tints and displays a vigor quite unusual in his work. Here also the influence of Classical art is clear. The tribune is decorated with niches between the pilasters, and there are statues in the niches; one of the statues carries a column, a symbol of strength. The whole scene is beautified by that historical sentiment which the saintly artist had imbibed from his study of Roman monuments. As Venturi says, Laurence on the Gridiron is like a fallen gladiator; from Byzantine times, indeed, we see the martyrs represented raising up their right hands towards the tyrant who looks down on them from his tribune.

These paintings must be placed among the last works of Fra Angelico. After them we have nothing but the painting of St. Bonaventure in the Wood in the Osservanza Church near Mugello, although he was perhaps the guiding mind behind the Armadi (cupboards) in the

The Martyrdom of St. Laurence
(Fra Angelico)

St. Laurence before the Emperor Decius
(Fra Angelico)

Annunziata Chapel built by Pietro de Medici. These paintings, then, that make up the last testament of the artist, are one of the most interesting pages in the history of art. All the qualities that go to make up the Angelic painter's art are here in their entirety, together with others of which he had previously given no sign. The accent of pure truth which characterizes all his creations is here enhanced by a freshness of minute observation which shows us the good monk in a new light, reveals him as a gifted observer of realities, and links him with the naturalistic school which was then in vogue in Florence, but from which he had previously kept aloof. We see him also as a close student of Classical antiquity and a restorer of ancient beauty in so far as his deep-rooted faith allowed him to dwell on secular things. This phase of his development we might least have expected to find in the painter of Paradise.

The influence of Benozzo Gozzoli has been seen by some in these changes in Angelico's art. Gozzoli may have had a hand in the decorative portions of the paintings, particularly in the finely executed borders wherein beautiful roses appear at intervals among the intricacies of the leaves, and also in the garlands which rest on the charming heads of the boys, and in the medallions showing the tiara and keys of Nicholas V. Furthermore, Gozzoli may have had charge of certain details, and there is a likeness between the background of his Assumption in the Vatican Picture Gallery and the background of the scene where Laurence appears before the Emperor Decius. It is, however, a very far cry from Gozzoli, as we see him at Montefalco, to Angelico. If by any chance he does for a moment grasp the movement of the master's figures, the result in his hands is rough and gross; the externals only have been caught, for the soul of Angelico always escapes him. In the matter of color the difference is equally great. The colors of Angelico are pure and spiritual; those of Gozzoli are heavy, full and realistic. To explain the change in Angelico's later style it is not necessary to introduce the influence of Gozzoli. It was a natural change in the style of a mystical artist forced by the very nature of his subject to deal with realities and reacted on by the things he saw. We have here, then, the fully developed Angelico—Angelico in the fullest control of his genius and with the serenity of his vision unimpaired. His ecstatic soul had previously found no outlet as full and free as in this chapel. In the Coronation at the Uffizi, in the tabernacle of the Linaiolo, in the paintings at St. Mark's, the artistic dreamer had free rein, his subject lending itself naturally to his ecstatic visions. But in the paintings of this chapel the mystic is face to face with the realities of daily life, and a new phase of his soul is lighted up, showing him to be the greatest of all religious painters—namely, a mystic who remains a mystic even when recording with his brush the humble happenings of earth. Who can forget the look on the faces of the women in prayer listening to the words of St. Stephen, or the gesture of the blind man poking his way along the road with the aid of his stick, or the children quarrelling, or the mother clasping her babe in her arms? When we remember the age of the artist at the time he wrought these master-pieces, we can hardly refrain from the astonishment which we feel in the Pauline Chapel when we stand before the wonders executed there by Michelangelo. Both artists show that they retained to the end the power of execution and the creative gift.

If Angelico is the last of the idealists of the Florentine School (and the few who follow, follow indeed afar off), his work is precious not alone because it perpetuates a type of ideal vision in an age of realism and naturalism, but because of the lessons which it transmitted to ages far removed from his own. When Melozzo da Forli, in 1477, painted Pope Sixtus IV in the act of creating Bartolomeo Sacchi, known as Il Platina, Prefect of the Vatican Library, he did nothing but call up to memory the scene painted by Fra Angelico in this chapel, depicting the ordination of St. Laurence by Sixtus II.

It was to Rome that Angelico left his last work, and it was in Rome, the heart of Christendom, that he died, in 1455, at the age of sixty-eight years. He lies buried in S. Maria sopra Minerva, in the convent of his Order, and on the slab of his tomb his ascetic figure is carved together with an epitaph said to be the work of Pope Nicholas himself:

> "Non mihi sit laudi, quod eram velut alter Apelles,
>   Sed quod lucra tuis omnia, Christe, dabam;
> Altera nam terris opera extant, altera cœlo.
>   Urbs me Iohannem *Flos* tulit *Etruriæ.*"

"Say not in my praise that I was a second Apelles; my only glory, O Christ, is that I gave to my brethren what my works brought to me. Thus earth keeps one portion of my work, but the rest is laid up in heaven. John was my name, and my native town was the *Flower of Etruria.*"

THE SISTINE CHAPEL

As it stands to-day, the Sistine Chapel differs somewhat from the work begun about 1493 by Giovannino de' Dolci (*Dominus et vir honorabilis*), at the request of Pope Sixtus IV. For instance, the end wall, where the famous Last Judgment of Michelangelo now stands, held originally a pair of windows, and the roof where the giant figures of the Sibyls and the Prophets are to be seen was once a blue-tinted sky dotted with gold stars. Of the original Palatine Chapel, which was built at the order of Nicholas III in 1278 near the Vatican Palace and gave way eventually to the Patriarchio Lateranense, we know very little; but at least we may picture it as having been rich in painting and sculpture. It was then the heyday of the arts in Rome. The Cosmati, the Vassalletti, and Pietro Cavallini and his school were bringing about a renaissance which anticipated the wondrous flowering of the arts in Tuscany. In that ancient chapel took place the canonization of St. Brigit of Sweden on October 7, 1391, and on Christmas night, 1468, Pope Paul II invested there with cap and sword Frederick III, Emperor of the Holy Roman Empire. Mention is made of the Chapel of Nicholas III in 1473, and again in 1477 in a document which hints at the building of a new chapel by Sixtus IV. This latter Pope consecrated a new sanctuary to Our Lady of the Assumption on August 15, 1482, and his historian, Giacomo da Volterra, tells us that the new building gave him such joy that he went there at all hours to fulfil his devotions and that he was never weary of praising the beauty of its decorations.

If we dwell a little on these things it is because most of them have come down to our day and help to complete one of the most glorious pages in the story of Italian painting in the period of the Renaissance. There was nothing in the interior of Pope Sixtus IV's Chapel to bear out the sternness it wore outside—a sternness which it owed to its builder, Giovannino de' Dolci (the man who had fortified Ronciglione and Civitavecchia), and which is still to be found in that part of the Vatican Palace that looks out on the Cortili del Papagallo and del Maresciallo.

The roof, with its lunettes and corbels, had much the same shape as it has to-day, and the side walls were more or less the same, being divided into three zones, each zone being subdivided by pilasters and windows.

General View of the Sistine Chapel

Very probably in the early days the painted curtains between the pilasters in the first zone were replaced by precious stuffs whose tints harmonized with the colors of the frescoes in the second zone. The third zone held the windows and little niches painted with figures. Such a division of walls into zones by pilasters was quite usual in Rome in ancient and medieval Christian monuments, and it is probably safe to say that it was adhered to in the original Chapel of Nicholas III.

Before Michelangelo painted his Last Judgment on the end wall, that wall also was divided into three sections. Above, there were two win-

Moses and Sephorah
(Perugino and Pinturicchio)

dows and four painted niches, and there were two large frescoes on the middle section. The entrance wall was also adorned with two frescoes. It was Giovannino de' Dolci's plan to add a choir, a screen, and a pavement in opus Alexandrinum. Whereas the decorations of the choir and the screen show the artistic output of the schools of Giovanni Dalmata and Mino da Fiesole, the splendid pavement is Roman workmanship following the lines of old Roman traditions. Among the broken marbles that go to make it up there are scraps of all kinds—bits of pagan inscriptions side by side with Christian ejaculations—and there are even whole patches of old pavements, the work of the Cosmati and probably belonging to the Chapel of Nicholas III which had been pulled down.

But we must hasten on to give an account of the decorations for which on October 27, 1481, a contract was agreed to by Cosimo Rosselli, Sandro Botticelli, Domenico Ghirlandaio, and Pietro Perugino, in which the decorators undertook to paint ten scenes for Giovannino de' Dolci, the architect. Later we mean to particularize the various artists and their assistants on each particular piece of the work, but for the moment our explanation must be more general.

The wall on the left contains the following scenes from the life of Moses: Moses's Journey, Moses in Egypt, Pharaoh Engulfed in the Red Sea, the Adoration of the Golden Calf, the Destruction of the Family of Korah, and the Death of Moses. The wall to the right contains the Baptism of Christ, also the Temptation of Christ, the Calling of Peter and Andrew, the Sermon on the Mount, the Giving of the Keys to Peter, and the Last Supper. On the end wall, where the Last Judgment is now seen, there were frescoes showing the Finding of Moses and the Adoration of the Magi. The entrance wall has frescoes, showing the Struggle for the Body of Moses and the Resurrection of Christ; these were lost when the wall went to

Detail from Moses and Sephorah
(Perugino and Pinturicchio)

ruin in the time of Adrian VI, about 1522, and some time later their places were taken by two paintings of the Michelangelo school from the brushes of Matteo da Lecce and Arrigo Fiammingo.

The very list of subjects shows that the old idea of correlating scenes from the Old and New Testaments in churches—the Law of Concordance, as it was called—held sway here in all its force. As a matter of fact, many stories from Genesis—*e.g.*, the story of Isaac, Abram, and Jacob, in whom early theologians found precursors of Christ—were all discarded and the figure of Moses dominates everything as sufficing in himself to symbolize the Old Testament face to face with the New, in which the redemption took place. The Child Moses Saved from the Waters balances the Adoration of the Magi; the Circumcision of Moses's Sons stands out against the Baptism of Christ; the Adoration of the

Moses and the Daughters of Jethro
(Botticelli)

Detail from Moses and the Daughters of Jethro
(Botticelli)

Details from the Passage of the Red Sea
(Rosselli and Pupils)

The Passage of the Red Sea
(Rosselli and Pupils)

Golden Calf finds itself opposite the Sermon on the Mount; the Struggle for the Body of Moses faces the Resurrection of Christ.

Thus we find in this Palatine Chapel of the Roman Pontiff at the close of the Quattrocento a matured and theological expression of those

The Adoration of the Golden Calf
(Rosselli)

wordless sermons in colors which for centuries had cheered the darkness of the Catacombs and lighted up the severe coldness of the Christian churches; pictures which, as St. Paulinus of Nola so elegantly said, served as silent teachers to the poor who could not read: *rusticitas indocta legendi.*

Now if we pass from the pictures themselves to the artists who painted them, it is instructive to observe that not one artist of note is a Roman. Antoniazzo, it is true, did some work of a very minor character in the chapel, but the great Lorenzo of Viterbo is not found there at all. There was an era of blossoming for art in Rome at the end of the Middle Ages, but the blossoms were nipped when the Popes went to Avignon. Art waned in the Eternal City, and Roman artists, among them the great Pietro Cavallini, to whom Giotto owed so much, were scattered throughout the cities of Italy. When the Popes returned to Rome about the middle of the Trecento and bethought them of decorating the Vatican Palace, they had to fall back on Tuscany, and Tuscans and Umbrians came to decorate the Sistine Chapel. Together with

The Punishment of Korah, Dathan, Abiram and On
(Botticelli and Signorelli)

The Testament of Moses
(Signorelli)

Detail from the Testament of Moses
(Signorelli)

Detail from the Baptism of Christ
(Pinturicchio and Perugino)

Sandro Botticelli, Domenico Ghirlandaio, and Cosimo Rosselli came Pietro Perugino, Pinturicchio, and Luca Signorelli, in whom the schools of Umbria and Tuscany blended so harmoniously. These great masters were aided in their works by assistants of all kinds, so that it is no easy matter to say whether a fresco from one painter's design has not been actually painted by another. As we go along from picture to picture, it will be our endeavor to point out, as far as we know it and as far as space allows, who were the collaborators in each masterpiece. Beginning, then, as usual, on the left wall, we will go round towards the right.

The first painting we come to shows us Moses together with Sephorah (Zipporah) and their sons and servants and handmaidens halted by an angel of God who forbids them to proceed because Sephorah's sons have not been circumcised. The caravan halts and the sacramental rite is performed. Here both design and coloring reveal the hand of Pietro Perugino, the great Umbrian master. It was one of the earliest works painted in the chapel, and was once looked upon as the gem of the whole decoration. Perugino painted four of the frescoes on the walls as well as the two on the end wall that were destroyed later. Moreover, the painting on the altar, representing the Coronation of the Virgin, is also his. In these works he was assisted principally by Pinturicchio, Andrea d'Assisi (known as L'Ingegno), Luca Signorelli, and Piero Dei.

Baptism of Christ
(Pinturicchio and Perugino)

The Temptation of Christ
(Botticelli)

On the first fresco above referred to he was assisted by Pinturicchio, whose lovely flowerlike
coloring is to be seen in the figures
his master designed. It was the
wondrous skill he showed in a
hundred ways on those paintings
that won for Pinturicchio the
honor of being chosen to decorate
the Appartamento Borgia. However the design neither of the
splendid figure of the angel with
the sword coming forward to meet
Moses nor of the virile heads of
those who assist at the circumcision can be attributed to him. They
speak too truly of Perugino. But
the landscape is exclusively by
Pinturicchio, and it was also he
who painted the fresco of the Bap-

Detail from the Temptation of Christ
(Botticelli)

tism of Christ, to which Perugino's sole contribution was the meek
figure of the Redeemer.

In the fresco showing the works of Moses in the land of the Midian-
ites we have a real example of the beauty and skill of Sandro Botticelli's
art—an art that knew so well how to link breadth of movement and
idyllic peace. Following the custom which was so dear to medieval
painters, he tells within the frame of a single fresco the whole
life story of the leader of the chosen people. From the fullness of his
own concept of the theme, he chose as central figure Moses with the
daughters of Jethro near the well. And so sweet is the charm of these
fair-haired maidens and so modest their bearing that they absorb the
attention of the visitor, who thus has no eyes for the story of Moses set
all around them. In one corner Moses is to be seen slaying the Egyptian and taking flight to Midian; in another he is pulling off his shoes
to adore God in the burning bush. In this as in the two other frescoes
Botticelli was assisted by the youth Filippino Lippi.

A work of less importance, by Cosimo Rosselli and his pupils, is the
fresco of the passage of the Red Sea and the engulfing of Pharaoh. The
attention to details and the accuracy of the drawing of the people who
accompany Moses do not save the fresco from criticism as a badly conceived and inorganic work.

It is thus with genuine relief that we turn our eyes to the painting

The Calling of Peter and Andrew
(Domenico Ghirlandaio)

Detail from the Calling of Peter and Andrew
(Domenico Ghirlandaio)

The Sermon on the Mount
(Rosselli)

Detail from the Sermon on the Mount
(Head of Rosselli to the left)

that comes next—the work of Sandro Botticelli and Luca Signorelli. Never had the souls of these two artists, so unlike in many ways, met so graciously as in this picture. The figures of the followers of Korah, Dathan, Abiram, and On, who have just been struck down by divine wrath, resemble nothing so much as the souls of the followers of antichrist and the damned painted by Luca in the Chapel of St. Brigit in the Duomo of Orvieto. To add to the magnificence of the scene, the artists have brought into the background, among other Roman ruins, the Arch of Constantine, and written on it we read: "Nemo sibi assumat

Christ Delivering the Keys to St. Peter
(Perugino)

honorem nisi vocatus a Deo tanquam Aaron"—a patent allusion to the rights and privileges of the Pope.

Concerning the fresco of the Testament of Moses, there was at one time a dispute among art historians, but Adolfo Venturi has banished every doubt and shown beyond debate that the design is by Luca Signorelli, that it was not included in the original contract drawn up in 1481, that he was called in to assist at it, and that the painting was actually done by Piero Dei, one of Luca's staff, with some slight assistance from Pinturicchio, who, being one of the least in that fair company of masters, was glad to lend a hand here and there as occasion offered.

The composition of the picture divides itself into episodes. In the foreground to the right Moses is reading the law, in the centre appears a naked Levite, and to the left Aaron is receiving his rod. In the background are shown the angel pointing out to Moses the Promised Land that his feet were never to touch, then Moses coming down tired from the mountain, and, last scene of all, the people of Israel weeping over their dead patriarch. There is an old tradition to the effect that the splendid figure of the Levite is the portrait of Luca's son, who was done to death by jealous painters. This glorious figure, which seems to herald the mighty works of Michelangelo, is a miracle of drawing for the time when it was done.

The Last Supper
(Cosimo Rosselli)

The series of frescoes on the right wall begins with the Baptism of Christ, the work throughout of Pinturicchio save for the masterful central figure of the Redeemer, which was designed by Pietro Perugino. Another gracious figure, recalling the Allegory of Springtime, is that painted by Sandro Botticelli in the Temptation of Christ, which is, on the whole, a feeble work overcrowded with characters and details. The sacrifice of the leper, with its background showing the Hospital of Santo Spirito restored by Pope Sixtus IV, the weird altar with its rising flames, and the curious crowd of onlookers, take the eye completely away from the little scene in which the demon appears vainly tempting the Saviour.

The series of stories taken from the New Testament begins, as we have said, on the right wall with the Baptism of Christ, which balances the Circumcision of the Children of Israel on the opposite wall. We next pass on to the Calling of Peter and Andrew, in the execution of which Domenico Ghirlandaio was assisted by his young brother, David. The method of grouping his subjects, so distinctive of the great Florentine, is clearly in evidence here. To the right, in the group of men, aged and youthful, he has painted for us, with all the accuracy he learned from studying the designs of the Dutch masters, the portraits of the

Portrait of Michelangelo
(Last Judgment)

great Florentines in Rome at the time. There, for instance, stands Guid'antonio Vespucci, Florence's spokesman to the Pope. But the whole composition is somewhat theatrical, as though the various characters had come to have their portraits painted and were bent on making as good an appearance as possible.

Weakest of all painters in the Quattrocento was Cosimo Rosselli, pupil of the mediocre school of Neri di Bicci. He seems to have lacked originality, and to have picked up a bit here and a bit there, but discovered nothing for himself. The best feature of his Sermon on the Mount is the landscape, which was painted by Piero di Cosimo, a pupil who modelled himself largely on the style of Leonardo and the Dutch school. To the left Jesus is addressing the crowds, and on the right he is healing the leper boy. Steinmann, in his great work on the Sistine Chapel, has successfully shown that the figure to the right in the first row is Giacomo d'Almedia, Knight of Rhodes, and that beside him stands his brother, the Portuguese ambassador in Rome. On the left side also, and a little behind these two, the painter has placed Carlotta of Lusignan, formerly Queen of Cyprus, together with her husband, Louis of Savoy.

A fresco of peculiar importance comes next, its subject being Christ Delivering the Keys to St. Peter. In the centre stands Christ, giving the symbolical keys to the kneeling Apostle. The lower portion of the pic-

Section of a Wall showing Popes Lucius and
Fabianus

Caryatid
(Michelangelo)

Pope St. Stephen I
(Botticelli)

Pope St. Soterus
(Botticelli)

ture is so painted as to stand out strong and dark against the pavement glowing with light; in the background rises a large octagonal building with porticoes, supposed to be the Temple of Solomon and typifying the Old Law, and a pair of triumphal arches, clearly Roman in architectural style. Six Apostles in various attitudes follow Christ, while five stand near Peter. On both sides are various personages in medieval robes, and one with brownish hair is said to be the painter himself. The background is filled in with figures of men in various costumes.

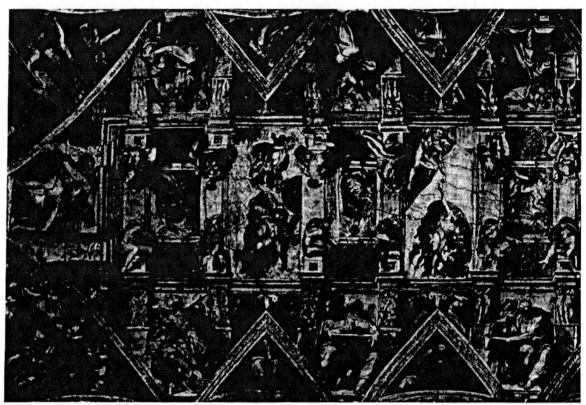

The Ceiling of the Sistine Chapel
(Michelangelo)

In this great fresco Pietro Perugino, who up to this had been working in Florence, gives us a new revelation of himself. The figures, nevertheless, have much of that Umbrian charm and sweetness which at times grow so wearisome in the works of this great master. But the whole work breathes so much power and majesty that it enables us to see the vivid impression the atmosphere of Rome had made upon him. There is no truth in the assertion that Luca Signorelli helped Perugino on this painting. His only helper was Piero Dei, who, as Adolfo Venturi has so clearly shown, designed and painted the figures of the two bearded Apostles who are seen one on either side of Christ.

The last fresco on the right is the work of Cosimo Rosselli, as empty

and feeble as anything he ever did. Not even the charming group of
the cat and dog at play, nor the excellent roof perspective he gives us,
nor all his pains at painting in the spaces on which the large windows
open scenes showing Christ in the Garden, the Betrayal of Christ, and
Christ on the Cross, can make us forget how mean and feeble the whole
composition is.

Even to-day, after the marvellous unity of this series of Quattrocento
frescoes has been broken, we cannot help feeling how beautiful and
eloquent it all is. Sixtus IV enjoyed this noble work but a short time,

The Ceiling of the Sistine Chapel
(Michelangelo)

for he died on August 12, 1484, almost a year after he had solemnly
consecrated the chapel on August 25, 1483. The chapel remained
untouched till 1508. In the meantime Innocent VIII had called Andrea
Mantegna to Rome to decorate his private chapel (which no longer
exists), and Alexander VI had enjoined Pinturicchio to decorate the
Appartamento Borgia.

When in May, 1508, Michelangelo Buonarroti set his hand to the
mighty task of decorating the roof of the Sistine, he had perforce to
give up work on the monument of Julius II which was the curse of his
life. He had already completed for Bologna a statue of the great Pontiff, which was smashed by the infuriated people in 1511. Michel-

angelo's first contract with the Pope for the decoration of the Sistine roof was drawn up May 10, 1508, and in putting his name to it the great master signed himself "a sculptor," as though to emphasize the pain it caused him to be obliged to cease work on the monument to which he desired to give up all the strength of his mind and body. It may well have been that, out of jealousy, Bramante had long been plotting to have the Sistine decorated so as to thwart the great Tuscan master whose recent works had so put him in the shade. However that may

The Deluge
(Michelangelo)

be, it is quite certain that Michelangelo was sincerely sorry to have to go to work as a painter, and he showed his disappointment openly.

His first plan for the roof was very different from what we now see, and studies for it are preserved in the British Museum. The design was a geometric one, cut up into squares of various sizes with sides running parallel to the walls of the chapel. In his preparations Michelangelo was assisted by his faithful friend, Francesco Granacci, who selected many painters to help in the great work. Among them were Jacopo di Sandro, Agnolo di Domino, Bastiano da Sangallo, Giuliano Bugiardini, and Jacopo, surnamed L'Indaco. They were all excellent

The Drunkenness of Noah
(Michelangelo)

The Sacrifice of Noah
(Michelangelo)

The Creation of Adam
(Michelangelo)

The Creation of Eve
(Michelangelo)

fresco painters who had come to Rome, and were all very eager for a chance of showing what they could do. For a time Michelangelo looked at them, let them talk, and then one day they found the chapel door locked against them. He could do no work with five painters around him, he said, and so he set about the mighty work all alone.

For four continuous years ending on October 31, 1512, he worked up there on his high scaffold, alone with his own creations, while down below the ceremonies in the church, changing from festivals of joy to

Original Sin and the Expulsion from Eden
(Michelangelo)

periods of mourning, marked the flight of time for common men. Day by day new visions came to fill his great mind, and, cut off as he was from the mass of men and rapt in superhuman ecstasy, he passed his time with the mighty children of his fantasy. Wounded by the endless plotting of his enemies, sorrowful over the infelicities of his home life that he could never forget, and suffering physical torture from being forced to draw and paint that roof with his head in a strained position, he found no relief save in ever-increased exertion and in the thought of the mighty work he was engaged on for the honor of God and the uplifting of the sons of man. Now and again Julius II unwillingly allowed him to recruit himself with a few days' brief rest. And on August 14, 1511, when the first part of the frescoes was uncovered, we

The Creation of Light
(Michelangelo)

The Creation of the Sun and the Moon
(Michelangelo)

find a brief mention of the fact in the diary of Paride de' Grassi, papal master of ceremonies, who forgot to mention the name of the great artist. The remainder of the work was completed and uncovered on October 31, 1512, at which time Julius II was on his death-bed.

Let us run over the subjects painted on the roof, beginning at the door where Michelangelo began to paint and where we find the Deluge—one of the earliest in point of time, and also one of the few subjects in which we can find any points of similarity between the master and the various painters or schools he had come in touch with.

The Separation of the Land from the Water
(Michelangelo)

Between the Deluge of Paolo Uccello, in the Green Cloister of S. Maria Novella, and this Deluge the links are ideal rather than real, but nevertheless they are there if one knows where to look for them. Around his vision of the horrible spectacle of Death, Michelangelo, as if to mitigate the view, has introduced two scenes from life—the Drunkenness of Noah and the Sacrifice on Leaving the Ark. In these two paintings the nudes and the draperies make us believe for an instant that Michelangelo is displaying his love for classical antiquity. If you look well into these paintings you will find that the figures are smaller than in the others. This was his first attempt, and he quickly found out that owing to the height and size of the roof he had to enlarge them.

The Prophet Zechariah
(Michelangelo)

The Prophet Joel
(Michelangelo)

The Delphic Sibyl
(Michelangelo)

The Prophet Isaiah
(Michelangelo)

The Cumæan Sibyl
(Michelangelo)

The Persian Sibyl
(Michelangelo)

The Prophet Daniel
(Michelangelo)

The Prophet Jeremiah
(Michelangelo)

Let us pass on from the Noah scenes to the Adam and Eve group in the centre of the roof. Here the very pinnacle of art has been scaled. The figure of Adam stands out against a solitary peak, alone with God, who comes forward from a crowd of angels through the calm sky. The limbs that spring into life at the divine touch, the fair body that seems, in its inertia, to be still a part of the very earth, are at once one of the greatest symbols and easiest lessons that the human mind has imaged to teach us that it is ever our tragic lot to struggle between the materialism of our bodies and the efforts of our imprisoned souls to wing their way to their divine Cre-

The Prophet Ezekiel
(Michelangelo)

ator. In the pictures showing the birth of Eve and the first sin the mind of the artist is more within our ken; and as we look on these scenes, our souls are not drowned in the infinite ocean of allegory which the master has known how to depict in his vision of man's first appearance on this earth. In representing God without crown or halo, Michelangelo introduced a conception, which was imitated by Raphael and others.

It is usual to call attention here to the relief of the Creation with which Jacopo della Quercia has adorned the façade of S. Petronio's at Bologna. There is, indeed, no denying points of contact between the two works, but one might search Bologna with lamps before finding one simple sculptured scene to equal that of the Creation of Adam. The synthetic quality which is so necessary for every great work of art— that synthetic quality which taught Giotto to build on the realism of the Roman and Sienese Schools of the Duecento the monumental simplicity of his compositions, in which not the passing events of a day but the eternal commerce of the human race with its Deity is set forth —that synthetic quality led Michelangelo to compose the Creation of Man and to place around it, as companion pictures, the Creation of Light, Land and Water.

The face of the Creator, which seems to lack all emotion in the first picture, is lighted up with paternal tenderness in the third, where he broods over the wide expanse of the seas that know not yet the shock

The Last Judgment
(Michelangelo)

The Figure of the Redeemer
(Last Judgment)

of the storm. In the lunettes above Michelangelo has painted in the purest types of human heroism: David slaying Goliath; the story of Judith; Esther and Haman; Moses and the Brazen Serpent. Next come the pictures of the Seven Prophets and the Five Sibyls, whose inner symbolical significance leads us to think that, from the very first touch of color Michelangelo put to the Sistine roof, he always entertained the idea of completing the decoration of the chapel by the Last Judgment —a work he did not really undertake until 1535.

Group of the Blessed around Christ
(Last Judgment)

Throughout the whole period of the Middle Ages the imposing figures of the Prophets and Sibyls had been used in decorations side by side with the Apostles and Saints of the New Law. The law of prophetic concordance between the Old and the New Testament is clearly manifest in the case of the Prophets, with whom were associated the legendary Sibyls as a proof of the spiritual union of the worlds of paganism and Christianity in their expectation of the new dispensation which was to knit them together in the bonds of its great love.

The Sibyl who on the Capitoline Hill foretold the Christ to Augustus is not here in person, but her spirit is here and speaks to us in the figures of her five companions. The Prophets and the Sibyls have each a deep meaning often transcending the historicity of the person or the legend, and the manner in which they are treated is an index to the meaning the artist would convey.

Zechariah, as a learned old man, seems to be seeking for light in the books of the old wisdom. Joel is reading there the dread prophecy of the great judgment day in the Valley of Jehoshaphat. Between them stands the Delphic Sibyl, calling up to the mind in this Christian church the temples of Apollo and the secrets of pagan worship. Lost in the very greatness of her vision, the Pythoness seems to be hearkening to

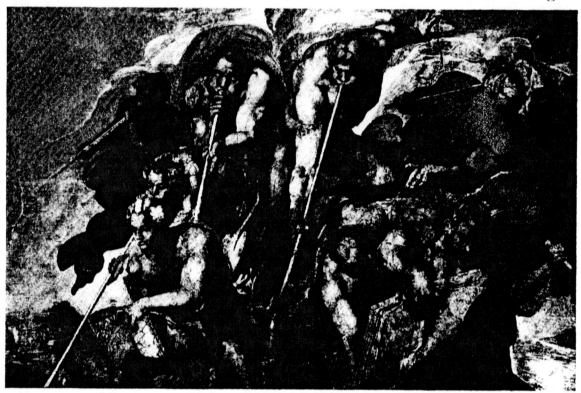

Angels Summoning the Dead to Rise
(Last Judgment)

a voice that tells her of the coming union of men of all times and climes in the great idea of a Supreme Deity. The Erythræan Sibyl is a more sympathetic figure, and recalls Zechariah, as he turns over the pages of Holy Writ. She seems to be carefully reading by the light of a lamp. The rapt attention of her attitude has been skilfully shown by the master in the unconscious grace of the left arm, hanging loosely by her side, while the right seems to have paused in the act of turning over a page whereon her eyes have caught the passage that she sought. The plump servant, who seems in the act of renewing the oil in the lamp, adds to the intimate charm of this scene.

Lost in deep interior vision, the youthful Isaiah hardly turns his head or lifts his eyelids, almost closed over the thoughtful eyes, at the eager call of the curly-headed youth by his side.

Angels bearing the Emblems of the Passion
(Last Judgment)

Angels bearing the Emblems of the Passion
(Last Judgment)

How much more alert is the figure of Ezekiel at the words of the
maiden near him, who seems as if
she were describing to him the
many-eyed animals around the
throne of the King of Glory. He
is surely here the prophet of the
Resurrection, impetuous as a tor-
rent and filled with faith in his God.

Figures of the Damned
(Last Judgment)

The Cumæan Sibyl that talked
with Æneas, Evander, and Pallas
has all the strength of ancient
Rome and with placid mien traces
the events of history in the great
book. Wrapped in her ample robes
from head to foot and with face
almost hidden, the Persian Sibyl is
in the act of writing. In conform-
ity with the traditions handed
down in the symbolism of the
Middle Ages, Daniel is there, the type of an upholder of the faith
against all threats. Jeremiah seems to brood over his Lamentations—
his attitude expressing the sorrow of his thoughts, and sorrow, too, is
written on the faces of his young followers.

Remarkable rather for corporeal than for symbolical beauty are the
Libyan Sibyl and Jonah. Jonah seems as if still confused by his deten-
tion within the belly of the leviathan, as stretched out under the traditional gourd he gazes at the Lord while he tells off on his fingers his
foolish reasons for doubting. The Preacher of Nineveh, the last type
of the Resurrection, closes the series of Prophets in the roof above the
Judgment which the Divine Judge pronounces over those risen from
the dead.

From the representation of the universal flood down to Jonah, the
figures seem to take on more life and dignity, and this is not only the
case in the scene pieces and in the Prophets and Sibyls, but even in
the nudes seated on the pilasters and holding the shields on which the
master has depicted the symbolic cycle based on Dante's Purgatory.

It was Carlo Borinski who discovered the meaning of these shields
whereon the personages bear the names of the various ancestors of
Jesus as given in the genealogy of St. Matthew's Gospel, and whom
Michelangelo, overcoming all difficulty and fatigue, has placed as
adornments for the eight beams of the roof and the corresponding

Candelabrum on the Balustrade
(Fifteenth Century)

Candelabrum on the Balustrade
(Fifteenth Century)

Side View of the Choir-loft
(Fifteenth Century)

Balustrade and Choir-loft
(Fifteenth Century)

twelve lunettes of the windows. Guided by a similarity between those figures and characters in Dante, Borinski has succeeded in showing that the figures typify certain moral and religious maxims in Dante's poem. Thus, in the composition to which the names Eleazar and Nathan have been added, we find reference to the Dantean nurse and the happy parents (Paradiso, xv, 121); that named Jacob and Joseph calls up the father who is worried over his daughter's dowry and marriage (Paradiso, xv, 103). Achim and Eliud remind us of the lines where he tells how bitter is the bread in the house of a stranger (Paradiso, xvii, 58). Ozias, Joatham, and Achaz call up the story of Caccia-

The Sistine Cantoria, or Choir-loft
(Fifteenth Century)

guida as Dante tells it (Paradiso, xv, 17). Rehoboam and Abiah remind us of the wife alone while her husband lies dead in France (Paradiso, xv, 19).

The two lunettes of the end wall once held Abram and Isaac with his load of wood, and Jacob and Judah, but these Michelangelo destroyed together with the Perugino frescoes twenty-three years later, when he came to paint the mighty vision of the Last Judgment. The subject was chosen by Clement VII, and Michelangelo made some early studies for it which were approved by Paul III. The choice of such a subject is quite in keeping with the spirit of the times, which was wont to pass lightly from the pagan joy of the Renaissance to the rigid orthodoxy of the Council of Trent and the asceticism of the Counter Reform. We must remember, too, that Rome had endured the dread sack of 1527, and Florence had fallen under the blows of her own citizens, who had formed an alliance with the Imperial party.

Michelangelo was sixty years old when he began this great work, which was to occupy him seven years. It was at one time intended to decorate the entrance wall with the Fall of Lucifer, but nothing ever

Portion of the Marble Balustrade
(1481–1483)

came of the idea. Moreover, by placing the Judgment on the wall facing the entrance door, an old tradition was broken which held that it should be on the entrance wall to the east whence the Judge was to come and facing the altar in the apse. It is so at Torcello, and at S. Angelo in Formis, and thus too it was painted by Pietro Cavallini in S. Cecilia in Trastevere and by Giotto in the Scrovegni Chapel at Padua. But the giant imagery of Michelangelo for the Sistine was not to be chained by an iconographic tradition. He retained the Christian idea, indeed, but he altered its form.

Michelangelo's masterpiece has come down to us darkened here and there by the smoke from the altar candles and repainted by Daniele da

A Panel of the Balustrade
(1481–1483)

A Panel of the Balustrade
(1481–1483)

Volterra, who, at the request of Paul II, whose feelings were shocked by so much nudity, dared to throw veils across the beauty of the limbs his master had painted.

Of its original form we can gain some conception from a copy painted by Venusti for Cardinal Alessandro Farnese, now preserved in the Museo Nazionale in Naples, and from a few engravings.

The figure of Jesus is not, as in other medieval Judgments, enthroned in glory and indicating with a gesture of his hand his approval or condemnation. Here he seems not to be concerned with the elect who are on his right hand, but to turn the wrath of his face towards the lost, who try to climb the mount of Paradise, struggling with the demons who drag them towards the eternal fire. Creation trembles before its Judge, and even Mary, the gentle adviser of mercy, turns aside as though in fright. Among the blessed around Christ are Eve, St. Peter, St. Stephen, St. Laurence, St. Bartholomew, and, lower down, St. Catherine of Alexandria with a broken piece of her martyr's wheel and St. Sebastian about to bend the bow of his own murderers.

In the centre of the lower portion of the picture angels with trumpets call on the dead to rise. Tombs open wide, and those about to be judged come forth heavy after their sleep of ages, and are either hurried on high by God's messengers or dragged down below by demons.

Charon is there as a black fiery-eyed demon, driving ashore with his oar those who have crossed in his accursed boat, and who now struggle to the shore, where one of the damned stands upright, bound about twice by the coiled tail of Mino, the judge of the infernal regions.

There is not in the whole work a single smile, a single trace of mercy; even the Virgin is afraid and dares not turn her eyes towards the awful sight. From the demons hurled headlong on the shores of Acheron to the giant angels on high who bear the emblems of Christ's passion, everything speaks of woe, pain, and terror.

The whole theme represents the state of mind of Michelangelo during the last portion of his life, and the gloom with which he gave himself up to that dark problem of life and death.

And so with the final Judgment the chain of pictures in the Sistine closes: a chain the first link of which was the charming idyl of Moses and Sephorah painted so joyously by Perugino and Pinturicchio among the green trees of a land smiling with the joy of springtime and joyous with the laughter of beautiful children.

THE PAULINE CHAPEL

THE Pauline Chapel, so called after Pope Paul III, was built according to plans made by the architect Antonio da Sangallo on the site where the Sacrament Chapel, decorated originally by Fra Angelico, had once stood. The decorations of the new chapel were the work of many artists. Lorenzo Sabbatini, known also as Lorenzino da Bologna (died about 1577), did the Stoning of St. Stephen and the Baptism of St. Paul. Federico Zuccari painted the Fall of Simon Magus and the Baptism of Cornelius the Centurion, works of little importance and calling for slight attention from either visitor or critic. There are, however, two masterpieces in the chapel—the Conversion of St. Paul and the Martyrdom of St. Peter, painted by Michelangelo in his last years.

Anxious to rival Pope Sixtus IV, the restorer of Rome, who had given his name to the Sistine Chapel, Paul III could entrust the decorations of his new chapel to none but the greatest living artist—the artist who had immortalized his titanic soul in the tomb of Julius II and a year before had finished the Last Judgment. So, in the year 1542, Michelangelo was called to decorate the new building.

The master was now an old man. The winters of sixty-eight years were weighing upon him, and twice, in 1544 and 1546, did illness beat him down and halt his labors. Fire caused an interruption in 1545, and it was not until 1550 that he completed his work. The ailments of the master were not all of the body: his soul, too, was wounded. The woes of his fallen city; the lack of appreciation of his own work; the profanation of his Last Judgment by Daniele da Volterra, whose meddling with its nudes won him for succeeding centuries the nickname of "Braghettone" (Breeches-maker); the taunts of Aretino in 1545, backed up even by Cardinal Biagio de Cesena, Papal Master of Ceremonies— all these oppressed his mighty soul. He had, however, but one real regret, and this regret finds an echo in the writings of Vasari: he was growing old, and his hand no longer answered true to fix in color the creations of his brain. "Fresco work was beyond the power of an old man," writes Vasari. In the sorrow of this giant mind there is something sublimely tragic that recalls the saying of the modern poet who speaks of "the anger of a god overcome by matter."

The Conversion of St. Paul
(Michelangelo)

Michelangelo has depicted on the walls two of the fundamental
scenes of nascent Christianity—Paul on the Way to Damascus and the
Crucifixion of St. Peter. No more heroic themes could have been
chosen than these, which may be regarded as the two culminating
points in the history of the Apostles.

In the Conversion of St. Paul the master has once more grappled
with the most difficult problems of aërial perspective. Christ, surrounded by a glory of angels, seems to swoop down on the Apostle
with the same power that the Angel has in the canvas by Tintoretto in
Venice. At the sight of the marvel, the affrighted Apostle cannot control his horse, which rears and unseats him. The legionaries gather
around their fallen leader, while one of their number holds by the

The Martyrdom of St. Peter
(Michelangelo)

bridle the wonderful white horse, the only thing Stendhal had eyes for. The majesty of Christ and the attitude of Paul are, as Burckardt has pointed out, among the happiest things Michelangelo ever did. But it is not fair to say, as the German critic does, that the whole subject fails through a sort of wilfulness which, even in Michelangelo, he does not hesitate to call mannerism. Nor can we agree with Blanc, who sees nothing in the choice of attitudes but an excuse to overcome drawing difficulties, and in the employment of nudes for the figures in the sky sees only a deliberate excuse of the artist to show his knowledge of anatomy and the infinite attitudes and poses into which the human body may be tortured.

Far different was Michelangelo's idea. Just as in the Sistine Chapel his vision went beyond the affairs of our daily life to a deeper and eternal reality, so was it here. Had he merely wanted to show off his skill as a draughtsman, it would have been easy for him to choose fantastic scenes like those revelled in by contemporary dwarfs. His use of the nude has a deeper meaning. By disrobing Paul's legionaries he meant to rid them of at least a part of their concreteness, and, as in the famous battle cartoon, make them stand less for the individual soldier than as an expression of human strength and vigor. The reality of the human body is for Michelangelo an ideal thing—a network of lines and curves suggesting the loftiest thoughts. His motives in painting the Conversion of St. Paul were the same as those that moved him when at work on the end wall of the Sistine; and, as Vasari tells us,—perhaps repeating what the master told him,—he was attracted only by the perfection of his art, caring nothing about such accessories as landscape, trees and houses, as though fearful lest such minor things should distract his genius. The whole motive of Michelangelo's art may be summed up in this phrase of Vasari's: "the triumph of the human body over every other form in creation—the body of man as the mirror of the world in which all else is reflected and through which all else may be shown."

The second picture is not quite so interesting as the first, as the artist seems to have confined himself more to the actual happenings. In the centre the executioners are raising the cross on which St. Peter is nailed head downwards in deference to his declared unworthiness to die exactly as Christ did. A newly dug hole has been prepared to receive the cross. To the right a group of women are awe-stricken witnesses, and foot-soldiers and men on horseback move around as though amused at the horrible sight. There is a blurred landscape of hills in the distance. The head of the martyred Peter is marvellously drawn. His is the same figure that in the Last Judgment gives back, with a noble gesture, the keys to the Saviour, and his face here is the face at once of a stoic and of one inspired. He looks beyond the moment's pain to the eternity of the Church which is built on his tomb.

One might almost take this figure as a symbol of Michelangelo himself. Racked and tortured as he was and weighed down by years, he must certainly have looked forward beyond his present bitterness to the eternal triumph of his art, all the more so as at that very time he was planning to raise into the sky the loftiest cupola in Christendom. It was, in fact, in 1547 that, after a delay of twenty years, he was recalled to resume the building of St. Peter's. At the age of seventy-three he took up Bramante's idea and planned the four mighty pillars that were to hold the wondrous cupola. What matter if the Fates cut short his life, and he never saw his work finished? He saw it complete in his own mind and more actual than it is even now, when it hangs in the clouds above Rome.

It was in such mighty thoughts that the giant's last days were spent. These two frescoes in the Pauline Chapel are the last paintings from his brush, the crowning works of a life spent in noting every movement and every gesture so as to fix it faithfully on his painted walls. From the calm triumph of the youthful David he had arrived at the awful majesty of Christ the Judge; and now, like his own dying Peter, he could face death unafraid, convinced that it would lead from this world of reality to the realm of the divine ideal of which he had more than once caught a glimpse.

THE APPARTAMENTO BORGIA

ON August 11, 1492, Rodrigo Borgia was elected Pope by the Conclave which had assembled upon the death of Innocent VIII, and took the name of Alexander VI. He was not far past his sixtieth year, so that he could not be called, for a Pope, an old man; but he knew only too well that he lived in an age when the termination of life did not depend exclusively upon age and natural ailments. Very intelligible, therefore, was his desire that his plans be promptly executed. A nephew of Calixtus III and raised to the Cardinalate at the age of twenty-five, he had found himself at an early age in possession of wealth which enabled him to indulge his taste for worldly pleasures and the Spanish temperament which inclined him to luxury. He could now freely indulge his luxuriousness with something like approval on the part of the ecclesiastical world, because, even before coming to the pontifical throne, he had broken through all ecclesiastical bounds, and, not yet a priest, had called down on himself the stern reproof of Pius II for his orgies in Siena. It was not until a much later period, however, that public indignation was aroused against him, and then not so much because of his own vices as because of the crimes of his son, Cesare. These crimes, with which he had no connection and which were indeed perpetrated to his exceeding sorrow, brought upon him more hatred than his earlier dissolute and immoral life. The victims of Cesare cast a darker shadow over the reputation of Alexander than his own amours with Vannozza and Giulia Farnese.

Alexander, then, had barely entered the Vatican when he resolved to prepare for himself a suite of apartments that would be a marvel of splendor, rich in reliefs, in gilding, in marbles, in majolica, in furniture, in hangings; a suite so magnificent that not a hand's breadth of ceiling or of walls should be left untouched. The eye and the mind were to find no repose. In the tiniest unoccupied space memory might lurk to awaken remorse or painful recollections. Everywhere, therefore, splendor and gaiety must prevail. Alexander summoned the artist who at that time gave the most satisfactory proof of his ability to comprehend his patron's disposition and satisfy his desires—Bernardino

The Hall of the Mysteries

di Betto, called Il Pinturicchio, a little decrepit creature, hard of hearing (and thus sometimes known as Il Sordicchio), frequently ailing,
and yet working indefatigably all his life to bring joy into the lives of
others, only to end in the claws of a worthless wife who paraded her
shame in the market-place of Siena. Pinturicchio had already worked
in Rome—in the Sistine Chapel with Perugino, and then in the Palazzo
dei Penitenzieri, and had also executed the frescoes of the Bufalini
Chapel in the Church of Ara Cœli and decorated the Belvedere of the
Vatican and various chapels in S. Maria del Popolo. He was, therefore, much in vogue as a decorator,—all the more so because, if not the
first to employ *grotteschi*, he had been the most enthusiastic cultivator
of that method, and had enriched the art with a variety of new and
lively forms. His attempts were at first confined to chiaroscuro, like
bas-relief, but by degrees, as the craze for excavations grew and new
forms of ancient pictorial decoration were revealed, he abandoned
himself to a grand revel of colors and gilding.

It is impossible to describe the fever for research and for the fantastic then in vogue. The animal and vegetable kingdoms were com-

David Enthroned   Door in the Hall of the Mysteries

bined in one wild, joyous riot of color. The recesses of the Domus
Aurea, which has been identified by some as the Baths of Titus, and
other buried monuments were invaded by a swarm of painters who
crawled on all fours, copied the decorations by the light of torches and
candles, and came out from their labor begrimed, half stupefied and
exhausted. As these buried chambers were called *grotte* (caves), the
ornamentations copied from them were given the name of *grotteschi*,
and Lorenzo Luzo, when he emerged from underground as pale as one
risen from the dead, was nicknamed Il Morto da Feltre (The Dead Man
of Feltre). That Pinturicchio was a remarkable portrait painter is
sufficiently proved by the Sanseverino picture; but, not to mention
Leonardo da Vinci, he was very far from possessing Signorelli's
strength, Perugino's feeling, Mantegna's power, the ideality of Giovanni Bellini, the grace of Botticelli, or the sincerity of Ghirlandaio.
He was inferior to many others also, and it is clear that he would never
have been sought after by princes, as he was, nor would he have
acquired such a reputation, had he not possessed in the highest degree
the qualities of a decorator. He liked to draw crowds in all their tumult
of form and color, perhaps because he recognized himself as lacking
in the gift of discerning individuality, divining character and depicting
personality. On the other hand, his genius was rich in such external
qualities as elegance and vivacity, and he was able to produce an art

The Adoration of the Magi
Hall of the Mysteries

The Annunciation
Hall of the Mysteries

The Nativity
Hall of the Mysteries

abounding in magnificence and calculated to please—an art which we may venture to call meretricious, for in it a wealth of ornament covered but a poverty of heart. This splendor it was that won him the smiles of princes. When Rodrigo Borgia became Pope, Pinturicchio was engaged in painting the Cathedral of Orvieto; but, having embroiled himself in a lawsuit there with the authorities in charge of the work, he returned to Rome, and was thus able to take over the decoration of the Appartamento in November, 1492. Taking shelter under the Pope's protection when the people of Orvieto angrily clamored for his return to complete the frescoes he had begun in their cathedral, he was able to finish his work in the Vatican by the end of 1494.

Any one who now looks at the immense amount of work in the Appartamento Borgia, must be astonished to learn that it was all done in about two years. To complete it, Pinturicchio gathered about him a number of assistants who, while distinguished by different methods in painting, have never, with one exception, been identified with any certainty. The work, examined in detail, shows traits of good and of mediocre artists, hints derived from Perugino, Signorelli and others from Tuscany or perhaps from still more distant climes. The unity of the whole was preserved, because a single brain conceived it all and presided over the work, guiding the hands of those who executed it and

The Ascension
Hall of the Mysteries

retouching, when necessary, what they had painted so as to bring it into harmony with the rest. It may be that this indispensable care on the part of Pinturicchio took away from every artist just that personal quality which might have guided critics in recognizing him, with the result that the merit and the glory of the work have been attributed to the spirit which conceived and animated it. The chambers decorated at that time are five in number, and we shall accept the names recently given to them by Ehrle and Stevenson: the Hall of the Mysteries, the Hall of the Saints, the Hall of the Liberal Arts, the Hall of the Credo, and the Hall of the Sibyls (Sala dei Misteri, Sala dei Santi, Sala delle Arti Liberali, Sala del Credo, Sala delle Sibille). Pinturicchio did a considerable amount of work with his own hands in the first of these, much in the second, very little in the third, and none in the last two. However, we must repeat, he conceived and directed the whole.

The Hall of the Mysteries is spanned by a great arch dividing it into two rectangular portions with four small lunettes and two large ones. In one of the latter, facing the window, the decoration is made to simulate two other lunettes with a corbel in which an angel stands holding in his uplifted hands a garland with the Borgia-Doms armorial bearings—an ox *passant* in the first half, and in the second a bend of gold and azure. The walls are decorated with large fillets, Greek fretwork, and gilded foliage surrounding green spaces, arabesqued in gold, and show a num

The Assumption
Hall of the Mysteries

The Coming of the Holy Ghost
Hall of the Mysteries

The Resurrection
Hall of the Mysteries

ber of representations of marble niches within which are sacred objects
and church furniture—vases, plates, a triple-crowned tiara, a reliquary
and a small bell. The painting above the cornice in this and in the
other halls is enlivened with stucco and papier-mâché designs of the
heraldic bearings of the Borgia, varied in every way, and interspersed
with garlands and tabernacles; and over everything falls a golden
shower of little compressed and flattened pellets of wax covered with
gilding. In each wall-veil is placed a disc. These discs show half-
figures, very badly done, of Zephaniah, Jeremiah, Joel, Micah, Malachi,
Solomon, Isaiah and David, the work of some Umbrian who seems to

Details from the Resurrection
Hall of the Mysteries

have followed Fiorenzo di Lorenzo, or, better, Antoniazzo Romano. Of the frescoes which adorn the semicircular spaces, only two are worth dwelling upon as the work of the master. The Annunciation is not Pinturicchio's; for, while it reveals Umbrian characteristics, it is not his, nor is it the work of any Lombard, as any one may see, for at this period *Lombard* would mean a disciple of Foppa. The same painter, in fact, keeps the exclusive Umbrian motives in the adjacent Nativity (Presepio), and at the same time recalls Pinturicchio's Nativity in the church of S. Maria del Popolo, as well as the Nativities by Perugino in the Sala del Cambio at Perugia and in the Villa Albani. On the other hand, the Adoration of the Magi has somewhat of a Tuscan character; it is perhaps by some artist who had appeared not much more than ten years before this as an assistant to the great masters who decorated the Sistine Chapel. Then again, the Ascension and the Coming of the Holy Ghost are evidently the work of another hand. The youthful faces with pointed chins, the old men buried beneath the heavy and inflated folds of their garments, the hands and feet with dislocated joints—all these produce a somewhat violent effect. The works, however, are not without a certain solemnity and pomp, evidently derived from Luca Signorelli, a sublime master, if rugged and uncouth.

But, while Pinturicchio supplied the designs and direction to those who executed the above-mentioned paintings, his own hands worked only on the Assumption of the Virgin and the Resurrection. In the figure of St. James and in that of Mary ascending to Heaven we see the pictorial characteristics of Antonio del Massaro of Viterbo, called Il Pastura, of whom we shall speak later on; but assuredly Pinturicchio's is the figure of the old beardless man, enveloped in a red robe, who, with sleek, flowing hair and with his hands joined, kneels to the right of the Sepulchre. This figure is said—and denied—to represent the papal treasurer, Francesco Borgia, son of Calixtus III.

We now come to the masterpiece of the room—and of all the rooms of the Appartamento Borgia—namely, the Resurrection, in which all except the figure of Christ is the work of the master. This figure is heavy and hard, like the work of Anton-iazzo Romano. The other fig-ures, artistically beautiful and very interesting iconographical-ly, are Pinturicchio's. In-deed, the im-portance of the models (Alex-ander VI and his sons) in this picture was such that no other hand but the master's could be per-mitted to touch them. The Pope, kneeling and facing to the right, is adoring the open Sepulchre. His mantle of gold brocade is surrounded by a wide border

The Madonna and Child
Hall of the Saints

which is a riot of pearls and gems; before him, on the ground, are set the triple-crowned tiara and the mitre. He has his hands joined; they are encased in gloves so thin as to interfere in no way with the contour of the shapely fingers. They are not conventional hands, but studies from life, just as are the plump head, with the gray of the beard and of the cropped hair, the hooked nose, and the full lips that truly reveal the luxurious character of the man. It is worthy of note, too, that the light falling on this extraordinary face suggests the thought that the Pope himself also mounted the platform and posed for the artist. Portraits also—as we may deduce from their type, costumes, grace and extreme youthfulness—are the three youths in this painting. These figures take the place of the usual rough, fierce soldiers who, sodden with wine and sprawling on the ground, are startled by the sudden commotion about the grave of the risen Christ. At that time there were actually living with Alexander

VI in Rome, besides Lucrezia, three of his four sons by Vannozza Catanei. And we shall presently see how even Pier Luigi, who died when about five years old, has found a place in the picture in a very strange way, which is always passed over unnoticed. The youth to the extreme right, dressed in red and turquoise blue (the heraldic colors of the Borgia), is evidently about twenty years old, which was at this time the real age of Giovanni, who about four years later was murdered and thrown into the Tiber; judging from his fair hair, the second

The Hall of the Saints

youth, a handsome youngster of about eighteen, with his left knee on the ground, is Cesare. His countenance is gentle and serene, for the shadow of his crimes has not yet fallen upon him. But the strangest figure is that of the gentle, blond Jofre, then twelve years old. He is dressed all in armor, but his cuirass is broken over his left breast, and within appears the image of Pier Luigi, Alexander's fourth son, who was then dead, but who remained ineffaceably imprinted on the heart of the youngest of his surviving brothers.

Giorgio Vasari writes that "over the door of one chamber" Pinturicchio painted "the Lady Giulia Farnese as a Madonna," and in the

same frame the head of Pope
Alexander; but Vasari's words are
simply one of the many proofs
which show how largely imagination has exaggerated the faults
and the audacity of this Pope. To
be sure, he had once been the
lover of Giulia Farnese, but he
neither caused his portrait to be
painted in the act of adoring her,
much less caused hers to be
painted in the halls of the Vatican
as a Madonna. While we see him
in the fresco adoring the Christ
rising from the Tomb, in the scene
of the Madonna with the Infant,
shown in a round frame in the
Hall of the Saints, we can discover

The Visitation
Hall of the Saints

nothing but the usual Pinturicchio type of Madonna—a delicate, gentle,
sweet, but altogether conventional type.

As we have said, it was in the Hall of the Saints that the master did
most work, beginning with the Visitation, a subject more suitable for
the Hall of the Mysteries. Amid all its architectural splendor, there is

St. Anthony and St. Paul the Hermit
Hall of the Saints

an intimate, familiar beauty in
this scene, with the children and
young women intent upon womanly tasks—an intimate beauty
which seems to give heightened
relief to the two central figures,
those of the Madonna and St.
Elizabeth, who meet and embrace
each other. More simple is the
adjoining picture, showing St. Anthony and St. Paul the Hermit in
the desert, faithful to the iconographic motive which lasted down
to the time of Velasquez and perhaps even later. The two hermit
saints, seated against a steep rock,
are sharing the bread which has
been brought to them by the
raven, which is seen cleaving the

Detail from St. Anthony and St. Paul the Hermit
Hall of the Saints

Detail from the Martyrdom of St. Sebastian
Hall of the Saints

The Martyrdom of St. Sebastian
Hall of the Saints

St. Susanna and the Elders
Hall of the Saints

air on its way back to the forest. But behind St. Anthony, in allusion to his temptation, there are three women in the bloom of youth and in aspect and gesture full of grace and seductiveness. If, however, you look closely, you will find there are horns sprouting from their heads, and below their skirts, instead of feet, the sharp claws of the falcon appear. Critics in general have been unwilling to admit that the three demonesses, and still less the two austere saints, come from the mild brush of Pinturicchio; but technical examination compels us to assign to him this interesting work, and with much more reason than the fresco representing the Martyrdom of St. Sebastian, in which perhaps nothing is his except the general idea—the fine, broad composition.

The Flight and Martyrdom of St. Barbara
Hall of the Saints

Characteristics resembling Perugino's are revealed by the painter—rather, perhaps, the painters—who worked here. In particular, the figure of the arrow-pierced saint shows its relationship to that painted by Perugino at Cergneto. Alone and apart is seen a singular figure of a Janissary seated on the ground with legs crossed; but of this we shall speak presently, when we shall have occasion to refer to other Turkish figures.

All the rest of the pictures in this hall are the work of the master—the St. Susanna, the St. Barbara, the St. Catherine, and, on the ceiling, the histories of Osiris, of Isis and of Argo. The garden of Susanna, with its gilded paling and hedges of rose bushes, the magnificent fountain with three basins, and the animals placidly resting on the grass, is not Joachim's Babylonian garden, but that of some rich palace or delicious villa of the Renaissance period. Susanna stands in the centre, about to enter the cool waters of the fountain itself, when she is attacked by two judges of the people. The attitude of the two elders refutes the story that Pinturicchio had painted Susanna nude, and that the blue robe was added afterwards. It is worth noting, too, that our painter, usually by no means strong in expression, has known how not

Detail from the Flight and Martyrdom of
St. Barbara
Hall of the Saints

only to put life into the scene, but to give an expression of greedy salaciousness to the senile faces. This and the next two pictures show that Alexander VI took pleasure in feminine beauty and youthfulness—even in his saints. Graceful indeed is the figure of St. Barbara fleeing, with her hands clasped, her drapery and hair streaming. The composition, however, is not so pleasing owing to that heavy tower which takes up two-thirds of the space to be filled and chokes it up—a tower which has the three windows that the Saint caused to open in it, in allusion to the Trinity, and the wide crack through which she miraculously escaped. One of the little episodes of the background is interesting: Barbara's father demands of a shepherd the direction of his daughter's flight, and the shepherd, in punishment for his betrayal of her, is beginning to become white, like the sheep around him, and turn into stone.

The large fresco, which is best lighted and most admired, is the Disputa, or Disputation of St. Catherine with the fifty philosophers brought together by the Emperor Maximinus. A reason has been sought for the preference for this Saint shown by Alexander VI, and, as she was born at Alexandria, there may be a suggested connection between the name of the city and that of the Pope. It is our opinion, however, that the Pope had chosen St. Catherine as the natural patroness to whose special protection he should commend his children. The scene, which is plentifully peopled, stretches over a valley, and the Disputation takes place near a great Roman arch like that of Constantine. Other painters also seem to have introduced this arch into their compositions, notably Perugino in his Conferring of the Keys. The figures cluster towards the sides in two spirited groups, which become more spare in the middle, thus leaving room for a few figures, the chief among which are the Saint and the Sage who is pointing out, in a book held by a graceful page, the passage which the Saint is at the moment

The Disputa of St. Catherine
Hall of the Saints

engaged in discussing. The group on the right—foot-soldiers and horsemen with a greyhound—seems to have returned from a hunting expedition, and has unexpectedly halted at the sight of the Court of Maximinus; on the left, the Emperor, seated on his throne and surrounded by his people, is listening attentively to what Catherine is saying. It is a truly marvellous effect of landscape, architecture, costumes, colors, intended perhaps to recall to posterity the great festivities which had been held not long before this for the coronation of Alexander, with the like superb attendance and with triumphal arches adorned with the Borgia device.

Several things in this fresco have engaged the attention of historians and art critics. In the first place, we must say that Vasari's observation

Details from the Disputa of St. Catherine
Hall of the Saints

Details from the Disputa of St. Catherine
Hall of the Saints

The Death of Osiris
Detail from the Ceiling of the Hall of the Saints

on the artistic impropriety of the reliefs introduced by Pinturicchio, even more in this picture than in the neighboring ones, seems to be just. "Having made in the said halls," he says, "a history of St. Catherine, he represents the arches of Rome in relief and depicts the figures in such a manner that, while the figures stand in front and the buildings behind, those things which are diminished in size come more forward than those which, according to the eye, are increased in size—a very great heresy in our art." It is certainly true that in some instances the shadow of the stucco buildings falls on parts of the figures which should appear in the foreground and in the light.

But more interesting still than this reflection, worthy as it is of Vasari's sagacity, are the different Oriental figures which are seen in this painting, and which were already foreshadowed by the seated Janissary watching the martyrdom of St. Sebastian—figures which seem, as Seitz says, to have "jumped in here out of another world." In point of fact, they have "jumped in here out of another world," because Pinturicchio, when he painted them, took them from the drawings which Gentile Bellini had made during a residence at Constanti-

Detail from the Ceiling of the
Hall of the Liberal Arts

Fireplace in the Hall of the
Liberal Arts

The Hall of the Liberal Arts

Grammar
Hall of the Liberal Arts

nople that lasted from the latter part of 1479 to the latter part of 1480.
They are drawings "of individuals," and are mentioned by Angiolello
as early as the beginning of the sixteenth century, and either the
originals or copies are still preserved in the British Museum, the
Louvre, and the Städel Institute at Frankfurt-am-Main. Pinturicchio
made use of them not only for these frescoes of the Appartamento
Borgia, but also for those of the Piccolomini Library in the Cathedral
of Siena. It is not improbable that such Oriental figures contained an
allusion to some particular Turkish personage, but, apart from various
and uncertain conjectures, historical iconography has made little prog-

Dialectic
Hall of the Liberal Arts

Geometry
Hall of the Liberal Arts

Arithmetic
Hall of the Liberal Arts

Rhetoric
Hall of the Liberal Arts

Archæology
Hall of the Liberal Arts

Music
Hall of the Liberal Arts

ress towards identifying them. In the Disputa of St. Catherine we see on the right a Turk on horseback, an Albanian on the left, and another Turk in full view near the Saint. Recalling the fact that Djem, called Zizim, a son of Mohammed II, was at that time in Italy, exiled from his own country for his attempt to wrest the Ottoman sceptre from his brother, Bajazet II, the art critics and historians would fain find his portrait here, some holding that he is the figure on horseback, and some the figure on foot. No greater credence, however, is to be placed in their opinions than is accorded to those who hold that Lucrezia Borgia is represented here by the Saint—a figure which surely does

Detail from the Ceiling of the
Hall of the Credo

not represent a girl who was at this period scarcely thirteen years.

Next to the Hall of the Saints comes the Hall of the Liberal Arts, and it may perhaps be remarked here without impropriety that the present writer has been generally admitted to have first discerned and identified one of Pinturicchio's collaborators—beyond question the greatest of his collaborators—in this hall. The scheme of the decorations in this anteroom is found in the *trivium* and *quadrivium* which formed the basis of learning in the Middle Ages. We see, accordingly, personifications of Grammar, Rhetoric, Dialectic, Astronomy, Geometry, Arithmetic, Music, with appropriate instruments and emblems, and figures of the learned personages and of artists, ancient and modern. In a work executed by many collaborators it is, as a rule, very difficult to determine which portion is due to one artist and which to another. How, indeed, is it possible to say where the brush of one painter stopped and another's took up the work? Artists who work together, besides coming usually from one and the same school or from the same locality and hence being already harmonized in type and color, naturally seek to merge the variety of their products in the same tonality and the same feeling, so long as they are engaged on the same work. Moreover, where there is one predominating spirit, all endeavor to keep pace with him and confine themselves to his manner, even when

Astronomy
Hall of the Liberal Arts

Another Hall in the Appartamento Borgia

Frieze in the Hall of the Saints

he does not retouch the various parts with his own hand and bring them into harmony with one another. If, however, an artist has been permitted to work upon figures and whole groups with a certain degree of freedom and breadth, then inevitably his personality cannot be altogether suppressed, but flashes out in traits which are fleeting, perhaps, but yet clear and revealing. And it was one such moment which revealed the great part played in the Hall of the Mysteries and in that of the Liberal Arts by Antonio del Massaro of Viterbo, called Il Pastura; for in the former hall his are certainly—and every one now agrees in this—the Coming of the Holy Ghost and the Assumption of the Virgin, and in the latter Music, Rhetoric and Astronomy. Venturi, who promptly accepted our view, next indicated Grammar, Geometry and Arithmetic as works of Tiberio of Assisi, and Dialectic as probably the work of Jacopo, called L'Indaco.

In the last two halls, which are included in the tower constructed by Borgia himself as soon as he became Pope, Pinturicchio's work appears no more, except in the way of directive conception. Here everything still turns upon the direction given by his decorative aims, but his own hand is altogether absent. The Hall of the Credo has on its ceiling elegant decorative motives and the usual Borgia devices, and in each lunette are two half figures, one of an Apostle and the other of a Prophet. And since, "according to a medieval legend, the Credo was composed by the Apostles before they separated to evangelize the world, in such a manner that each one of them wrote one article of it, so one verse was attributed to each one of them," which verses may be read on great flowing scrolls. It seems to us that in these figures, as in those of the Sibyls, which give its name to the next and last hall, there are considerable indications of the hand that painted Grammar, which, according to Venturi, would be that of Tiberio of Assisi. In the selection of the Sibyls, the artist, or whoever advised him, "let himself be

The Hall of the Sibyls

guided by the little books then in popular use, in which the appearance and dress of each [Sibyl] is described, the oracles of each one being accompanied by an analogous passage from one of the Prophets or a text from the New Testament." The artist "did not invent, but drew from these books the figures and the legends which appear on his scrolls." But here the ceiling is particularly interesting. For, besides the subjects which are taken from Egyptian mythology and glorify the

Frieze showing Portrait of Alexander VI
Hall of the Saints

ox, the device of the Borgia (just as did the histories of Isis and Osiris on the ceiling of the Hall of the Saints), it displays, in octagonal settings, crowded scenes representing terrestrial actions under astrological influences. Through the heavens proceed the chariots of Saturn, Venus, Mercury, Jupiter, Diana and Apollo, drawn by dragons, bulls, stags, eagles, dolphins and horses respectively. In another octagon is displayed an armillary sphere, the emblem of Astrology. The Signs of the Zodiac are set among the clouds, and below are unfolded the human activities which are favored by their influences. Saturn, with his scythe, protects the works of justice, piety and love, over which he presided after Janus received him into Latium; Venus, with Love speeding the dart, watches over various couples of lovers, while Mercury, devoting himself to students only, overlooks a number of other matters entrusted to him. Under Jupiter pass the hunters, with dog and falcon; and under the Moon, fishermen. Mars is watching a battle; Apollo looks down on a quiet assemblage of "great souls." Lastly, geomancers and astrologers stand under the astrolabe, engaged in discussion. The artist of these designs was some follower of Perugino.

That, as a whole, the work completed under the sole direction of Pinturicchio fully satisfied Alexander VI is proved by the fact that the Pope soon afterwards commissioned him to decorate with frescoes other chambers on the Courtyard of St. Peter's. These frescoes have since perished, and a hall constructed for this Pope by Antonio da Sangallo in the great tower of the Castel S. Angelo was destroyed by order of Urban VIII. The artists who had enthusiastically labored at this great work and acquired the master's festive methods of decoration were scattered throughout Rome and all its territory to paint in churches and dwellings, where they left works commonly ascribed to Pinturicchio.

As soon as the star of the Borgia had set in a lake of blood amid a tempest of curses, Alexander's suite in the Vatican was straightway abandoned as a place accursed. Scratches and inscriptions made with the point of nail or knife are found there, dating from the years of the early Cinquecento and leaving us to suppose that by that time the halls of the Appartamento had become the abode of servants or of soldiers. Later they were divided into a number of cells for use during the Conclave, and still later they were given up to the minor officials of the palace, who had their quarters there during Holy Week. It was only in 1816 that Pius VII caused them to be restored, as restoration was then understood, to afford accommodation for the pictures returned from France after the Treaty of Vienna. At a later period Pius IX, finding the halls too dark, removed the pictures and replaced them by the library of Cardinal Angelo Mai. This remained there until the day when it seemed to Leo XIII that the Appartamento Borgia ought to be cleared of all encumbrances, restored, and solemnly opened to the public, an event which took place in March, 1897.

To-day the Appartamento Borgia presents a calm and smiling aspect, but our thoughts travel back to the terrible hours when the splendor of the gilded ceilings and the graceful paintings on the walls had no longer power to assuage the grief of Alexander VI or to lessen the paroxysms of the anger of Cesare when, from the tower built by his father, he had to witness the ruin of his own fortune. All his dreams of glory had melted away, but the dreams of Pinturicchio remain for ever.

THE STANZE OF RAPHAEL

O N November 26, 1507, Julius II gave up living in the Appartamento Borgia, where everything spoke of the abhorred Alexander VI, and took up his rooms on the next floor above, in that portion of the Vatican Palace formerly occupied by Nicholas V, where there was and still is a glorious chapel with frescoes by Fra Angelico. Bramante, the architect, set to work at once to get together artists to decorate worthily these rooms, which, if we are to believe Vasari, though his opinion has been recently contested, had already many important frescoes by such men as Andrea del Castagno, Bonfigli, and Piero della Francesca.

Vasari will have it that Julius II caused these works to be destroyed to make room for new works by modern masters. In the autumn of 1508 the work began. In one of the rooms—that of the Fire in the Borgo—Perugino painted the groinings of the roof with the Trinity between the Twelve Apostles, Christ between the allegorical figures of Grace and Justice, Christ tempted by Satan. Giovanni Antonio Bazzi, known also as Il Sodoma, painted the roof in the Hall of the Signatura, and Baldassarre Peruzzi the roof in the Hall of Heliodorus. But towards the beginning of 1509 these masters, together with Bramantino and Lorenzo Lotto, who worked with them, were dismissed and the entire decorative scheme was put in the hands of Raphael of Urbino, a young man hardly twenty-five years old, who had recently come to Rome and had at once won over the Pope. It may have been harsh on the part of the Della Rovere Pope to dismiss the elderly Perugino and his companions, but in doing so he gave Raphael a chance to create his masterpieces. The Pope's act gave birth to a new era in the art of Italy, and the Stanze painted by Raphael were a new triumph for the human mind.

Raphael began with the room which as early as 1513 was already known as the Signatura and seems to have been intended as the private library of Julius II. Therein he created one of his masterpieces which has been ever since the wonder of art lovers, and has inspired pages of rapture as a work that breathes the spirit of all time and expresses not only the esthetic ideal of its own age, but breathes a very breath of eternity.

The Hall of the Signatura

To grasp the link between the various paintings in the Hall of the Signatura we must dwell a little on the paintings on the roof, where we find four medallions containing, under female forms, Theology, Philosophy, Poetry, and Justice. These four beautiful figures, throned on the clouds, stand out against a golden background of imitation mosaic and are surrounded by angels holding labelled scrolls. Theology (*Divinarum rerum notitia*) is seated crowned with olive leaves and holds a closed book on her knees, while with her right hand she

Fortitude, Prudence and Temperance

seems to be pointing out the painting on the wall below where the Disputa is shown. Philosophy (*Causarum cognitio*), seated on a throne supported by two figures of Diana of Ephesus, is holding massive tomes on which are written *Moralis* and *Naturalis*, and seems to be absorbed in deep thought. The School of Athens is shown below. Poetry (*Numine afflatur*) is an attractive winged figure crowned with laurel, holding in her left hand a lyre and in her right hand a book, her eyes afire with inspiration. Below Parnassus is shown. Lastly comes Justice (*Ius suum unicuique tribuit*) with the sword and the scales.

In the presence of these figures the mind calls up the allegories of the Trecento and the Quattrocento, but how are we to trace even an ideal

Theology

Poetry

The Ceiling in the Hall of the Signatura and Details

connection between them? Raphael drew his wonderful creations
from his own mind and brain, clothed them with colors all his own,
nurtured them on his own lofty thoughts, so that whereas the symbolical attributes used by the painters of former days with their figures
served as a label to identify and point out the subject, the very use of
such symbols seems superfluous in the case of the figures in the Hall
of the Signatura, since at sight the figure of Theology actually calls up

Parnassus

divine thoughts, and the eyes of Philosophy are filled with understanding, and Justice has all the dignity of Law, and Poetry has all the divine
fire of Art.

In the four oblong spaces in the angles of the roof, set in frames of
rich borders, he has painted for us Original Sin, Astronomy, Apollo and
Marsyas, and the Judgment of Solomon, subjects closely related to
the larger pictures below them, and all treated with charm and
originality.

On the walls of the hall Raphael has depicted scenes relating to the
four great powers that rule the life of man. On the wall opposite the
windows is the least intricate of all: the Glorification of Jurisprudence.
In the centre of the wall is set a window, and in the lunette above it the

The School of Athens

painter has placed the three in-
separable companions of Law,
Fortitude, Prudence, and Temperance. They are three wonderful
studies in womanhood and admirably arranged to fit the space.
Fortitude, armed with helmet and
breastplate, carries instead of the
usual sword a leafy branch of oak
—the oak of the Della Rovere family. Temperance, on the opposite
side, is a gentle, modest figure
holding a bridle in her hand and
turned towards a winged genius
who is pointing towards the sky;
higher up in the centre is noble,
serious Janus-headed Prudence
together with two boys, one of
whom presents a mirror, and the
other a torch. Here again the mas-

A Detail from Parnassus

ter has conveyed his idea without the aid of adventitious symbols.

To the right and left of the window he has painted the Giving of
Civil and Ecclesiastical Law. On the narrower part of the wall to the
left the Emperor Justinian, seated on a throne, is handing his book of
Pandects to Tribunianus, who is kneeling before him, in the presence
of the chief jurists. The scene is treated after the manner of the ancient bas-reliefs. To the right of the window, where there is more
space, we see Gregory IX depicted as Julius II handing his Decretals to
the consistorial jurist kneeling at his feet. Around him are many
prelates and characteristic portraits. The scene is full of nobility and
simplicity at the same time. When at work on it Raphael must have
had in mind the fresco by Melozzo da Forli representing Platina kneeling before Sixtus IV.

On the opposite wall, with the window looking on the Cortile di Belvedere, Raphael has represented the Triumph of Poetry. This Parnassus is a joyous composition wherein all is charm, grace, and
elegance. On the top of the sacred mount Apollo is seated playing a
viola, and ringed around him are the Muses and laurel-crowned poets:
Homer, Sappho, Pindar, Virgil, Dante, figures of rare elegance scattered in groups, are conversing among the laurel trees under a sky of
limpid blue. The whole picture in its ease and grace breathes the very
soul of the Renaissance. The poets of antiquity live again in Raphael's

A Philosopher

Francesco della Rovere

Raphael and Sodoma

Plato and Aristotle

Details from the School of Athens

Sts. Bernard and Jerome

Dante Alighieri

The Disputa del Sacramento and Details

The Ceiling in the Hall of Heliodorus

fresco as if they were sharing in the Humanist movement of the Cinque-cento with their Christian brothers, and it seems as if at the playing of the young god a wave of delight is filling the spaces of the air.

Now we come to the magnificent composition on the left wall known as the School of Athens, and as the breath of Poetry came to us from the Parnassus, here we are face to face with a gravity and dignity of thought that win our admiration and claim our respect. No longer do we see the clear sky of Parnassus, but we find in the background a noble cruciform building surmounted by a cupola and with steps lead-ing up to its entrance. From the door are seen coming forth with majesty between the opening lines of their disciples the two great mas-ters of philosophy, Plato and Aristotle, who are making their way to the edge of the steps where Diogenes, the philosopher of simplicity, humbly reclines. From the figures of the two princes of knowledge the divine light of intelligence radiates. Aloof to the right of the cen-tral group there are two beautiful figures representing a boy writing and an old man deep in thought. To the left a band of dialecticians is gathered around Socrates, who is counting off syllogisms on his fingers.

The Hall of Heliodorus

The Mass of Bolsena

In this group a fair youth with helmet and body armor represents Alcibiades. Farther on around the base of a pillar there are other figures, one a youth reading a book, and near him is a beautiful study of a child's head, said to be the young Federigo Gonzaga. In the foreground stands a group of arithmeticians and musicians. Pythagoras is there kneeling on one knee and writing in a book, and on his right a boy stands holding a slate showing the Pythagorean numbers. A

Detail from the Mass of Bolsena

man in Oriental garb, Averroes, and another said to be Boetius are reading what Pythagoras writes. To the right of this group is a young man in a white robe trimmed with gold, whom tradition identifies as Francesco Maria della Rovere, Duke of Urbino, and before him is a handsome personage pointing out what is written in his book. Farther over in the centre of the steps a philosopher is engaged in writing. Over in the opposite corner there is a group of geometricians and astronomers. Euclid, depicted as Bramante, is there explaining a figure on a slate, and four of his pupils are looking on. Behind this group there is a king holding a terrestrial sphere. He is Ptolemy, and another figure holding a celestial globe showing the stars is Zoroaster, and

Detail from the Mass of Bolsena

Detail from the Expulsion of Heliodorus
from the Temple

The Expulsion of Heliodorus from the Temple

The Meeting of St. Leo IV and Attila

The Freeing of St. Peter from Prison

in the extreme corner on the right we have pictures of Raphael himself and of Sodoma, his co-workman.

Many explanations have been made concerning this wonderful work; efforts have been made to find symbolism in it everywhere, and to give a name to every figure. All that is but a waste of time. Enough for us that we see in that miracle of harmony and beauty the noblest glorification of the activities of the human mind, of the unending quest of man's spirit for truth and knowledge, and of the power and light of man's unaided human reason. It is very probable that Raphael was aided in his choice by some of his learned friends, and Sadoleto is one often mentioned, but to the youthful artist alone belongs the glory of having created this noblest expression of the activity of the human mind in a new and striking way. We are no longer face to face with thrones or seats, with ambiguous personifications and allegories; we are no longer confronted with the attributes so dear to medieval schoolmen; but the pure light of thought finds its expression in the human figure in a setting where the architectonic lines remind us of the beauty and grace of Classic times. In this same Hall of the Signatura, on the wall opposite the School of Athens there is another important and most beautiful

Ancient Mosaic in the centre of the
Hall of Heliodorus

composition known as the Disputa, a very inappropriate title, as the picture, rather than a dispute, presents a hymn of glory in honor of the mystery of the Redemption. A girdle of clouds divides the composition into two parts, separating heaven from earth. In the centre of heaven, surrounded by a golden glory, Christ is seated on clouds, stretching out his wounded hands as though offering himself in oblation and food for the faithful. Beside him are the Baptist and the Madonna in adoration. Above appears the bust of the Eternal Father, holding in his left hand the earthly globe and blessing with his right; lower down, on either side of the Redeemer, there are two groups representing the elect in heaven, sitting in semicircular rows, saints, apostles, and martyrs. Beneath the figure of Christ the Holy Spirit in the form of a dove is coming to earth, forming, so to speak, a point of union between the two parts of

The Hall of the Fire in the Borgo and Ceiling

Details from the Fire in the Borgo

the picture. The dove is turned towards the altar, which holds the
centre of the lower half of the fresco. On the altar stands a golden
monstrance showing the sacred Host, which is the central point of the
whole composition, catching the eye of the onlooker at once. On either
hand are the doctors of the Church, saints, popes, cardinals, hermits,
representatives of the sciences and arts. They are engaged in meditation, disputation, adoration. St. Ambrose is there, and Augustine and
Jerome and Gregory and Thomas and Bonaventure. Innocent III and
Dante are on the right, and on the left we see a Franciscan, a Dominican, and a hermit, and the portrait of the angelic painter, the blessed
Giovanni da Fiesole (Fra Angelico). Poets and artists are there, too,
around the altar whereon rests the mystic food.

It is quite certain that Raphael had advice in making the selection he
gives us here, and it may well be that Julius II himself went so far as
to suggest the fundamental idea. But the master, in this work, which
he began in 1508 and finished in 1511, gives proof not only of theological insight but above all of a spontaneous understanding of divine
love. No other artist has ever so well expressed the closeness of the
bond that links the visible and the invisible world, the heavens and the
earth. In the background of a landscape to the right we see the massive
foundations of a building said by many to be the new St. Peter's, Rome,
and on the left a lordly edifice round which men are busily working.

Detail from the Fire in the Borgo

The Victory of St. Leo IV over the Saracens at Ostia

The two buildings are said to symbolize the decadence of Paganism and the building up of Christian Theology, which is never destined to be completed.

Much has been written about the use to which this Hall of the Signatura was put. Nowadays nearly every one agrees that it was the private library and workroom of the Pope, that therein he signed (*signare*) his papers and documents. We find the name first mentioned in 1513.

The Coronation of Charlemagne

The decoration of these walls and roof upholds the traditions of the Church and the Papacy and marks once more the alliance of intellectual culture and sacred knowledge, the blending of ancient philosophy, poetry, and law with the tenets of the Faith. The work came to an end in the course of the year 1511.

The wonder caused by Raphael's skill in bringing to a close the decoration of the Hall of the Signatura determined the Pope to entrust to him also the decoration of the hall near by, which was later called the Heliodorus. The original plans for this hall contained scenes taken from the Apocalypse to harmonize with Peruzzi's pictures on the roof,

The Hall of Constantine

which were taken from the Old Testament; and there is to be seen in the Louvre a design by Raphael showing the Breaking of the Seal on the Book of Life.

But important events in those very years brought new glory to the Papacy and brought about a change in the plans, so that it was resolved to depict on the walls of this room the triumph of Julius II. On the wall opposite the window Raphael painted, at the suggestion of

Ancient Mosaic Discovered near the Scala Santa
(Hall of Constantine)

the Pope, the Mass at Bolsena. The subject is the famous miracle that took place at Bolsena in 1263 and led to the building of the Duomo of Orvieto. A German priest had doubts as to whether the sacred Host at the moment of consecration really contained the blood of Christ. As he was saying Mass one day in the Church of St. Catherine in Bolsena while making a pilgrimage in Italy, blood flowed from the Host in his hands and stained the corporal a red color. To commemorate this miracle the feast of Corpus Christi was instituted. Julius II, while on an expedition one day to Bologna, stopped over at Orvieto and venerated with particular devotion the blessed corporal preserved in the

Duomo, and it may well have been that he made a vow that in case of victory over his enemies he would glorify the miracle by a fresco in the Vatican. Raphael caught up the spirit and intuition of his patron most wonderfully, and in the centre of the arch he painted the altar with the young priest before it, all confused and astonished at the sight of the miracle; behind him are assistants and congregation adoring the wonder, and on one side, kneeling at a velvet-covered faldstool, is the

The Vision of Constantine

Pope, resembling Julius II, in no way surprised by the miracle, but looking severely at the priest as if to reprove him for his lack of faith. Two cardinals and two prelates, together with the officers of the Papal Court, make up the Pope's suite and are all characteristic paintings and speaking likenesses.

The victory over the schismatics is symbolically depicted on the wall to the left, whereon is shown the Expulsion of Heliodorus. As we learn from the Scriptures, Heliodorus was the treasurer of the King of Syria, and he was ordered to carry off the treasures of the temple of Jerusalem. As he was in the act of carrying out this order, a horseman with

The Battle of the Milvian Bridge

stern countenance and gorgeous robes, accompanied by two young men, appeared, struck him down, and flogged him. In the background of the fresco, under the columned altar, we see the high priest in prayer before the seven-branch candlestick. To the right is the horseman with his assistants in golden robes, attacking and flogging Heliodorus, whose followers take to flight. To the left there is a group of women and children in amazement at the sight, and in the corner of the fresco we see Julius II, borne on his *sedia gestatoria,* towering over the crowd and affirming through the miracle the sovereignty of the Church. We have here a clear allusion to the triumph of the Papacy over the rebel cardinals who in the time of Julius II bethought them of holding an antipapal council.

Opposite the Heliodorus fresco is the meeting of Pope Leo the Great and Attila. Julius II being dead by the time this fresco was painted, the Pope bears the likeness of Leo X and is seen moving tranquilly on to meet the fierce king of the Huns surrounded by his warriors; in the upper portion of the scene the princes of the Apostles appear with swords in their hands. At the sight Attila spurs his horse in dismay and the Huns are terror-stricken. The flight of the French troops from Italy in 1512 is here paralleled. In the background Raphael has painted in, as though the meeting with Attila had taken place near Rome, various Roman scenes, including the Colosseum.

On the wall with the window looking on the Belvedere he has painted the Freeing of St. Peter from Prison, a subject well in harmony with the many others in this hall—that is, the victory of the Church and its head over every human plot. The lighting effects in this fresco are wonderful: the light within the prison comes from the Angel who awakens the sleeping Peter; then the light outside is also from the Angel as he accompanies the Apostle in his freedom; but there is also the moonlight on the stairway to the left, where the astonished soldiers rouse each other and find their prisoner gone. Julius II was Cardinal of the title of St. Peter in Chains and went on a pilgrimage to this church in June, 1512, to give thanks for the withdrawal of the French: hence we may conclude that although the hall was not completed until 1514, under Leo X, yet it was planned and begun under Julius II.

If we compare the pictures in the Signatura Hall and those in the Heliodorus Hall, we cannot help noting that Raphael had been altering the tonality of his coloring and putting more effective movement in his compositions. There is more vivacity in these later frescoes, and instead of the classic purity and coldness of the

Detail from a Door in the Stanze
(Giovanni Barili)

pictures in the Signatura we find here more of the warmth of life. The coloring alone may have a lot to do with this effect, and his coloring owes much to the Venetian Sebastiano del Piombo, who came to Rome in 1511 and affected the schools of Michelangelo and Raphael with some of the glow he had learned from Giorgione. This is true in a special manner of the Bolsena Miracle, the Heliodorus, and the Freeing of St. Peter. The fresco of the meeting of Pope Leo and Attila is widely different from these. It is weaker in coloring and in design, and it is not difficult to recognize that it is largely the work of the master's pupils.

Raphael was now overweighted with work. He was engaged not

only in painting the Stanze, but he was charged with drawing the designs for the tapestries for the Sistine and he had commissions for sacred pictures and portraits, so that he was constrained to hand over much of his work to his pupils, particularly to Giovanni Francesco Penni, styled Il Fattore, and Giulio Lippi, known as Giulio Romano.

In the summer of 1514 Raphael and his disciples brought the painting of the Heliodorus Hall to a close, and he was already commissioned to paint a third room. We have a letter from him in which he tells his uncle Simone Ciorla about it, and from other documents we learn that the painting of this third room was completed in June, 1517. In the third room, which we named above as that of the Fire in the Borgo, the pupils were given even a freer hand. We might almost go so far as to say that Raphael himself did not paint any part of that room, and had very little to say in the matter of the drawings for it. Perugino's fresco showing Christ glorified was left on the roof, and the pupils decorated the walls, out of deference to Leo X, with scenes from the life of Leo III and Leo IV, who had been canonized, taking such events as had some connection with their own day. In all these paintings the Medici Pope plays the parts of Leo III and Leo IV.

The one painting wherein, if not the hand, at least the mind of Raphael is to be discerned is that of the Fire in the Borgo, which records one of the miracles of Leo IV, who with the sign of the cross extinguished a devastating fire that had taken hold of that quarter of the city. The story is told in episodes rather than in unit form. There is no real connection between the incidents, no unity of ensemble. The background shows the Pope in the act of blessing from a balcony behind which appears the façade of old St. Peter's; in the foreground on either side are buildings where the flames are raging. To the right men are engaged fighting the flames and women are carrying water to them: among the women there is one with her back to us, who is much admired. In the building to the left, where the flames are fiercest, a woman is throwing her child from above to the father below; one sturdy youth is saving himself by flight, and another is carrying off his aged father on his back, as Æneas carried Anchises from the fire of Troy. In the centre women and children in despair appeal for help to the Pope. The execution of the foreground of this work mainly belongs to Giulio Romano, and Francesco Penni is responsible for the background. Raphael designed the finer groups, which his pupils afterwards transferred to fresco without paying overmuch attention to the harmony of due proportions.

In the second fresco, depicting the Naval Fight at Ostia won by Leo IV over the Saracens, the Pope is again Leo X seated on a throne and surrounded by cardinals. He raises his eyes to heaven, while in the foreground the Saracen prisoners are being hurled to the ground and in the background the fight rages. In this picture Raphael's sense of order is entirely lacking, and we are undoubtedly face to face with a painting of his school, very probably by Giulio Romano. The master himself did no more than give studies for some of the principal figures in it.

Of the two other frescoes in the room, one depicts the Justification of Leo IV, or the oath by which on December 23, in the year 800, that Pope in the Vatican Basilica absolved himself from false charges that had been brought against him. This work is entirely

The Chiaroscuri Hall with frescoes by Giovanni da Udine and P. Maratta

from the hands of Raphael's pupils, perhaps mainly by Penni, who followed out the scheme laid down in the Bolsena Miracle; the other painting represents the crowning of Charlemagne by Leo III, a splendid scene in which Penni displays such genius in depicting the glories of Court ceremonial, with all its magnificent trappings, that for the moment we forget the defects of the composition before us. Charlemagne is shown with the features of Francis I. The root idea of the decorations in this third room has reference to the paintings in the Heliodorus room. The power and greatness of the Papacy are glorified especially in the war against the infidels. The Battle at Ostia is an allusion to the Medicean Pope's idea of calling a new crusade; the Coronation of Charlemagne reminds the imperial power that it must bow to the authority of the Church; the Fire in the Borgo is not so easy to explain in symbols, but it must have some reference to the rebuilding of St. Peter's; and the Oath of Pope Leo III is connected with the end of the Schism and the Lateran Council, pointing out that the Supreme Head of the Church can be judged by God alone.

Having thus completed the frescoes in the Hall of the Borgo Fire, there remained to be decorated the large room near the Heliodorus Hall and leading on to the Loggie. Here, instead of continuing scenes alluding to his own pontificate, Leo X gave orders that the main events

The Chiaroscuri Hall
(Leading from the Stanze to the Chapel of Nicholas V)

in the history of the Church should be depicted: *e.g.*, the life of the Emperor Constantine, under whom Christianity was officially recognized, and whose legendary donation or gift was associated with the beginnings of the Papal States.

Now, it came to pass that the paintings in this room were begun after the death of the master, and the pupils, in order to prevent the work being entrusted to Michelangelo, pretended that they had all Raphael's drawings for it. It is certain in any case that, while in all the other frescoes, as for instance the Vision of the Cross, the Baptism of Constantine, the Donation and the figures of the Eight Popes, there is no trace of Raphael, we do find in the scene showing the Battle of the Milvian Bridge a hint of the master's style. The work is hastily done in many places, the gray and cold coloring shows the hand of Giulio Romano, but its breadth of movement and its sweep and dash, which make it one of the finest battle scenes in the world, all speak of Raphael. Details of beauty that miss the eye at first sight reveal to us the master's aim to produce something truly great, but on seeing what Giulio Romano has done with it in paint, and how it differs from the master's plan, we only understand the better what a painter Raphael was, and how much above his pupils he towered, so that their greatest efforts fall far short of his stature. Not in the following of the canons of his art, not because of any secrets of technic, not by tricks of the trade, but through genius only Raphael's art touches the topmost peaks.

In this same room the two allegorical figures of Justice and Clemency are from studies by the master, the one being executed by Penni, the other by Romano. Romano's also is the fresco showing the Vision of the Cross, but the Baptism is by Penni, and the Donation is the work of Raffaellino del Colle. The roof of this room was painted a long time afterwards by the Zuccari brothers. The Exaltation of Faith, in the centre, is by Tommaso Laureti of Palermo.

The Hall of Constantine ends the cycle of frescoes in the Stanze, the masterpieces of Raphael and his school. In his sacred paintings and his gentle Madonnas, the artist poured out all the sweetness of his soul. There is insight in his portraits, and power of thinking, too, but in the frescoes in these halls is the whole man, the artist who is equally at home with the charms of Poetry, the stern visage of Philosophy, the recesses of the mysteries of Faith, and the awe-striking tones of the voice of Divine Judgment. A poem of beauty and thought passes here before our eyes. Whatever humanity has thought or imagined that is great and sublime speaks to us from these frescoes in a voice that has all the mystery-awaking melody of art.

The lyric note dominates the Hall of the Signatura; the dramatic chord vibrates around the scene of Heliodorus; an epic voice is heard through the flames of the Borgo. Raphael has touched every chord on the lyre of the Muse of painting. The Bible, Classical antiquity and the Middle Ages, humanism, philosophy, theology, the liberal arts, law, peace and war, temporal and divine power have found in him a singer who has clothed them in beauty; and as to-day the dead religions of Pagandom live again for us in our wonder at the images of their gods, so too, even where Faith is dead, Raphael's art speaks and will ever speak to humanity in the eternal language of the beautiful.

THE LOGGIE OF RAPHAEL

FTER the frescoed rooms and the tapestries comes in the order of chronology another important work by Raphael, namely, the decorations ordered by Pope Leo X for the galleries opening on the Cortile di S. Damaso.

The building of these galleries was begun by Bramante in 1513, and after his death was completed by Raphael in 1518 or thereabouts.

They comprise three tiers, of which the centre one is the most famous because it contains the Bible pictures designed by the master. We are not quite certain as to when these decorations on the walls and pilasters and vaulting were begun, but we may safely say that the work was advanced in the summer of 1519 since we find in a ledger in the Vatican Archives an entry, on June 11, of twenty-five ducats paid to Raphael's assistants for work done in the galleries, and on June 16 Baldassarre Castiglione wrote to the Marchesa Isabella d'Este as follows: "The Pope is more than ever taken up with music, and in one way or another delights in architecture. He is always planning some new work in the palace here, and his latest fancy is a painted gallery adorned with stucco work of an antique character. The whole is the work of Raphael and is really fair to see and perhaps surpasses anything done by the modern school." Moreover, the Venetian Marc Antonio Michiel tells us that in May, 1519, Raphael had decorated one very long gallery and was about to paint two others.

The first tier of the galleries is adorned with leaf designs and arabesques, which unfortunately have been largely restored. They follow a plan similar to that which we shall describe later in the upper tier, but are characterized by greater simplicity and more hasty execution.

In the second tier or story the decorations are spread over thirteen arcades, and here it may truly be said that Raphael has poured out liberally the treasures of his artistic genius: paintings and sculpture go hand in hand, and the beauty of the imitation antique stuccos and the friezes depicting pagan scenes on the pilasters blend wonderfully with the scenes from the Bible represented on the domed roof. The whole makes up a noble tribute to the art and spirit of the Renaissance. The

sacred scenes on the roof are fitting in the palace of the ruler of
Christendom, and the pagan touch
along the walls carries to us a
memory of Leo's mighty love for
classic antiquity. The decoration
of the roof is divided into thirteen
compartments, each of which contains four scenes set in an appropriate frame of color, and in the
centre of the seventh is the Pope's
coat of arms. Of these fifty-two
frescoes, forty-eight are scenes
from the Old and four from the
New Testament. The set is known
as Raphael's Bible.

The great artist was face to face
with a difficult task. It is a far cry
in art from the faltering steps
of Christian painting in the dim
light of the Catacombs to the Loggie of Raphael. The master was
confronted with a theme that had
been attempted time and again by
artists in every age, and he had to
find a new expression for it; he
had to recreate it, so to speak, in
the language of the Renaissance.

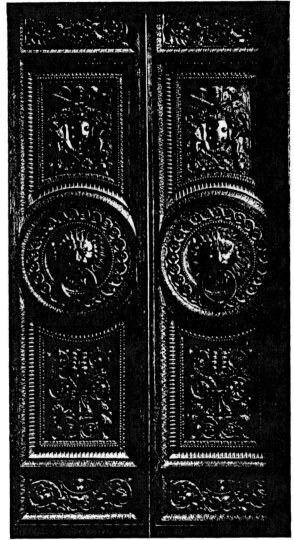

Door leading to the Loggie
(Sixteenth Century)

The painters in the Catacombs of Rome in the early days of Christianity employed subjects taken from the Bible and the Gospels, but
their choice was limited to the smallest possible number of symbolic
elements. The symbol and the dogma it taught were for them the great
thing. Hence they paid no great attention to biblical accuracy. The
mosaics in the central nave of S. Maria Maggiore in Rome, dating back
to the fifth century, and the miniatures on the purple parchment Codex
of Genesis in the Imperial Library in Vienna, dating from the sixth
century, as well as the faintly colored designs of the parchment roll of
the Book of Joshua in the Vatican Library, a tenth century copy of a
fourth century original, all have Bible subjects of a more or less complex character but along fixed lines and all inculcating lessons of
religious belief. Art therein is the thrall of faith. The picture cycles
in Monreale, in St. Mark's, Venice, in the upper church at Assisi, the

One of the Loggie of Raphael

The First Toil of Man

Quattrocento work of Paolo Uccello in the Green Cloister of S. Maria
Novella, and the works of Benozzo Gozzoli in the Campo Santo at Pisa
are, on the other hand, more or less *genre* pictures, episodes depicted
with sincerity and truth and with particular emphasis on certain figures and details of special importance.

On the roof of the Sistine, eight or ten years before, Michelangelo
had painted the scenes of the Creation, but his imposing, dominating
figures and the tragic strength of his compositions could be of no service to Raphael, so totally different were the place and the space allotted to him for decoration. So that we may say Raphael took up the
well-known theme afresh and gave it a new utterance. No longer are
we face to face with the fearsome visions of the Middle Ages in the
titanic struggles of the giants in the Sistine, but we look on at a graceful
idyl told by Raphael in these galleries, where he has known how to
clothe the sacred stories with all the charm and grace of the fables of
antiquity.

It was long a matter of dispute—and, for that matter, it is so still
—among critics how much of these galleries is actually the work of the
master himself.

Vasari, in speaking of the Loggie, says:

"Moreover, Raphael designed the papal stairways and the galleries begun by the architect Bramante, but left unfinished at his death. These galleries were designed anew by Raphael, who made a wooden model of them, and were not only better planned but gave more scope for decoration than did Bramante's plan. Seeing that it was Pope Leo's wish to leave a record of his greatness, magnificence, and generosity, Raphael not only designed the stucco ornaments and the scenes to be used in the decoration, but he placed Giovanni da Udine in charge of

Lot and His Family Leaving Sodom

the stucco work and the arabesques, and Giulio Romano in charge of the paintings, though Giulio did little of the work himself. Giovan Francesco Penni, il Bologna,[1] Perino del Vaga, Pellegrino da Modena, Vincenzo da San Gimignano, Polidoro da Caravaggio, and many other painters worked there on the scenes and figures and details of that work, which Raphael was so intent on making a masterpiece that he brought even a Luca della Robbia pavement from Florence for it. Thus it is that we may safely say that for paintings, stucco work, skill and inventive genius it is impossible to better it or to imagine anything more perfect."

Hence we see that Vasari attributes the whole plan and its designs to

[1]Bartolomeo Ramenghi, called also Bagnacavallo.

the master and the work itself to his pupils. Some recent critics have attempted to exclude Raphael from all part in it save one of general supervision, but there is no foundation for such a theory. No doubt there is no trace of Raphael's brush anywhere in these galleries, but his spirit animates the whole place, and nowhere is it more in evidence than in the arcades, of which the paintings in the first eight are truly the children of the master's brain. His guiding hand is also seen in the two that follow. As for the remaining three arcades, we are perhaps justified in attributing them in their entirety to Raphael's pupils.

One of the Loggie

As far as the actual work is concerned, owing to the wretched restorations that have been made from time to time, it is not easy to form any very accurate judgment to-day, but it is generally believed that the painting of the first nine arcades was the work of Francesco Penni, called Il Fattore, save for the landscape scenes and the pictures of animals, which are said to be the work of Giovanni da Udine. The other pupils shared among them the work on the remaining arcades, and the name of Perino del Vaga heads the list. All thirteen arcades leave the impression that the wondrous designs which ought to have guided the painters were weighed down with colors too warm and brick-colored flesh tints, and with landscapes whose lines are not sufficiently toned down, so that at times we might almost say the whole presents the effect of a Cinquecento work interpreted by men living under the spell of the barocco period in art.

Students and critics have striven to find out the sources from which Raphael drew his plan for these compositions. The Creation scenes and those relating to Noah recall Michelangelo's work in the Sistine, but only for their iconographic merit, not by any means in their vigor and severity. Not a few find traces of Masaccio, and there is a hint of Dürer in the scene where Jacob meets Rachel at the well, while there is also a strong memory of classical sculpture.

But these petty thefts, to which every artist has recourse, do not take away from the importance of this work; and we have no hesitation in saying that we are about to run through one of the most beautiful creations of the Renaissance—a simple moving poem full of beauty and serenity. The landscape scenes by Giovanni da Udine, so filled with atmosphere and light, add to the idyllic charm of the whole cycle. We might almost say that the work breathes the spirit of Virgil from beginning to end. After the ninth arcade the character of the work changes; the dramatic elements dominate and the coloring becomes brighter.

Isaac and Rebecca

When we reach the thirteenth the work is somewhat feeble, and we recognize that the pupils are working without the aid of the master hand. This is where the scenes from the New Testament begin, which, owing to the death of Leo X, were never completed. The decorations framing the frescoes (painted tapestries, pilasters, grotesques, mosaics and flying angels) remain the same for each two arcades.

FIRST ARCADE: (1) God Separates the Light from the Darkness. With a motion of his whole being, which is here enlarged and exaggerated after the style of the Michelangelo figures, God brings about the separation. The dark red of the flesh tints used bears out what Vasari says, that this cupola is the work of Giulio Romano. (2) God Divides the Land from the Waters. Beneath the figure of God, suspended in the bright heav-

Jacob and Rachel

ens, the terrestrial globe takes its rounded shape, on which the waters are distinct from the land, whereon a clump of trees has begun to appear. (3) Creation of the Sun and the Moon. This design is also a reminiscence of Michelangelo. The figure of God is as in the former design, but his back is turned to the spectator and he is stretching forth his arms towards the globes of the sun and moon. The world is rolling through space below. (4) The Creation of the Animals. Moving through the earth, God causes all the animals, some of them of fantastic shapes, to appear upon it. The figure of God is no longer in the strong Michelangelo style, and

Portion of a Loggia

we here discern unmistakable traces of the hand of Giulio Romano.

SECOND ARCADE: (5) The Creation of Eve. In a fertile landscape, God, who has put foot on earth, is showing Adam his helpmeet. We have here a new method of treating the subject in art. The folds in the drapery of the Eternal Father's cloak are wonderful. Vasari says that Giulio Romano worked in this arcade, but it is by no means certain. (6) Original Sin. In the centre stands the tree, around which is coiled a serpent with a human head. Eve, erect to the left, is in the act of offering a fruit to Adam, who is seated on the other side. The background is a wondrous piece of landscape painting. There is a tradition that Raphael himself painted this figure of Eve, but the coloring is too severe for such a tradition to be accepted without reserve. (7) The Expulsion from Paradise. An angel with a flaming sword stands at the gate of Paradise driving away the two sinners. The shame-stricken woman seeks as best she can to cover her nakedness with her hands, and Adam strives to hide his face. These two figures are copied from the fresco by Masaccio in the Carmine Church at Florence. (8) The First Toil of Man. Adam is seen sowing in a field, and Eve appears spinning, while Cain and Abel play around her.

THIRD ARCADE: (9) The Building of the Ark. Noah, an old man, is showing his sons how they must set about preparing the timber for the ark, the hull of which is seen in the distance. The work bears traces of

Moses Saved from the Nile

Francesco Penni's style. (10) The Universal Deluge. In the background the ark is seen on the waters, and in the foreground a rider is drowning. One man looks in terror on a woman who dies in his arms, and another, holding up a child, is trying to rescue a woman from drowning by grasping her hair. (11) The Coming Forth from the Ark. While the animals are leaving the ark, Noah and his family are seen lamenting the ruin of the flood. (12) Noah's Sacrifice. In the centre Noah is praying before an altar, while one of his sons slaughters a lamb and another son holds a second victim ready. In the rear two young men are seen leading two bulls, and a camel appears in the background. Here again, if we are to believe Vasari, we have the work of Giulio Romano, but it is not quite certain.

FOURTH ARCADE: (13) Abram and Melchisedeck. Melchisedeck, King of Jerusalem, brings forth to Abram two baskets of bread and four jars of wine. He is surrounded by warriors and shepherds. (14) God's Promise to Abram. The patriarch is on his knees in the foreground, his back to the onlooker, and God appears to him on high, promising him a numerous offspring. (15) The Visit of the Three Angels to Abram.

Candelabra in the Loggia decorated by
Mantovani

Detail from the Ornaments in the
Pilasters

Decorations showing the Arms of Gregory XIII
over a Door in the Loggie

Candelabra
(Mascherini, Sermoneta and Nogari)

In the front of his house Abram is on his knees before the three young men, who are speaking to him. Sara is looking on from the door. The background is a charming landscape. The fresco is thought to be the work of Penni. (16) Lot and his Family Leave Sodom. In the background is to be seen a burning city, and in the near distance Lot comes

Moses Presenting the Law to the People

forward, leading his children by the hand. The wife, who looked back at Sodom, has been turned into a statue of salt. This work also is said to have been executed by Francesco Penni.

FIFTH ARCADE: (17) God Appears to Isaac. In a fair landscape Isaac is seen on his knees, and God appears to him in the clouds. Rebecca is seated to the left. (18) Isaac Embraces Rebecca. In the atrium of a palace, whose background is a balcony looking on the open country, Isaac and Rebecca are seated in embrace. King Abimelech watches them from a window. The work is Penni's. (19) Isaac Blessing Jacob. The aged patriarch, on his couch, raises his hand to bless Jacob, who is kneeling at the foot. Rebecca is seen encouraging her son. The background shows Esau hunting in a wild country. This is certainly the work of Francesco Penni. (20) Esau Asking Isaac to Bless Him. At his father's bedside Esau is asking a blessing, while the patriarch shows his surprise. Rebecca and Jacob are seen looking in at the door. The work is in the style of Penni.

SIXTH ARCADE: (21) Jacob's Ladder. Jacob lies asleep in the foreground and in ecstasy turns his head towards the centre, where six angels are seen ascending and descending a ladder the top of which is lost in a glory surrounding the figure of God the Father. (22) Jacob and Rachel at the Well. Rachel and a bond-servant who holds her by the hand are standing before a well while the flocks quench their thirst. Rachel is speaking to Jacob, who has a pilgrim's staff on his shoulder.

David and Bathsheba

The poetry of the whole scene is enhanced by a charming landscape. (23) Jacob Seeking Rachel's Hand. Jacob goes to see Laban, who has his daughter Leah with him. Near Jacob stands Rachel, tending the flock. The fresco is badly injured. (24) Jacob's Flight. Jacob, seated on an ass and accompanied by his women and children on camels, is returning to his own country. The flocks and shepherds are seen on the road ahead.

SEVENTH ARCADE: (25) Joseph Telling of his Dream. Joseph, represented as a young boy, is standing while he tells his brethren of his dream. They are reclining on a sloping ground. The flock is to one side. In two luminous circles in the sky are depicted the events of the dream. The work is attributed to Giulio Romano. (26) Joseph Sold by his Brethren. The open well is in the foreground. Joseph has just been handed over to four merchants who are counting out the agreed price to one of the brethren. (27) Joseph and Potiphar's Wife. The woman is seated on a couch and tries to draw Joseph to her. He is in flight and leaves his cloak in her hands. The room is adorned with rich tapestry designs, and the work is perhaps very properly attributed to Giulio Romano. (28) Joseph Interpreting Pharaoh's Dreams. On a portico with a landscape background the king is seen puzzled, and Joseph is explaining to him the meaning of his dreams, the events of which are represented in two circles of light on the upper portion of the picture.

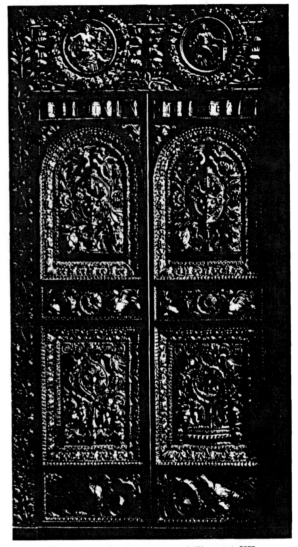

Door showing the Arms of Clement VII
(Sixteenth Century)

EIGHTH ARCADE: (29) Moses Saved from the Water. With the Nile as a background, Pharaoh's daughter and six beautiful maidens are looking at a male child that one of the women is taking from the basket. The landscape, with the river losing itself in the distance, is very fine. Vasari says the work is Giulio Romano's, but it is uncertain. (30) The Burning Bush. Moses, with his face hidden in his hands, is kneeling before a bush within which God appears. This work is by the same artist as the preceding one. (31) The Crossing of the Red Sea. The host of Israel, with their baggage, are moving off to the right. Moses stretches his rod over the sea, in which Pharaoh and his army are drowning. (32) Moses Striking the Rock. Moses hits the rock, from which water gushes forth, while the Hebrews look on in amazement. The figure of God is seen among the clouds.

NINTH ARCADE: (33) Moses Receiving the Tables of the Law. God the Father, in the clouds and surrounded by a glory of angels, is seen on the summit of Sinai handing over to Moses the sacred tables. Moses is kneeling. In the plain below the tents of the Israelites are shown. (34) The Adoration of the Golden Calf. The Hebrew people, on their knees, are worshipping a calf of gold set upon an altar, while dances are going on to the right. On the left Moses is seen coming down from the mountains, and as his eyes meet the spectacle he drops the tables and breaks them. (35) The Pillar of Cloud. The pillar of cloud rises

Solomon and the Queen of Sheba

up among the encamped Hebrews, the figure of the Eternal being concealed in it. Moses is seen kneeling before it. (36) Moses Presenting the Law to the People. From a raised mound Moses shows the tables of the law to the assembled people. This is one of the finest compositions in the galleries.

TENTH ARCADE: (37) The Passage of the Jordan. The river Jordan, personified as an old man as in classical days, separates its waters to allow the priests carrying the ark, the people of Israel, and the warriors to cross over dry-shod. (38) The Taking of Jericho. While the warriors, followed by the ark, make the circuit of the city, the walls and towers fall, giving free entry to the besiegers. It is doubtful whether Raphael designed this picture. (39) Joshua Halts the Sun. Joshua, on horseback in command of his fighting men, makes sign to the sun and moon to stop in their courses so that the warriors of Israel may complete their

victory over the Amorites. (40)
The Division of the Lands. Joshua
and the high priest Eleazar are
seated on thrones before two
urns, from one of which a boy
takes out a paper which he gives
to the head of the tribe. It is a
feeble work. Vasari assigns all
the works in this arcade to Perino
del Vaga.

ELEVENTH ARCADE: (41) David
Anointed King by Samuel. In the
temple, David, surrounded by his
brothers, is anointed by Samuel,
while sacrifice is made ready on
an altar. There are suggestions
of Giulio Romano here. (42)
David Slaying Goliath. The giant,
hit by the stone, is stretched on the
earth, and David, with one knee
pressing his chest, is about to cut
off his head with his sword. At
the sight the Philistines flee and
are being pursued by the Hebrews.
(43) David's Triumph. Like an
ancient conqueror, David stands
upright in a chariot, surrounded

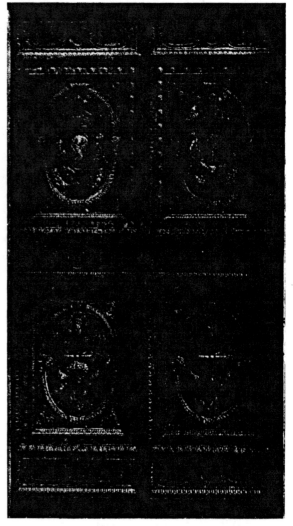

Door showing the Arms of Gregory XIII
(Sixteenth Century)

by his warriors, who bear along the prisoners and the booty. (44)
David and Bathsheba. David, at a window of his palace, is looking at
his soldiers marching out against the Amorites when he chances to see
Bathsheba on a terrace.

TWELFTH ARCADE: (45) The Anointment of Solomon. In the presence
of an applauding crowd, the high priest anoints Solomon as king of
Israel. In the foreground the reclining figure of an old man symbolizes
the river Tigris. (46) The Judgment of Solomon. In the background
Solomon is seated on his throne, and in sight of the two mothers, one
of whom is a suppliant on her knees while the other asks him to divide
the child in two, he orders a soldier not to harm the infant. The wise
men express their admiration. The picture has very little, if any, inspiration drawn from Raphael. (47) The Queen of Sheba. The queen,
followed by her servants laden with gifts, advances towards the throne
of Solomon, who bends to embrace her. The design is faulty and can

The Adoration of the Magi

hardly be the work of Raphael. (48) The Building of the Temple. Solomon has come out to visit the foundations of the Temple, and is examining the plan shown him by the architect. In the foreground the workmen are busy hewing stones and sawing wood.

THIRTEENTH ARCADE: (49) The Adoration of the Shepherds. The Virgin is kneeling before the Child, on whom two angels are dropping flowers. To the left the shepherds are seen coming with gifts. On the other side Joseph beckons to a shepherd to draw near. The fresco has been damaged considerably. (50) The Adoration of the Magi. In the centre the three kings are on their knees before the Virgin and the Child. The oldest king is kissing the Child's foot. The slaves follow behind. To the left Joseph is lifting with much curiosity the lid of one of the vases brought by the kings. (51) The Baptism of Christ. Christ stands with joined hands on the river bank and St. John is pouring water on his head. Behind the figure of Christ a group of men are disrobing for baptism. Two angels near St. John hold the garments of the Saviour. (52) The Last Supper. The Apostles are seated around the table and the Saviour is in the centre. The figures of the Apostles are full of movement.

Having thus briefly described the sacred scenes on the roof that go to make up Raphael's Bible, it remains for us to run over the rich decoration and stucco work and coloring on the pilasters and arches and windows of the Loggie. The name usually given to these details is that of "grottesche," because they were copied from Roman monuments long buried away, which were and are known as *grotte*.

It is certain that these ornaments are derived from Roman remains, notably from Nero's Domus Aurea, which was at one time called the Baths of Titus.

Vasari, in his life of Giovanni da Udine, tells how that artist, together with his master Raphael, visited the rooms of the Domus Aurea, which had just been discovered near San Pietro in Vincoli, and how Raphael was so pleased with their decorations that he ordered his pupil to make copies of them for use in the Loggie. Moreover, quite recently, on the roof of one of the galleries in that House of Nero a graffito has been discovered recording the very name of this painter: JUAN DA VDENE FIRLANO. Antiquity, indeed, was laid under tribute for the ideas in these galleries, but there was no real plagiarism. Giovanni da Udine adapted the ancient models, and he did so with exquisite taste and judgment. He took the parts and made a new whole of them, and the result is one of the finest creations of the Renaissance, a story-book in colors full of dreams and fancies. The pilasters and walls are dotted with stucco work and pictures: mythological subjects, cupids, plants, fruits, vases, animals, landscapes, fantastic originals and copies of ancient statues, musical instruments, fishes, birds, flying ribbons, are to be seen on every hand; and in a charming stucco frame in a window nook Raphael himself is painted together with his pupils, some of whom are mixing colors, others drawing, others painting on a wall, while the master is busy making a dainty design on a canvas supported on his knees, and lower down Fame blows a trumpet to proclaim the excellence of the whole work.

It is truly not easy to imagine any work more excellent. Classic antiquity, Bible story, legend, poetry and faith, heaven and earth, and the winds of heaven are here drawn into one great poem in which the world of Pagandom meets the world of Christendom without shock, save for those who do not understand the spirit that was at work in the Renaissance. Giovanni da Udine, to whom under Raphael the work is due, has known how to avoid the pitfalls of excess into which the artists of that time were so liable to fall. The arabesque style became prevalent in the second half of the Cinquecento, but the ornaments employed became stiff and heavy and too thickly laid on, and hence it came to pass that the method soon began to pall. But we must not confuse the cold imitations of a later day with the beautiful creations of Giovanni da Udine, in which we find again an outcropping of the beauty of classic times.

PART THREE

—

THE VATICAN MUSEUMS AND COLLECTIONS
AND THE MOSAIC FACTORY

THE NEW PICTURE GALLERY

I is very difficult for the Popes nowadays to rival their predecessors of the Renaissance period as patrons of the arts. With the best will in the world, they enjoy neither the means nor the opportunity to do so. Nevertheless, Pope Pius X was able on several occasions to follow up the course laid down by Papal traditions. Two artistic undertakings in particular he initiated with so great success that they alone are enough to win him the gratitude of all artists. We refer to the institution of the New Picture Gallery and to the complete restoration of the Chapel of Nicholas V, famous for its glorious frescoes by Fra Angelico. The present writer had the great honor of being entrusted with the latter work, and succeeded in bringing back to light the small windows with the painted sides.

Up to the year 1909 the paintings that made up the Old Pinacoteca were gathered together on the top floor of the Palace, in what was known as the Apartment of Gregory XIII. It was a steep climb up there, and the visitor could hardly fail to lament the fact that these priceless artistic treasures were sequestrated in a place entirely unsuitable in lighting and space accommodations. Moreover, the safety of the pictures was not sufficiently provided for. The works contained there were mainly those which Antonio Canova and Marino Marini, representatives of Pius VII, had succeeded in recovering by the Treaty of 1815 out of the countless treasures taken by the French in 1797 from the Vatican and the churches in the Papal States. The Pope's envoys had to overcome the prejudices of the Allies and difficulties of every kind, and were forced to give up all claims to the collection of imperial coins, before they got back the more precious of these paintings. Sixty-seven pictures were allowed to re-cross the Alps by agreement of the Congress of Vienna on condition that they would not be returned to the original owners, but would be exposed for public view in the Vatican to be studied and copied by art lovers. Thus began the Old Picture Gallery, which, under the direction of Cardinal Consalvi and Canova, was first of all opened in the Appartamento Borgia. Soon afterwards it was transferred to the Apartment of Gregory XIII on the third floor of the Loggie; then to what is now the Hall of the Tapestries; later to the Apartment of Pius V, where the modern paintings now are; then back to the Apartment of Gregory XIII, whence Pope Pius X removed it to its present ample and worthy quarters.

In bringing about this last change, Pius X availed himself of the technical experience of Architect Sneider of the Apostolic Palaces, of the refined taste of the Sub-prefect, Monsignor Misciatelli, and of the great culture of Professor Seitz and Professor d'Achiardi, the present writer's

One of the Halls in the Old Picture Gallery

predecessor. For Professor Seitz it was a labor of love: he was not, however, destined to see his work completed, for on the day when Raphael's Transfiguration was lowered with cords and pulleys from the top of the Cortile di Belvedere, he was so overcome with emotion that during the night he succumbed to an attack of heart disease. Besides the paintings in the old collection, the New Gallery has the collection of Primitives, hidden away previously in the glass cases of the Library, the small but celebrated Lateran collection, the Byzantines of the Christian Museum, and other works of singular value that had been scattered throughout the storerooms and apartments of the Apostolic

The Ceiling of a Hall in the Old Picture Gallery,
showing the Signs of the Zodiac (L. B. Alberti)

Palaces. The halls which were to receive this collection were arranged
and decorated with a nobility in keeping with the best artistic traditions
of the Vatican. In admiring the severe elegance of the halls wherein
the pictures are so favorably displayed and their safety so amply provided for, no one would imagine that these quarters on the east of the
Cortile di Belvedere were formerly the storerooms of the Floreria and
the coach-house of the Vatican. The halls are nine in number, and are
reached by that street which leads to the Museums and is so well known
to thousands of Vatican visitors. Over the entrance door is a slab with
an inscription and a bust of Pius X carved by the sculptor Seeback.
The inscription is from the pen of Monsignor Aurelio Galli, Secretary
for Latin Letters, and reads:

Pius. X. Pont. Max.
Pinacothecam Vaticanam
Laudatorum operum Accessione Auctam
Heic splendore Attributa Sede
Statuendam Ordinandam Curavit
Sacri Principatus Anno VI.

The light enters through the windows which overlook the Cortile

The Hall of the Trecento or Primitives

di S. Damaso. These windows were cut according to ancient designs, so that the plans of Sneider entailed to a certain extent a restoration of one side of the majestic Cortile. The decorations of the hall are uniformly severe and noble. The doors are framed with white marble slabs, and over the architrave the name of the Pope appears in carved gilt lettering. The ceilings are adorned with stucco-work in pure Cinquecento style, interspersed with the coat of arms of Pius X. The walls are covered with olive green silk, against which the rich gilding of the picture frames stands out boldly; the heating arrangements are skilfully concealed in the walnut panelling near the floor, and to complete the comfort and nobility of the room there is an abundance of chairs and elegant lounges, of the shape called *raffaelesca,* and decorative pieces of precious marble.

One of the chief charms of the Vatican Picture Gallery is the great variety of its most rare and valuable paintings, for the visitor can pass from the early imitations of the Greeks down to the modern paintings of a Lawrence. The task of arranging such a collection so as to satisfy at once esthetic demands and sound scientific requirements fell to the painter Seitz and Professor d'Achiardi. On the death of Seitz, d'Achiardi had to complete the glorious work alone. In the first room, to the right of the vestibule, are to be found the Primitives and Byzantines, paintings hitherto for the most part kept in the Library or Christian Museum. In the second room—known as the Melozzo Hall, because it has the famous fresco of the Romagnolo painter— are examples of many Italian schools of the Quattro- and Cinquecento. Then comes the Hall of the School of Umbria and the Marches, which precedes the hall devoted to the School of Raphael. Beginning again at the vestibule, to the left, we meet successively the Hall of the Venetian School, the Hall of the Secentisti, and the Hall of

The Hall of the Trecento

Foreign Painters. In all, then, including the atrium and the storeroom wherein are kept all the paintings that are not considered worthy of a place in the Gallery, there are nine rooms skilfully and logically planned.

The Primitives in the first hall represent the most tasteful novelty of the Gallery, but have never yet been satisfactorily identified or criticized. They are all small-sized paintings, and were until recent times kept in glass cases in the Library, where, owing to the poor light and the reflections of the glass, it was difficult to examine them. For the most part they date from the fourteenth century, though there are some of earlier date, and the majority belong to the Central Italian Schools— Florentine, Sienese and Bolognese. A framed painting belonging to the first school is of special interest. It shows in the upper half the Crucifixion, in which the Virgin falls beneath the weight of her sorrow and is being supported by the holy women; at the foot of the Cross are Sts. Francis and Mary Magdalen, Sts. John the Apostle and John the Baptist. In the lower half are seated in hieratic attitudes before some draperies Sts. Paul, Peter and Louis of Toulouse. This is a truly masterly work not only because of its breadth of treatment, but also because of its dramatic force. In our opinion, therefore, it has been very properly attributed to Giotto: such is also Berenson's opinion, and he is supported by Cochin, who, in view of the fact that the Bishop of

The Hall of the Quattrocento, or Melozzo Hall

Toulouse here portrayed was a near relative of Robert of Anjou, for whom Giotto was painting at Naples from 1330 to 1332, holds that the work belongs to this period in the activity of the famous painter. Grouped around the painting are many smaller ones in the Giotto manner from various parts of Italy, testifying to the great influence exercised by the Florentine master in his own day; one of the best of these is a Madonna and Child against a golden background, the work of Bernardo Daddi. Faithful to the Giotto tradition, but heralding the dawn of the Quattrocento and the advent of Angelico, are a group of pictures by Lorenzo Monaco, some of which—for example, the Story of St. Benedict, the Crucifixion, and the Nativity—are certainly by his own hand.

The Sienese School is even more fully represented. Among those that give particular evidence of the Giotto influence are Bartolo di Fredi's Angel Appearing to St. Joachim, and the Death of Mary by his pupil, Taddeo di Bartolo, whose name is linked with the decorations of the upper chapel in the Communal Palace of Siena. The latter little tablet shows with charming simplicity the soul of the Virgin in the

The Madonna and Child, with Saints and Angels
(Fra Angelico)

Episodes from the Life of St. Nicholas of Bari
(Fra Angelico)

form of a young child wrapped in golden draperies and resting in the
arms of Christ, while several apostles and angels stand round the dead
body. A work of great importance, not alone for its intrinsic value but
also for the history of art, is the Christ Blessing by an artist who had
pronounced influence on the Sienese School, and helped to free it from
the Greek influence of Duccio di Boninsegna. This picture by Simone
Martini, and especially the Crucifixion by Lippo Menni, in view of its
excellent state of preservation, are among the most precious docu-

The Miracles of St. Vincent Ferrer
(Francesco del Cossa)

ments for the study of the beginnings of the art of painting in Italy. The Crucifixion is the central panel of a triptych, of which the wings are missing. Of no less importance is Pietro Lorenzetti's tablet Christ before Pilate, a work known to and described by Cavalcaselle. The manners of the two Lorenzetti can be advantageously studied and distinguished in many paintings in this group, particularly in eight tablets which even to-day cannot be attributed to either with certainty.

The Bolognese Primitives are well represented; there is, for example, a table by Vitale Cavalli, showing the Madonna and Child blessing a group of kneeling disciples, which bears the signature, Vitalis de Bonomia I.

Mention must here be made of one of the important works of the ancient Florentine school, the Madonna Enthroned with her Son and Four Saints and with other figures in the cusps of the polyptych. This work is dated 1372, and is noteworthy for its exceptional size, but above all for the signature of the artist, Giovanni Bonsi, of whom no other work is known. Indeed, the painting itself was unknown until the New Picture Gallery was opened, for it had previously lain neglected in the Vatican storerooms. This polyptych, however, possesses a peculiar interest as an example of Tuscan painting from the second half of the Trecento. It is also of great intrinsic interest, especially for the expression of the saints on the sides of the central panel; this expression becomes especially effective in the wild face of the hermit St. Honuphrius, in the panel on the left.

The Miracles of St. Vincent Ferrer
(Francesco del Cossa)

The Oncagna School and its traditions are represented by a picture of the first rank, the Regina Sanctorum by Giovanni del Biondo. The scene shows the Madonna and Child enthroned against a background of gold and purple drapery held by two angels. To the left are four male saints, to the right four female saints, and in the sky above an angel is seen purifying with a live coal the lips of the prophet Isaiah. This beautiful tablet, which glistens with gold, is framed with the motif of the Annunciation, while on the predella is seen a figure dear to the artists of the Trecento—a decaying corpse, the object of salutary fear and meditation.

From the Florentines who followed Agnolo Gaddi we have many valuable paintings; the Madonna and Child with St. John and St. Catherine is attributed to Niccolò di Pietro Gerini, and the St. Nicholas Freeing Three Knights is said to be by his son, Lorenzo di Niccolò.

The icons taken from the Christian Museum are for the most part arranged on the sides of the deep apertures of the windows in this room. While it is not unusual to hear it said that these are fabulously old works—for instance, the Burial of St. Ephraem is said to be a work of the tenth or eleventh century, whereas it is really signed by Emanuele Zanfurnari, a sixteenth-century artist—the truth is that they are early Renaissance works done by Greek artists or artists under Greek influence. The oldest of the group, and that which bears the clearest traces of the Byzantine style, is a painting by Margaritone d'Arezzo (*Margarito de Aretio me fecit*) from the second half of the Dugento,

The Miracles of St. Vincent Ferrer
(Francesco del Cossa)

depicting St. Francis Showing the Stigmata. The painting is a venerable and most important relic, and, like other pictures of the same period at Siena, Pisa and Arezzo, as well as the earlier one at the Sacro Speco of Subiaco, is a noteworthy iconographic document of the Poverello of Assisi, who was the first in the obscurity of the Middle Ages to feel the breath of the coming dawn, and with whom is linked the idealism revealed in the works of art gathered in this very room.

The various currents of Italian art in the fifteenth century are represented by works of exceptional importance in the second room, which exceeds all the others in size, and holds a surprise for visitors to the New Gallery, since the majority of the works were not on view in the Old Picture Gallery. Here are, for instance, three undoubtedly authentic works by Fra Angelico, of which one, in an excellent state of preservation, shows the Virgin in glory with the Child, St. Dominic and St. Catherine. The two others contain episodes from the life of St. Nicholas of Bari: the first of these panels tells the story of his birth, the gift of a dowry to the three poor sisters while they are asleep, and the preconizing of the holy youth as bishop at the entrance to a church, while a crowd of the faithful are assembled on a flowering sward; the other panel tells the miracles of the multiplication of the sacks of grain and the apparition of St. Nicholas to save a vessel from shipwreck. These two panels formed part of a predella painted by Angelico about 1437 for the Chapel of S. Niccolò dei Guidolotti in the Church of St. Dominic in Perugia, and some parts of the third panel are still treasured in the Picture Gallery of that city.

The Miracles of St. Vincent Ferrer
(Francesco del Cossa)

Around these most precious works have been judiciously grouped paintings depicting episodes in the life of Christ: the Birth, the Adoration of the Magi, Jesus in the Temple, the Transfiguration, the Entry into Jerusalem; all these were formerly kept in the Library, and evidently belong to the school of Fra Angelico. One scene, which is an early work of Benozzo Gozzoli and was painted in the middle of the Quattrocento, shows so clearly the influence of Angelico that it was long attributed to him. It is a painting in tempera, done for the Church of St. Fortunatus near Montefalco, and shows the Virgin surrounded by a choir of angels and giving a girdle to St. Thomas. On the predella are six scenes from the Virgin's life—her Birth and Espousals, the Annunciation, the Birth of Christ, the Circumcision and the Dormition; here the influence of Fra Angelico is still more evident, just as the admirable power of the drawings speaks of Gozzoli. Under the central part of the altarpiece is a rectangular hole, which tradition declares was used in giving Communion to cloistered nuns.

Among other Tuscan works of the early Quattrocento two are attributed to Masolino da Panicale—the Crucifixion and the Dormition. The school of Fra Angelico and Masolino are seen united in the famous triptych by Fra Filippo Lippi, which is held to be one of the most characteristic works of the master, and, notwithstanding the great progress made by painting technique, still astonished Vasari by its freshness of coloring. As is well known, the work was ordered by Carlo Marsuppini, secretary to the Florentine Republic, who is shown in a panel to

Portrait of Francesco Sforza
(Bernardino de' Conti)

St. Jerome
(Leonardo da Vinci)

the left offering it to the Chapel of St. Bernard at Mount Oliveto. The central panel shows Christ on a throne of precious marble crowning the Virgin; the panel on the right shows the donor in ecclesiastical garb being presented by two monastic saints; the panel on the left also shows a personage, in an ermine-lined cassock, assisted by two monastic saints. In the background of the panels appear three angels playing on musical instruments.

Coming from the private apartments of the Vatican, and therefore hitherto unknown to art students, is a precious painting showing St. Francis Receiving the Stigmata against a marvellous background of landscape-work. It

Head of St. Jerome
(Leonardo da Vinci)

is a fifteenth-century work, and shows some characteristics of Piero della Francesca, as well as traces of the Florentine influence exercised by Angelico and Lippi.

In this same room there is a very interesting group of small tablets taken from the Library and belonging to the Sienese School of the fifteenth century, the works of which are now so much sought after by art lovers. This school is represented by the most prominent artists.

To Stefano di Giovanni, known as Il Sassetta, is attributed a graceful work showing St. Thomas Aquinas in his monk's robes adoring Christ crucified, who speaks to him, saying: "Bene scripsisti de me, Thoma." There are many works by artists who imitated Il Sassetta, such as Pellegrino del Mariano and Sano di Pietro. To the latter are attributed various tablets of which some depict episodes from the Golden Legend; but most elegant of all is the Espousals of the Virgin, which is crowded with the figures of boy and girl musicians, and is an admirable embodiment of the delicacy of the Sienese School during the Quattrocento. Among other celebrated masters of the Sienese School must be mentioned Giovanni del Poggio, one of whose works here shown was used as a cover for the tax-register of Siena during the years 1444 and 1445, a very significant instance of the wonderful love of art in those days. Who can conceive a ledger to-day with such a cover!

Pope Sixtus IV and Il Platina
(Melozzo da Forli)

Details from Pope Sixtus IV and Il Platina
(Melozzo da Forlì)

But the visitor to this room is confronted by even more splendid relics of the Italian Renaissance, the most famous masters of the epoch being here represented. We have the celebrated predella of Francesco del Cossa, showing the Miracles of St. Vincent Ferrer; this work comes from the Old Picture Gallery, and, as Frizzoni has shown, belonged (like the St. Peter and St. John, now in the Brera at Milan, and the St. Vincent Ferrer, now in the National Gallery of London) to the altar of

The Hall of the School of Umbria and the Marches

the Griffani Chapel in St. Petronius's at Bologna. It is true that Vasari attributes the predella doubtfully to another Farrarese, Ercole de Roberto; but all critics now agree that the great artist who painted it is the same as the one who decorated the Schifanoia Palace. The predella shows the healing of a leprous woman, the healing of a sister of the Queen of Aragon who had been struck down by a rock, a mason's assistant falling from a house in construction and kept suspended by the saint, and the restoration to life of a child who had been torn to pieces by his insane mother. All these scenes, which take place against a background of fantastic and luminous landscape with ruins and archi-

Madonna and Child
(Francescuccio Ghissi)

tecture, are nothing more than a pretext for the artist to crystallize for ever by the magic of his incisive drawing the costumes and the every-day life of Ferrara in the days of the Renaissance.

In this room are also seen two large figures of apostles, a St. Peter and a St. Paul, by Fra Bartolomeo della Porta; these were formerly in the Church of St. Silvester of Montecavallo, and, if we are to believe Vasari, one of them was finished by Raphael. Both certainly were influenced by Raphael and Michelangelo. The Virgin and Child is a beautiful painting of the pure Tuscan School; the Virgin is seated at a window opening on a bright landscape, and the whole is the work of Lorenzo da Credi. A

small painting, showing the Madonna and Child with St. John and St. Anne, is attributed to Andrea del Sarto.

The rare gem of the room is Leonardo's St. Jerome, a vigorous work revealing the master's technique at its best and bringing out his perfect knowledge of form, which has never been surpassed. This picture, which is among the very few executed by the master's own hand, has had a strange history. It belonged to the Cardinal Fesch collection, and the story runs that His Eminence was so lucky as to come into possession of the two pieces of the canvas at different times; no one seems to know how it ever came to be torn and separated. The church in the

The Camerino Triptych
(Niccolò Alunno)

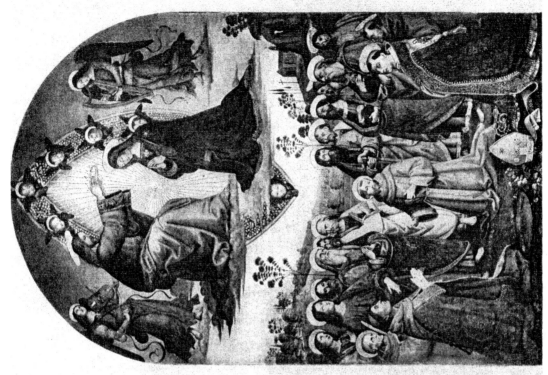

The Coronation of the Virgin
(Pinturicchio)

The Madonna della Spineta, or the Adoration of the Magi
(Lo Spagna)

The Virgin of the Rota
(Antoniazzo Romano)

background reminds one of the architecture of S. Maria Novella, and from this we may fix the date of the sketch as being before 1489, that is, in the master's Florentine period.

In this room are exhibited some of the paintings belonging to the Northern Italian School. Among these is a portrait of the boy Francesco Sforza by Bernardino de' Conti, signed and dated and containing a legend which identifies the boy as the five-year-old son of Galeazzo Maria Sforza. A portrait of a man reveals the characteristics of Gian Battista Moroni of Bergamo, the great portraitist. Here too, though it might more fittingly be placed with the Venetian School, is a Madonna and Child with St. Jerome and St. Bartholomew by Il Moretto; this painting is known as the Madonna of the Pears from two piles of fruit near the foot of the throne. The work apparently belongs to the later period of the Brescian master, when the characteristic brightness of his silver tones began to be a little dulled.

But this whole room is appropriately known as the Melozzo Hall from Melozzo da Forli, whose celebrated fresco is given the place of honor between two good canvases by one of his pupils, Marco Palmezano. These two canvases come from the Lateran. One is a Madonna Enthroned with her Son, dated 1537; the central figures are surrounded by six saints, while an angel plays a musical instrument. The other painting is a variation of the same theme with fewer personages. Both pictures, which are practically the same size, bear traces of Venetian influence, and belong to the last period of the artist's activity, although they give no evidence of enfeebled powers.

The Madonna Enthroned with Saints
(Perugino)

We now come to Melozzo's masterpiece. When Sixtus IV was rearranging the Library in 1477, he had this fresco painted for the space between two windows of the hall now known as the Floreria Apostolica, where even to-day traces of the original decoration may be seen on the ceiling and majolica floor. As in his time the fresco was in a poor condition, Leo XII had it transferred to canvas so that it might be given a more worthy setting, and since then it has been preserved in the Picture Gallery. Melozzo shows Pope Sixtus IV in the Library investing the humanist Bartolomeo Sacchi, called Il Platina, as Prefect of the Apostolic Library. The scene is rendered with miraculous truth, and the perspective of the Library is perfect. The Pope is accompanied by his nephews, Raffaello and Gerolamo Riario (later Governor of the Papal States), and Giovanni and Giuliano della Rovere, who was afterwards Pope Julius II, and whose reign was immortalized by the works of Raphael and Michelangelo. The work is nothing but a grouping of entirely distinct portraits, without any special connection with the action which the painting aims at representing; but we must go to Mantegna to find anything equal to the perfection of drawing, which is here intensified by the artist's profound penetration into the characters of the persons portrayed. The figures have the relief of living persons, and reveal to the spectator at the first glance their peculiar characteristics. The satirical and indomitable spirit of the humanist is shown in

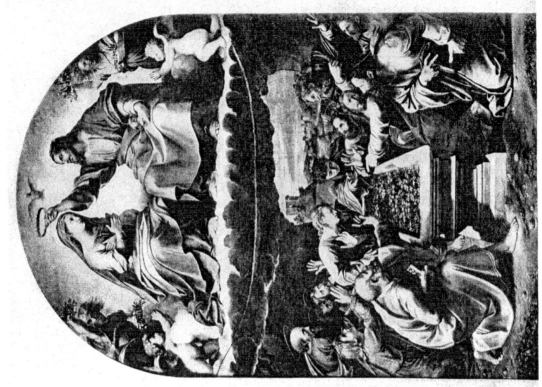

The Madonna of Monteluce
(Designed by Raphael and Painted
by Giulio Romano and Penni)

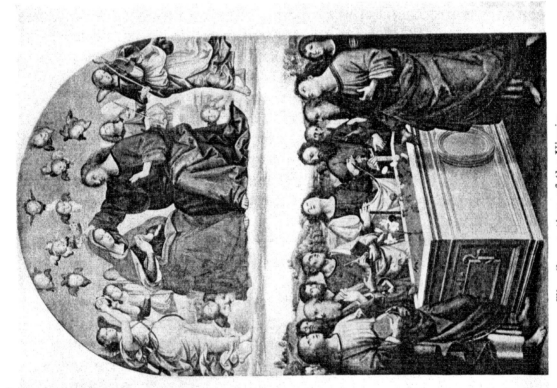

The Coronation of the Virgin
(Raphael)

The Annunciation
(Raphael)

his sharp visage and tightly closed lips, while the vigorous will of the
future Pope appears in the firmness of his powerful jaw. It is impossible to appreciate the true artistic worth of this great Romagnolo master of the fifteenth century unless one has seen and studied this fresco.
The later developments of painting may perhaps prevent us from sharing in all the enthusiasm of Vasari and Luca Pacioli for Melozzo's grasp
of aërial perspective, but even to-day we are astounded at the incredible
skill of the execution and the unrivalled lucidity and splendor of the
coloring.

The third room is given over exclusively to the School of Umbria
and the Marches before the coming of Raphael, whose works, being
assembled in the next room, thus receive a logical introduction.

The influence of the Florentine, and more especially of the Sienese,
School on the Primitives of the Marches is very evident in the beautiful
triptych by Allegretto Nuzi da Fabriano, dated 1365, wherein the
gentle grace of the Virgin and of St. Ursula, painted on the panel to the
right, is accentuated by the masculine vigor of the Archangel Michael
in armor. Another artist who shows Sienese influence is Francescuccio
Ghissi, also a native of Fabriano and a precursor of Gentile. He has
a characteristic painting here, formerly kept in the Library, showing
with incomparable simplicity and candor the Virgin suckling her Child.
To Gentile are attributed four small tablets which, according to Siren,
once formed part of a predella belonging to the polyptych of the Gonfaloniere Quaratesi at St. Nicholas's in Florence. These paintings de-

The Adoration of the Magi
(Raphael)

pict the miracles of St. Nicholas of Bari: his Birth, the Gift to the Three
Maidens, the Freeing of the Three Young Men, and the Apparition of
the Saint to save a vessel from shipwreck. They certainly approach
very close to the style of this master, who exercised such a great influence on painting in Italy, and actively paved the way for the advent of
the Renaissance.

The rapid spread of Gentile's art is evident in the Madonna and Child
(known as the Madonna of the Butterfly because a large coleopter is
painted near the Virgin's shoulder), by Francesco di Gentile, supposed
to be the son of the great Fabrianese master; also in the graceful fragment, the Virgin and St. Anne, which shows the Virgin having her head
encircled with a cloth of woven blue and gold. This painting is attributed to Lorenzo (Jr.) d'Alessandro di Sanseverino. It may be interesting to know that the restoration of this picture is due to the diligent
research of Professor d'Achiardi, who, having noticed that the gold
background to the Virgin's head was a recent addition, removed this
background and discovered beneath it a part of the head of St. Anne.
He was then so fortunate as to find the remainder of the painting hidden away in a storeroom.

The three principal Umbrian masters, Perugino, Pinturicchio, and
Niccolò di Liberatore (known as Niccolò Alunno), claim the visitor's
attention in this room. Niccolò has a complicated polyptych from
Montelpare, dated 1466; it is divided into many zones, and has two rows
of male and female saints around a central panel representing the

The Presentation in the Temple
(Raphael)

Coronation of the Virgin. More famous than this work is the triptych known as the Camerino, because it comes from the Collegiata in that town. Its three compartments are richly framed with peaks decorated with Gothic flourishes. The central panel shows the Crucifixion with the Madonna, St. John, and the Magdalen at the foot of the cross, together with four angels; the panel on the right shows St. John and St. Porphyry; that on the left shows St. Peter and St. Venantius. The upper parts of the triptych have scenes showing the Resurrection, David and Isaiah. The intensity of the Folignese artist finds an outlet in the expression of piety and grief in the Crucifixion scene; the anguish indeed which distorts the face of St. John almost reaches the grotesque.

A fresco fragment showing the Virgin and Child is attributed to Pinturicchio, but it has been so much restored that discussion of its authorship is now useless. Assuredly Pinturicchio's is the Coronation of the Virgin in a luminous oval surrounded by cherubim. This was painted, as Vasari says, about 1500 for the Friars Minor of the Fratta near Perugia. In the lower part of the painting are the twelve apostles and several saints of the order of Friars Minor.

This room also contains Perugino's well-known Resurrection, painted for the Church of St. Francis in Perugia in 1502. The drawing is so pure that tradition has seen in this painting the collaboration of Raphael, and even declares that the sleeping figure and the figure fleeing at the sight of the risen Christ are portraits of Raphael and Perugino. Unfortunately, the picture has been many times restored.

In a better state of preservation, and more intense in color and expression, is the picture of the Three Saints (Placidus, Flavia and Benedict), a fragment from the great altarpiece in St. Peter's, Perugia, which was carried away to France at the end of the Settecento, and of which only this section and a few smaller pieces now at Perugia were ever recovered.

A very fine painting of the Umbrian school, formerly in the Pope's private apartments, is Antoniazzo Romano's Virgin of the Rota, showing the Virgin between Sts. Peter and Paul receiving the homage of the

The Madonna of Foligno
(Raphael)

twelve Auditors of the Rota. The striking individuality expressed in the faces of the Auditors confirms the fame of Antoniazzo as a portraitist.

Cola dell'Amatrice's triptych of the Assumption, dated 1515, is another important work, as also is the Madonna della Spineta, painted about 1507 by Giovanni di Pietro, better known as Lo Spagna or Lo Spagnolo. It was formerly in the Convent della Spineta near Todi, and depicts in a most novel way the Adoration of the Magi. So beautiful is this work that it has at times been attributed to Perugino, to Pinturicchio, and even to Raphael. It shows the Child on a cushion, being adored by his Mother, St. Joseph and three angels. The background is a bright landscape in which are seen the retinue of the Magi and the angels announcing the good tidings to the shepherds. The noble composition is bounded above by three angels holding a scroll. Notwithstanding the replica which is to be seen in the Louvre, this painting must not only be regarded as an original, but it is one of the best works by that rare artist who united in himself all the graces of the Umbrian School, and whose fame would have been even greater were it not over-shadowed by that of the great Urbinate himself.

In the next room, the fourth to the right from the vestibule, are the works of Raphael Sanzio. In this unrivalled shrine the genius of the marvellous artist first appears under the influence of Perugino in the Coronation of the Virgin; it later develops its immortal characteristics in the Madonna of Foligno, and finally surpasses itself in the Transfiguration, wherein it epitomizes preceding art and all the forms of art as yet unborn. These paintings, the noblest of all ages and countries, are too well known to need a long historic treatment here. It was a wise plan to leave these works of the great master by themselves, save for a minor work of his—the predella of the Baglioni Deposition—and three other paintings which bear a special relation to Raphael's work. The first of these three paintings is a work by the master who had the most influence on Raphael, namely, the Virgin Enthroned surrounded by

Detail from the Transfiguration
(Raphael)

Sts. Laurence, Louis, Herculanus and Constantius; this was painted with special vigor of coloring by Perugino for the chapel of the Communal Palace of Perugia in 1496. The second painting, the Madonna of Monteluce, was ordered from Raphael by the nuns of the Convent of Monteluce near Pistoia, and was executed after his death, according to the designs of the master, by Giulio Romano and Penni; this was one of the two works which most actively spread the style of Raphael. The third, the St. Jerome by Giovanni Santi, Raphael's father, is a painting in tempera, and bears no comparison to the mighty works around it; it does not even belong to the same school, since, as is well known, Giovanni died when Raphael was only eleven years old, and consequently before it was possible to influence him in any way. But, apart altogether from the sentimental significance of placing this work near the Transfiguration, the arrangement serves a valuable purpose by showing the marvellous artistic evolution which took place in a brief interval of time.

It will, however, be more instructive to compare the Coronation with Perugino's painting. Raphael's work, completed in 1503, is in the Perugino manner, but has greater breadth of treatment; the drawing is purer, and the composition and the individual figures already reveal that beauty the attraction of which Raphael alone is able to convey. The development of the great painter, who was then hardly twenty years old, is still more evident in the predella of this same altarpiece depicting the mysteries—that is, the Annunciation, the Adoration of the Magi, and the Presentation in the Temple. The scene of the Annunciation is set in an atmosphere full of intimate charm and mystery; in the Adoration of the Magi the artist is given an opportunity to represent, in accordance with the Umbrian tradition, a rich cavalcade; while in the third picture the well-balanced composition is directly inspired by the work of Perugino in Fano and the Sistine Chapel. Here, however, Raphael affirms his own personality and incomparable sureness of design much better than in the altarpiece of the Coronation.

Raphael attained his full artistic maturity in the Madonna of Foligno, which was painted in 1511, and marks a great advance over his Coronation of the Virgin, both in the modernity of its composition, the purity of its form, and the splendor of its coloring. This masterpiece was ordered by Sigismondo Conti as an *ex voto* for his escape from a bomb which fell on his house in Foligno during a siege. The prelate is shown praying with St. Jerome, St. Francis and St. John the Baptist at the feet of the Madonna, who is seated with her Son in a glory of angels. In the distance is seen the house of the donor, against which a fiery-tailed projectile has been hurled. In the foreground is the celebrated boy bearing a tablet. This painting was taken to Paris in 1797, together with many other precious canvases, which must have suffered much during that long journey in ox-wagons and by sea; for not only small tablets like the Mysteries, but such large tables as the Madonna of Foligno, had to be transferred to canvas—a very delicate operation even to-day, and in those days such a novelty that a special report of it was written by the restorer ("Rapporto dei cittadini Guijon Vincent Tannay e Berthollet sul ristauro dei quadri di Raffaello conosciuto sotto il nome di Madonna di Foligno," Parigi, piovoso anno X).

The Transfiguration has suffered also the vicissitudes of a great number of the pictures in the Vatican collection, if to a less extent. Thus, the picture, which is still on wood, has become dulled, principally

The Transfiguration
(Raphael)

on account of the drying of the colors resulting from the absorption of the varnish into the wood. As a consequence, certain corrections which the artist made can be detected—for instance, that on the foot of the woman, said to be the Fornarina, who, kneeling, points out to the apostles the boy possessed by the demon—and we thus recognize the infinite care and zeal bestowed by the master on this painting, which he wished to make his greatest, as he felt it would be his last work. If the table were freed of the old varnish, and if the coloring could display again that "aria lucida" (transparent air) spoken of by Vasari, even though it was then blackened on account of the "nero fumo da spampatori" (soot-black) used by Raphael, it would be more evident that the work of Giulio Romano, who completed it after the death of Raphael on Good Friday in 1520, is almost negligible, and must have been restricted to a few details of the landscape, particularly the flowering plain on which the figures in the foreground stand. A comparison of this work with the Madonna of Monteluce— so inferior in coloring and relief — which has been fitly placed beside the Transfiguration, will dissipate the prejudices once felt by even profound critics towards the work which was exhibited near the dead body of the Urbinate as a true expression of his mighty soul.

Although Vasari is not favorable to Raphael as a rule, and although his judgment was warped by exaggerating the rivalry between Raphael and Michelangelo and their schools, no more touching words occur in his "Lives" than those which he applies to this great work: "The most famous,

Madonna and Child
(Carlo Crivelli)

Pieta
(Carlo Crivelli)

most beautiful and most divine work of Raphael," he says, "who here
seems to have strained every effort of his genius to set forth all the
power and wealth of art in the face of Christ; and when he had finished
it, as though nothing else remained for him to do in life, he put down
his brush for ever and death came and called him."

The rich collection of Venetian paintings is shown in the first room
to the left of the vestibule. The earliest among them is a polyptych by
Antonio Vivarini; this work is divided into ten compartments, in which
painting and sculpture contribute equally to the decorative splendor.
In the centre below is a painted statue of St. Anthony, Abbot, seated
and in the act of blessing; in the side panels are Sts. Christopher, Bas-
tianus, Venantius and Vitus. In the upper portion of the panels are
Sts. Peter, Jerome, Paul and Benedict, with the bust of Christ in the
centre. Under the chair on which St. Anthony sits we read the signature: "Antonius de Murano piẍit, 1469." It was one of the last altar-
pieces executed by Antonio in which he reproduces in the architecture
of the polyptych the archaic form of an ogival flourish, like that
which the Masegne Brothers had employed at Venice a century earlier.
The painting comes from the Church of St. Anthony at Pesaro, and is
of importance for the evidence which it gives of the great spread of
Venetian art in the centres of culture along the Adriatic coast.

Near Vivarini's work are two admirable paintings by Carlo Crivelli
of the Marchesian School—a characteristic Pieta, a lunette showing
Christ, the Madonna, St. John and the Magdalen, and a Madonna and
Child, dated 1482, formerly kept in the Lateran Gallery. The latter

St. George Slaying the Dragon
(Paris Bordone)

The Madonna of St. Nicholas dei Frari
(Titian)

is one of this singular master's latest and best works, and is remarkable for its deep sentiment, its decorative splendor, and the vigor and strength of its design. Near these works, which are certainly authentic, is the ancient copy of Crivelli's Madonna and Child and Saints (dated 1481), an altarpiece with five compartments, in which St. James of the Marches is represented. This copy was formerly preserved in the Lateran Museum, and is thought by some to be the work of Carlo di Vittore Crivelli; the original is in the Louvre. After the careful research work of Gustavo Frizzoni (see "The Burlington Magazine," February, 1913) there can be no doubt that the Pieta is by Carlo Crivelli. It formed the upper part of an altarpiece planned by Giovanni Bellini for the Church of St. Francis at Pesaro. Its many restorations, and the peculiarities common among the best pupils of Giambellino, led many to attribute to Bonconsigli or Bartolomeo Montagna this monumental work, which is dominated by the piteous figure of Christ, the pathetic grief of the Magdalen and the virile sorrow of St. John.

After Giambellino, Venetian art of the Cinquecento blossoms forth in all its splendor. The famous table by Titian, the Madonna of St. Nicholas dei Frari, finished in 1523, awakens to-day no less admiration than it did at Venice in the Cinquecento because of the wonder and richness of its coloring and the nobility of its composition. In a sky of marvellous lucidity the Madonna and her Son, between two angels bearing garlands of flowers, hang from the clouds over a group of six saints near a ruined exedra. The solemn dignity of St. Nicholas, garbed in rich episcopal dress, the gentleness of St. Catherine, and the virile figure of St. Sebastian in this picture are well known to art lovers. The painting, however, has been somewhat damaged and restored, and the upper portion was also cut so that it might face the Transfiguration in the Old Picture Gallery. Among the figures most damaged is that of St. Sebastian, which nevertheless seems flesh and blood rather than paint.

Titian's Portrait of a Doge is another example of his masterly simplicity, but it has unfortunately suffered greatly from many restorations. Paris Bordone's St. George Slaying the Dragon, painted against a fresh landscape, brings out in a vivid manner the genial fantasy of Venetian art; but the painting has suffered at the restorer's hands, as has also that of Bonifazio Veronese, the Virgin and Child with Joseph, St. Zechariah, St. John the Baptist, and St. Elizabeth offering a basket of fruit. This last work is distinguished by the artist's characteristic fancy and wealth of coloring. Worthy of note here also is a large painting by Sebastiano del Piombo, showing against a background of architectural detail and landscape St. Bernard crushing a chained

The Deposition
(Caravaggio)

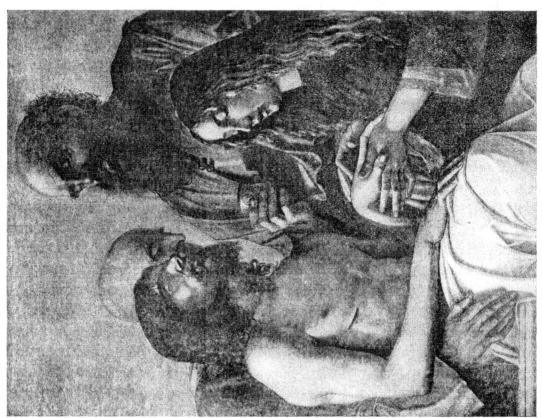

Mary Magdalen Anointing the Dead Christ
(Montagna)

demon. The painting dates from the artist's Roman period, and is in a bad state of preservation.

The influence of the Papacy on the art of the Seicento was enormous, and during that period Rome became the centre of the civilized world. Hence it is natural that we should find a large number of works by the great painters of this period in the sixth hall of the Gallery. Among these works some possess so high a value that one can explain why the Seicento has been depreciated in the past only by referring to the tyranny of fashion, from which even the greatest works of art cannot escape. The dominating picture in this hall is Caravaggio's Deposition, a work of sculptured

Detail from the Last Communion of St. Jerome
(Domenichino)

solemnity in which the ideals and spirituality of the preceding epoch are sacrificed for a stern realism and a rude sincerity based upon direct observation. The large picture itself, in which we see Nicodemus and John, followed by the Holy Women, carrying the dead Christ to the tomb, embodies all the canons of modern painting and proclaims the new gospel of Caravaggio in opposition to the tradition of Caracci, whither painting had taken refuge in the strife between the school of the spirit and the school of the world.

Very rightly this monumental work has been offset by Domenichino's Last Communion of St. Jerome, a work which combines the concepts of the eclectic school of Bologna. This glorious work, which depicts with touching efficacy the tottering old man assisted by his friends, while a group of angels hover against a charming landscape, seems to symbolize the eternal youth of the spirit freed from the trammels of the flesh. Towards either of these poles, Caravaggio's realism and Domenichino's eclecticism, veer all the greatest artists of the Seicento. The four paintings of Il Guercino (Giovanni Barbieri) which are exhibited in this room serve as an index to the worth of this painter. These are entitled the Incredulity of St. Thomas, St. John the Baptist, Mary Magdalen, and St. Margaret of Cortona. The influence of Caravaggio, still felt in the painting of the Incredulity of St. Thomas, dis-

The Last Communion of St. Jerome
(Domenichino)

appears in the Magdalen, which remains one of Il Guercino's greatest works, even though it has been restored by Camuccini.

Guido Reni, Caravaggio's imitator in the Martyrdom of St. Peter, veers towards the Caracci method in the Madonna in Glory with St. Thomas and St. Jerome, painted for the Cathedral of Pesaro. Sassoferrato's Madonna and Child, with a glory of cherubim, and his Portrait of a Cardinal are faithful to the Caracci influence and to the Bolognese School, the soft graces of which he accentuates. The spirit of the Seicento

The Martyrdom of St. Laurence
(Ribera)

and its hunger for new forms are expressed with rare efficacy by Ribera in his famous Martyrdom of St. Laurence, a work probably dating from the old Spanish artist's last period, if we are to believe the tradition which declares that the figure of the old man, seen in profile apart from the scene, is a portrait of that master himself.

The Roman painter Andrea Sacchi gives us a completely different aspect of the art of that period, and acts as the herald of the Settecento. A new elegance of color and technique is evident in his Miracle of St. Gregory the Great, wherein the saint is seen causing blood to flow from a corporal on an altar in the presence of a kneeling old man and some soldiers. His Vision of St. Romuald shows the founder of the Camaldolese monks, seated at the foot of an aged tree, relating to his monks his vision or dream of the mystical ladder of heaven, which is shown

A Rest during the Flight into Egypt
(Baroccio)

St. Margaret of Cortona
(Il Guercino)

The Espousals of St. Catherine
(Murillo)

by the painter in the background. The whole work is characterized by a simplicity most rare in the Barocco age, and, notwithstanding the monotony of the faces in the scene, it was so highly valued that in 1797, when seized by the French, it was held to be one of the four great paintings in Rome. It had an undoubted influence on French painting in the eighteenth century.

The paintings of Federico Baroccio form a distinct group among the works of the Seicento. The recent celebration of the tercentenary of the death of this artist, which took place on September 30, 1612, has called more attention to the exaggerated sweetness of his palette, to his skill in contrasting light and shade effects, derived from Correggio, and to his marked and really majestic power of design. Besides his Ecstasy of St. Michelinus on seeing Jerusalem, and his glorious Annunciation painted for Duke Francesco Maria d'Urbino, both of which were in the Old Gallery, we have to-day one of Baroccio's most beautiful works, which was thought to be lost and was previously known only from copies and engravings. This work, entitled A Rest during the Flight into Egypt, was painted in 1573 for Simonetto Anastagi of Perugia, who gave it to the Jesuits; it found its way to Rome in the time of Clement XII, but was then lost sight of until discovered by d'Achiardi in the Private Apartments of the Vatican in 1909. In a landscape gilded by the setting sun, the Virgin is seated at a spring taking water in a bowl, while St. Joseph is seen plucking fruit from a cherry tree for the Infant Jesus. In this scene Baroccio gives his predilection towards naturalistic observation free reign; as a consequence, the character of the sacred scene takes on a domestic charm, the artist's technique is not so excessively sweet as usual, and his coloring loses its conventional virtuosity. Besides this fortunate discovery, the New Gallery has been enriched with a canvas showing Peter Denying Christ before the Handmaiden. This has been attributed to Caravaggio. There is, moreover, a Holy Family by Carlo Maratta, whose name could not be absent from such a complete assemblage of Roman artists of the Seicento.

The New Gallery has a room given over to the works of foreign artists. While few in number, these works possess, besides their intrinsic value, an additional importance here for the study of the characteristics of religious painting in foreign schools. Many of them show such direct dependence on Italian art of the Seicento that they might well be hung with the works of the Seicento artists in the room we have just described. For instance, Valentin, a Frenchman, in his Martyrdom of Sts. Processus and Martinianus, has all the characteristics of Caravaggio. While retaining all his own peculiar individuality, Nicolas Poussin shows the influence of Domenichino, and especially of Sacchi, in his Martyrdom of St. Erasmus, the only work which he signed: "Nicholaus Pusin fecit." There is, however, no lack of works more truly expressive of foreign art. The Spanish School has an authentic masterpiece in Murillo's Espousals of St. Catherine, which shows the saint bending in intense rapture before her mystic Spouse. The German School has a Pieta by Lucas Cranach the Elder, a painting previously kept in the Private Apartments of the Vatican. Thence were also transferred to the Picture Gallery the paintings of the Flemish School by the famous painter of flowers, Daniel Seghers. In one of these, showing the figure of St. Ignatius, painted after the manner of Rubens, surrounded by a crown of flowers held by two angels, we may read the initials "D. S." The most attractive painting in the room is the large portrait of George IV of England by Sir Thomas Lawrence, a splendid symphony in gray tones and a work at once of great intrinsic value and of remarkable importance in the history of modern painting. Consequently, in the writer's opinion at least, this work is out of place in a collection which does not extend beyond the Seicento.

This is but a brief and hasty survey of the most famous works in this Gallery, but it will serve to show that the New Gallery is among the most famous of the world, not for the number, but for the intrinsic worth of its paintings. The storerooms annexed to the Gallery hold many other works which, while they might figure properly in other public galleries, have been rightly excluded from this carefully chosen collection of highly valuable works. For instance, there are a Basaiti, a Garofalo, a Sassoferrato and many Palmezzanos. Only a few of the seven paintings from the Papal palace at Castel Gandolfo, containing realistic episodes expressive of the Seven Sacraments, are worthy of being exposed in the Room of the Seicento as a singular indication of the artistic currents of the time; these are the work of that most original artist, Antonio Maria Crespi Bolognese (called Lo Spagnolo). Furthermore, there are many gems scattered throughout the Vatican, which, if added to this collection, would increase its already great artistic and esthetic value. Thus Melozzo's famous fresco might very fittingly be surrounded with the eleven fragments of his Ascension, painted for the Church of the Apostles, including those radiant figures of the angel musicians which constitute a revelation of beauty never surpassed. These are now badly hung in the Sacristy of St. Peter's, where the public seldom sees them. There is also Giotto's famous triptych, known as the Ciborium of Cardinal Stefaneschi, an ingenuously profound expression of the religious sentiment of the master, and in the highest degree representative of his work. The present writer expects to see this added to the Picture Gallery. A further source of increase will be supplied by the restoration of fragmentary works. As in all other important galleries, the canvases and tables which need care and retouching are many. The artistic world, however, may feel confident that the authorities will neglect no measures necessary for the proper preservation of the precious treasures entrusted to their safe-keeping.

THE GALLERY OF TAPESTRIES

I N his "Life of Raphael" Vasari says: "Pope Leo X, wishing to have most rich tapestries made of gold and silk, got Raphael himself to paint the colored cartoons of the right shape and size. These were sent to Flanders to be woven, and, when finished, the tapestries came to Rome." There were ten of these tapestries, depicting scenes from the lives of Sts. Peter and Paul (mostly from the Acts of the Apostles), and they completed the decorations of the Sistine Chapel, which already had on its walls scenes from the Old Testament and the Gospels. The subjects chosen for the new tapestries were the Miraculous Draught of Fishes, the Giving of the Keys, the Healing of the Lame Man, the Death of Ananias, the Stoning of St. Stephen, the Conversion of St. Paul, Elymas Stricken with Blindness, the Sacrifice of Lystra, St. Paul in Prison, and St. Paul before the Areopagus. Including the friezes, they measured about 4.80 metres deep by 42 metres long, and were to be hung on the walls below the frescoes painted by the artists of the Quattrocento, where the imitation curtains are now painted— four on the left wall, two on the end wall, where the Last Judgment is, and four on the right wall. One of the tapestries for the right wall, St. Paul in Prison, was made narrower than the others, owing to the limited space between the balustrade and the choir. It was presumably on the right side that all the St. Paul tapestries were placed, while those dealing with St. Peter ran along the opposite wall. The vertical friezes were placed between the tapestries in continuation of the pilasters which separated the frescoes above; friezes were also added at the ends of the walls so that each tapestry was bounded by two lateral friezes. In view of the narrowness of the space, an exception to the latter rule was made in the case of the tapestry showing St. Paul in prison. The two tapestries on the back wall were most probably separated from each other, and there were thus two lateral friezes for each tapestry. The tapestries had no horizontal frieze above them.

The idea of decorating with tapestries the lower part of the walls of the Sistine did not originate with Leo X. It is fairly certain that his service was simply to replace old tapestries which were in poor con-

The Miraculous Draught of Fishes

dition, and which were no longer in harmony with the taste of the age, with more appropriate works. In the inventory of Papal effects before Leo's time mention is indeed made of a number of pieces of woven draperies, depicting scenes of the Passion. The designing and weaving of the new tapestries were completed in a very few years. Begun about 1515, the tapestries were ready in 1519. As may be seen, the work was somewhat hastily performed, and to this hastiness may be referred the defects shown by the tapestries, especially in details. The cartoons were prepared under the direction of Raphael himself, but were not entirely from his hand. He drew, perhaps, the sketches for the general composition and for some figures, but many of the sketches were left to his pupils to enlarge. Vasari himself confirms this hypothesis in his "Life of Giovanni Francesco Penni" (Il Fattore), where he says that this painter "was of great help to Raphael in painting a large part of the cartoons for the tapestries of the Pope's chapel, and especially for the friezes."

The weaving was entrusted to Peter Van Aelst of Brussels, under the

Detail from the Horizontal Frieze of the Miraculous Draught of Fishes

The Giving of the Keys, or "Feed My Sheep"

Detail from the Lateral Frieze of St. Paul
before the Areopagus

Detail from the Lateral Frieze
of "Feed My Sheep"

supervision of the artist Bernard Van Orley, who belonged to the
School of Raphael. The first seven were set in their places in the
Chapel in December, 1519. On the twenty-seventh of that month a
Roman correspondent of the famous Venetian dilettante, Marcantonio

The Healing of the Lame Man

Michiel, wrote as follows: "On Christmas day last the Pope displayed in his Chapel seven tapestries woven in the west. They are considered the most beautiful work of the kind ever done, notwithstanding the fame of other tapestries, such as those in the Antechamber of Pope Julius II, or those of the Marchese of Mantua from designs by Mantegna, or those of Kings Alfonso and Federico of Naples. The designer is Raphael of Urbino, an excellent painter who has received from the Pope one hundred ducats for each design. Silk and gold have been used in great quantities. The cost of the weaving was one thousand five hundred ducats for each tapestry, silk and all included; so that the total cost was, as the Pope said, one thousand six hundred ducats each, though gossip has it here that they cost two thousand ducats each." This means that, in our modern money, the tapestries cost $150,000, and Raphael was paid about $1,000 for each design.

Small-sized copies of the cartoons of these tapestries were made in Rome immediately after the completion of the originals, since Agostino Veneziano reproduces the Death of Ananias in a cut dated 1518. The cartoons were then sent to Brussels to be copied, and were cut in

The Death of Ananias

strips for the various weavers. Seven of them remained in the workshop of Peter Van Aelst and his successors at Brussels throughout the
sixteenth century. Only the Conversion of St. Paul was sent back to
Rome in the days of Pope Leo X, and between 1521 and 1528 we find
it mentioned in the Grimani Collection. Then we lose sight of it. Two
others were soon lost. In Brussels, however, copies must have been
made, and from these were woven the many reproductions now scattered among the various collections. On the advice of Peter Paul
Rubens, Charles I of England bought seven of the originals as models
for his weavers, and allowed them to be cut into sections. In 1662 the
French ambassador came to an agreement with Charles II for their
purchase, as Louis XIV was then thinking of establishing the manufacture of the gobelins. The English ministers, however, annulled the
contract and the cartoons remained in England. Towards the close
of that century William III ordered William Cook to piece together and
restore the fragments, after which they were preserved in the Hampton
Court Gallery near London. From there they passed in 1865 to the
South Kensington Museum, London, where they may be seen to-day.

The subjects are: the Miraculous Draught of Fishes, the Giving of the Keys, the Healing of the Lame Man, the Death of Ananias, the Sacrifice of Lystra, Elymas Stricken with Blindness, and St. Paul before the Areopagus.

The fate of the tapestries themselves was no less stormy. In 1521 they were in the Sistine Chapel; in 1527 they were removed to the Vatican Palace; in that year some of them were stolen; in 1553 the Connétable de Montmorency had two pieces returned to Pope Julius III. In 1798 they were again taken from the Vatican, but Pius VII succeeded in having them returned. The lower part of the Elymas tapestry was cut off and

The Stoning of St. Stephen

burned in 1527 to melt the gold of the texture. Fortunately, the yield was not enough to tempt the vandals to treat the remainder in like fashion. A great portion of the above information may be read in the inscriptions on the tapestries and in the Gallery.

Vasari gives his opinion of the tapestries in his "Life of Raphael": "The work was so wonderfully done that it was a marvel to the beholder how the weaver could possibly have succeeded with his thread in giving softness to the cheek and gloss to the hair and beard so faithfully. It is a miracle rather than the work of man; water, animals, and houses are so truly reproduced that the whole seems the work rather of a painter than of a weaver." This eulogy of the great critic of the Renaissance is intended exclusively for the professional merits of the work of Van Aelst, who then initiated a new textile taste which was to secure universal allegiance. Thanks to this new method, the weaver's work became much more valuable, since it resembled so closely a real painting as to give the spectator the delusion of having before his eyes, not a woven texture, but a painted canvas.

This work of Van Aelst, however, shows a distinct stiffness of design and a certain discord of coloring, strong tones appearing isolated in a field of mezzotones and color gradations. Despite these defects, however, they must have evoked universal admiration when they first appeared on account of their great novelty, since they foretold a veri-

The Conversion of St. Paul

table revolution in the technique of tapestry. The new method was nothing more or less than the combining of the breadth and majesty of Italian fresco-work with the illustrative and decorative analysis of Flemish painting. If the work did not completely succeed, this was to be attributed to the variety of the hands which were engaged on it. Although executed by Raphael with the extensive collaboration of his pupils, the cartoons preserve a unity of pictorial vision and a fineness of execution that quite disappear in the tapestries. No matter how the Italian School may have influenced their development, and no matter how much they were bound by their Italian models, Van Orley, who directed the work, and Van Aelst, who executed it, could not quite rid themselves of their Northern temperament and their Flemish taste. An adaptation of himself to his models was the less to be expected in the case of Van Aelst, whose methods had become crystallized owing to his long years of work and countless repetitions.

Another important new feature was the importance given for the first time to the friezes. Hitherto all such woven tapestries were set in narrow frames of flowers or geometric ornaments. Raphael, however, employed vertical friezes similar to the parietal decorations of pilasters and horizontal friezes below similar to bas-reliefs. Each tapestry thus assumed the aspect and served the function of a frieze of the Renaissance, and the similarity extended even to the framing. The vertical friezes contain decorative and allegorical figures, but the horizontal ones are filled with scenes from the life of Cardinal Giovanni de' Medici, who was later Pope Leo X.

Many copies of the tapestries were made. Copies of seven of them were made in 1534 for Francis I of France, but they were burned in 1797. Henry VIII owned a superb duplicate copy, which was acquired by the Spanish Ambassador in London during the English Revolution

Elymas Stricken with Blindness

of 1649. One of the most precious replicas is that now in Vienna; this formerly belonged to the Dukes of Mantua, and was made at the commission of Ercole Gonzaga, who died in 1563. The Imperial Collection has another set of nine, and the Spanish Crown owns a similar set; mention of the last-named set is made in the inventories of Philip II (1527–1598).

The Miraculous Draught of Fishes depicts an event related to St. Luke's Gospel (v, 4 sqq.). The lateral friezes contain ornaments and decorative figures; the horizontal frieze shows Cardinal Giovanni de' Medici entering Rome and being received by the Pope. The fishing scene is one of Raphael's finest creations, and the most successful of the tapestries. The perspective shows the defects of the time; the plane of the water is not horizontal, but inclined towards the horizon, just as though seen from above, while the figures are shown on the level of our eyes. Moreover, the houses, figures, and vegetation far away have the geometric proportion of great distance, but preserve the clearness of outline of objects in the foreground. These, however, are scientific defects which would not detract anything from the esthetic effect if it were not for the real artistic discord: for example, the deep red in some of the costumes which forms too violent a contrast to the general mezzo-tints of the scenery, the faulty modulation of the strong tints of the shore, several instances of harshness in the outlines and in the folds

The Sacrifice of Lystra

of the dresses, and the unpleasant crudity of the various tints of the dresses. These defects in details, however, do not prevent us from enjoying fully the sublime and serene scene created by the Urbinate. All the illustrative skill of Raphael in the interpretation of physical beauty and of the human mind is here requisitioned. Admirable are the beautiful bodies of the youths who draw in the nets, and the noble countenances of the two apostles in the presence of Christ, which so clearly express their marvel and worship at what He has done. The fishes and the birds on the bank are drawn with astonishing truth; the representation of the water and the illusion of the reflection are wonderful. But more admirable still is the expression of the purely artistic elements—for example, in the linear rhythm which moves with continuous and soft curves in the outlines of the figures and in the folds of the garments, and lulls our souls to rest in the contemplation of the sweet and endless undulation of that tranquil sea. A clear sense of majestic serenity pervades us as we gaze on that placid and transparent expanse of water, which deepens obliquely in the scene, and loses itself in the distance on the right. No less exquisite are the linear arabesques and the delicacies of color of the vertical friezes. More sonorous is the slightly gilt yellow monochrome which characterizes the lower frieze, reproducing the solidity and plasticity of a very clear composition in bas-relief.

The Giving of the Keys, or "Feed My Sheep," is founded on an incident in St. John's Gospel (xxi, 15–17). Three fragments of the original cartoon are preserved in the Chantilly Museum, and show the heads of eight of the apostles. On the lateral frieze to the left are shown the Four Seasons, and on the right the Parcæ (Fates). The frieze shows the flight of Pietro and Giuliano de' Medici from Florence in 1494. The scene of the Giving of the Keys is inspired by the Perugino fresco in the Sistine on the same subject; of particularly beautiful coloring is the figure of Christ, with its pearl-like tones. In the other figures the work of the master is much altered by the interpretation of his pupils and of the weavers.

The Healing of the Lame Man shows the miracle worked by St.

St. Paul in Prison,
or the Earthquake

Peter at the door of the Temple, as related in Acts iii, 1–11. In the horizontal frieze we see the capture of Cardinal Giuliano de' Medici after the Battle of Ravenna and his subsequent escape. The figure of the lame man and the two chief female figures in this scene deserve particular attention. The Death of Ananias represents a miracle which is re-

St. Paul before the Areopagus

lated in Acts v, 1–11. The theological virtues are shown in the vertical friezes, and on the horizontal frieze we see the Gonfaloniere Ridolfi addressing the Florentines, and the return of Cardinal de' Medici to Florence in 1512. Particularly fine are the figures of Ananias and the young man on the right. The attitude of St. Peter recalls the Christ in the Tribute fresco by Masaccio in the Carmine Church at Florence.

The Stoning of St. Stephen is a scene from Acts vii, 1–59. The cartoon of this picture has been lost since the sixteenth century, and the work bears abundant traces of the collaboration of Raphael's pupils, particularly of Giulio Romano. The horizontal frieze shows the entry of Cardinal de' Medici into Florence in 1492 as Papal legate.

The Conversion of St. Paul is founded on Acts ix, 1–9. The cartoon

The Adoration of the Magi

The Adoration of the Shepherds

of this tapestry has been lost. The horizontal frieze shows the sack of Prato in 1512, and the protection extended to its inhabitants by Cardinal de' Medici. In a fresco on the same subject in the Pauline Chapel, Michelangelo has copied the terrified horse of the falling rider.

Elymas Stricken with Blindness, or the Conversion of the Proconsul Sergius Paulus, is based on an incident told in Acts xiii, 6–12. The first suggestion of the attitude of St. Paul is to be traced to frescoes by Masaccio in the Carmine Church at Florence. This tapestry was mutilated during the sack of Rome in 1527, and the lower part is missing. The figure of Elymas is one of the most expressive Raphael ever created.

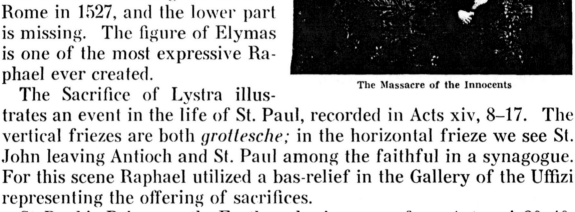

The Massacre of the Innocents

The Sacrifice of Lystra illustrates an event in the life of St. Paul, recorded in Acts xiv, 8–17. The vertical friezes are both *grottesche;* in the horizontal frieze we see St. John leaving Antioch and St. Paul among the faithful in a synagogue. For this scene Raphael utilized a bas-relief in the Gallery of the Uffizi representing the offering of sacrifices.

St. Paul in Prison, or the Earthquake, is a scene from Acts xvi, 20–40. Its narrow shape is due to the demands of wall space. The cartoon is lost. To show that Giulio Romano performed a large portion of the work, we need only compare this tapestry with the Gigantomachia fresco in the Palazzo del Tè of Mantua. The horizontal frieze completes the scene of the sack of Prato.

St. Paul before the Areopagus is a scene from Acts xvii, 19–34. In the left vertical frieze are represented Fame and Hercules holding a globe; in the right are arabesques. The horizontal frieze contains several incidents from the life of St. Paul. The first-mentioned frieze was mutilated during the sack of Rome in 1527, but the missing portion was replaced in 1553 by the angel holding the coat of arms of the Connétable de Montmorency who gave back the tapestry to Julius III and an inscription added recording the fact. The angel is by a French artist.

The Massacre of the Innocents

The Massacre of the Innocents

The Apparition of Christ to the Magdalen

The Supper at Emmaus

The Resurrection

The Presentation in the Temple

The Ascension   The Descent of the Holy Ghost

The Coronation does not belong to the set of the scenes from the Acts, which are called the Series of the Old School. It was woven in Flanders and given to Paul III by Cardinal Everard de Marck of Liège in 1537 after the death of both Leo X and Raphael. There is at Oxford a design by Raphael treating this subject in a notably different way. In the tapestry the lower part has been almost entirely altered, the change being certainly due to some pupil. In the new composition Sts. Peter and Paul have been replaced by Sts. John the Baptist and Jerome, two figures copied from the Disputa and the Madonna di San Sisto respectively; even the angels are an addition. This tapestry measures 3.55 meters in height by 2.93; the friezes measure 30 centimeters in breadth, and are adorned with flowers, fruits, birds, sirens and small, variously colored boy genii against a gold background. The tapestry is now in the Pope's private apartments. The scene shows Christ on a throne crowning the Madonna, who is between two angels. Sts. John the Baptist and Jerome are on either side, and in the foreground, at the foot of the throne, are two angels reading.

TAPESTRIES WITH SCENES FROM THE LIFE OF CHRIST.—These are known as the Series of the New School, to distinguish them from the scenes from the Acts, which are called the tapestries of the Old School. They were originally intended to decorate the Halls of the Consistory, and were ordered by Leo X, who in 1520 commissioned Peter Van Aelst to furnish within three years a series of tapestries more than five meters high and sixty long. The weaver was to receive 3,600 gold ducats (about $40,000 in modern money) over and above the cost of the gold thread, which reached the enormous amount of 14,000 ducats. The work was long drawn out. The death of Leo X and the indifference of Adrian VI towards the arts probably halted it. But when Clement VII became Pope he took up and modified the contract with Van Aelst. In October,

The Three Virtues

1524, he had 12,000 gold ducats paid to Van Aelst on account of 20,750 gold ducats to be paid in all for tapestries woven in gold and silk, "of the same quality and of the same perfection as the histories of the Apostles Peter and Paul." The contract was to be completed in eighteen months after the payment on account of the 12,000 ducats, but it was not until June 14, 1531, that the tapestries were approved at Rome by the artist Angelo de Farfengo of Cremona and Johannes Lengles of Calais, who declared that the tapestries of the Nativity of Christ were "well and loyally wrought, were superior to those of the histories of Sts. Peter and Paul, sent by the same Van Aelst to Leo X, and finally richer in gold and silk." The subjects were: the Nativity of Christ, the Adoration of the Shepherds, the Adoration of the Magi, the Presentation in the Temple, the Massacre of the Innocents (in three pieces), the Descent into Limbo, the Resurrection, the Apparition of Christ to the Magdalen, the Supper at Emmaus, the Ascension and the Descent of the Holy Ghost. Until the end of the Settecento they were in the Vatican, but in 1798 they were sold at auction, and all found their way to the Louvre, except the Descent into Limbo, which disappeared at this period. They were brought back to the Vatican, together with the tapestries of the Acts, and are now in this Gallery.

Francesco d'Olanda, a sixteenth-century writer, states that the cartoons for these tapestries were colored by Tommaso Vencidor of Bologna. As a matter of fact, Vencidor did go to Flanders in 1520, on a mission from Leo X. Moreover, Francesco mentions Antonio, his father, as having taken part in the work. But without further proof it is enough for one to compare the tapestries of the Massacre of the Innocents and the Marcantonio print reproducing the same subject to realize the difference between Raphael's design and the interpretation of it by those who composed and colored these cartoons. Those who designed these tapestries, whether they were Italian or Flemish, may have used a rough sketch of the subjects by Raphael, but the arrangement, the composition and the execution are all their own. Only here and there does a figure preserve a touch which Raphael might have accepted as his. The scene that comes nearest to Raphael's style is the Adoration of the Magi. The Adoration of the Shepherds is distinct from the others, and the figure of the young shepherd with the basket of eggs is well worth noticing. The Resurrection and the Descent of the Holy Ghost are a pair of compositions showing exaggerated agitation in the movements. Other groups with monumental figures are found in the Ascension, the Presentation and the three scenes of the Massacre of the Innocents. Two of the tapestries show a taste purely Flemish, namely, the Apparition of Christ to the Magdalen and the Supper at Emmaus, in which there is a better harmony of tints. In the Apparition a vivacity of mezzotints smiles over all the landscape and flowers; the Supper at Emmaus glistens with the brightness of the great table-cloth, the transparency of the glassware on the table and of the glasses in the vase on the floor. The other tapestries are characterized by a monotony of strong colors such as red, turquoise, green and yellow, and violent crudities are seen in the shading of the tones in accordance with the decadent taste of the Mannerists of the end of the Cinquecento.

The tapestry of the Three Virtues, or the Lions, has long been considered part of this series of the Life of Christ. Like the others, it is 5.11 meters high, including the friezes, and the lateral friezes are 80 centimeters broad. The arms of Pope Clement VII are seen above, and in the middle of the horizontal frieze is a falcon with the word *Samper* (*sic*), the motto of the same Pope. The friezes of this tapestry are richer than those of any other work of the same school. The tapestry shows Religion seated in a glory of light, with her feet on the world and with Justice and Charity on either side. Below, in the foreground of the broad landscape, two crouching lions support Papal standards —two keys surmounted by a baldachin. The lions are an allusion to Pope Leo X. The cartoon of this tapestry shows the hand of one of Raphael's pupils—the same, perhaps, who designed the more graceful figures throughout the series illustrating the Life of Christ. In the landscape the Flemish weaver has overloaded the original design in many instances, but the tonality of the friezes, a grayish mezzotint, is very fine.

THE EGYPTIAN MUSEUM

 THE Egyptian Museum was founded by Pope Gregory XVI, and opened in 1839. It was formed at considerable expense by uniting various collections, by bringing some objects all the way from Egypt, and by purchasing others from dealers in antiquities. The various objects here collected may be grouped as follows: (1) statues brought to Rome in the days of the Roman Empire or statues carved in Egyptian style and found in the ruins of Hadrian's Villa at Tivoli; (2) the Borgia Collection, made by the learned Cardinal Stefano Borgia at Velletri, the greater part of which, however, found its way to the Museum of Naples; (3) Monsignor Gaddi's Collection; (4) the De Palin Collection, made by the Swedish Minister to Turkey, who bought many rarities in Egypt; (5) the collections made by the travellers Silvestro Guidi and Pietro Gavazzi in the time of Pope Pius VII, and those made by the antiquarians Baseggio and Spagna between 1835 and 1838; (6) the Collection of Papyri, comprising the documents brought to Rome by the Franciscan missionary Angelo da Pofi in 1818, and others presented by Belzoni, the explorer, to Cardinal Consalvi. During the pontificates of Leo XIII and Pius X the Museum has been enriched by many important gifts, such as those sent by the Khedive's government, by Franciscan missionaries in Egypt, and by private individuals—as, for instance, Cavaliere Pelizeus, the Spanish consul at Cairo, and M. Emile Guimet, head of the famous Guimet Museum in Paris.

From the very start the Egyptian Museum was excellently arranged by Father Luigi Ungarelli, a Barnabite, and one of the first followers of Champollion in Italy. The Egyptian decorations in the Museum are the work of Cavaliere de Fabris, a sculptor of eminence, who at this period was in charge of the papal museums. A few slight changes have been since made to make room for manuscripts subsequently acquired, and to provide for the better display of those already housed here. This is particularly the case in the Hemicycle and in the smaller rooms, in which new cases have been set up for the smaller objects, and which now accommodate the Collection of Papyri, recently increased by the papyri from the Library. The antiquities in the Egyptian Museum have been described in special illustrated works by the following Egyptologists: Ungarelli (1839); Wiedemann (1885); Piehl (1888); Marucchi (in various works from 1889 down to the present time).

The rooms given over to the Egyptian Museum are on the same floor as the Pio-Clementino Museum, and were formerly occupied by the Cardinal Librarian. There are two entrances: the main entrance, from the Hall of the Greek Cross, near the staircase leading to the Etruscan Museum; the second, in front of the screen dividing the Pio-Clementino from the Chiaramonti Museum. The various rooms have special names, and were catalogued in 1912 as follows: (1) Hall of the Coffins and Sarcophagi; (2) Hall of the Statues; (3) Hall of the Naophorus; (4) the Hemicycle; (5) Hall of the Gods and Objects of Worship; (6) Funeral Hall; (7) First Hall of the Papyri; (8) Second Hall of the Papyri; (9) Third Hall of the Papyri; (10) Hall of Roman Imitations.

Whereas the history of Greece and Rome is well known, at least in outline, by all educated people, and every one has a more or less clear idea of the main personages and legends of Classical mythology, there are very many who have never heard, or who have forgotten what they heard, of the history and mythology of ancient Egypt. Hence it may not be unnecessary to preface to the description of this Museum a brief survey of ancient Egyptian civilization, so as to allow the general reader to grasp more clearly the importance of the antiquities in the collection.

OUTLINE OF ANCIENT EGYPTIAN HISTORY.—It may be said with truth that Egyptian civilization is the oldest in the world, if we speak of civilizations of which important monuments have come down to us, and of peoples about whose history we possess accurate information. For, though of course it is certain that, in the order of chronology, the civilization of the primitive inhabitants of Chaldea dates farther back than that of the Egyptians, yet we know very little indeed about the early Chaldeans. Concerning Egypt and its history, on the other hand, we have important historical monuments from the remotest periods, and it is safe to say that its first beginnings date back to about 5000 B.C., if we accept that year as the approximate date of the foundation of the kingdom of Egypt under Pharaoh Menes of the first dynasty. After Menes the civilization of Egypt went on developing through fifty centuries and under thirty practically successive dynasties, and was spread by Phœnician traders along the whole basin of the Mediterranean. After exercising a powerful influence on the glorious dawn of Greek culture, it was later in turn influenced so much by Greece that Egypt became Greek under the Ptolemies, although she remained true to the hieratic form of her ancient cult even when she was lashed to the triumphal chariot of conquering Rome. Later, however, her speech and her writing began to be forgotten, especially after the victorious advent of Christianity; they were utterly lost when Arab hordes swept over her territory, and remained buried and dead throughout the Middle Ages down almost to our own day. Thus, the long historical inscriptions over the temples that remained standing, and the writings on the tombs of the Pharaohs and other famous personages, which contained precious data for Egypt's history, and which even during the Roman era could still be understood by a few, became in course of time a closed book for the whole world. And when, at a later epoch, the study of antiquity took on a new life, and the student was anxious to know something of this land of mystery, he had to be content with the few notices preserved in the Bible and with the more or less inaccurate stories handed down by Greek or Roman writers, who very commonly confused and altered the names of the Pharaohs, and ignored whole periods of the history of a great people, because they were incapable of appreciating its civilization, and especially its religion.

This almost complete eclipse of Egypt's story would have persisted down to our own times had there not occurred, in the beginning of the nineteenth century, the wonderful discovery of Champollion,

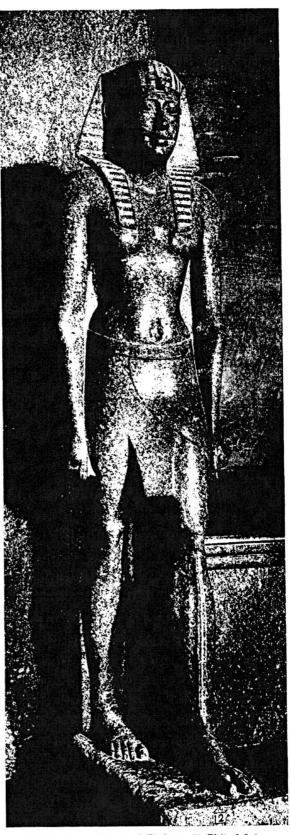

Red Granite Statue of Ptolemy II Philadelphus
(285–247 B.C.)

which lifted the veil of Isis and re-vealed the secrets buried in the hieroglyphics of Egypt. It is well known that the deciphering of Egyptian hieroglyphics was made possible by the discovery of the famous Rosetta stone (now in the British Museum), with its bilin-gual inscription (Greek and Egyp-tian), wherein it was possible to read the name of Ptolemy. The discovery was verified by com-parison with another bilingual in-scription from the Temple of Isis on the Island of Philæ, containing the name of Cleopatra. From that day to our own, the study of Egyp-tian antiquities has made great progress; very successful excava-tions have been made in various parts of Egypt; museums have been opened in Cairo and in the principal cities of Europe; nu-merous works have been written, dealing with Egyptian monuments of every kind, hieroglyphic texts, and hieratic and demotic papyri. And thus it has come to pass that the mistakes of the ancient Greek and Roman writers in connection with the history and civilization of Egypt have been gradually cor-rected; Egyptian chronology has been verified; the lists of the Pha-raohs of the various dynasties and the spelling of their names have been revised; the religion of Egypt, so misunderstood by Classical writers, has been fathomed and explained; her literature has been restored; poems, legends, religious and philosophical treatises, cover-

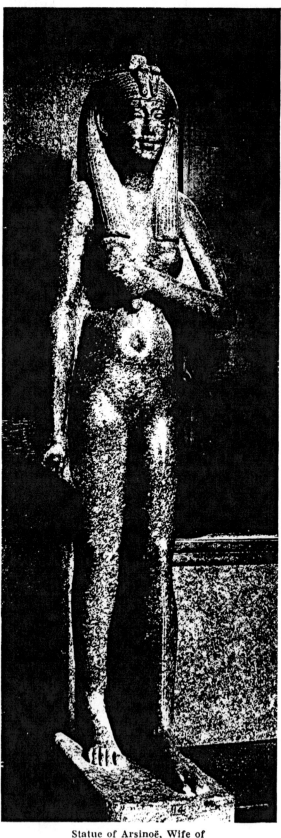

Statue of Arsinoë, Wife of
Ptolemy Philadelphus

ing thirty centuries, have been once more brought to light. In a word, the Egyptian world has been restored to us in all the manifestations of its private and public life. On the fortunate discovery of Champollion the science of Egyptology has been erected.

The first period of Egyptian history is generally known as the "Ancient Empire," or as the Memphitic period, because Memphis (the modern Bedrashein, near Cairo, in Lower Egypt) was the residence of the Pharaohs. This period comprises the first ten dynasties, of which the most important was the fourth, including the reigns of the three great pyramid-builders, Cheops (Chufu), Chephren (Kafra) and Mycerinus (Menkaura). The date is about 4000 b.c. The eleventh and twelfth dynasties followed; the twelfth is very important, and one of its kings was the Pharaoh of Abram (about 2000 b.c.). This great period, of which we possess rich monumental remains, was succeeded by a less known epoch, which might be designated the "Middle Period," and lasted from the thirteenth to the seventeenth dynasty, thus including the domination of the foreign Hyksos, or Shepherd Kings. It was during this time that the Hebrews settled in Egypt. Independence was restored in the eighteenth dynasty, and with this "New Empire" began the most glorious period of Egyptian civilization, during which the authority of the Pharaohs was extended as far as the banks of the Tigris and the Euphrates. Its apogee was reached in the reigns of Tuthmosis III (eighteenth dynasty) and Rameses II (nineteenth dynasty), who is now generally identified as the Pharaoh who persecuted the Hebrews, and in whose reign Moses was born. Under the next Pharaoh, Meneptah I, the people of Israel were led from the land of captivity (thirteenth century b.c.).

This glorious era was followed by a period of decadence, which lasted from the twenty-first to the twenty-fifth dynasty, when the Assyrians under the Sargonides conquered the land of Egypt. A brief spell of freedom and glory followed in the Saite period of the twenty-sixth dynasty, when Egyptian civilization felt in turn the influence of Greek culture. It was quickly followed, however, by the conquests of King Cambyses of Persia, who put an end to the ancient kingdom of the Pharaohs (525 b.c.). Alexander the Great came fast on the heels of the Persians, and then the rule of the Ptolemies began, only to give way in turn to the eagles of Rome in the days of Augustus. The last stage in this decay of a people arrived with the Arab conquest in the seventh century after Christ.

Originally the religion of ancient Egypt was probably monotheistic, but corruption crept in, as happened in all ancient religions, and a form of polytheism arose, with certain modifications for the initiated

and the learned. The next step on the part of the masses was to fetich-
ism, including the worship of animals, which, in the ancient theology,
were regarded merely as symbols and various attributes of the deity.
The religion of Egypt, at least at the time when we know it better, was
based on sun worship, the sun being taken to represent the most glorious manifestation of the deity; and all the other gods of its complex
mythology were nothing but solar emanations, typifying one or other
beneficial effect derived from the sun or referring to its mysterious
generative power. There were many deities, divided into groups or
triads, each having its special locality in Egypt. The underlying idea
of each group or triad is as follows: (1) a male deity, emblem of the
action of the sun and the generative power of the divinity; (2) a female
deity, emblem of the sky within which the action of the sun takes
place; (3) a sun-god born of these two, that is, of the activity of the one
within the other. The most famous triad, and the one most widely
worshipped in Egypt, was that of Osiris, Isis and Horus. The deity
became incarnate in the ox Apis, who was adored during life and even
after death; but the deity also manifested himself in the person of the
Pharaoh, who was held to be a real god while on earth, and to whom,
after death, temples were raised and sacrifices offered.

Just as from the supreme deity the lesser deities emanated, so from
these lesser deities came forth the race of men, composed of a soul and
a body. Man was to obey the laws of the deity, and after death his soul,
separated from his body, was to live a life beyond the tomb. The dead
were believed to pass through mysterious regions and present themselves for judgment before the tribunal of Osiris. If found guilty, the
dead were subjected to various tortures and then annihilated; souls
which were adjudged just had in every case to purify themselves of
the faults committed in the body, and wander through the regions beneath the earth, exposed to many trials. Having cleansed themselves
of every stain during this painful pilgrimage, they were at length
absorbed back into the divinity and became one with it. But during
their long wanderings, lasting perhaps for centuries, the souls were
transformed and returned occasionally to earth and to their tombs to
visit the body, which they had to find well preserved if they were to
rest there and live over within the tomb the same life that they had
lived in this body on earth. This belief gave rise to the custom of em-
balming corpses, so that they might retain as long as possible their
human shape for the comfort of the soul which was to rest there.
Hence also arose the custom of decorating tombs with pictures representing the earthly life of the deceased, and with inscriptions containing lengthy prayers, so that the returning souls might delight in the

scenes and recite the formulæ prescribed for use during their long
wanderings.

The funeral monuments usually
seen in museums are fragments
of the walls or doors of tombs,
stelæ, sarcophagi, painted coffins,
vases, statuettes, mummies with
their amulets, and papyri. The
walls and doors of tombs are often
splendidly decorated with extensive scenes showing the carved
figure of the defunct in adoration
before a god, and with long inscriptions giving the names of
kings, the titles of dignitaries, and
phrases taken from the sacred
books. Shorter texts of a similar
nature are found on the funeral
stelæ, which also give us important information concerning the
religion and social organization of
the ancient Egyptians and preserve for us various religious
and funeral symbols, particularly
scenes depicting the offering of
sacrifice. The sarcophagi of sandstone or granite are sometimes
carved to resemble houses with
doors and windows, thus symbolizing the eternal dwelling-place of
the dead, and are decorated with
texts in hieroglyphic characters
like those on the walls and the
stelæ. Sometimes, too, they take
the shape of the mummies, and the
lid is in many cases surmounted
by a representation of the head of
the defunct, adorned by the peculiar head-dress known as the
calantica. Within these enormous
receptacles were placed the coffins

Statue of an Unknown Princess
belonging to the House of
the Ptolemies

of sycamore wood, painted inside and out with figures of the deities, the gods of the underworld, and hieroglyphic inscriptions reproducing in most instances verses or whole chapters from the "Book of the Dead." In these coffins were placed the mummies, wrapped tightly in swathing bands and covered with little pious objects or amulets. The chief amulets used were: (1) the scarab, symbol of the resurrection; (2) the *tat,* or easel, symbol of stability; (3) the *uta,* or eye, symbol of the all-seeing deity; (4) the *anch,* symbol of life; (5) the *ureus,* or serpent, symbol of the female deity; (6) the *usech,* or necklace, the reward of the just, spoken of in the "Book of the Dead." There are many other amulets, not to mention the diminutive statues of the minor deities.

Near the coffins were also placed four vases crowned with the heads of animals. These vases may be seen in almost any museum, and are known under the erroneous name of *Canopi,* or Canopic vases, because they resemble the grotesque figure of the god Canopus of the Alexandrine era. They are more properly called funeral vases, because they

Statue of Queen Tuaa, Wife of Seti I
and Mother of Rameses II
(Fourteenth Century B.C.)

contain the viscera of the embalmed defunct. They were four in number, each containing one of the viscera, and were dedicated under the protection of the genius whose head appeared on the lid. The names of these genii were: (1) Amset (man-headed); (2) Hapi (baboon-headed); (3) Tuaumautef (jackal-headed); (4) Kebsenuf (hawk-headed). Usually the inscriptions on the vases tell of the protecting influence of these genii, and speak of the four divinities, Isis, Neftis, Neit, and Selk.

The papyri found in the tombs deal with various subjects. They contain poems, tales, moral treatises, and even works on medicine and mathematics. They are thus precious records showing the high

Sandstone Head of Mentuhotep (Eleventh Dynasty, between 3000 and 2000 B.C.)

degree of civilization reached by the ancient Egyptians even from the remotest days of their history. Most of the papyri found in museums are funeral papyri, particularly those which contain a portion or all of the text of the sacred book which was called in Egyptian *Sciat per em heru* ("Book of the Going Out in the Daytime"), but which Lepsius, who was the first to publish it, called the *Todtenbuch,* and which has thus been since known as the "Book of the Dead." It was divided into one hundred and sixty-five chapters, each bearing at its head "Ro en . . ." (*i.e.,* "Chapter of . . ."), and decorated with plain and colored vignettes showing the various incidents in the travels of the souls in the underworld. As these papyri were prepared in advance by the scribes, and were bought when the funeral took place, the space for the name of the dead person was left blank, and we thus see the name inserted by another hand.

The "Book of the Dead" is of great importance for the study of the mysterious religion of Egypt, and it has been rightly called the "Bible of the Ancient Egyptians." Its text is very obscure, and even to-day, as Navilli frankly confesses, we have not been able to penetrate into its mystical secrets. The principal editions of this book are those of Lepsius and Navilli; there is a good French translation by Pierret, and a good English one by Le Page Renouf. Another important document is the book of the *Ap en Ro* ("The Opening of the Mouth"), usually known as the "Book of Funerals," and often wrongly identified with the "Book of the Dead." It contains the burial service used from the moment the embalmed corpse was taken from the house where it had been exposed, during the journey to the tomb, and during the long ceremonies in the necropolis until the tomb was closed. Exceedingly rare are the papyri containing this document, which is of the highest importance. It was published by Schiaparelli in 1881–1882.

Seated Statue of Seti I (1366–1333 B.C.)

There is something so peculiarly distinctive about Egyptian art that we can at once distinguish Egyptian productions from those of any other ancient people. In architecture the pyramidal effect predominated, the pyramid being the symbol of the radiant sun. The columns are crowned with strange capitals of lotus flowers, and the architraves are ornamented with solar discs and *urei*. Everywhere on the walls, doors and columns are accumulated figures of gods and Pharaohs, and everywhere long hieroglyphic inscriptions form a real and appropriate decoration of the monuments. This style of art, which had been developing from the remotest periods of the first dynasties, was preserved almost unaltered in its hieratic form through forty centuries of Egyptian history, so that only an Egyptologist, by a chronological comparison of the monuments, can succeed in distinguishing the characteristics of the paintings and sculptures of the various ages. This singular art caught the fancy and pleased the taste of the Greeks and Romans, who, when they conquered Egypt, attempted to imitate it, either as a salve to the wounded pride of the conquered people or owing to the attraction of strange artistic forms, as we to-day imitate the productions of the Far East.

And, just as in this imitative process Egyptian art underwent a change, Egyptian religion likewise took on a new form—that of the worship of Isis, which grew up in the Græco-Alexandrine period and lasted during a large part of the Roman period. Of all the divine triads worshipped in the land of Egypt in the olden days, the only one that survived was that of Osiris, Isis and Horus, in connection with whose worship the old ceremonies were retained with a newly invented ritual. The worship of Isis spread rapidly throughout the Empire, and · from all parts people flocked to be initiated in the mystic religion wherein souls that turned in loathing from the polytheism of Greece and Rome sought a higher and purer doctrine. Thus it happened that in Rome and in the principal cities, from the first days of the Empire, splendid temples were erected in honor of

Green Basalt Statue of the Priest Ut-a-hor-resent
(Sixth Century B.C.)

Isis and Serapis, containing statues and inscriptions brought from Egypt, or imitations of them made at home.

In a museum it is well to distinguish the truly Egyptian antiquities, belonging to the epoch of the Pharaohs, from those of the time of the Ptolemies and from those dating merely from the period of the Roman domination. Nor is it hard to do so; since, putting aside the Græco-Roman reproductions of Egyptian deities which may be unfailingly recognized from their Classical style, even the sculptures and inscriptions in which the imitation of the national art of ancient Egypt has been attempted present a remarkable difference from indigenous productions, and bear the clearest marks of imitation.

ROOM I. HALL OF THE COFFINS AND SARCOPHAGI.—On the right as you enter is the painted lid of a mummy coffin, with a hieroglyphic inscription (No. 1). It belongs to a priestess of Ammon, named Neschonsu. The inscription of six vertical lines contains sacrificial prayers, and there is a prayer that the dead lady may come forth as a living soul, and that it be granted her to see the radiant disc of the sun together with the spirits of light. On the left is the coffin (No. 2) to which the lid (No. 1) belongs. It is decorated with paintings and an inscription. The dead priestess is shown clad in a white robe before an altar. Her name and that of her husband, Tet-Hor-auf-ank, are given. There are, moreover, the royal

Naophorus, or Shrine-bearing Statue

cartouches of Pharaoh Amenophis I (eighteenth dynasty), cartouches which are to be found even on monuments subsequent to his time, as this ruler was held in great veneration. The coffin dates from the Bubastitic dynasty (tenth century B.C.).

No. 4 is a coffin lid similar to No. 1, belonging to a priestess of Ammon and Chonsu-pa-krat named Tet-maut, and dates from the same period. No. 5 is the coffin belonging to the above cover, and shows well-preserved painted figures and hieroglyphic inscriptions. On the outside, to the right as you face it, is a remarkable scene showing the funeral cortège of the mummy, which goes from the house to the tomb, exactly as described in the "Book of Funerals." The mummy is shown resting on a boat-shaped vehicle drawn by oxen and surrounded by priests reciting prayers and carrying the sacred instruments and the ritual papyri.

In front of both walls of the hall, and to the right and left as you enter, are three large sarcophagi in basalt with closely written hieroglyphic inscriptions which refer to the twenty-sixth or Saite dynasty (seventh and sixth centuries B.C.). The sarcophagus on the right belonged to a courtier of the time of Psammetichus II (596–591 B.C.), who was called Nefer-ab-ra-meri-Neit, the first part of which is the same as the prenomen of the above Pharaoh. Of the other two sarcophagi on the left, one belongs to a high-priest of the temple, a favorite of a king named Necht-Hor-menk-ab; the other is placed upside down so as to show the inscription, which must have

Naophorus, showing the Carved Figure of Osiris

reached to the ground. This belonged to another priest, named Psamtik, and the brief inscription breathes the wish "that his name may live in eternity."

ROOM II. HALL OF THE STATUES.—No. 8, to the right as you enter, is a colossal statue of the goddess Sechet, which has the head of a lioness surmounted by the solar disc and the serpent (*ureus*). She is seated on a throne, holding the symbol of life (the *anch*). This goddess was the symbol of the devouring heat of the sun, and presided over the punishment of the lost in the Egyptian hell. There were a long series of such statues erected by Amenophis III of the eighteenth dynasty in the city of Thebes, and from that city undoubtedly came this and the other statues of the same goddess, several of which are in the Museum. On the other side of the hall is another statue of the goddess, in the same attitude (No. 26). On the front of the throne on the right, and to the left of the figure of the goddess, still remain the royal cartouches of Amenophis III (dating from about the middle of the fifteenth century B.C.), under whose reign Egypt reached the zenith of its power and culture.

No. 12, standing out from the wall to the right as you go in, is a colossal red granite statue of Ptolemy II Philadelphus (285–247 B.C.). The cartouche with his name is inscribed on the front of his girdle, and is repeated in the hieroglyphic inscription on the small obelisk on which

he leans. The reign
of this sovereign is
memorable in his-
tory for the splendor
Egypt reached under
him, especially in the
sciences, which were
cultivated in the
famous schools at
Alexandria, where he
founded his great
library. To his time
also belongs the fa-
mous translation of
the Hebrew Scrip-
tures into Greek
known as the Sep-
tuagint. On the right
and left of this statue
are placed two other
red granite statues
of princesses of the
house of the Ptol-
emies. No. 14, on the
right, is a statue of
Arsinoë, sister and
wife of Ptolemy
Philadelphus; and
No. 10, on the left, is

Opisthographic Sandstone Stele
(Fourteenth Century B.C.)

the statue of an unknown princess. No. 17, before the end wall, is a
statue in gray veined marble of Queen Tuaa, consort of Seti I and
mother of Rameses II (fourteenth century B.C.). On the diadem
crowned with *urei,* which she wears on her head, are carved the cartouches of Rameses II and of the Queen herself. To the left is the figure of her daughter, with the *ureus* on her head, and with a cartouche
telling her name: "Royal daughter of the Royal Mother, Het-ma-ra."

To the right and left of the statue of Tuaa, two lions, in gray veined
marble and larger than life, are stretched on rectangular plinths and
bear the cartouches of Nectanebo II of the thirtieth dynasty, the last of
the Pharaohs (362–340 B.C.). These two magnificent pieces of sculpture were brought to Rome in the time of Augustus and set up near the
Pantheon, where they were found when some alterations were being

made in the time of Pope Eugene IV (1431–1447). In the time of Sixtus V (1585–1590) they were set up as ornaments near the Fountain of the Termini which this Pontiff had built. Finally they were brought to the Egyptian Museum by Gregory XVI (1831–1846), its founder, who had four imitation statues set up in their places around the fountain, bearing copies of the original inscriptions.

We now come to the left wall where the windows are. Here is No. 20, a basalt statue of the goddess Sechet, standing erect and bearing in her right hand the *anch* and in her left the sceptre. No. 23 is the lower portion of a seated granite statue of the famous Rameses II of the nineteenth dynasty, who was probably the Pharaoh who persecuted the Hebrews, who is spoken of in the Book of Exodus, and during whose reign the birth of Moses took place. According to recent computations of Egyptian chronology, Rameses II reigned from 1349 to 1288 B.C. Near the same wall, before the window, is No. 25 A, a sandstone head representing one of the kings of the eleventh dynasty who bore the name of Mentuhotep (before 2000 B.C.). The name of this Pharaoh is written in a rectangular cartouche on the side of the monument, to the right as you look at it. This is the oldest royal statue in the Museum, and the reign of this Pharaoh antedates the era of Abram, who went down into Egypt in the twelfth dynasty. Close by is No. 25 B, a seated statue, in green granite, of King Seti I of the nineteenth dynasty, father of Rameses II. According to Brugsch's chronology, he reigned from about 1366 to 1333 B.C.

ROOM III. HALL OF THE NAOPHORUS.—In the centre of the hall is No. 113, the famous statuette, in green basalt, of the priest Ut-a-hor-resent, custodian of the Temple of Neit in the city of Sais about the end of the twenty-sixth dynasty (sixth century B.C.). The priest is represented as carrying in his hands a small shrine (*naos*), within which is seen the carved figure of the god Osiris. The long-haired head of this statue is a modern restoration. The body of the statue is literally covered with one long hieroglyphic inscription, which begins at the front, to the left as you look at the statuette, and extends all around it. The inscription tells us that the priest held many important offices during the long reign of Amasis II (564–526 B.C.) and under the brief rule of Psammetichus III (526–525 B.C.). He was priest of the temple of Neit at Sais when Cambyses, King of Persia, won the battle of Pelusium and reduced Egypt to a Persian satrapy (525 B.C.). The new ruler, it tells us, conferred on the priest the dignity of the Grand Sun, and charged him to prepare the royal name in Egyptian, which he did under the form of Ra-mesut (*i.e.,* Born of the Sun). He then showed Cambyses the monuments of the city of Sais, and explained the meaning of the religious

worship of the
itiating him into
the Egyptian re-
finally able to
country the anger
thus meriting the
his people. This
monument, which
of the collection,
excavations car-
of Hadrian, near
we may infer that
Rome by Hadrian's

Two other shrine-
(*naophori*), dating
twenty-sixth dy-
92, are to be found
is the statue of a
named Patebchu;
other priest of Sais,
dignity of the Grand
Psamtik Seneb.
scription on the
taken partly from
the "Book of the
union of the soul and

On the wall con-
is a table of offer-
yellow granite base,
with hieroglyphics
touches of Pharaoh
eighteenth Theban
B.C.). On the hori-
this table or altar,
are six sacred loaves,
stands a libation
four sides of the
scription in hori-
ing cartouches with
cognomen of the
Pharaoh, Tuthmosis

Mummy-cover (Third Century
after Christ)

goddess Neit, in-
the mysteries of
ligion. He was
avert from his
of the conqueror,
great gratitude of
most valuable
is perhaps the gem
was found during
ried on at the Villa
Tivoli, and hence
it was brought to
orders.

bearing statues
also from the
nasty, Nos. 91 and
in this hall. No. 91
priest of Neit,
No. 92 shows an-
who also bore the
Sun and was named
There is a brief in-
back of the statue,
Chapter LXXXIX of
Dead," where the re-
body is spoken of.
taining the window
ings (No. 87) on a
rectangular in form,
and the royal car-
Tuthmosis III of the
dynasty (1503–1439
zontal surface of
carved in low relief,
in the midst of which
bowl. Around the
altar runs an in-
zontal lines, contain-
the prenomen and
above-mentioned
III.

No. 86 is an opisthographic sandstone stele set on a pivot. On the front we see in outline the seated figures of a husband and wife; the man leans on his left hand, which grasps a stick, and in his right hand holds the sceptre, called the *sechem*. The wife grasps his arm with her right hand, while her left rests on his shoulder. There is an inscription on the figure, showing part of the cartouche of King Amenhotep, and we thus learn that the monument belongs to the nineteenth dynasty. Following this inscription is the name of the defunct, Neb-sen, and of his wife, Amen-tu-tut. In front of the couple are the standing figures of their three sons and a daughter, together with their names. Below the figures of the children are seen various oblations, including some vases, a casket to hold the funeral statuettes, and a round mirror. Below the whole is the figure of a girl harpist

Table of Offerings of Tuti-mes (Eighteenth Dynasty)

who, in a crouching posture, plucks the strings of her instrument in front of a table of offerings. Near her are the words: "The Singer of Ammon."

No. 70 is a statuette of black granite, showing an Egyptian officer crouching and wearing the *calantica;* his arms are resting on his knees. On the front of his robe, under the arms, are three vertical lines of hieroglyphics reading from right to left, telling us that the dead man's name was Aa, that he was a cavalry officer, and that he was the son of an officer named Pa-un. This work belongs to the Saite period. No. 94 is a small basalt statue of a priest standing with his arms relaxed along his sides and leaning against an obelisk. From the inscription we learn that he was a priest of Ammon, a royal scribe, and called Pesatah, son of Hori and of the lady Asit-ur. No. 97 is the statuette of a *naophorus* with a long inscription on the back. He holds before his breast a cylindrical base on which crouches a baboon, and on which is carved an inscription in four vertical lines with an invocation to this animal, which was sacred to the god Thot. From the inscription we learn that the priest was named Chet-hir, and that he was guardian of the treasury, and son of Men-chat and the lady of the household, Nefer-tau. The statuette belongs to the Persian period. No. 99 is a fragment of a yellow alabaster vase for holding the sacred oblations. It is shaped like a truncated pyramid set upside down. This work belongs to a late period. It shows scenes depicting the worship of various divinities.

Room IV. The Hemicycle.—To the right as you enter is No. 120 A, a well-preserved unpainted sycamore coffin, containing a mummy wrapped in its bands. It belongs to the lady Chen-em-hat, daughter of Samtaui, of the latest Saite period. It is worthy of notice that the funeral wreath of flowers around the mummy's neck is still well preserved. In the glass case near the wall are the cloths and other Coptic objects found in the excavations at Antinoe, and given to the Museum by the Guimet Museum of Paris in 1903. The most important among them is a mummy-cover, which probably belongs to the third century of the Christian era. It shows the body of a woman standing upright, with the left hand pressed to the breast and the right raised in gesture of acclamation. Around it runs a cornice surmounted by a solar disc

Funeral Carving showing the Deceased seated before a Table of Offerings
(Nineteenth Dynasty; Fourteenth Century b.c.)

among *urei*. To the right are two pictures: one of them shows a man and a woman struggling; and the other shows a man seated while dictating to a woman who writes in an open book. The head painted on this mummy-cloth is important as a rare example of an ancient portrait. In this same glass case there are a small collection of Egyptian Christian lamps, and a few terra-cotta ampullæ, on which is depicted the famous St. Menna surrounded by camels, with the inscription "Oil of St. Menna." No. 118, in the recess of the window, is a rectangular sandstone block, divided into compartments separated by numbers in Egyptian characters. This is a table of oblations, various numbers indicating the quantity of the offerings. No. 125, also in the recess of the window, is a fragment of a funeral bas-relief, showing animals surrounded by lotus flowers and reeds. It is a reproduction of a bas-relief from the Egyptian tomb. No. 127 is a table of offerings of the eighteenth dynasty. The inscription around the cornice of the table contains a prayer to Ammon Ra and Osiris that the dead scribe, Tuti-mes, may receive all his funeral offerings.

On the wall of the Hemicycle containing the windows are a few mummy-coffins of the twenty-second dynasty with painted symbolic scenes and hieroglyphic inscriptions relating to various priestesses of Ammon. These coffins come from the famous *cachette* at Deir-el-Bahri. Towards the end of the Hemicycle, near the window, is a sandstone fragment of a scene showing two divinities in the act of pouring from two vases the symbolic signs of life (*anch*) over Tuthmosis III. No. 130, in the corner, is a large panegyric stele of Queen Hatasu, or Ramaka, of the eighteenth dynasty, daughter of Tuthmosis I, wife of Tuthmosis II, and adviser of Tuthmosis III. In the centre is the figure of the god Ammon, with feathers on his head and holding his sceptre in his hand. Before him stands the Queen, offering gifts to the divinity. Behind is Tuthmosis III, wearing the crown of Upper Egypt, while on his right the City of Thebes is personified, with arrows in the left and the *anch* in the right hand. Under the carvings runs an inscription of five horizontal lines in which the cartouches of the above Queen appear. This monument is important since it refers to a woman who was celebrated in Egyptian history on account of her glorious deeds and the magnificent monuments she erected.

No. 131, below No. 130, is a cabinet containing a noteworthy collection of archaic vases. One vase is inscribed with the name of King Den, one of the most ancient kings of Egypt and referred to the first dynasty. This collection comes from the excavations at Abydos. Along the wall of the Hemicycle opposite the windows we find four life-size statues in dark granite representing the goddess Sechet. They date

Funeral Stele of Apa (Sixth Dynasty)

from the time of Amenophis III, as do the two already described in Room II, and all were found in the Theban temple at Karnak. No. 136 is a sandstone sarcophagus, the lid of which culminates in a man's head wearing the *calantica*. It dates from the Saite epoch. The inscription mentions an official, scribe, and priest named Ti-hotep. No. 135 A is a sepulchral stele in sandstone belonging to the priest Pasetach, who bore the title of Amiasi, or Priest of the Sepulchres. It bears seventeen horizontal lines of hieroglyphics, running from right to left and containing prayers and invocations to the Sun, Osiris, Neit, Ma, and Tafnut. These divinities, together with their names, are seen above, and the defunct is shown in adoration before them. The text of this inscription is very important, because it is an extract from the sacred work of the ancient Egyptians called the "Book of the Crossing of Eternity."

No. 137 B is a fragment of a funeral carving of the nineteenth dynasty, representing the deceased seated before a table of offerings, wearing an elaborate head-dress and the necklace *usech*. Written on the table is a list of the offerings he has made. The workmanship of this sculpture is very fine, and belongs to the classic period of Egyptian art. No. 139 is a wooden coffin, decorated with paintings and containing a fairly well preserved mummy wrapped in its bands, with the face uncovered and the arms crossed on the breast. The coffin is placed against the wall, as is also the lid, which is decorated in like manner. On the left of the coffin the dead woman's name is given as Hotep-hir-tes. No. 139 A is a lid of the

Stele of Hori (Thirteenth Dynasty)

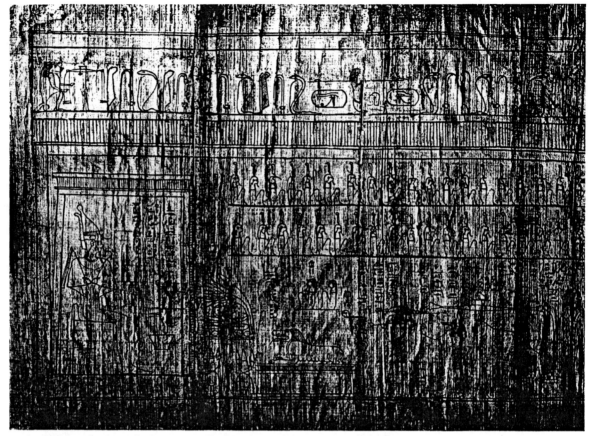

Hieratic Papyrus of the "Book of the Dead," belonging to Neskem and showing
the Tribunal of Osiris

above coffin. Just below the breastplate there are portraits of Hotep-
hir-tes praying to the gods of the nether world, Amset, Apis, Kebsenuf,
Tuaumautef, and to the deities Thot, Chnum, Osiris, Ra and others.
The inscription contains a portion of Chapter LXXXI of the "Book of the
Dead," relating to the transmigration of the soul of the dead into a lotus
flower; a part of Chapter LXXVI, which tells of other transformations;
and a part of Chapter XLIV, concerning the life of the soul in the nether
world. The goddess Neit is depicted on the inside of the lid. She stands
before the sacred tree, and offers with both hands the water of life to
the soul of the dead woman, which is represented with the body of a
bird and a human head. There is, moreover, a long vertical inscription
containing Chapter XXVI of the "Book of the Dead," which is headed
"Chapter for giving back a man his heart." At the end of this there are
a few other lines containing prayers for the dead, one of which has the
phrase: "May she go in peace towards the good Ament." This is regarded as one of the most important coffins in the Egyptian Museum,
in view of both the nature of its inscriptions and its excellent state of
preservation.

No. 143 C is a funeral stele dating from the Ancient Empire (sixth

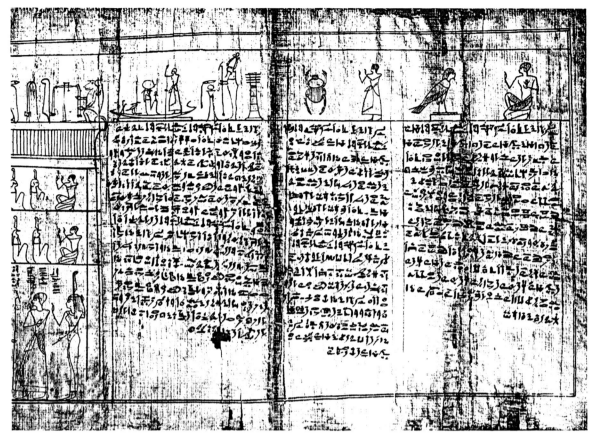

Hieratic Papyrus of the "Book of the Dead"
(Continued from opposite page)

dynasty), and belonging to a man named Apa. It is shaped like a door, as was usual under the Ancient Empire, and on the lower part of the front are carved four figures, of which two (a man and a woman) are on the door, and the two others (of men, one in prayer) are on the sides. They represent the family of the dead man, perhaps his wife and three children, who come to fulfil the funeral rites, as may be seen on many similar monuments.

The cupboard in the centre of the Hemicycle contains a stele of the time of the Ancient Empire, with a hieroglyphic inscription telling that the dead man to whom it belonged was called Ara, that he was a priest belonging to the cult of the pyramid of King Chufu, or Cheops, of the fourth dynasty (4000 B.C.). Above it is placed a fragment of a sepulchral sculpture of the Ancient Empire, showing a head represented in profile and painted. The glass case on the left contains a papyrus case with an inscription giving the name Tuthmosis, a priest who was guardian of the Temple of Ammon. The glass case on the right contains a wooden funeral boat with small figures of oarsmen. It belongs to a tomb dating from the days of the twelfth dynasty.

No. 145 is a sarcophagus with a lid terminating in a human head wearing the *calantica,* and with pointed beard. The name of the deceased is Samtaui. No. 146 B is a stele from the thirteenth dynasty belonging to a man named Hori, who is shown sitting before a table of offerings. We also see the kneeling figures of his wife, his mother and his sister, together with their names. No. 149 is the lid of a sycamore coffin in the form of a mummy; the head wears the *calantica,* and the eyes are painted black. A necklace is carved around the neck, and below it is the winged image of the goddess Neit, with the solar disc on her head and the two symbols of life in her outstretched hands. Below the image of the goddess is written a portion of Chapter LXII of the "Book of the Dead." The name of the dead man given in the inscription is Ua-ab-ra, which was the name of a king of the twenty-sixth (Saite) dynasty, and it is probable that the monument dates from that time.

HALL OF THE GODS AND OBJECTS OF CULT.—After the Hemicycle follow some small rooms containing the lesser objects and the papyri. The first of these rooms contains statuettes of the gods and sacred animals as well as objects of cult. In the cabinet on the left as you enter, the first glass case contains statuettes of the god Bes and of the goddess Hathur and also small bronze figures from the Roman epoch, noteworthy among which are an Aphrodite and a female figure of rosso antico wearing a long robe. In the second glass case are bronze and wooden amulets, also boxes with amulets of various shapes, especially noteworthy being the small figures of the god Bes, symbolic eyes, small vases of the heart and the feathers of Ammon. In the bottom of this glass case are exhibited some statuettes of baboons. In the upper part of the third glass case are mummies of hawks and crocodiles, presented by the Franciscan missionaries of Luxor near Thebes. The fourth glass case contains thirty-five cats in bronze, stone and wood.

In the fifth glass case of the central cabinet are fourteen *urei* and fourteen *situlœ* (including a noteworthy one in bronze with graffiti figures). In the middle is the altar for presenting the offerings to Osiris. Twenty-four statuettes of the god Nefer-tum in enamel, bronze and stone are also exhibited in this glass case. The sixth glass case contains eighty-two statuettes of Osiris in stone, bronze and wood, five being seated with their backs against a small obelisk. A small group in bronze represents the Egyptian triad Osiris, Isis and Horus. In the seventh glass case are twenty small figures of Isis feeding Horus at her breast; only two of the figures are standing. On the third shelf is seen a rare and precious object, an ancient censer, like those we see in the bas-reliefs. To the right a small bell and some sistra may be seen. In the centre are some stilettos, nails and spoons (one wooden). Below these are

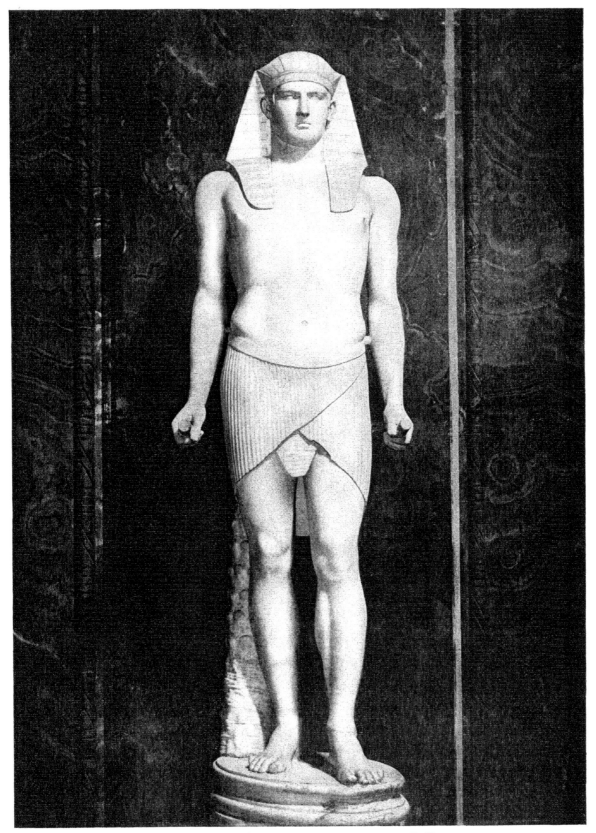

Statue of Antinous ("The Egyptian Apollo")

nineteen small figures of Isis, three of the god Bes and three of Ammon Ra. In the eighth glass case of the cabinet on the right hand are four statuettes of the goddess Sechet, seven of the god Ptah, nine of Anubis and twenty-seven of Harpocrates—that is, the child Horus with his finger near his mouth. This attitude, which was meant to suggest the childhood of Horus, was later interpreted by the Greeks as an action calling for silence. The child Horus was thus confused with the god of silence, Harpocrates. In the ninth glass case are five statuettes of

Princess holding a Table of Offerings, and Two Canopic Vases

the goddess Sechet, four of the god Kem, three of Imhotep and five of Horus. In the lower part are exhibited sacred animals: crocodiles, frogs, lions, small serpents and ten sacred oxen. The tenth glass case contains fourteen sacred hawks in wood, various birds and birds' claws. The eleventh glass case is devoted to terra-cottas of a late period, including votive heads and arms. On the wall where the window is, to the right is a large terra-cotta vase. To the left of the window and high up on the wall is a wooden figure of Osiris; below this are five sacred *urei* in bronze, a wooden Osiris and a bronze Osiris. Finally, on glass case six stands a wooden Osiris; beside this figure, and standing on glass cases five and seven respectively, are two cats, one in wood and the other in bronze.

FUNERAL HALL.—The first glass case of the cabinet to the left contains forty-one funeral statuettes called *Usebtiu* (that is, *respondentes*), because the Egyptians believed that they helped the dead in their labors beyond the tomb. Owing to this belief, they were placed in great numbers on graves, and all of them contained Chapter VI of the "Book of the Dead." One of these statuettes still rests in the sandstone coffin. In the second glass case are twenty-eight complete funeral statuettes, and five others of which only the lower part has been preserved. The third glass case of the central cabinet contains twenty-four terra-cotta funeral cones, which were substituted for the ancient funeral offering of grain bread. Below are preserved three wooden cases containing funeral statuettes and some painted sections of similar cases. In the fourth glass case are exhibited four small glass vases with long necks and one of white alabaster. Objects of funeral adornment, consisting of small vases, necklaces of turquoise blue enamel, three necklaces of stone scarabs, a bracelet of gold and two gilded slats with inscriptions, are also found here. In the lower part of the glass case are sections of small painted caskets. The fifth glass case is devoted to the collection of scarabs. On the third shelf we see the honorary scarab of Queen Tii, wife of Amenophis III (eighteenth dynasty), together with ten other scarabs and a chalk impression of the inscription on another scarab. The lower two shelves contain ninety-four scarabs of various sizes. The sixth glass case contains lamps, bronze vases and funeral ornaments. Worthy of notice is the sandstone figure of a dead man standing in his tomb. Here also are many bronze mirrors and five discs with white rosettes. Many of these objects used as funeral ornaments are of domestic origin. In the lower section are preserved grains in eight Canopic vases.

The seventh glass case of the cabinet to the right contains forty-four funeral statuettes in wood, alabaster and enamel. The eighth glass case contains twenty-four funeral statuettes, of which some are from the tomb of Seti I, father of Rameses II; almost all are of wood. Especially noteworthy is the funeral statuette of Prince Ka-em-uas, son of Rameses II (nineteenth dynasty), whose name is painted on the enamel. In the middle of the room is a painted mummy-coffin.

On the wall containing the window, to the left is glass case nine. This contains domestic objects which were used as funeral ornaments: baskets, three wooden chairs, seven insoles, three funeral statuettes resting in a small casket, and a statuette of sandstone. The tenth glass case contains fragments of the canvases in which the mummy of Queen

Lion from the Monument of Nectanebo II, last of the Pharaohs
(Fourth Century B.C.)

Nefertari, wife of Rameses II (nineteenth dynasty), and that of Prince Khopeshef, son of Rameses III (twentieth dynasty), were wrapped. Lids of painted caskets, two funeral statuettes in wood, and two others resting on a casket are also exhibited here. On the central cabinet rest four or five fragments of petrified wood.

First Room of the Papyri.—This room contains ten papyri enclosed in wooden frames. Only the most noteworthy can be referred to here. On the left-hand wall is a hieratic papyrus of the "Book of the Dead" (No. 11), belonging to Neskem, whose mother was Set-ar-bant. Beginning at the right, we meet Chapters xxvi, xxx, c, cxxv, and finally the scene of the Judgment (Saite period). In this Judgment scene, which is fairly well preserved, we can see the tribunal of Osiris and the figure of the dead Set-ar-bant, who is introduced into the room where are placed before Osiris those scales in which the deeds of the dead are weighed. On the back wall is a hieroglyphic papyrus of the "Book of the Dead" (No. 7). It belonged to Amen-em-apt, son of Abai (eighteenth dynasty), and contains part of Chapters i, xvii, xviii and clxxxi. It is in a very fragmentary condition, and its headings are written in red. On the right-hand wall is a hieratic papyrus (No. 6), with magic text of the nineteenth dynasty; both the beginning and the end are missing, only five fragments having been preserved. The papyrus contains headings in red. No. 5 is a hieratic papyrus of the "Book of the Dead," belonging to the priestess of Ammon, Ii-mut (twenty-second dynasty); this papyrus also has red headings. Near by on the same wall is a hieratic fragment of the "Book of the Dead," belonging to the woman Ta Arpit (Saite period); to the right we see the scene of the Judgment. On the wall containing the window we see, to the left, two hieroglyphic papyri of the "Book of the Duat" (*i.e.,* of the Nether World). Below are nineteen fragments of *ostraca* in demotic and Coptic characters, contained in a wooden casket covered with glass.

SECOND HALL OF THE PAPYRI.—Low down on the wall to the left is No. 35, a fragment of a funeral hieroglyphic papyrus with sacred amulets; here also are six demotic fragments. On the rear wall, beginning low down on the left hand, are: No. 32, a papyrus with a scene from the "Book of the Duat," representing the punishment of the damned; No. 23, a hieratic papyrus with sacred funeral text of Chonsu-Tot, son of Patu-asar and Sat-Chonsu (of late origin); a well-preserved hieroglyphic papyrus of the "Book of the Dead," which belonged to Asit-urt, daughter of Na-asit, and contains on the left the Judgment scene (Saite period); a hieratic papyrus of the "Book of the Dead" of Nes-chonsu, priestess of Ammon (of late origin); a badly preserved hieroglyphic papyrus of the "Book of the Dead," belonging to Hor, son of Ta-sat-Kem (twenty-second dynasty); three hieratic fragments of accounts kept by a scribe of the nineteenth dynasty. On the upper portion of the wall on the right hand are hieratic fragments. Low down is the fragmentary hieratic papyrus of the "Book of the Dead," belonging to the priestess of Ammon, Asit-ur. On the lower part of the wall containing the window are a hieratic papyrus of the "Book of the Dead," belonging to the priest of Ammon, Pa-tu-amen-neb-res-taui; a rather fragmentary hieroglyphic papyrus of the "Book of the Dead," belonging to the scribe of the treasury, Kenen-hor (nineteenth dynasty); a funeral hieratic papyrus of Hor (of late origin).

THIRD HALL OF THE PAPYRI.—In this last hall is exhibited under glass, in two large cases, the most complete papyrus of the "Book of the Dead" possessed by the Museum. It contains thirty-one large squares, written in hieratic characters with painted scenes, and comes from the tomb of a priest named Pa-chen-ah (twenty-sixth dynasty). In the walls of this same room are inserted some sculptures and cuneiform inscriptions obtained during the excavations of Nineveh. The most remarkable are: No. 26, Assyrian deity; No. 23, assault on a city during the war of Sennacherib; No. 19, cuneiform inscriptions from the Palace of Sargon; No. 18, another similar inscription from the same palace; No. 8, sacred tree with the name of King Assur-nazir-habal. Here may also be seen an inscription in Nabatæan characters, dating from the first century of our era. Finally, high up in the hall are fixed some

Mussulman inscriptions in Cufic characters (ancient or early Arabic). The oldest of these inscriptions dates from the year 1133 of our era.

HALL OF ROMAN IMITATIONS.—The monuments in this hall date mostly from the first period of the Empire (first two centuries of our era), and are very important for the study of the imitation style of the Roman artists, who strove to reproduce the Egyptian type while maintaining the form of Classical art. This section surpasses all the other sections in the number and excellence of the monuments, most of which have been secured from the Villa of Hadrian, near Tivoli. Antinous, Hadrian's favorite, is represented as an Egyptian god in a colossal statue, which, on account of its beauty, is also called the "Egyptian Apollo." Near the wall opposite the window is No. 27, a large recumbent study of the River Nile, who leans his arm on a Sphinx, symbolizing Egypt. The latter holds in front between her claws an amphora, the emblem of the beneficent inundation of the sacred river. This statue was secured from the Museo Capitolino. In the middle of the hall is the reproduction of a portion of the obelisk erected by Emperor Domitian, which stands to-day in the middle of the magnificent Piazza Navona, above the Fountain of Bernini. With this are united some fragments of the original monument, namely, a large portion of the cusp with a figure of the Emperor in front of various divinities, and also a piece of the southern surface of the obelisk. On the last fragment may be seen some hieroglyphic characters, which have been completed in this model. On the side of the model have been painted the royal cartouches of the Emperors Vespasian, Titus and Domitian. They are placed in the same order as that in which they are found on the corresponding sides of the original obelisk. A sample of the numerous sculptures in this hall is given on page 276, where our illustration shows an Egyptian priestess holding a table of sacred offerings, while on each side is seen a Canopic vase. These vases derive their form from the antique funeral vases which were used to contain the viscera of the corpses, but which, in the period of imitation, were supposed to represent the god Canopus of Alexandrine origin. In this hall may be also seen the following monuments: a very fine basalt statue representing the Dea Isityches, that is, Isis-Fortuna (No. 28 A); a basalt hermes of the goddess Isis and the bull Apis (No. 46); statue of the god Anubis, represented as Mercury (No. 49); colossal statue of the veiled goddess Isis, obtained from the Iseum of the Campus Martius (No. 50); awesome figure of the god Bes (No. 63); two sacred crocodiles, one in marble and the other in basalt; granite figure of a crouching baboon (No. 68 A). On the base of the last, which was obtained from the Iseum of the Campus Martius, is a Greek inscription with the name of the artist.

THE GREGORIAN ETRUSCAN MUSEUM

THIS remarkable collection occupies the second floor of the building which stands on the north side of the Cortile della Pigna. In the seventeenth century and the first half of the eighteenth the suite of rooms on this floor was known as the Appartamento di Ritiro, or di Belvedere. It was given the former name because the Popes were wont to retire thither for rest, and derived the latter title from the fact that it looked out on the huge court which was known as the Cortile di Belvedere until it was divided by Sixtus V. Towards the end of the eighteenth century, in the reign of Pius VI, Cardinal Francis Xavier Zelada, Librarian and Secretary of State, had his quarters here, which became known as the Appartamento Zelada. After his tenure of office these rooms were still occupied by the Cardinal Librarian, and such continued to be the case until Pius VII incorporated them in the Museums. This last fact is commemorated in an inscription, dating from the year 1829, which may be read on the wall of the room containing the Regolini-Galassi Tomb.

It is by no means easy to say at present what pieces of sculpture were placed in these rooms originally, and in November, 1836, when the Museum was under discussion, we find no mention whatever of sculptures, but of many smaller objects, such as vases, terra-cottas, small bronzes and gold-work, which had been collected by various Camerlenghi and placed here as the nucleus of a museum. This Museum, the formation of which was approved at the end of 1836 and which was formally opened on February 2, 1837, was called the "Gregorian" after its founder, Gregory XVI, and the title "Etruscan" was added, first, to distinguish it from the Museum at the Lateran founded by the same Pontiff, and, secondly, to define the special purpose which it was to serve. A more correct title would have been "Antiquarium of the Vatican Museum," or "Museum of Classical Antiquities," since the strictly Etruscan objects formed only a small portion of the collection, and the dominant idea in its formation was to furnish more suitable and safer quarters for the smaller, more fragile or more precious objects, which could not without grave risk be exhibited in the spacious rooms of

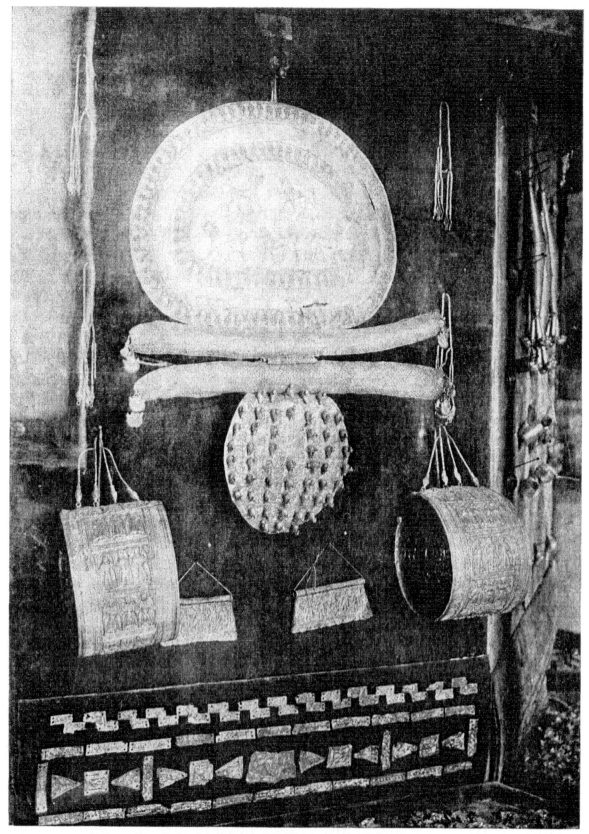

Objects found in the Regolini-Galassi Tomb (Seventh Century B.C.)

the Sculpture Gallery. When it was opened the Museum comprised the small vestibule and the rooms overlooking the Cortile della Pigna, but soon after 1838 other rooms were added on the northern side, including the Hall of the Bronzes and the hall now occupied by the Regolini-Galassi Tomb. Later, in 1903, when Leo XIII acquired the Falcioni Collection from Viterbo, the room immediately beyond the last-named hall was added; this has been since known as the Leonine Hall.

Step by step with the increase of space proceeded the accumulation of exhibits, but unfortunately the plan adhered to in all museums during the first half of the last century was followed: the objects were grouped according to classes

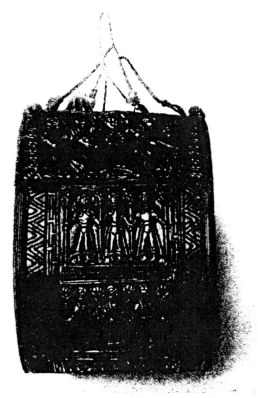

Golden Armlet from Regolini-Galassi Tomb
(Seventh Century B.C.)

(regardless of their relation to other objects found with them), and were arranged in such a way as to form decorations of the halls or rooms in which they stood. This method of arranging objects prevailed until very recent times. The first three rooms were devoted to sarcophagi, funeral urns of travertine or alabaster, and fragments of sculpture; the fourth room was allotted exclusively to terra-cotta objects; the fifth, sixth, seventh and eighth rooms were given over to pottery; bronzes and jewelry occupied the ninth room; copies of the paintings found in some tombs at Tarquinii, rough terra-cotta and *bucchero* vases, with wine jars of the seventh and sixth centuries B.C., were exhibited in the tenth room; the Falcioni Collection was placed in the eleventh, and some bronze ornaments from Bolsena and a reproduction of a chamber tomb in the twelfth.

Such an arrangement can be justified only when the antiquities exhibited are of uncertain origin, and can never be defended in the case of correlated objects forming a separate group and described in detail when excavated. Hence the directors of the Gregorian Etruscan Museum, with the encouragement and coöperation of the general administration of the Vatican Museums, have undertaken a fundamental rearrangement of the exhibits—a difficult task requiring much work

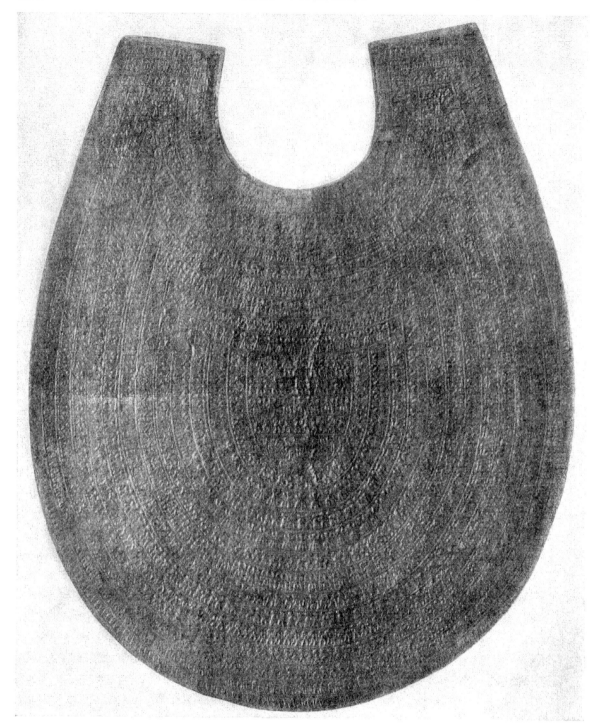

Golden Rere-piece from Regolini-Galassi Tomb (Seventh Century B.C.)

of a technical and practical nature and much time to carry through successfully. One of the first results of this work has been the proper arrangement of the objects found in the famous Regolini-Galassi Tomb, discovered at Cervetri in 1836, which, in its relation to the history of Etruscan civilization, has an importance not inferior to that of the tombs discovered by Schliemann at Mycenæ. Thanks to the studies

Amphora made by Exechias, showing Ajax and Achilles playing dice (Sixth Century B.C.)

Red-figured Attic Amphora with full-length figure of Achilles

and researches of Professor Pinza, it has been possible to reconstruct, from the fragments preserved, the chariot, the wooden chair covered with bronze plates with incised ornamentation, and the rest of the furniture or trappings buried with the corpse. And whereas these objects were formerly shown separately,—the gold with the gold, the bronze with the bronze and the terra-cottas with the terra-cottas,—it is now possible to see in the tenth room (opened to the public at the time of the International Archæological Congress in October, 1912) the whole collection assembled in appropriate glass cases. Thus the visitor can form a fairly accurate idea of the art and culture which flourished in one of the most celebrated cities in southern Etruria in the seventh century B.C., and even persons without any special interest in antiquarian studies cannot fail to marvel at work which shows a correctness of technique and a wealth of ornamentation which are worthy of the most highly developed civilization.

To the gold objects in this exhibit only a very few words can be devoted. Especially noteworthy are a *fibula,* or brooch, in the shape of a disc, the largest known specimen, and two armlets with granulated ornaments. This style of ornamentation is a distinctive feature of Etruscan jewelry, intricate designs being worked out on a gold object by soldering on it minute grains or globules of gold. There are, more-

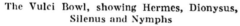

The Vulci Bowl, showing Hermes, Dionysus,
Silenus and Nymphs

Terra-cotta Objects, including
Frieze in Bold Relief

over, a large rere-piece of gold with incised ornaments, which probably ornamented the back of a mantle shaped like a chasuble, and a necklace formed of a chain from which hang three amber discs set in gold rims. Attached to each rim is a spindle-shaped tassel terminating in a flower. Among the silver objects of note are: three plates and a goblet decorated with hunting scenes, the figures and the borders being worked in gold relief. These works are entirely unlike the other ornaments, and were therefore probably imported from the East by traders.

After the Regolini-Galassi Tomb, the most notable possession in the Museum is the collection of pottery in Rooms 5, 6, 7 and 8. It comprises examples of Corinthian and Attic work and specimens from Apulia, Campania and Etruria, and, though inferior to some collections in the number of its exhibits, it rivals any in the beauty and importance of several of its treasures. It is sufficient to mention here, among its black-figured vases, the famous Cyrenaic Cup, as it is called, on the lower part of which is depicted a scene said by some to be the punishment of Prometheus and by others to be that of Tityus and Sisyphus. There is, moreover, an amphora with the trade-mark of Exechias, an Athenian potter in the second half of the sixth century B.C.; it shows on one side Ajax and Achilles playing dice, and on the other the return of Castor and Pollux to their father's house. Among the red-figured Attic vases the principal are: a large amphora with a

Bronze Statuettes of Boys with Bullæ and Inscriptions

full-length figure of Achilles armed with cuirass and spear; a water-jar showing Apollo playing a lyre while, seated on a winged tripod, he skims over the surface of the sea; an *œnochoë*, or wine-jar, depicting Menelaus grasping his sword and rushing on Helen, who takes refuge near the statue of Athena, while Peitho (Persuasion), Aphrodite and Eros interpose and appease the fury of the outraged husband. There is, above all, a unique bowl found at Vulci. Seven figures are painted on a white background. On one side we see Hermes carrying the infant Dionysus in his arms to the aged Silenus, who is sitting on a rock, while two nymphs, one on each side of the scene, look on. On the reverse a nymph, or Muse, is seated, playing a lyre; a second nymph stands before her, holding another lyre and seeming about to sing, while a third wrapped in a mantle seems to be making ready to dance.

The principal vases from southern Italy are: a glorious voluted amphora from Apulia, on the main surface of which is seen Triptolemus in a winged car drawn by serpents, while Demeter, holding a torch in one hand, offers him ears of corn with the other; a bowl from Lucania (perhaps the work of the famous potter Asteas), depicting a comic scene in which is shown a woman at a window while Zeus, in the guise of an old man holding a ladder, looks up at her, and Hermes, wearing a wide-brimmed hat (*petasus*) and holding his wand (*caduceus*) in one

hand, holds a lantern in the other.
These vases must be numbered
among the most beautiful remaining specimens of Greek ceramic art.

Among the funeral monuments
(Rooms 1, 2 and 3) is a sarcophagus in travertine, found at Cervetri; this shows traces of polychrome work in the rich figuring
on the lid and in the bas-relief
there, which depicts some festive
ceremony, perhaps a nuptial procession. Among the terra-cotta
objects (Room 4), the principal
are a frieze in bold relief showing
hints of Hellenic influence, and a
sepulchral urn (known as the Urn
of Adonis), showing the figure of
a boy stretched on his death-bed,
with a gash in his left thigh and
wearing his hunting-boots, while a
hound crouches in the foreground.
Both of these monuments are full
of life and beauty, and give evidence of a technique truly perfect.

Chief among the bronzes (Room
11) are: a votive *biga* (two-horse
chariot), the ornaments on the
shaft and wheels being extremely
well preserved; two *cistæ*, or caskets, one oval in shape and ornamented with incised designs—elegant borders of flowers and the
battle between the Amazons under

Statue of Mars, bearing an Umbrian Inscription

Penthesileia and the Greeks under Achilles; two figures of boys, of
which one has an inscription on the left upper arm and the other on
the right leg, and an endless collection of mirrors, candlesticks, tripods,
and dishes of various forms. There is also the famous statue of Mars
found at Todi in 1835, which bears on the border of the cuirass the name
of the donor in the Umbrian language: AHAL TRUTIOIS DUNUM DEDE.

From the foregoing brief account it is evident that the Gregorian
Etruscan Museum is a most worthy complement and, so to speak, the

crown of the Sculpture Museum. Owing to the distribution of the objects in the various halls, and their comparatively modest number, the distracted or weary visitor might pass them by without appreciating the interest, the rarity and the importance of the monuments. But whosoever visits this Museum in quiet, receptive mood will find in it vital nourishment equal to that which one derives from the great works of literature. The Etruscan Museum is for most visitors a hidden gem, but it is to be hoped that the fascination of mystery which envelops it will attract an ever-increasing number of art-lovers and students, for there are few collections which promise a fuller recompense for the time and attention devoted to examining its unique exhibits.

THE MUSEUM OF SCULPTURE AND
ANCIENT PAINTINGS

J ULIUS II, the della Rovere Pope, during the ten years of his pontificate (1503–1513), collected among the laurel and orange trees and around the murmuring fountains in the Cortile di Belvedere a few pieces of ancient sculpture. These were the nucleus of the Vatican Museum, which in the course of four centuries was to receive from the soil of Rome and the surrounding territory many artistic heirlooms of bygone ages, which the ignorance of intervening centuries had neglected and buried. In the three niches of the end wall, to which Bramante had lent architectonic grace, were placed the Apollo Belvedere, an Empress in the guise of a naked Venus, and the Laocoon. The young god seemed about to hurl himself in vengeance on mankind, recalling the image of Homer which describes him as swooping down "like the night"; Laocoon, punished in himself and in his sons, a victim to the inexorable vendetta of the gods, raised his "dread clamor to the stars," as Virgil tells us; and between the Homeric deity and the Virgilian creation, between the poem that embodied Greece and that which imaged Rome, between the avenging god and the chastised mortal, was personified the obsequious flattery which worshipped in the bold pose of a Venus a Roman empress—perhaps Sallustia Barbia Urbiana, the wife of Alexander Severus. In front of the niches, between the shrubs, the supposed statue of the Tigris poured its inexhaustible stream into a Roman sarcophagus; and on a second sarcophagus, Ariadne, whom cultured and popular imagination of the time identified as Cleopatra, slept her restless sleep between the flight of a hero and the arrival of a god. On one of the sarcophagi was blazoned the triumph of the Greeks over the Amazons; on the other, the submission of barbarians to a Roman general. Other pieces of sculpture of less importance were scattered here and there; some of these are still in the Vatican, but others have found their way to Florence as the result of one or other of the vicissitudes which later befell the Vatican collection. Thus it was that Julius II, the warrior Pope who, as the epigram has it, laid down the keys of St. Peter to gird on the sword of St. Paul, never ceased even during the political turmoil of his pontificate to be what he had

The Gallery of Statues

been as a Cardinal—a Humanist. The sword of St. Paul occasionally rested on the codex of the man of letters. Some of these marbles, indeed, belonged to the private collection which he had made as a Cardinal at his palace at S. Pietro in Vincoli.

In turning his eyes to Classic antiquity, Julius II simply continued the work of his Humanist predecessors from Nicholas V to Innocent VIII. Hitherto, however, Humanism had found an entry to the Vatican only in a literary guise. The codices of the Library spoke of Greece and Rome, of gods and heroes, only to those who sought out their pages; but Apollo, the Venus Empress, and the Laocoon displayed their virile, soft or tortured beauty to the eyes of all who passed through the Cortile di Belvedere. Julius's predecessor, Sixtus IV della Rovere (1471–1484), had not ventured to invade the austerity of the Vatican with such pagan images; for, when he gave Rome its first collection of ancient art—a collection of bronzes—he relegated it far from the Vatican to the Capitoline Hill. The Capitol had been the hill of the glory that was Rome, just as the Vatican region embraced the valley of Christian martyrdom.

The Gallery of Statues

Hence we cannot withhold our admiration from the Pontiff who committed this breach of ecclesiastical austerity with the same courage and success with which he nerved his army at the siege of Mirandola when he changed the mitre for the helmet.   His victory here was a victory of the spirit which was destined to have a far more lasting effect than his victory of arms.   Nor can we help admiring the invincible and ageless youth of the art of the ancients which captivated the stern Pontiff's heart, and under his auspices penetrated where for centuries its strength and its youth had been ignored.

But even more marvellous was the slow evolution of the Italic spirit, which, bending itself with the Renaissance to the contemplation of the joys of life, had first led Nicholas V (1447–1455) to build on this very spot a battlemented tower whence the eye could roam at will over the Roman Campagna and find in the beauties of nature the source of art. A few decades later this spirit had the tower torn down to make way for the Casino of Innocent VIII (1484–1492), with the graceful architectonic lines given it by Giacomo di Pietrasanta and the pictorial decorations of Mantegna and Pinturicchio.   This same Italic spirit in Julius

II won an entry into the Cortile near this Casino for the first pieces of ancient sculpture. Contemporaneous Christian art had paved the way for the art of ancient Greece and Rome. Certainly, these marbles placed in niches or adorning fountains were there to fulfil a decorative purpose rather than as objects of admiration; they were part of the architectural ensemble, so to speak—an adjunct of the art of Giacomo di Pietrasanta, of Mantegna and of Pinturicchio. To-day, however,

The Gallery of Statues

owing to the successive alterations, the house built by Innocent VIII has almost disappeared: save a few figures, but little remains of its frescoes, whereas a whole army of statues have come to join the Apollo, the Laocoon and the Venus Empress of the Cortile di Belvedere. The art of the ancients, which stole in timidly as a handmaiden, now rules as a queen.

The events which caused the present Vatican Museum to develop from the few marbles introduced by Julius II for decorative purposes, reflect the intellectual and political experiences through which the Papacy and Church have passed. In so far as the Renaissance of an-

cient art is concerned, Julius II certainly introduced it into the Vatican.
At this period the Renaissance had already devoted about a century to
the study of Greek and Roman literature. Through the works of the
ancient poets, philosophers, historians and rhetoricians a better real-
ization of the life of Classical times had been secured between the
Trecento and the Quattrocento, for literature is always the surest and
quickest means of establishing an intellectual understanding between

The Sala della Rotonda

different ages. And when literature had done its part, when it had
awakened an admiration for the greatness of ancient Greece and Rome,
Classical monuments—first the buildings and then the masterpieces of
sculpture—might finally claim their meed of appreciation.

The buildings of ancient Rome were for the most part in ruins, and
had either been allowed to remain as pathetic witnesses of a civilization
gone forever, or had been rifled for their marbles, lead and bricks, just
as if, instead of being the ideal patrimony of a whole people, they had
really belonged to nobody. Now they began to be cherished, studied,
measured and hypothetically restored, because their greatness and
grandeur offered a living commentary on the words of the writers.

The Hall of the Greek Cross

Finally came the sculptures. To appreciate them properly presupposed not only a particular quality of imagination of a high order—a gift which is rare, and is usually the fruit of a lofty intellect—but also a thorough preparation of the mind, which could be attained only through the long study of Classical literature. It was an easier matter for a Quattrocento Christian to harmonize the philosophy of Plato with his religious instructions, or to link the greatness of contemporaneous Rome with the glorious Rome of Livy's pages, than to appreciate the unveiled beauty of an Apollo or a Venus. Between him and this appreciation lay the world of Romanesque and Gothic art, which, in its exclusive preoccupations with the ideal, had overlooked the form, or had above all ignored the human body. When Romanesque and Gothic art had run their course, and when the renaissance of Christian religious art began, it was indeed possible for Nicolas Poussin to hint in his reliefs at the figures on the Roman sarcophagi, and for the artists of that period to look on nature with eyes different from their predecessors'—paganized eyes, one might say. But ancient art as a whole required a much more radical change in sentiment and taste than that which was required for the appreciation of ancient literature. This change took place later. And whereas in the second half of the Trecento and the first half of the Quattrocento great libraries had been instituted and enriched with Greek and Latin codices—museums of

Portico of the Cortile Ottagono

literature, as one might call them,—it was not until the second half
of the Quattrocento that the collections of sculpture, or museums of
art, began.

GROWTH OF THE MUSEUM.—It chanced that a Cardinal who had made
one of these collections—Giuliano della Rovere—became Pope. Thus
the Vatican, which as an institution founded for all time could offer
the greatest promise of continuity of development, entered into a race
which had previously interested only private individuals (càrdinals or
princes), whose work had for the most part been interrupted at their
death. Leo X (1513–1521) and Clement VII (1523–1534), the two
Medici Popes, had already family traditions urging them to keep up
the work begun by Julius II, since the Medici were the first among
the princes of Italy to form a collection of their own at Florence. Paul
III Farnese (1534–1549) continued in the footsteps of his predecessors.
And, while it is true that at this time not many pieces of sculpture were
sent to join the Apollo and the Laocoon, all that were sent were excellent. Leo X is responsible for the Nile group; Clement VII for the
Torso of Apollonius, associated with the name of Michelangelo; Paul
III for the so-called Antinous, that is, the statue of Hermes as a youth.

But while these Popes were indulging their Italic nature in the admiration of Classical art, clouds were collecting to the north, and the
storm of the Reformation was at hand. To cite these "shameless"

marbles as the final proof that the Church and the Papacy had fallen away from the purity and humility of the original Christian doctrine, was a most unfortunate error. They proved only that the Pope, while the Shepherd of the Church, was besides a secular prince, and appreciative of natural joys. The marbles were indeed in the Vatican, and most of them remained there; to exile them now would not have helped to reconquer Protestant Europe, so that only a few, and those not the

The Cortile Ottagono

best (thanks to the Pope's discrimination), passed to other collections outside Rome. But from this moment the collecting activity of the Vatican stops. It was the time of the Counter-Reformation and the Council of Trent. And even though, in the face of the attacks of Puritanism, which would destroy even Christian art, the Council defended this art and declared that a love of art was not a material worship of images but a contemplation of the noble works of God or of works executed under his inspiration, it would have been excessive audacity to go on collecting within the walls of the Vatican sculptures in defence of which no religious need could be cited, but which, on the

The Hall of the Muses

contrary, spoke only of a pagan civilization and a religion the Church
had perforce to destroy.

But not even the threats of Puritanism could kill the spirit of the
Renaissance that had come to life in Italy. The Pope, as head of the
Church, ceased to add to the Vatican collection of marbles, but, as an
earthly prince and an Italian, he built himself far from his spiritual
home a villa in which he might indulge his passion for both ancient and
contemporary art. And thus it came about that Julius III del Monte
(1550–1555) extended from the beginning of the Flaminian Way to
the Milvian Bridge and to the Parioli, between the river and the hill,
his wonderful villa, to which Michelangelo, Vasari, Vignola, Ammanati
and Baronino lent their architectural skill, while Prospero Fontana
and Taddeo Zucchero were entrusted with its pictorial decoration.
Here were collected, along every walk and around each fountain, ancient statues and reliefs exceeding far in number those treasured in
the Vatican itself. Yet the venerable Pontiff, if not in his spirit, must
have borne at least in his body the memory of the struggle between the
Reformation and the Church; for, even if he could forget that he was
Paul III's delegate at the Council of Trent, he must assuredly have
remembered the anger of the Lanzichenecchi during the siege of Rome
in 1527, when he nearly lost his life.

The Hall of the Animals

The Hall of the Animals

Sixtus V Peretti (1585–1590), a vigorous Pontiff famous as a protector of agriculture and industry and as a restorer of church discipline, can hardly be conceived as a restorer of Classical art. Yet he displayed no less eagerness than preceding Pontiffs in collecting old marbles in his Villa Montalto. If some of these (such as the Caryatid,

The Hall of the Animals

now in the Braccio Nuovo, or the seated Greek statues, said to be of Posidippus and Menander) found their way at a later date to the Vatican Museum—just as some of the statues from Pope Julius's villa also found their way thither—this should be referred to a kind of destiny which willed that these Pontiffs, even when they acted as private individuals, should work for the ultimate glory of the Papacy. For, besides the reaction of the Reformation, another cause halted the growth of the Vatican collections, namely, Papal nepotism. Under the inspiration of the Popes, members of their families began to build villas and form private collections of marbles for their own gratification and glory. Julius III's collection was indeed of such a character, and, if his brother Baldwin and his nephew Fabian did not reap much profit from it, it was because the Pope had lavished the funds of the Papacy on his own villa. Pius IV (1559–1566) interfered in the settlement of the complicated will of his predecessor, upholding the claims of the Holy See; but while he gave lands and villas to the Medici of

The Gallery of the Candelabra

Milan and to the Borromeo family, only one statue—that of the sophist Elios Aristides—entered the Vatican, and this was exhibited, not in the Belvedere, but in the Library.

To Cardinal Scipio Borghese, nephew of Paul V (1605–1621), Cardinal Ludovico Ludovisi, nephew of Gregory XV (1621–1623), and Cardinal Camillo Pamphilj, nephew of Innocent X (1644–1655) are due the Borghese, Ludovisi and Panfili villas and collections. And thus it would have come to pass that, notwithstanding its masterpieces, the Vatican collection would have remained a modest adjunct of the Cortile di Belvedere after the first thrill of the Renaissance had died away, had not the second half of the eighteenth century brought about a profound change in the general attitude towards Classical antiquities.

In 1768, Johann Joachim Winckelmann, a little over fifty years old, met a violent death in Trieste, but he left an everlasting monument to his genius, which had been nurtured on the vital sap of ancient art, especially in Rome. This was his "History of Ancient Art" ("Geschichte der Kunst des Alterthums"). Winckelmann had approached the works of Greek and Roman sculpture, not with the esthetic eyes of

The Gallery of the Candelabra

the Renaissance period, but permeated with the historic spirit with which, from the Seicento to the Settecento, men had begun to examine the manifestations of human activity. The statue, the relief and the engraved gem were for him not only beautiful forms to be admired, but also documents revealing another conception of nature and life—that is, reflecting the attitude of another intellect towards the one and the other. To appreciate this attitude, to make it live again in all its phases, was to possess a true knowledge of Classical art.

It is by no means one of the least boasts of archæology that the historic spirit, which had hitherto busied itself with its researches into human actions, had recourse first to art, not to literature, when it began the study of the intellectual manifestations of mankind.

Art was a late-comer in the esthetic march of the Renaissance; it leads the way, however, as the touchstone of all modern history. Winckelmann's "History of Ancient Art" appeared long before any similar plan for the reconstruction of literature occurred to the minds of philologists, and may thus be said to have given a new impulse to ancient art. If Classical sculpture were a document to be studied for

The Gallery of the Candelabra

the further development of human thought, rather than a thing to be
admired in a civilization that Christianity had supplanted, it might well
receive a hospitable welcome even in the austere halls of the Vatican.
And, if the Humanist Popes might be blamed for laying too much stress
on earthly enjoyment in their zeal for Classical art, no such charge
could be brought against Popes whose aim in fostering collections of
marbles was to further the study of archæology.

A new era for the Vatican collections began indeed with Clement
XIV Ganganelli, who became Pope in 1769, the year after Winckelmann's death. And the personality of Ennio Quirino Visconti, the
illustrious archæologist who with his father Giovan Battista Antonio
presided over the formation of the Pio-Clementino Museum in the pontificates of Clement XIV (1769–1774) and Pius VI Braschi (1775–1799),
proves conclusively, if proof be required, the purity of intentions
which underlay the new work. Through the activity of these Popes
the small collection of Julius II, which could all be grouped in the space
of the Belvedere, developed into what is now known as the Vatican
Sculpture Gallery. By altering a few rooms and the chapel of the Villa
of Innocent VIII, these Popes established the existing Gallery of Statues and Hall of the Busts. The chief credit, however, is due to Pius VI,
who in 1775 not only transformed the Belvedere, added the interior
portico and the columns, and built the Hall of the Biga, the Hall of the

Greek Cross, the Rotonda, the Hall of the Muses, the Hall of the Animals and Gallery of Masks, but also gave its present form to the Gallery of the Candelabra, which originally was an open corridor.

The finishing touch was put on the work by Pope Pius VII Chiaramonti (1800–1823), when in 1803 he gave its final arrangement to the Cortile di Belvedere, transforming the atria at the corners into cabinets, and allotted to his Museo Chiaramonti the northern hall of the great

The Museo Chiaramonti

gallery which Julius II and Bramante had built to connect the Belvedere with the Vatican Palace. Finally, between 1817 and 1821, he added the Braccio Nuovo, which runs parallel to the new Library and joins Bramante's gallery with the opposite wing.

But the Napoleonic storm broke with equal violence over the artistic and political plans of Pius VII. After Classical art had finally won its spiritual fight against the Puritan forces within and without the Church, and had been installed with honor in the galleries and halls of Clement XIV and Pius VI, the material violence of Napoleon, who revived the conduct of the Roman conquerors of old when they spoiled the Greek cities of their treasures of art, stripped these galleries and halls, and carried the booty to Paris. Only three fine works of Canova,

Part of the Braccio Nuovo

the Perseus and the Boxers (Kreugas and Damoxenus), were left in the Belvedere, and these were as dreary-looking as the plaster copies of the Apollo and Laocoon which took the place of the originals. Canova's works were indeed a genuine echo of ancient Greece, but the empty grace of a Perseus showing his spoils could never compensate for the godlike advance of the Apollo, nor did the brute violence with which the Boxers gathered themselves for their encounter offer any comparison with the shudder that ran through the crushed flesh of Laocoon.

But, just as it had triumphed over intellectual oppression, the Vatican Museum was destined also to triumph over material violence. After five years of exile, the greater number of the old treasures were restored in 1816, so that Napoleon left less trace of his passage here than elsewhere. Canova's marbles, however, were retained in the collection as a souvenir and in token of gratitude. For, if the proximity of the masterpieces of Greece overshadows them, they at least are political documents dealing with the vicissitudes of the Museum. They are also, as it were, a seal on its history, for since the days of Pius VII no chapter has been added to it. Gregory XVI (1831–1846), Pius IX (1846–1878), Leo XIII (1878–1903) and Pius X (1903–1914) added a few pieces here and there, but the aspect of the Museum is unchanged. Gregory XVI devoted himself to the Etruscan Museum, and Pius IX

Part of the Braccio Nuovo

had but little time for things of art, so deeply was he preoccupied with the clouds on the political horizon of his time.

When we to-day look back over the road the Museum has travelled from its humble beginnings in the days of Julius II, we are forced to admit that no museum in the world has such a remarkable history. Some museums, like the Glyptothek at Munich, owe their existence to the collecting zeal of a prince; others, like the British Museum, spring from an educational function of the state; others, like the National Museum at Athens, satisfy the patriotic devotion of a people to its glorious past. The Vatican Museum has, on the contrary, enjoyed the zealous support of both prince and state and people, and of something still more important than all of these—namely, the world of Catholic Christendom, which looked towards the Papacy for its rule of life. For, just as the Vatican Museum owed its origin to a world-wide current of thought, the Renaissance, it called its first halt in answer to a Catholic current of thought, the Counter-Reform; it owed its new lease of life to the awakening sense of the teaching function of the state, since the work of Clement XIV and Pius VI in aid of archæology can only be interpreted as such; and it owes its continuity of existence, throughout good and evil fortune, to the spirit of the Roman people, who have always aided the Papacy in its work, recognizing in the ancient marbles the documents of their own mighty past.

But if currents of thought which affected the whole civilized world; if functions of the state which were confined within a small dominion; if the historic pride of a people, confined within limits even smaller than those of a state, have been co-operating agencies in this monumental work, this has happened because the success of the work did not depend on the more or less brief life of individual princes, whose tastes and predispositions might vary, but rested on the organic principality of the Papacy, in which each Pope, bowing his head humbly

The Braccio Nuovo

before the glorious traditions of his dynasty and confidently regarding himself as the predecessor of an endless line, lent his temporary co-operation in the work, filled with trustful strength.

GENERAL CHARACTER OF THE MUSEUM.—But now, after following the history and development of this Vatican collection, if we stop to consider it as a whole so as to grasp its distinctive character, we must admit that from the esthetic standpoint it is disappointing. With the exception of a few Greek originals and some excellent Roman works, all of the exhibits are copies—and often mediocre copies—of Greek masterpieces or modest creations of the Roman chisel.

If we were asked what, in our opinion, would be the impression received by an ancient Greek or Roman on entering the Vatican Museum, we could only reply that he would probably experience the same feeling as we do when we visit a museum of medieval and modern art composed of the works of the cheap copyists who infest our galleries and those of the marble-workers who cater mainly for cemeteries.

Unlike the National Museum at Athens, the Vatican Museum is not the archives of the creative spirit of a whole people, whose original documents date back to the Mycenæan age and down through the mid-

One End of the Braccio Nuovo

dle ages of ancient Hellas to the dawn of Classical art, tracing this art from the crude essays of the archaic period to the most precious manifestations of Greek genius. Neither has it, in the midst of Roman copies, the little Greek oases one meets in the Glyptothek at Munich, with its Æginetan sculptures; nor, like the British Museum, far from the sky of Greece, can it show the relics of the Parthenon, the Temple of Phigalia, the Monument of the Nereids, and the Mausoleum. The original Greek works brought to Rome after the conquest have nearly all been destroyed; and the original works which Roman art succeeded in creating—honorary reliefs—very luckily still adorn for the most part the monuments for which they were intended. Thus the Vatican Museum had to be content with the scattered parts of the decorative works executed to adorn Roman gardens, squares, baths and cemeteries.

But while even from the esthetic point of view the Roman copies of Greek masterpieces, ill treated as these were in the process, call forth our admiration and make us feel still more keenly our great loss in being deprived of the originals, historically the Vatican Museum, just because it has grown up out of the very soil of Rome, has a value that is lacking in collections formed in other countries with works violently

Part of the Braccio Nuovo

torn from their native home. It reveals, if not the creative quality of the Roman spirit, the attitude which Roman taste adopted towards Greek art. In contrast to the National Museum at Athens, which gathered the pure flower of Greek creative genius, it shows originality only in its discriminating function and in the re-elaboration of what it has chosen. From this collection we learn how Roman genius was affected by the manifestations of Greek genius, and we carry away the same impression as when we read Virgil after Homer, Terence after Menander, and Catullus and Horace after Sappho and Pindar.

Before the glory of Rome had yet unfolded itself, in the seventh and sixth centuries before our era, merchants and artists from the East and from Greece had established a trade in sculptures with Latium, just as they had previously done with Etruria and Campania. Rich decora-

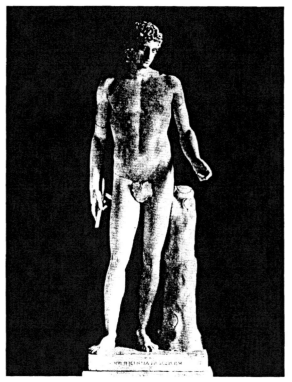

Seated Apollo Citharædus (Fig. 1)   Nude Figure of Apollo (Fig. 2)
(Archaic Period)   (Archaic Period)

tions for tombs and pretentious ornaments for temples gave evidence of the social comfort and prosperity rather than of the artistic taste of the purchasers. This art, indeed, was a thing external to the real life of the country, and did not spring from any urgent religious need. The Latin conception of the gods and of death was altogether untouched by the artistic external trappings with which trade and the fashion of the moment decked their religion. Unlike their neighbors, the Etruscans and Oscans, the Latins were more moderate in their adoption of foreign art. They remained particularly conservative of their funeral art, and, as a matter of fact, in Latium we never find those hypogea so common in Etruria and Campania.

Conditions in the fourth and third centuries B.C., when Greek art exercised undisputed sway in Latium, were marked by no great change. Latin art, indeed, would have remained an insignificant provincial episode in the story of Greek art, and would have had very little influence on the life of the country, if the rise of her military greatness had not brought Rome, through her conquests of Greece and Asia Minor, into direct contact with Greek art in its native home. The artistic booty brought home by the Roman generals gave the Romans an acquaintance with the masterpieces of Greek sculpture and painting, which were used to adorn the temples and public buildings of Rome. This work of the state found, now as ever in the life of Rome, many imita-

The Three Graces (Fig. 3)
(Archaic Period)

tors among the private citizens. Magistrates sent out to govern distant
provinces either bought or took by force (as we know Verres did)
works of art wherever they went, and, when this taste for works of art
had grown to such an extent that the market of antiquities of the time
could no longer supply sufficient original works to meet the numerous
demands, there arose a new industry which has been of the greatest
value for our knowledge of ancient art—namely, the industry of copying. The Roman who could not have originals for his house or garden
could at least have copies of them in bronze or marble; and to such a
pitch was this industry developed that the copyist often went so far as
to add his own signature, so that we have a Sosicles claiming an Amazon by Cresilas, an Antiochus appropriating the Athena Parthenos,
and an Apollonius boasting authorship of Polycletus's Doryphorus.

Girl Runner (Fig. 4)
(Archaic Period)

Penelope (Fig. 5)
(Archaic Period)

Young Gymnast and his Slave (Fig. 6)
(Archaic Period)

The Discobolus (Fig. 7)
(Myron, Classical Period)

Doryphorus (Fig. 8)   Amazon (Fig. 9)
(Polycletus, Classical Period)   (Polycletus, Classical Period)

Seeing, however, that these copies were intended mostly to decorate
houses and gardens, it is only natural that not all the subjects of Greek
art should have been equally copied. An erudite eclectic, like the owner
of the villa of the Pisos at Herculaneum, might desire a specimen of all
the styles and periods of Greek art; an emperor with a cultured taste
like Hadrian might assemble in his villa near Tivoli—whence most of
the Vatican treasures have come—what one might call an exposition
of all the architecture and sculpture of antiquity; but in the main the
Roman imitator chose as his models subjects best suited for the decorative effect he had in mind. How much more appropriate among the
rocks of a fountain, or along the green borders of a garden, was the
train of Dionysus or Poseidon—the sea-horses, nymphs, satyrs and
mænads—than the awesome figures of the major Olympic gods! And
as it was Hellenistic art which had lent so much grace and sentiment to
the gracious denizens of the sea and the woods, it was this same Hellenistic art that gave its chief inspiration to this Roman marble industry.
And when at a later period the Roman sculptor wished to associate with
these demigods, who had all the passions and weaknesses of man, gods
and divinities whose forms in stone would give joy to the beholder, he
turned his eyes, not to the awe-striking figures of Phidias, whose fitting
home was the cloud-kissing peak of Olympus rather than the sanded
walks of a garden, but to the artistic creations of Praxiteles, whose

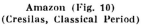

Amazon (Fig. 10)
(Cresilas, Classical Period)

Amazon (Fig. 11)
(Phidias, Classical Period)

gods are so human and so sensual. The Aphrodite of Cnidus, laying aside her robe as she entered the bath, lost little of her modesty in being transported from the little round and open temple at Cnidus, where on every side she was exposed to the gaze of the curious, to become a *genre* figure beside a fountain. The Apollo Sauroctonus, slaying a lizard on the trunk of a leafless tree, might very appropriately fill the space between two trees laden with foliage.

As a further proof that Roman taste was swayed in its choice by the decorative possibilities of the statues, we have only to remember that, when it was a question of decorating not gardens but gymnasiums, it spurned the soft and delicate carving of the fourth century and went back to the fifth in search of the rugged and stern canon of Polycletus. Not in the nimble-limbed Apoxyomenus of Lysippus—that personification of an age when even the athlete seemed to harbor deep thoughts behind a knitted brow—but in the solid frame of the Doryphorus of Polycletus was the Roman to find the model which, in preparation for the wars of world-conquest, would teach him to prize bodily strength more highly than the subtleness of the brain.

On the whole, however, we may say that "refined" Roman society of the later Republican and Imperial days grew sated with, and almost ashamed of, the old simplicity which had given it the strength to establish a world-empire, and went coquetting with strange tastes and ideas until at last it found itself more in sympathy with the output of the fourth century and the Hellenistic period—*i.e.,* the sensuous, learned and sceptical epoch of Greece—than with the archaism of the fifth century—the period of Greece's simplicity and severity of ideal. The anatomic rigidity and superficiality of the archaic works seemed but gross insipiency when placed beside the tortured beauty of the Laocoon. When the Roman desired simplicity in art he did not seek it in the true archaic works, but succumbed to the soft gracefulness of Hellenistic imitations. He did not turn to the severe and commanding Demeter in the Rotonda, whose presence suggests a crowd of devout worshippers, but to the sensual Aphrodite of Dædalus, crouching in her bath under the stream of cold water the better to reveal the plastic charms of her body. This soft quality it was that delighted the intellectuals of Rome, who no longer believed in the gods, or at least did not identify their own gods with the creations of Greek art. And, if in our review of the principal works in the Vatican Museum the disproportionate represen- tation of works of the archaic period and of the fifth century as compared with those of the fourth century and the Hellen- istic period

Pericles (Fig. 12)
(Cresilas, Classical Period)

(*circa* 290–150 B.C.) should appear less evident than to a visitor passing through the halls of the collection, we would ask our readers to remember that this lack of proportion has been here intentionally corrected so as to give a complete and balanced survey of the development of Greek and Roman art. The works of the archaic period and the fifth century have almost all been chosen for criticism with this end in view, while many works of no little importance dating from the fourth century and the Hellenistic period have been left unnoticed. It should also be remembered that to the former class belong some originals which reached Italy either in the Roman or the intermediate period.

Roman art thus consists, for the most part, of copies of Greek masterpieces belonging in the main to fixed periods. The Roman copyist,

Demeter (Fig. 13)
(School of Phidias, Classical Period)

Artemis (Fig. 14)
(School of Phidias, Classical Period)

Caryatid (Fig. 15)
(School of Phidias, Classical Period)

Athena (Fig. 16)
(School of Phidias, Classical Period)

however, was not a mechanical imitator. In saying this we do not refer to infidelities wherein even fairly able Roman sculptors libelled their original, nor do we refer to the special Graeco-Roman School of Pasiteles, which flourished at the end of the Republic and the beginning of the Empire, and which deliberately combined in its copies (of individual statues or groups) parts of figures or whole figures belonging to different styles and periods. There is not a single work of this school in the Vatican. We desire rather to call attention to a general phenomenon which characterizes all the work of the Roman copyists. In addition to the servile work of

Discobolus Preparing for the Throw (Fig. 17)
(Classical Period)

copying mechanically, the Roman aimed at introducing something of his own showing that he was the conqueror; but being a mediocre artist, with a jumble of all styles and periods in his brain, he often succeeded in producing a work that was true to no style in particular and had no style of its own. Such works are a riddle for the archæologist, who does not know whether to attribute them to the fifth or fourth century, or to the fourth century or the Hellenistic period. As a rule, he humbly pleads ignorance in cases of this kind; but in reality such statues belong to the hybrid mass dumped on the market by the Roman marble-worker as his own original productions, although in the eclectic purchasers of the time they aroused none of the doubts which torment the archæologist of to-day. All this material, which affords little esthetic satisfaction, still awaits the patient archæologist whose careful classification will determine the historic stratum to which each work belongs. Here also, as in the case of the copies of originals of the various periods, our review will convey to the reader an impression far different from that derived from an actual visit to the Museum. Having to choose between flower and flower, and to cull only a few dozens of specimens, our attention must be confined to works which have a well-defined style and characterize a period, a school or an artist. The Vatican Museum has a remarkable stock of these non-classifiable works, amounting to many hundreds. To these so many sections of

the collection owe their monoto-
nous aspect; for, after examining
them, we feel the same boredom
as is conveyed by the rhetoric of
the Empire, with its didactic va-
riations of the great Greek and
Roman orators.

But, after thus indicating the
deficiencies of Roman art, we
must not overlook its positive
achievements. Though Rome attached so little importance to art;
though she considered it a pursuit
unworthy of a citizen, and even
under the Empire left its cultivation to the Greeks, she not only
exercised a certain discrimination
in her copying, but also created
something that Greece until then
had never had. In two of her

Bœotian Relief of Horseman (Fig. 18)
(Classical Period)

customs, one domestic and one political, Rome found the source of
inspirations which were original in art. In the *imagines maiorum,*
which preserved the remembrance of the deceased for future generations, lay the germ of portraiture; the great tableaux in which the victorious generals displayed in the Forum the principal incidents of their
campaigns paved the way for historical reliefs.

But if Rome had remained a republic, and if the imperial idea had
not brought one individual—the Emperor—to the forefront of public
life, the art of portraiture and of honorary reliefs would have remained an unimportant episode in the life of Greek art, like the temple decorations and the tomb ornaments in contemporary Latium.
This is proved by the laurel-crowned bust from the tomb of the Scipios,
which is now in the Vatican Museum and is said to be a portrait of the
poet Ennius, and by the fragment of a painting recording the exploits
of M. Fannius and Q. Fabius, now in the Museo dei Conservatori; the
bust is an insipid imitation of the Greek idealistic style, while the painting treats a Roman subject in a purely Greek manner.

The imperial idea modified all this. To Rome came the great artists
to place themselves at the service of the Empire. From the *imagines
maiorum,* hitherto confined to the privacy of the home or the family
tomb, developed the portrait of the Emperor, which either flattery or
loyalty multiplied in every corner of the Empire. The eulogistic no-

The Barberini Hera (Fig. 19)
(Fourth Century B.C.)

Aphrodite of Cnidus (Fig. 20)
(Praxiteles, Fourth Century B.C.)

Apollo Sauroctonus (Fig. 21)
(Praxiteles, Fourth Century B.C.)

Torso of an Eros (Fig. 22)
(Praxitelic School, Fourth Century B.C.)

tices, which for a few days attracted the attention of the loungers in the Forum, were replaced by monuments of stone, and thus we have the historical reliefs on the honorary slabs which perpetuated through the centuries the memory of the Emperors.

Here again, as always, the imperial example influenced private citizens. Every prominent citizen was a lesser emperor among his own clients, and his daily routine of business was, so to speak, his empire, concerning which posterity was to be duly notified through the instrumentality of art. Hence arose those countless honorary portraits that studded the squares of the small provincial towns, immortalizing the not always very intellectual features of insignificant magistrates. Hence, too, arose the excessive desire of private citizens to glorify their past in honorary monuments. Nor did these sarcophagi belong only to the magistrate who had faithfully served the ideal of Rome and wished to immortalize the salient facts of his administration, or to the general who had himself represented in all the turmoil of battle. Even an M. Virgilius Eurisaces, a wealthy baker, had a costly tomb built for himself on which the reliefs show the successive processes of bread-making, the trade in which he had made his fortune; while in a modest sepulchral painting Farnaces, a boatman, has bequeathed to us the picture of the tub with which he eked out a meagre living!

In this art of portraiture and honorary reliefs Rome not only introduces subjects untouched by the Greeks, but treats these subjects in a way of her own. Though this art was practised by Greek artists, the honor of originating it must be conceded to Rome. From the early days of the Empire down to Constantinian times and even later, the art of Rome rises and falls as it pursues a path which we may call naturalism based directly on life. Rome took up the burden of art at the point where Hellenism laid it down, namely, at the point of idealistic naturalism, because the Greek art of this period was still ideal even when it represented the unesthetic and drew its subjects directly from nature. Hellenism could never quite shake off the tradition of ages. Thus the first output of Imperial art, in the period from Augustus to the Flavii, is strongly tinged with idealistic naturalism. Between the Flavii and Trajan a change came: more freedom is given to nature as seen directly, and the form becomes less delicate and accurate. Decadence was rapid from the days of the Antonines to Constantine and Theodosius, when the compositions became poor and the figures ungraceful.

We have seen that the inspiring influence of Rome was limited to the two branches of portraiture and relief work. But even in these Greece was always the tutoress, and often an indiscreet one. Under the traditional idealistic forms she introduces her gods even into the honorary reliefs. Unable to pour the full plethora of her myths into the architectural decorations, since the Roman architecture had abolished the metope and generally left the friezes and façades without ornaments, she employed them as wall decorations in the *triclinium* to delight the eye of the banqueters, and crowded them on the surfaces of the sarcophagi to supply subjects of meditation to the bereaved. And when Rome was called on to lend artistic aid to the new Oriental cults which the mingling of races under the Empire had diffused so

widely, Greece was again the agent. It seemed as though Greece had a monopoly of the ideal, and especially of the divine ideal. How ill would the gods have fared had they been subjected to the rough mentality of the Romans! Greece, moreover, had already performed a similar task for the Ptolemies when she presented Egypt with the figure of Serapis.

That the Roman mind, engrossed with material conquest, had no capacity for the divine ideal is shown by the fact that neither in her literature nor in her art was Rome able to create an heroic myth of her own. She did not know how to till the soil

Antinous del Belvedere (Fig. 23)
(Praxitelic School [?], Fourth Century B.C.)

wherein the human germ might develop into the divine. The Romans, who were above all makers of real history and not fantastic creators of the unreal, could not conceive even their own origin as a myth; for them it, too, was history. And if in literature and in art the first figures in her history, Romulus and Remus, are illuminated by an aureole of myths, we must not forget that this is due, not to the Roman, but to the Greek spirit, which, through the pious Æneas, Stesichorus and the *tabulæ iliacæ,* linked the origin of Rome with the ruin of Troy. Thus, in the Base Casali, a votive altar to be found in the Belvedere, the artist celebrates on one side the birth of Romulus and Remus, and on the other harks back, through the Trojan War, to the Judgment of Paris.

In general, therefore, these are the works in which Roman art is expressed: copies of Greek masterpieces (preferably of definite periods), arbitrary combinations of the elements of these masterpieces in figures devoid of a definite stylistic character, portraits, honorary reliefs, sepulchral monuments glorifying Roman life (even the humble life of the tradesman), pictures and sarcophagi with Greek myths, Oriental gods executed in the Greek style, and some scenes dealing with the beginnings of Rome. This is all that Rome produced during the centuries of the Empire, and this was for the most part executed by Greek hands. Here undoubtedly we do not behold the straight and uninterrupted line of development followed by the spirit of one people. Roman art does not offer an enjoyment, logical as well as esthetic, such as is afforded by the evolution of the art of Greece. Mental categories formed and crystallized in the school of scientific evolutionism are worthless in the presence of this collection of works created under the various influences exerted simultaneously by different epochs, artists and sentiments. But just for this very reason Roman art is a faithful mirror of life under the Empire. Far better in it than in the other manifestations of the era do we see the clash, the repulsion and the final coalescence of Greek and Roman elements; we see in it the contrast between myth and history, between the ideal and the real, and we trace in it the tortuous course of the destiny of the Empire. The contemplation of Roman art as the amalgamation of different civilizations affords us exactly the same enjoyment as was experienced by an early Roman of refined taste when he walked along the paths of a public garden and examined the great variety of works which the eclectic spirit of the times had collected there. But, descending from the peaks of art to the plane of every-day life, we derive from Roman art an even stronger sense of that vastness of the Empire which must have been conveyed in the Forum by the multicolored crowds of spiritual Greeks and fanatical Orientals who made a motley picture against the background of dignified Romans.

Apollo del Belvedere (Fig. 24)
(Leochares[?], Fourth Century B.C.)

The Vatican Museum is composed of all these works, but here
the original mixing of ages, styles
and subjects is still further complicated as the result of the history
of the collection. The most dis-
parate works have been placed together, either because the order of
their acquisition has willed it so,
or because esthetically they are
better adapted to a certain place.

It is only the uncultured person
who, on passing rapidly through
the halls, receives the impression
of having before him a long series
of marbles, almost all alike. The
student who views them with an
historic eye is compelled to take
giddy leaps of ages and ideas as
he passes from marble to marble.

Apollo Citharædus (Fig. 25)
(Fourth Century B.C.)

The sarcophagus to which the remains of some poor mortal were
piously consigned under the protection of Greek heroes, and which in
its treatment of death hints at the life beyond the grave, supports an
honorary relief which was detached from a commemorative monument and treats of Roman victories in this life of ours. The figure of
an athlete, offered as a model of vigorous health to the youth frequent-
ing the gymnasia and baths, stands near the dignified statue of an
emperor, general or high priest, which from its place in some public
forum once spoke of the authority of rulers. In front of the solemn
image of a fifth-century Greek divinity, which formerly towered in the
mighty niche of a temple, we are greeted by the immodest smile of an
Hellenistic satyr which earlier diffused its coarse joviality among the
trees of a villa. The Sacrifice of Mithra, venerated by his Oriental followers in the dim recesses of his mysterious shrine, is lost among the
countless figures of animals which once struggled or reposed around
the fountains of some courtyard. Thus, in capricious succession, the
Vatican Museum presents us with the phases and characteristics of
Roman civilization. We witness in turn its melancholy preoccupation
with the ultramundane life, its proud satisfaction at the political glory
of Rome, its worship of physical energy, its faithful devotion to the imperial idea, its sincere and solemn religiosity, its light and sarcastic
scepticism, its fanatical practice of strange cults, and the calm serenity

Melpomene, Muse of Tragedy (Fig. 26)
(Fourth Century B.C.)

Thalia, Muse of Comedy (Fig. 27)
(Fourth Century B.C.)

of its domestic life. This collection takes us wherever the rich and tumultuous life of Rome developed and ended—to the home and the temple, to the Forum and baths, to the public gardens, and to the cemetery. Visitors who possess the sense of historic evocation, and who nurture this sense as a delightful extension of their own lives, can feel no greater joy than that which is derived from this vertiginous flight through the ages and this profound penetration into the heart of ancient man.

It is true that archæological science, which would catalogue and arrange everything with punctilious care and thus destroy the vitality of the collection, feels restless at the sight of the very chronological disorder which makes of the Vatican Museum a living thing. But, for our part, we must confess that, from the historic point of view, not the wise distribution of the marbles of the Parthenon, of the Temple of Phigalia, of the Monument of the Nereids, or of the Mausoleum in the British Museum, nor the meticulous classification of the funeral monuments in the National Museum of Athens, has given us that pleasant sense of intellectual exhilaration which we felt when, looking from the Rotonda in the Vatican and casting our eyes over the scene below, our thoughts cantered through the ages as we caught a glimpse of schools and of places far removed. What a wealth of historical messages are conveyed by the belligerent attitude of the Juno Lanuvina, the ridicu-

lous banality of Claudius posing
as Jupiter, the suffering expression of the aged Nerva, the benevolent indulgence of the Hera Barberini, the crude bravado of the
Hercules Righetti, the severe calm
of Demeter, and the morbid melancholy of Antinous! And alter-
nating with these messages come
the no less charming notes which
vibrate from the genial but agi-
tated Zeus of Otricoli, the feminine
energy of Faustina the Elder, the
open and kindly countenance of
Hadrian, the pathetic and sensuous hermes personifying Poz-
zuoli, and the mystic concentration of Serapis. So varied and at
once so harmonious an expression
of ancient life has never been of-

Artemis (Fig. 28)
(Fourth Century B.C.)

fered us by the perusal of any Latin texts,—even those texts which the
all-conquering Greek tradition has filled with so many elements from
the past. In fullness and precision the evoking power of the image far
transcends that of the written word. But to enjoy the gratification of
grasping every note in this concert of various voices we must first train
ourselves to appreciate each individual sound; every image must needs
have already delivered individually its full message concerning its origin, age, significance and function. The message of each work must
be mentally correlated with that of its most intimate sisters, so that we
may go through the Vatican Museum, not on the alert for every note,
high or low, strong or feeble, which each marble may emit, but lending
an ear only to those sounds which are concordant and are reminiscent
of other sounds previously ignored but now contributing towards a
fuller and higher harmony. That is to say, by following historical cri-
teria and making ourselves humble disciples of that archæological science which is so upset when, as here, it—which is order itself—receives
the confused voices of so many works, we shall seek out in this great
collection those marbles which better characterize an age, a school, an
artist, an idea; and we shall thus retrace the grand line of development
of ancient art from the archaic products of Greece to the late Roman
works which herald on the horizon the dawn of another civilization—
the Christian. Those whose ears are attuned to the grand harmony of

this fundamental line will detect with much deeper gratification the individual and precious motifs which run through the apparent discord of the ensemble.

THE ARCHAIC PERIOD.—Figures of gods and votive reliefs, mythological scenes and figures of athletes, statues and sepulchral reliefs are the first products of Greek art. These sufficed amply to satisfy the desires of a civilization which craved for a material expression in images. The figures of the gods and the votive reliefs owe their origin to the mystical sense which inclined men, who were desirous of the constant protection of superior beings, to the hope that this protection would be more readily vouch-safed to them if their prayers were recited and their offerings made before material images of such beings, or if they immortalized their prayers and offerings in some scene in which the figures of the protective deities and their own, or even the former only, appeared. The mythological scenes originated in a sense opposite to the mystical one — namely, in the commemorative and honorific historical sense, which regarded the gods and heroes, not as protectors of the living, but as the agents of great past enterprises. To this very same honorific

Zeus of Otricoli (Fig. 29)
(Fourth Century B.C.)

sense, translated into the human atmosphere, we owe the figures of the athletes; for these were the heroes of the immediate yesterday, just as Hercules and Theseus, who also were athletes, were the heroes of the dim past. The mystic sense and the honorific sense, variously combined, can be recognized in the statues and sepulchral reliefs, because, while on the one hand these, in perpetuating the figure of the deceased, aimed at securing his peaceful ultramundane existence through the mystical power of the image, on the other hand they aimed at perpetuating his memory among his surviving relatives and friends. For this reason the sepulchral reliefs most commonly show the deceased engaged at one of his usual earthly occupations.

The ability displayed at first by Greek art in the cultivation of all

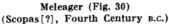

Meleager (Fig. 30)   Headless Statue of a Niobid (Fig. 31)
(Scopas[?], Fourth Century B.C.)   (Fourth Century B.C.)

these branches was not greater than that shown by Egyptian or Assyrian art in the interpretation of nature; in fact, Greece shows as yet
no superiority whatever over any other country where art developed
and ran its independent course. In statuary, the figures are conceived
rigidly in perspective, without any lateral or oblique motion which
might disturb the stern line of the trunk, and with few angular movements of the limbs. In reliefs, which are the transference to stone of
decorative scenes, the figures, instead of being represented with the
natural coördination of their parts, are the result of the arbitrary reconstruction of parallel views. Thus, the thorax in perspective is crushed
between the head and legs in profile; the eye in perspective is represented in a head in profile.

But, however little it may be apparent from these rigid and distorted
designs, Greek art from the very beginning looked on nature with keen
observation of the real, and ennobled this reality by idealizing it.
And, as it gradually advanced in the knowledge of the human body,
it succeeded in correcting the errors of design which had rendered the
figure rigid and distorted. In the statue the head inclines towards one
shoulder; one leg bends at the knee, relieving itself of the weight of the
body; the arms move in smoother gestures, and the trunk from the
shoulders to the hips begins to accompany with greater freedom the
motions of the limbs. A similar advance is made in the representation

Ganymede Carried up by the Eagle (Fig. 32)
(Fourth Century B.C.)

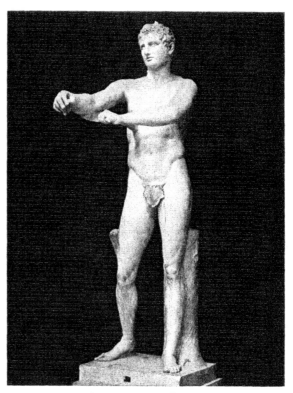

Apoxyomenus (Fig. 33)
(Lysippus, Fourth Century B.C.)

Crouching Figure of Aphrodite (Fig. 34)
(Dædalus[?], Hellenistic Period)

Jupiter Serapis (Fig. 35)
(Bryaxis, Hellenistic Period)

of the draperies, which at first
smothered the body like a sheath;
the folds, which previously fell in
regular parallel and superficial
lines, now diverge, curve and
deepen. Then, in its turn, the
trunk in the reliefs begins to
deviate from its rigidly vertical
position, and to assume a more
natural posture between the legs
and the head. Gradually this
slight obliquity is extended to the
limbs, increasing still further the
naturalness of the posture; and
that enormous eye shown in perspective, which had previously
gazed into vacant space as if entirely detached from the action of
the figure, loses some of its size.

Personification of Antiochia (Fig. 36)
(Eutychides, Hellenistic Period)

It is easy to indicate the tech-
nical ways and means by which Greek art gradually accomplished its
liberation, raising itself thereby to a plane high above Oriental art, and
opening for itself a horizon shut off from the latter for ever. But we
can never know why to Greek art was granted that which was denied to
art elsewhere. To attain to the truth in such a research, we should
need to know the causes which occasioned the peculiar psychological
constitution of the Greek people; that is to say, we should need a knowledge of things which time has obscured for ever. But, if we must perforce abandon our inquiry into causes, we may at least take cognizance
of the fact. Greek art slowly approaches to reality, and idealizes it.
This preparatory work was performed during the archaic era—that is,
between the second half of the seventh century and the first half of the
fifth century before Christ. During the early part of this era—the period of crude archaism—Greek art is rigid in its statuary and distorted
in its reliefs, like all primitive art; in the latter part of this era—the
period of mature archaism—it corrects both excesses, and makes
natural and idealizes both subjects and forms.

Of the output of crude archaism the Vatican possesses nothing. This
period, with which the excavations in Greece, Asia Minor and Sicily
have so familiarized us, produced crude figures of which no intelligent
Roman would have desired a copy. The Vatican indeed possesses very
few works from the period of mature archaism, and even these date

rather from the end than the beginning of this period. Still, with the exception of the mythological reliefs, which were peculiarly an ornament of the temples and of which therefore it was not easy to find specimens or fragments in the soil of Rome, all the genres of Greek art are represented in these few specimens—the statue of the deity, the votive relief, the athletic and mythic statue, and the sepulchral relief. And we even have one work wherein, according to our interpretation, we may see the figure of a goddess, or of a heroine, or of a mortal.

The first of the above-mentioned genres is represented by three

The Nile (Fig. 37)
(Alexandrian School, Hellenistic Period)

statues of Apollo. As the most archaic of these has been transformed by the copyist into a Latin god, Semo Sancus, and thus characterizes a special tendency of the Roman religious spirit, it will be examined by us when we shall later speak of the art of the Empire. Of the other two statues, the older shows the Apollo Citharædus Seated (Fig. 1). The copyist has here translated into marble a bronze original which dates from the beginning of the fifth century, as the following technical details show: the skilful carving of the hair and of the folds of the chiton (tunic) and the cavity of the eyes, which was to be filled with metal or a glassy paste to give the illusion of the living glance. The restorer has been guilty of some inaccuracies in the reconstruction of the two arms with the plectrum and lyre, but in general his restoration of these members has been well conceived. He has, however, been less fortunate with the feet, which he has enveloped in too clumsy footwear, and with the added mass of curls which fall on the shoulders; the latter accords ill with the original coiffure, which gathered all the hair in a knot at the nape of the neck. Yet not even the infidelities of the copyist or the disfigurements of the restorer can destroy the expressive gracefulness of this work. The young god, with his delicate and oval face, and with his body lightly wrapped in a chiton with fine and superficial folds, in-

The Marine Centaur (Fig. 38)
(Hellenistic Period)

clines his head slightly towards his left shoulder to catch the sounds which he draws from his instrument. If the cavity of the eyes conveys to the modern spectator the impression that he stares astonished into vacancy, we must remember that this was not so in the original. In the attitude of the figure all is composure and calm. Hardly perceptible is the inclination of the head; the face is inert; the trunk is firm; the left foot is slightly in advance of the other. As yet we have nothing of that Apollonian fury, of the enrapturing power of music, which, a little more than a century later, we shall find in another figure of Apollo, also in the Vatican Museum. Greek art is studying the human body, but it is as yet unable to breathe into it a soul.

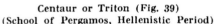

Centaur or Triton (Fig. 39)
(School of Pergamos, Hellenistic Period)

Centaur Crowned with Vine Leaves (Fig. 40)
(Hellenistic Period)

The other figure of Apollo, a few decades later than the preceding one, is not only an ideal nude body (Fig. 2): it also shows increased research into expression. It too has suffered at the hands of the copyist and the restorer. The copyist, who lived probably in the time of Hadrian and was therefore imbued with classical smoothness, has so far exaggerated this quality as to refine down almost completely the muscles and bones. He has besides, for the sake of contrast, created pronounced shadows in the mass of the hair by ruffling it and increasing its size. In this instance the restorer's work has been less detrimental than the copyist's. He is mistaken, however, in his restoration of the left arm, which ought to have been more bent at the elbow, and he has besides shown poor taste in adding the big arrow when reconstructing part of the right arm. On the whole, he has well reproduced the rhythm of the legs. In any case neither the copyist nor the restorer has been able to obliterate the original character of the work, which is linked with a whole series of figures of Apollo dating from the first half of the fifth century, and showing the two aims of Greek artists: first, to make the figure of the god ever more delicate, while retaining the squareness of the shoulders and the firmness of the trunk; and secondly, to give to the figure a benevolent expression and a subdued melancholy through the inclination of the head and the shape of the eyes and mouth.

Silenus with the Infant Dionysus (Fig. 41)
(Hellenistic Period)

Young Satyr Carrying Dionysus (Fig. 42)
(School of Lysippus, Hellenistic Period)

From the statues of the gods we pass to the votive reliefs—that is, to that genre in which the believer gives material expression to his prayer for divine protection. That the Vatican Museum among its statues of this period does not possess those of the great and solemn gods (for example, Zeus or Hera), but only statues of the young and graceful Apollo, is due entirely to chance. It was, however, not chance, but a particular characteristic of the Greek spirit which willed that the Vatican Museum should possess only one votive relief, and this dedicated to the Charites or Graces (Fig. 3). Like the material vows of more modern days, the ancient *votum* was above all a need of the uneducated, who, desiring especially health of body and earthly benefits, addressed themselves to secondary and more humble divinities rather than to the high gods of Olympus. The belief was that the lower gods, as such, were more accessible, and therefore more inclined to satisfy human desires. The Greek thus addressed himself to Æsculapius, Hygeia, the Nymphs, and the Graces. That the Vatican Museum has in this relief a copy of a celebrated original is shown by the existing fragments of duplicates. Whether the original, which stood at the entrance of the Acropolis in Athens, was the work of an artist Socrates (perhaps the Bœotian), will never be determined. In any case we cannot accept the ancient tradition to the effect that this work is a youthful creation of the great philosopher who, before constituting himself the gadfly of the Athenians, sought in sculpture a means of placating the excitable, if wise housewife, Xanthippe; for this work was executed between 480 and 460 B.C., when the philosopher was still a child.

Faun in rosso antico (Fig. 43)
(Hellenistic Period)

The three Graces in this relief could not be taken as models of gracefulness; they have indeed the heavy and stiff appearance of three aged spinsters. The cumbersome gowns add nothing to their grace, and the rigidity of their legs suggests that, instead of being engaged in a round dance, they are taking part in a slow parade. But, if the work has no attraction for the expression of the figures, it is of great value in view of its form and its technique.

The artist not only tries to pay attention to bodily forms—and does it in such a way that they appear even through the heaviness of the clothing—but he also tries to vary the drapery and above all to render with the highest possible fidelity the various courses of the folds. Besides, with the help of the technique of high relief which, in its greater body, allowed the correction of the distortions contained in the design, the individual parts of the body have been coördinated in each of the figures, which have been differentiated by varying the positions of the head and the trunk. The first is foreshortened; the second in perspective; the third in profile. Thus, at once, have been established the motion of the figures and their relation to the spectator, for the two side figures indicate the movement of the group, while the central one shows that the movement is made for the benefit of a spectator supposed to be out of the relief—that is, for the real spectator. In our opinion, the artist has succeeded in conveying the dynamic and static functions of the three figures even in the variety of hair-dressing, which is simple and superficial in the two side figures, but is elaborate and heavy in the central Grace, who seems to make a display of it as a Byzantine icon displays its nimbus. Though quite devoid of Attic sweetness and grace, and displaying all the heaviness of the Peloponnesian School, this relief is the work of an artist who could coördinate effects and strove to liberate Greek art from its archaic uniformity.

Mænad (Fig. 44)
(Hellenistic Period)

Fugitive Niobid (Fig. 45)
(Hellenistic Period)

In its Girl Runner (Fig. 4) the Vatican Museum possesses, not one of
the numerous and ordinary statues of athletes, but the most singular
of all athletic figures. This work is perhaps both an athletic and a
mythic figure, because, as we view this slim and graceful girl, our
thoughts inevitably turn to the athletic heroine *par excellence*—Atalante, the rival of Peleus and Meleager, who, outdistanced through a
ruse in her race with Hippomenes, became his bride. The palm engraved on the tree-stump beside her seems in contradiction of such
defeat. This stump, however, is an addition of the copyist; and, while
from one point of view the palm may be reminiscent of the other victories of the heroine, it may also contain merely some arbitrary meaning attached to it by the copyist, who did not appreciate the true historical significance of the statue. The fact that girls' races were held at
Olympia and in other ancient cities on the occasion of the feast of Hera
has led some to suggest that this was the honorary statue of some winner. One detail, however, does not harmonize with the idea of a girl
competitor at Olympia: the short chiton worn in such races reached
almost to the knees, whereas this statue wears the very short chiton
which is peculiar to the divine and heroic figures (for example, Artemis and the Amazons), and which no mortal maid would ever have
worn in public. But this modification might be attributed to the artist,
who desired to represent in all their grace and vigor the agile limbs of

the winner. Evidently, however, the posture of the figure better corresponds to that of Atalante. Even granted that the arms should be closer to the body than as shown in the modern restoration (the left at least certainly should), their position is not such as to balance the body during a race, for which purpose they should be held lower and not so extended; their position seems rather to express surprise, and accords well with the poise of the head, which suggests attention concentrated on the ground. Again, the girl is caught by the artist in the act of running, not in the act of starting, because the little block underneath her right foot is an addition

Ulysses (Fig. 46)
(Hellenistic Period)

of the copyist, who only thus could give the figure stability in translating it from bronze to marble. In the original the right foot was free in the air, and the girl was represented at a moment of unstable equilibrium—that is, at a moment when, surprised by some object on the ground, she stops running. And this object which halts her may well have been the golden apples which the crafty Hippomenes employed to overcome her speed and win her hand. Such an explanation alone can account for the fixity with which the girl gazes upon the ground. Neither the motion of the arms nor the poise of the head would be justified under different circumstances. If, for example, she were concentrating for the start, the girl, instead of looking down, would have looked straight ahead; instead of extending her arms as in the figure, she would have drawn them nearer the body; instead of drawing back with one foot in the air, she would have bent forward at the knees.

We have stated that the figure offers an example of unstable equilibrium. Our thoughts thus turn immediately to the artist of movement, Myron, and particularly to one work of his which deals with a similar situation—Marsyas viewing on the ground the double flute cast away by Athena. There are certainly some Myronian traits in the face of the Girl Runner, especially in its general conformation and in the eyes. Some of the other elements, however, seem too archaic for Myron—for example, the hair and especially the folds of the chiton, which, confined by a pectoral sash under the partly uncovered breast, descends with folds so superficial and undulating that the figure must be regarded as archaic. On the other hand, it is true that the greater part of Myron's works were executed during the latest period of mature archaism (that is, between 480 and 460), to which period our statue belongs. But even if it is not by Myron, it must certainly be attributed to the Attic School in view of the elegance of its proportions and its

Ariadne (Fig. 47)
(Hellenistic Period)

delicate treatment of the nude—particularly of the lower limbs. It contains no trace of the Peloponnesian style, which, however, is suggested to us by the contest of Olympia and the Doric spirit of such a custom.

Even more uncertain is our interpretation of another singular statue in the Vatican Museum. This is the so-called Penelope (Fig. 5)—a poor copy of a celebrated original, of which other duplicates exist, not only in statuary but also in relief. It should properly be regarded as simply a torso, since a large part of the right leg, the left foot, and the right hand are restorations, while the youthful head which has been added to the statue, though ancient, does not belong to the figure. The attraction of this work thus consists altogether in its posture. In so far as its technique is concerned, this posture is simply the translation into statuary of a scheme conceived in relief, which allowed the sculptor to establish definite relations between his figure and the spectator. As for the significance of this posture, various hypotheses might be offered. The statue is the figure of a woman concentrated on grave thoughts or buried in grief; and as in the other duplicates the figure is seated, not on a rock, but on a sedile (chair) beneath which is a basket, the statue was immediately identified as the pensive Penelope seated before a loom at her interminable task of weaving the shroud for Laertes—her pretext for rejecting the advances of

Menelaus (Fig. 48)
(Hellenistic Period)

her importunate suitors. But the posture and the basket agree equally well with the figure of Demeter mourning the loss of her daughter Persephone, or with that of any mortal woman who, through this image placed on her grave, would convey to the passer-by her housewifely industry and her regretful longing for her earthly life.

But whether it be the figure of a heroine, a goddess, or a mortal, this statue certainly personifies the commemorative spirit of Greek art, and reveals on how few technical resources this art could rely at the end of the archaic period (470–450 B.C.) in its research into expression. Though given greater body, the folds of the chiton and the himation (mantle) are still artificial, as also are the curls which fall on the shoulders, and the position of the right leg, which is crossed over the left, is stiff and unnatural. But the figure, even unaided by the expression of the face, clearly reflects, in the bending of the head and of the trunk, in the position of the arms and the legs, the interior state of the soul. With equal sobriety of gesture the surprise and sudden halt of Atalante were expressed, and this sobriety, coupled with certain characteristics of style, helps us to recognize in this work also a product of Attic art.

In so far as the Vatican Museum is concerned, the archaic period closes with the sepulchral stele of the Young Gymnast and his Slave (Fig. 6). This is not a Roman copy, but a Greek original, belonging to the Attic School of the middle of the fifth century B.C. The study of expression which we have noticed in the two preceding works is here accentuated, and the clearness of the subject and the purpose of the stele distinctly reveal the intention of the sculptor—namely, to represent at his daily occupation a gymnast who has died in the flower of his youth. The gymnast looks at and salutes with his left hand the little slave who tenders to him the ariballus (oil flask) and the strigil (scraper) for use in the palæstra. What eloquence there is in the attitude of the two figures! The gymnast salutes, but his face is suffused with melancholy, and the slave stares wonderingly in return. This has indeed been one of their daily occupations, but now it is never to be repeated. Never again will the young slave tender to his beloved master the ariballus and the strigil, and he looks towards him as if death had already separated them. Yet, to express this silent grief, the sculptor has but very few technical means at his disposal. The gymnast inclines the head, while the little slave raises his towards his master. The wonder and sadness which we perceive in the two heads do not exist in the physical forms, but spring from the looks which the figures exchange. And, confronted with such expression, we forget the irregularities of the bodies, which are to be attributed partly to the technique of bas-relief; we forget the disproportionate size of the gymnast's head and arms, the unsuccessful foreshortening of the slave's thorax, and the eye, which is still almost in perspective in the faces of the figures.

THE CLASSICAL PERIOD OF GREEK ART.—The surprise and sudden halt of Atalante, the concentration and sorrow of Penelope, the melancholy and surprise of the Gymnast and his Slave—these archaic art has successfully rendered simply by a movement of the head, of the arms, or of the legs. It also displays increased ability in the rendering of the human body; it corrects the rigidity and the superficiality of the drapery; it modifies the posture both in statuary and in relief. Amid such developments the great artists of the fifth century were nurtured, since at least part of the activity of Myron, Phidias and Polycletus must be referred to the period of mature archaism. Uplifted on the wings of genius, these sculptors within a few decades raised Greek art to the pinnacle of perfection in the reproduction of movement, of divine dignity and of the undraped body of the athlete.

The Vatican Museum possesses a poor copy of the Discobolus of Myron (Fig. 7), the earliest of these three sculptors. The work indeed looks as if the copyist and the restorer had vied with each other in their endeavors to render the figure as little athletic and impressive as possible. The copyist has almost made the figure lean against an immense tree-trunk, and has smoothened the body so much that the bone and muscular reliefs have been greatly diminished. Besides adding the left

The Laocoon (Fig. 49)
(Agesander, Polydorus and Athenodorus, Hellenistic Period)

arm and right leg, the restorer not only has given the figure a modern head, but has applied this head so badly that it seems to drag down with it the rest of the body. In the bronze original the athlete's right arm was drawn back, and he was represented at the moment of pausing before bringing forward his arm to hurl the discus. To obtain a better swing, he had his right foot set firmly on the ground, bending his body over the right knee, and was ready to follow the swing and direct it by raising and advancing his left foot, the toes of which graze the ground. From the standpoint of athletics, much might be said concerning the naturalness of the athlete's posture; viewing the statue from the technical point of view, we may say that Myron is less of an innovator than at first appears, since he has only introduced into statuary a motive which, in a distorted form, was already found among the decorative designs of the relief. Nevertheless, this work of Myron must be characterized as a distinct stroke of audacity, for he aimed at destroying the stability of statuary, which is the stable art *par excellence*. When compared with the Atalante, the Discobolus shows what great progress in expressing movement Greek art made within a few decades.

As the Vatican does not possess any copies of works that can with certainty be attributed to Phidias, and as his greatness is here conveyed to the visitor rather through sculptures coming from his school, our references to this artist may be postponed while we speak of the works of Polycletus.

Archæological research has established beyond doubt that in our sculptural inheritance from antiquity we possess copies of three works of the great Argive master—the Doryphorus, the Diadumenus and the Amazon. Of these three the Vatican Museum has copies only of the first and last. In the Doryphorus (Fig. 8), Polycletus, the artist of the robust athletic nude, established practically the rule for those ideal bodily proportions which he had already determined theoretically in his writing called the "Canon." The traditional admiration felt for the Doryphorus was fully shared by Pliny and Quintilian; the former admires its "virile youthfulness" (*viriliter puerum*), and the latter sees in the statue a youth "equally fit for the battle-field and the gymnasium." But artistic criticism of antiquity, while attributing to Polycletus the innovation of making his sturdy figures stand on one foot, blamed him for making these figures square and uniform. The Doryphorus contains all the excellences and defects which are characteristic of the works of Polycletus. The copy in the Vatican is not one of the best, but, apart from certain insignificant elements, the restoration at least is confined to the right arm and the left forearm, and on the whole is well conceived. In contrast to the violent movement of the agile Discobolus, we see in the Doryphorus a powerful inert figure, which bends the left leg at the knee and draws it a little aside to relieve it of the weight of the body. To this slight movement of the lower limbs—which now appears for the first time in Greek art in the case of static figures, although we have already seen instances of it in moving figures—corresponds a similarly placid movement of the left arm, which bends at the elbow as it rests the javelin on the shoulder. Equal calm and firmness characterize the head, which is slightly inclined and faces towards the right. The effect of the movement is felt but superficially by the trunk; on the right side, which supports most

of the weight of
shoulder de-
loin ascends.
lateral solid
one of a pilaster.
mand of art vio-
which are partly
acrobatic poses,
significance in
unemotional fig-
of the Dory-
but his head is
his forehead no
passes, and to
calmness of his
on a closer ex-
this figure, the
will find what a
the study of the
Greek art has
work, whose fas-

Torso del Belvedere (Fig. 50)
(Apollonius [?], Hellenistic Period)

the body, the
scends and the
And this quadri-
body reminds
Those who de-
lent emotions,
the result of
will find little
this inert and
ure. The body
phorus is full,
empty. Behind
great thought
this is due the
movements. But
amination of
student of art
great advance in
human body
made in this
cination no per-

son of taste can escape. The Doryphorus is as restful to the eye as a reflection in still water. We feel that, in refining the light lines of the contour and the calm planes of the body, the artist wished to create the image of a conscious physical robustness which need have no recourse to violent movement to win appreciation. For this reason he has treated the head, not as the mirror of the internal condition of the soul, but simply as one of the parts of the body all of which must be equally calm and robust. And when we view the ample dimensions of the head, the firm outline of the face, the smooth forehead, the large and oval eyes, and the careful and regular arrangement of the hair, we must acknowledge the success with which his efforts have been crowned.

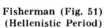

Fisherman (Fig. 51)
(Hellenistic Period)

Demosthenes (Fig. 52)
(Polyeuctus, Hellenistic Period)

After this inquiry we can well understand why the Doryphorus of Polycletus appeared to the settled Roman the ideal expression of the human body. This glorious figure may have been created by the artist for the sole purpose of serving as a model for athletes, as is suggested by his describing it as the "Canon" (or "Type"), and by his also general title of Doryphorus. It may be that Polycletus wished to honor herein an athlete who really lived, and to whom this statue was erected in some sacred enclosure; or finally, as some to-day believe, the figure may be the image of a god. In the eyes of the Romans, however, the Doryphorus was nothing else than a Greek anticipation of their own ideal soldier.

An anecdote told by Pliny in connection with four statues of Amazons at Ephesus, states that these statues were works of Polycletus, Phidias, Cresilas and Phradmon; that the artists made them in competition with one another; and that, when invited to pass judgment on the works, the three others unwittingly surrendered the palm to Polycletus, for, while all claimed first place for his own statue, the statue of the Argive sculptor was placed second by his three rivals. We possess in numerous Roman copies three types of Amazon belonging to the second half of the fifth century B.C.; two of these are entire, while the third is headless. It is our opinion that, even in ancient times, the copyists applied the head of one type to the body of another, because only

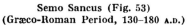

Semo Sancus (Fig. 53)
(Græco-Roman Period, 130–180 A.D.)

Juno Sospes Lanuvina (Fig. 54)
(Græco-Roman Period)

thus can we explain why we find numerous heads of one type, and of another only the body.

These three types have undeniable affinities both in posture and costume. Persons who hold a similar conception of originality in the case of both ancient and modern art, and regard as original only that which differs absolutely from what has preceded it, may find in the affinities between the three types of Amazon a reason for denying the authenticity of Pliny's anecdote and for holding that the three figures were made successively by the artists after the one was already acquainted with the work of the other. In fact, if we were not acquainted with the anecdote of Pliny, we might, in accordance with our modern canons of criticism, attribute after a superficial examination the three figures to a single artist who had repeatedly attempted the same problem. Originality in ancient art, however, consisted in the temperate variation of traditional types. No great artist was ashamed to take up a subject already treated by his predecessors, and to approach it from the same standpoint as they had done. Thus, while from one point of view the affinities between the three Amazons might suggest the possibility of the figures being the successive works of three artists, they do not necessarily contradict the story of the contest, since all the competitors may have followed a preëxisting traditional type. That such a traditional type was associated with the Temple of Artemis at Ephesus may be all the more readily admitted, since the myth tells us that there the vanquished and wounded Amazons found a refuge. And, when we turn to the examination of the different statues, we shall see that the originality which is wanting in the ensemble is visible in the details— so much so, indeed, that each of the three figures reveals an artistic individuality expressive of its bodily and mental attributes. Inasmuch as Pliny speaks of four Amazons, and duplicates of only three are extant, it is an obvious hypothesis that the missing one is that of Phradmon, the bronzist—the least known and least capable of the four artists.

Remembering that Polycletus was censured for making all his figures uniform, we can immediately determine which of the three extant types must be attributed to him (Fig. 9). We are here confronted by a full sister of the Doryphorus, both in the general conformation of the body and in the rhythm of the lower limbs. It is true that the left leg and the right, from the knee down, are restorations, but the restorer has here correctly divined the posture of the original. He has, however, been less fortunate in his restoration of the right arm, which should have been nearer the head, and of the left, which should have rested on a pillar. The young woman has been wounded near the right breast; and, although her light armless chiton does not touch the wound, with the instinctive movement characteristic of physical pain she raises her arm to her head, forgetting that this movement opens wider the edges of her wound. The figure is expressive, not alone of physical pain, but especially of mental dolor. The bent head, the large eyes with wandering looks, the parted lips, also give mute utterance to the suffering of the spirit. The indomitable virgin has been defeated—and defeated by a man! Ancient feminism has met with failure. But how calm and contained is this sorrow! This composure indeed well befits the strong virgin who, not even in defeat, deigns to be a woman and to appeal to our pity. In this supreme composure breathes the spirit of the Doryphorus.

How different, on the other hand, is the Amazon attributed to Cresilas (Fig. 10)! She resembles the Amazon of Polycletus in the position of the lower limbs (which, however, is here reversed), in the inclination of the head towards the right shoulder, in the raising of the right arm; but all these details are utilized to convey an impression less dignified. In the original the figure rested with her right hand on a spear, and, drawing aside the edge of her chiton, showed to the spectator the wound underneath her right breast. She knows that she is observed, and expects compassion, for, unless the language of forms deceives us, she seems to say: "See, how wounded I am!" Such sentiments, while suiting well a feeble mortal woman, characterize ill the woman warrior. The Amazon of Cresilas is undoubtedly more expressive of pain. With a higher delicacy of form, her head is also more ideally pathetic, and it has therefore been more frequently copied, even to the extent of being applied to the bodies of other types of Amazon. But, on the whole, the Amazon of Cresilas is less virile—that is, she is less an Amazon. Her body is more hampered by the long himation (cloak) which surrounds her neck and falls below her knees; and how rigid is her chiton with its rectilinear lower edge and parallel folds! When we

The Sacrifice of Mithra (Fig. 55)
(Græco-Roman Period)

compare these details with the Amazon of Polycletus, whose soft draperies offer so fine a contrast to the solid nude and terminate below in a harmonious undulating line, we appreciate well why even in antiquity the palm of victory was yielded to Polycletus.

A similar detailed comparison cannot be made in the case of the third Amazon (Fig. 11), which is referred by most critics to Phidias, since the head of this type is missing, and its original posture uncertain. In the Vatican copy the head is borrowed from the Cresilas type, and the restorer, in adding the arms and parts of the legs, has represented her in the act of taking her bow from her shoulder and surrendering her-

Isiac Procession (Fig. 56)
(Græco-Roman Period)

self defeated to her adversaries. Such a restoration, however, is arbitrary, and no less doubtful seems to be that which makes the Amazon lean with her two hands on her spear as she prepares to spring on horseback. It is far more probable that this figure too was wounded and resting; that she sustained her body by leaning with her two hands on her spear, while dragging her left foot lamely behind. In view of this uncertainty, our examination must be limited to the torso. Here we must certainly admire proportions of greater elegance than is shown in the two other figures; this elegance is especially conspicuous in the drapery, which, though masking excessively the bodily forms, falls in the finest and most vivacious folds, and approaches nearest to the style of the Parthenon. Nevertheless, even without knowing the head we may safely declare that this is the least successful of the three Amazons in attitude and expression. She is less womanly than the Amazon of Cresilas, and less virile than that of Polycletus.

Cresilas has been a lucky artist, for, while according to literary tradition his works were few, numerous duplicates of these few works have been preserved. The Vatican Museum possesses a copy of his portrait of Pericles (Fig. 12). The great Athenian is represented as a strategus (general)—that office which allowed him to leave the impress of his genius on a famous epoch of history. Through the eyes of the high comitial helmet we can see the peculiar elongated skull which an ancient comedist called "squill-shaped." Certainly the artist has not flattered Pericles, either in this matter or in the features of his face—

particularly in the short and curly beard.   But, if Pericles is not handsome, he is ideal.   Behind this thoughtful brow and behind those eyes
to which the accentuated upper eyelids lend a strange shadow, we feel
that deep preoccupations lurk.   This is not the empty face of the Doryphorus!   Cresilas has given us above all the grave image of the states-
man, and it is not without a certain historic emotion and a sense of
gratitude to figurative art, which preserves through the centuries what

Procession of Sacrificers to Artemis (Fig. 57)
(Painting, Græco-Roman Period)

otherwise would have been lost for ever, that we see reëmerging from
the shadows of antiquity the goodness, the dignity and the nobility of
Pericles, which are mirrored in his own words in the panegyric of
Athens recorded by Thucydides.

Myron has taught us audacity of movement; Polycletus, the robustness of the body; Cresilas, the strength and power of the portrait; but
Phidias alone was able to render the dignity of the gods.   From the
Phidiac School have come four statues, representing different figures,
but similar in their composure and drapery; and all four embody the
divine ideal.   One is the Demeter of the Rotonda; the second is the
Artemis of the Gallery of the Candelabra; the third is the Caryatid of
the Braccio Nuovo; the fourth is the gigantic statue of Athena.

Of all the glorious works which we inherit from ancient art, none
gives such a perfect expression of matronal dignity as the Demeter
(Fig. 13).   This figure might be also identified as Hera, for the two
arms are restorations, and consequently the ears of corn in the right

hand (the symbol of Demeter) are
a modern addition. The goddess
is dressed in a heavy peplum; this
gown falls in deep and parallel
folds along the right leg, on which
rests the weight of the body, but
moulds the left leg, which is free
and bent at the knee. The figure
thus has the stability of a Doric
column, and this impression is
accentuated by the proud carriage
of the head, which looks straight
before it without any benevolent
inclination towards mortals. Since
the goddess may not reveal to
humanity her physical beauty, the
peplum conceals her ample breast.
But the naked arms, emerging
from the coronet of folds at her
shoulders, bear witness to her di-

Charioteer (Fig. 58)
(Græco-Roman Period)

vine charms, and remind one of the epithet "splendid-armed," which
Homer applies to Hera. But the beauty of the goddess lies above all in
her majestic face, with its firm and yet delicate planes, its serene eyes,
and its pure brow under the harmonious arch of the hair. Reverence is
the sentiment inspired by such a figure, and, while Greece will later make
her gods more human, never again will she make them so divine. In his
Rhamnusian Nemesis Agoracritus, a pupil of Phidias, must have represented in similar manner the austere firmness of the goddess of fatality.

And yet the same elements, with little variation, serve to give character to a figure entirely different, the Artemis (Fig. 14). It is not possible for us to seek guidance from the head in determining the type,
since it, while emanating from the Phidiac School, seems to belong to
some other figure. We feel, however, that this peplum which falls in
folds along the firm right leg and suggests a channelled column, covers
the youthful body of the Virgin Huntress rather than the matronal
body of a Demeter or a Hera. In this statue the folds are more sober,
particularly at the sides; the belt is here rectilinear, while in the Demeter its arch reveals the fullness of the hips, and the longer apoptygma
of the peplum gives more litheness to the figure. The arms in this figure are a restoration: in the original they extended along the sides, and
must thus have increased still further the litheness of the body.

A comparison of these figures with the third statue of the Phidiac

School, the Caryatid (Fig. 15), shows how great is the significance of the drapery in Greek art. To give more stability to the figure, which had to fill an architectural function (that is, to support an entablature), the artist has not completely relieved the left leg of the weight of the body, for, though bent at the knee, it still rests firmly on the ground. Desirous of lending as nearly as possible to the body that same strength and elasticity which was conveyed to the column by the entasis (or convex curve below the middle), the artist has given the Caryatid great development at the hips, and has created the illusion of still greater development by the numerous folds of

Pasiphaë (Fig. 59)
(Painting, Græco-Roman Period)

the peplum below the apoptygma of the colpos—that is, the fold made by pulling the chiton over the belt. In fact, while the breast is draped and almost flat in front, channelled folds descend along the sides to join the folds of the colpos, and the curved line of the colpos accentuates the ampleness of the hips. This general effect is crowned by the arms, which from the elbows down have been (like the head) reproduced in accordance with the original Caryatid from the Erechtheum. For, while the arms cling to the body, and thus make the breast appear narrow, they increase the roundness of the hips. Draping and posture thus contribute alike to give the impression of architectural stability.

To the Phidiac School finally belongs a statue of Athena (Fig. 16), the many duplicates of which prove that the original was a celebrated one. To this statue, as to the Demeter, the artist has communicated the divine bearing—not, however, that of the dignified matron, but that of the austere virgin. Clad in a light chiton with delicate folds, over which is thrown an ample himation, the goddess shows nothing of her body except the forearm, and even her face recedes into her high Corinthian helmet. But in this overshadowed and almost sad face, which seems to occupy so small a part of such a towering figure, the expression is dominating. Here is really the goddess of wisdom and of war, concentrated on her own thoughts.

That a new spirit animates all Greek art at this period is shown also by an athletic figure of a Discobolus, who, before taking the swing, scrutinizes the ground (Fig. 17). The most admirable characteristic of this figure is not the delicate nude, free as it is from the emptiness of Myron; nor is it the rhythm of the posture, at once so elegant and so free. It is the concentration with which the athlete makes his examina-

The Nozze Aldobrandini (Fig. 60)
(Painting, Græco-Roman Period)

tion—a concentration which is exaggerated if you will, but which ennobles and almost intellectualizes the action which the Discobolus is about to perform. The figure seems to warn us that, to win in the contest, it is not sufficient to possess a trained body; we must also have a trained mind. In this we recognize the influence of the art of Phidias.

That the spirit of Phidias dominated Greek art throughout the second half of the fifth century may be seen also in a fragment of a Bœotian funeral relief—an original showing the figure of a Horseman (Fig. 18). Noble and dignified, this bearded man evidently wished that, in the image which he bequeathed to posterity, he should be represented at his favorite diversion. But not less noble and ideal is this horse, with its ample neck, its intelligent eyes, and its spirited head, which tosses proudly at the touch of its master. In both figures we have an echo of the Cavalcade of the Parthenon.

GREEK ART DURING THE FOURTH CENTURY.—Nobility in the figures of the gods and dignity in the figures of men—such are the qualities which characterize the great artists of the fifth century. But in time these gods in their nobility grew remote from men, and the men in their dignity grew remote from reality. The art of the fourth century therefore endeavored, in the works of its chief masters, to make the gods more human and men more real, and this spirit proved especially productive of figures of deities.

Even the Barberini Hera (Fig. 19), which belongs to the first part of the fourth century, bears no affinity to the austere matron whom we

Detail from the Nozze Aldobrandini (Fig. 61)

have seen in the Demeter of the Rotonda; she is the benevolent goddess who bends towards mortals. Instead of being buried in a heavy peplum, her upper body is scarcely veiled by a fine chiton, the himation being added only from her waist downwards. Under the chiton may be seen the breast, a portion of which is uncovered. Here too the suggestion is human, and not divine. And human grace also is to be found in the delicate oval of her countenance, and in the eyes fixed on her worshippers. Not reverence but confidence is the feeling which the goddess inspires.

But with the Barberini Hera we are only half way, for she is still a goddess. It remained for Praxiteles to make gods who were truly human and shared their characteristics with mortal men. The Vatican possesses a copy of his Aphrodite (Venus) of Cnidus and of his Apollo Sauroctonus.

In the Aphrodite (Fig. 20), not only has the restorer been mistaken in the position of the right forearm, which he places too low, and in the left arm, which he raises too high; not only has he given a wrong position to the head, which belongs to another copy, and should in this figure have been raised somewhat more and face more towards the left shoulder: but he has encased the lower portion of the figure with a

Detail from the Nozze Aldobrandini (Fig. 62)

heavy mantle of tin, varnished to resemble marble, and has thus completely altered the original aspect of the figure. Praxiteles had represented the goddess at the moment when she was about to enter her bath, and when she was laying aside her last garment on the water vase near her. No profane look was supposed to fall upon the goddess, but yet her natural modesty and bashfulness impel her to conceal her naked body. No fear of profane looks, however, is to be seen in the delicate head, which seems to look into the distance, and which reveals, in the humid eyes and half-open lips, the slight tremor of a yearning that transcends mortality. In the work of Praxiteles, Aphrodite is a woman, but she is still a modest one; and, if she lacks divine dignity, she has still divine charm.

Another graceful image is that of the Apollo Sauroctonus (Fig. 21). The god is here represented as a gentle youth with almost feminine forms, and effeminate also is the coiffure which ends in a knot behind and is held by a large band. With beautiful curves, which make the unmasculine development of his hips conspicuous, he rests his left arm against a tree-trunk, and awaits the moment when he can transfix the lizard with his arrow. Such an occupation certainly accords ill with the dignity of a god, but is rather a prank of naughty children. And,

Detail from the Nozze Aldobrandini (Fig. 63)

even though at the root of this conception of Apollo there was originally a religious significance, the spectator no longer recognizes in this
figure either the god of the bow or the god of the lyre.

The spirit of the Praxitelic School is also seen in the Torso (Fig. 22),
which some seek to identify as one of the Erotes created by Praxiteles.
Very few statues have the delicacy of this nude figure, and still fewer
have the fascination of this beautiful head. The boy's forehead and
neck are hidden under a wave of juvenile curls, and he seems as preoccupied and melancholy as if he knew what great disturbance his
work of inspiring love has wrought in the heart of man. Perhaps, indeed, he has fallen a victim to his own art!

With still less certainty may we refer the so-called Antinous del Belvedere (Fig. 23) to the Praxitelic School. This is a replica of a statue
of Hermes which the copyist, by adding the palm-trunk, has changed
to a Hermes Agonisticus, and which the restorer has somewhat disfig-
ured by reattaching badly the legs, which were broken when found. It
is most probable, however, that the original was an image of Hermes
Psychopompus—that is, of the god who conducted the souls of the dead
to Hades. How beautiful is this firm but delicate body, in which the
trunk makes a sideward movement with such soft grace! But even

more beautiful is the shadow which suffuses the face, and which is emphasized by the voluminous mass of curls on the forehead, by the deep furrows beneath the eyebrows and by the firm planes of the jaws and chin. The god is fulfilling his office, but he fulfils it with compassionate humanity; he shares in the sorrow of the souls who relinquish life with yearning and regret. If the nude body and the rhythm of the lower limbs seem more reminiscent of the School of Lysippus, the face and above all the forehead remind us of the Hermes of Praxiteles at Olympia.

Even outside the Praxitelic circle, the fourth century created a

Head of Athena (Fig. 64)
(Mosaic, Græco-Roman Period)

plethora of juvenile and human gods. We have Apollo as the god of the bow in the statue of the Belvedere (Fig. 24). This also is a copy, but an excellent one. The restorations are few, and are limited for the most part to the left hand and the right forearm. The god certainly grasped a bow in his left hand, and in his right hand held a branch of laurel bound with ribbons, as traces on the tree-trunk show. The deity is represented in the two aspects of his divinity—as a numen who chastises and a numen who purifies. He wreaks vengeance on men when they do wrong, but relieves them of their guilt when they approach him humble and repentant. This is the god who in the first book of the Iliad chastises the Achæans for their outrage at Chryse, but later benevolently accepts their expiatory hecatomb. In the posture of the statue the artist has succeeded admirably in rendering these two aspects of the numen. Rising almost on the point of his toes, Apollo advances with great strides, so that the litheness of his body is still further emphasized. But his enemies are not in front: before him are his faithful worshippers, to whom he brings the lustral branch. His enemies are on the left, and towards them he turns his head, menacing them with his bow. And if the delicate oval of his face and the broad forehead suggest that the god is good, his stern and frowning eyes, his slightly dilated nostrils, and his half parted lips indicate that he can also feel ire—and terrible ire. We cannot identify with certainty the artist who could thus, in the language of forms, give expression to, not one, but two states of the soul. Some have suggested Leochares, an Athenian artist of the second half of the fourth century, of one of whose authentic works the Vatican possesses a copy.

Not with the stride of an avenger, but to the rhythm of musical sounds, does Apollo advance in another statue in the Vatican Museum (Fig. 25). The quiver has been exchanged for the lyre, which also is

Sarcophagus showing the Slaughter of the Niobids (Fig. 65)
(Græco-Roman Period)

supported by the balteus. His body sways under his long flowing chiton, and is buried in his large mantle as in the shadow of a niche. His head is bound with the crown of laurel, but at this moment his thoughts are not directed towards the purification of men, but are enraptured by his music. His face looks upwards, and in the oval eyes and small mouth we feel the sweetness of the music which soothes the heart of man. How long a road we have traversed in less than two centuries from the archaic Seated Apollo! This figure of the Apollo Citharædus bears clear evidence of the influence of Praxiteles.

Together with this Apollo were found several statues of Muses who encircled him. Among these were the images of Melpomene, the Muse

of Tragedy (Fig. 26), and Thalia,
the Muse of Comedy (Fig. 27).
Though the artist has not been so
happy in these two figures as in
the Apollo, they bear evidence of
his power of precise characteriza-
tion. Some of the attributes of the
figures are of course restorations,
but they seem to have been correctly divined, and correspond
with those in other ancient statues.
In the Melpomene the left forearm with the sword, and in the
Thalia part of the left forearm
with the tympan, are restorations.
Ancient, on the other hand, are,
except for some elements, the
tragic mask of Hercules and, in
Thalia, the comic mask of the servant and the pedum (crook).

Augustus (Fig. 66)
(Græco-Roman Period)

These attributes in themselves distinguish between the literary genres
over which the Muses preside. The mask of Hercules hints at the abundant material with which the adventures of this hero had furnished
Tragedy; the servant's mask and the pedum indicate the great part
which domestic and rural life played especially in the New Comedy.
Melpomene's crown of vine and Thalia's crown of ivy both refer to the
Dionysiac origin of dramatic literature. But, entirely apart from their
attributes, the two figures express in their bodily forms different sentiments. The posture of Tragedy, who rests her left foot on a high block,
suggests her agitation; Comedy sits calmly on a rock. Tragedy's dress
is simple and heavy with deep folds; Comedy wears a fine chiton, while
a rich mantle is wrapped around her lower limbs. In Tragedy the hair
falls loose to the shoulders and descends over the brow, reminding one
of the oncus which lent majesty to the tragic mask; Comedy's hair is
soft and elaborately dressed. The face of the former is energetic and
serious; on that of the latter there is a wondering look, not untinged
with melancholy.

Full sister to the Apollo, even in her posture, is the statue of Artemis
(Fig. 28). Critical examination of this figure must be limited to the
body, since the head, though ancient, belongs to another figure, and the
two arms which make the statue an Artemis Lucifera (Selene, or the
Moon) are restorations. The quiver behind the right shoulder shows,

however, that in this statue the goddess was represented as a huntress, and held the bow in her left hand, perhaps as she approached her quarry. As the goddess advances, the robustness and beauty of her youthful body, which reminds us of the Apollo del Belvedere, show through the draperies which mould her limbs. Even the austere Virgin Huntress has been made a mortal woman by the sensual age of Praxiteles, which has sacrificed divine dignity for bodily grace.

Caius, Nephew of Augustus (Fig. 67)
(Græco-Roman Period)

Even in the statues of the supreme gods, with whom art was less inclined to tamper in deference to the great strength of religious tradi-tion, is reflected this spirit of dominant hu-manity. Far dif-ferent from the Zeus of Otricoli (Fig. 29) must have been the Zeus of Phidias at Olympia. Ac-cording to an-cient writers, the latter was solemn, digni-fied and calm; but in the agi-tated forehead of the Zeus of Otricoli, which appears to be lashed by the stormy waves of his hair, and in the deep and kindly eyes, which seem so small under the great arched eye-brows, we read not serenity and calm, but care and disturbance. Rather than the father of the gods, he is the father of men—and of men filled with anxious agitation.

While, in comparison with the numerous statues of gods, the fourth century created few figures of heroes or mortals, all of these figures show the general tendency of the period to aim at the expression of spiritual rather than purely physical attributes. That we cannot trace such an expression in the Meleager (Fig. 30) is due to the copyist. The original is attributed to Scopas, one of the great artists of the fourth century. But not only is it probable that the copyist has added the dog, the head of the boar and the chlamys; not only is the excessive smooth-ness of the body to be credited to him: but he has furthermore failed to retain in his copy that characteristic pathos which we see in other replicas, particularly in a head in the Villa Medici. Why did the artist choose this hero for a subject? Perhaps to represent a beautiful youthful body, or perhaps to celebrate an adventurous victory like that over the Calydonian boar; but he also wished to show that not even the heroes are happy—not even they can escape adverse destiny. In the profound and melancholy look of Meleager is expressed the presentiment of his approaching end, of which his own mother is to be the voluntary instrument.

Art now begins to seek in the myths for figures which, besides the struggles of the body, will indicate also the struggles of the soul. Niobe, receiving in her bosom all the arrows which Apollo and Artemis hurled against her fleeing children, was taken as the most expressive symbol of mother's love. A headless statue of a Niobid (Fig. 31) belongs to a group of this kind, of which we can now gather only one of the characteristics—that of movement. But, though perforce judged apart from the group, what an eagerness there is in this draped figure to escape the inexorable vengeance of the gods! What a longing for the safety of a mother's arms do we witness in the violence of the movement whereby the girl tries to evade death by rushing to her who gave her life! If, in the Demeter of the Rotonda, the fifth century gave an insurpassable embodiment of calm dignity in the folds of a peplum, the fourth century has with no less majesty expressed hurried flight in the flowing folds of a chiton and himation.

Not a horizontal motion but an ascending one has been attempted in the group of Ganymede Carried up by the Eagle (Fig. 32). Although, from archaistic times, Greek art had grappled with the problem of flight, in all previous attempts the figures (for example, of Iris or Nike) were represented as passing before the spectator or descending towards him. Ganymede, however, ascends to Olympus; and if the problem was too difficult for statuary, which is the art of stability, the sculptor has at least succeeded in conveying his intention pretty clearly. The eagle, as if conscious of its precious booty, holds Ganymede's body tenderly behind the shoulders, grasping with its claws, not the nude flesh, but the chlamys. A minute ago Ganymede, lying with his dog under a tree, was amusing himself by playing on the syringa (Pan's pipes), but now he is being borne aloft towards the sun. The heads of the dog and the eagle, which, like Ganymede, look upwards, are correctly restored. And in these three bodies of varying heights, which are placed near one another like the reeds of the syringa, the artist has well expressed the fundamental idea of the scene and the ascending flight. The eagle looks toward Olympus; Ganymede towards his captor; the dog towards its master.

The Vatican Museum, which has so many fourth-century figures of gods and heroes, has only one athletic figure. Such a lack of propor-

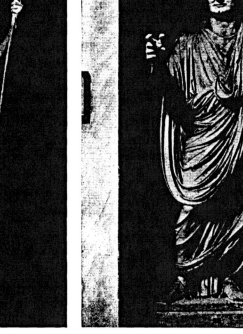

Claudius (Fig. 68)
(Græco-Roman Period)

Titus (Fig. 69)
(Græco-Roman Period)

tion cannot be due to chance. The fifth century was a period of glory for the Hellenic games. In the fourth century, however, just as literature had no longer a Pindar and a Bacchylides to celebrate the winning heroes, sculpture likewise, grown more inquisitive about the soul than the body, pays rarer visits to the palæstra. But the Argolic tradition which had developed around the name of Polycletus was not extinguished; for from the School of Sicyon came Lysippus, the greatest bronzist of the fourth century. Of his Apoxyomenus (or athlete scraping the sand and oil from his body) the Vatican possesses an excellent and almost intact copy (Fig. 33). A moment's comparison of this figure with the Doryphorus of Polycletus shows the new method adopted by art in treating the body of the athlete. Lithe forms, elastic movement, and small head—such was the canon or standard which Lysippus substituted for the robust and heavy type of Polycletus. But what is still more striking in this figure is the thoughtful and almost nervous expression of the face. How can we explain so much emotion in so banal an action as that of scraping one's body? The concentrated attention of the Discobolus as he examined the ground (Fig. 17) could be appreciated in view of the action which was to follow, but the vague stare of the Apoxyomenus can be explained only as a "manner" of an age which, even to the athlete, was unable to give the empty brains assigned by Polycletus to his Doryphorus.

The Hellenistic Period of Greek Art.—The fourth century had produced an abundance of figures of gods, and these had already become too human. Hellenism finished the work, and the gods, after losing their nobility, are deprived of their divine gracefulness. We recognize no longer a goddess, but a mortal in the Crouching Aphrodite (Fig. 34), the original of which was perhaps the work of the Bithynian artist Dædalus. Far from being disturbed by a sense of modesty, she boldly takes her bath. Having composed her body so as to show a harmonious outline, she places her back under the jet of cold water. In the presence of the Aphrodite of Praxiteles the spectator feels a certain embarrassment at having indiscreetly surprised the modest goddess; the goddess of Dædalus, on the other hand, seems to invite attention. This statue touches no spiritual chord; its appeal is simply sensual. Divine reverence has been exiled from Greek art.

And if this epoch can still point to the Jupiter Serapis (Fig. 35), by the Carian artist Bryaxis, as the image of a numen which still retains a solemn dignity, we must not forget that this work was created under the inspiration of another religion—the Egyptian—which possessed a greater richness of faith. The Serapis, in fact, was intended to embody at once the Greek Hades and the Egyptian Osiris. And while to the Greek conception is due the benevolence of the face, the impress of the Oriental conception must be recognized in its occultness, which is lent by the confused masses of the hair, and in its fanaticism, which seems indicated by the upturned eyes.

Unable to create gods any longer, Greek art, as it came in touch with the new countries which welcomed Greek civilization, creates personifications of nature. In these images the divine sense takes refuge as in a final retreat. Thus a pupil of Lysippus, named Eutychides, cast in bronze an image of the city of Antiochia on the Orontes (Fig. 36). The Tyche, amply wrapped in her mantle, sits on the rocky Silpios, and at her feet the river Orontes, represented as a youth, emerges with the gesture of a swimmer. The city thus dominates as a queen the river which rendered her plains so fertile. The head of the goddess is ancient but not the original one, while the right forearm with the ears of corn and the arms of the Orontes are modern. But even if we leave these details out of consideration, we can appreciate well the naturalistic value of this group in which city, mount and river are united in a harmonious ensemble.

Not swimming with the powerful strokes of a youth, but as a venerable man reclining comfortably on his ample couch, is represented the figure of the Nile (Fig. 37). Reliefs running around the plinth show the flora and fauna of the river's banks. Leaning on the Sphinx, which

Julia[?] (Fig. 70)
(Græco-Roman Period)

Hadrian (Fig. 71)
(Græco-Roman Period)

Faustina the Elder (Fig. 72)
(Græco-Roman Period)

Venus Empress (Fig. 73)
(Græco-Roman Period)

The Antinous Braschi (Fig. 74)
(Græco-Roman Period)

Head of Dacus (Fig. 75)
(Græco-Roman Period)

symbolizes Egypt, the river-god holds in his left hand the cornucopia
(or horn of abundance), and in his right the ears of corn—the symbol
of the fertility which his inundations bring. Sixteen little boys (mostly
restorations) personify the cubits which the level of the waters rises,
and their grouping around the gigantic body of the god, from those
who play with the crocodile near his right foot to those who have victoriously clambered to the top of his shoulder and of the cornucopia,
suggests the gradual rising of the flood. Never before in Greek art were
infantile and adult bodies united with such grace and humor, and
we easily recognize in this work the Greek spirit which was trans-
planted to Egypt in the Alexandrian epoch.

But if the period of Hellenism was poor in gods and endeavored to
express the divine idea in personifications of nature, it was the age *par
excellence* of those semi-divine, semi-human beings who formed the
cortège of Poseidon and Dionysus; it was the epoch of the Tritons and
the Nymphs, of the Centaurs, Satyrs and Mænads. These figures became as abundant as the gods were in the fourth century, and in them
were personified every human passion and sentiment.

Bearing in his arms a gentle nymph, the Marine Centaur (Fig. 38)
dashes boldly over the waves. Though the left arm, with the marine
trumpet, is a restoration, we believe that it is in correspondence with
the original. The Centaur drowns with his victorious blasts the pro-

tests of the nymph, to which one Cupid lends an ear, while another imposes silence.

Not buoyant triumph but the infinite melancholy conveyed by the immense plane of the sea is reflected in the eyes of this other being, of whom only the human part remains, and who may therefore have been either a Centaur or a Triton (Fig. 39). The companions of Poseidon are not joyous like the companions of Dionysus, and it seems as if a deep sigh escapes from the lips of the Triton—like the sigh of a wave. The grandiose character of the forms proclaims this work a product of the School of Pergamos rather than a replica of a figure by Scopas, who was the first to portray the train of Poseidon and of Amphitryon.

Similarly unjoyous is the terrestrial Centaur crowned with vine-leaves (Fig. 40). He too looks sighingly upwards, and from some extant intact replicas we know the cause of his sorrows: he is the victim of a little Cupid who has perched on his back and guides him at will.

Greater composure is found in the companions of Dionysus, who are susceptible of more soothing affections and healthier joys. An image of fatherly tenderness is seen in the Silenus holding the Infant Dionysus in his arms (Fig. 41). With what affection Silenus gazes at the young god, and how delicately his rough hands rest on the tender body of the child! In the gracefulness of the group, in the rhythm of the posture, and in the fullness of the nude is still reflected the Praxitelic School.

Gay brotherly camaraderie characterizes the group of the Young Satyr carrying Dionysus astride of his shoulders (Fig. 42). The many restorations have certainly misrepresented the original. Besides elements of minor importance, the arms and legs of the Satyr are restorations, and so are the head and a large part of the arms and legs of the child. We cannot be much astray in thinking that the little Dionysus had a whip in his hand, and urged onward tyrannically his improvised steed. The lithe forms and the agility of the movement bespeak the School of Lysippus.

Finally we find an expression of purely animal joy in the Faun in rosso antico (Fig. 43). He has replenished his hide with rural fruits, and gazes rapturously at a bunch of grapes—his master's gift for the recreation of the mind! Though his right hand with the grapes is a restoration, its correctness is attested by extant similar figures. The red marble (*rosso antico*), which was perhaps meant to reproduce the earthy color of the skin; the animal elements, which are accentuated in the face and the neck; the coarse laugh, which causes the numerous wrinkles about the mouth—all of these make the figure a significant personification of primitive rural life.

Sepulchral Tablet of Lucius Vibius and His Wife and Son (Fig. 76)
(Græco-Roman Period)

Just as in the group of the Marine Centaur the delicate body of the
nymph was retained in contrast to the coarse form of her captor, the
Mænads were (unlike the Satyrs) never represented as coarse or
brutish by Greek art.   On the contrary, Hellenism accentuated their
feminine elements, and thus offers a sharp contrast to the archaic art
on the vases.   The Mænad (Fig. 44) is an image of delicate grace.   The
beautiful forms of her body are visible through the light chiton, the
graceful curves of her mantle remind one of the sails of a ship, and the
light rhythm of her step seems that of a dance.   We cannot extend our
examination to the head, which, though ancient and that of a Mænad,
does not belong to the body.

Its preference for subjects of the emotional strength which it strove
to lend to the marine and Dionysiac beings, led Hellenism also to the
investigation of the myths.   From the fourth century we witness a return to the myth of the Niobids, and to such a group, more recent than
that already referred to (cf. Fig. 31), belongs the figure of a young fugitive Niobid (Fig. 45).   This cycle of statues, the most complete copy of
which is to be seen in the Uffizi Gallery at Florence, was artistically

conceived as radiating from the central figure of Niobe. In the Vatican statue is preserved the youngest of the children, who, as he hurries with long strides towards his mother, looks upwards in horror at the vindictive gods.

With the statue of Ulysses (Fig. 46) was originally grouped the figure of Polyphemus. The foxy hero tenders to the Cyclops the wine which is to win him liberty; but in the original his gesture was different from, and the wine bowl larger than, that shown in the modern restorations. The attitude of the figure admirably suggests the hero's cautious advance and his readiness to withdraw hurriedly if he should detect any sinister intention in the movements of the giant shepherd. Art has here given eloquent expression to a dubious state of soul.

Buried in sleep and panting with her emotion, Ariadne (Fig. 47) dreams of the desertion of Theseus and the arrival of Dionysus. Thus, though the statue is an isolated one, we reconstruct it mentally as a group, and witness the departure of the hero with his companions and the approach of the god with his train. This pregnant conception, which is so characteristic of Greek art, has been somewhat inadequately treated in the composition: too matronal are the bodily forms of the young woman, and too irregular her face. The drapery, however, with its sumptuous richness of folds, gives to the work a distinguished beauty which not even the carelessness and lack of appreciation of the copyist could destroy.

Tension of body and mind is seen in the head of Menelaus (Fig. 48), a work which was once part of a group representing an episode of the Trojan War, and of which numerous duplicates are extant. Menelaus has grasped the body of Patroclus, and, though hard pressed by the enemy, endeavors to drag it out of the mêlée. The divine dignity which Hellenism can no longer give to her gods, she has given finally to one of her heroes, but from this open mouth also escapes a human outcry of rage.

Hellenism reached the apex of expression in the Laocoon (Fig. 49). The work is an original by Agesander and his two sons, Polydorus and Athenodorus, artists of Rhodes who lived in the first century B.C. The right hand of the elder and the right arm of the younger son of Laocoon are restorations. But especially mistaken is the restoration of the right arm of Laocoon, which, instead of stretching away from the body, should have been bent over the head; the group, which has now an unstable appearance on the left side, would then acquire again its pyramidal aspect. Twin serpents have enmeshed in their coils the Trojan priest and his sons, and proceed to accomplish the divine vengeance for Laocoon's act of desecration. This is the terrible and blind vengeance of a god who chastises even the innocent sons for the fault of their father. The group is expressive of a paternal anguish with which the maternal grief of Niobe alone can compare. The two serpents have hurled the father and the younger son violently against the altar on which they were sacrificing, and hold firmly near it the elder son. Already strangled by the huge coils and bitten in the breast, the younger boy breathes his last as he turns his glassy eyes upwards seeking his father. The elder son, less involved in the coils, makes a mechanical effort to loosen the coil which surrounds his left foot, but it seems as if almost his sole concern is for the suffering of his father. Laocoon, bitten in the side, strives to push away the serpent's head, and in the tension of the movement draws in his breath, while a convulsive shudder passes through his body. Conquered in a moment, his dread outcry will "rise to the stars." In his thrown back head, as at the apex of a triangle, culminates the huge wave of dolor which rises from his sons and his own tortured body. The spasmodic contraction of the muscles makes of the face the vital target of the divine vengeance. Marvellous unity of composition, profound anatomic knowledge, and an incomparable fusion of physical and mental dolor make the Laocoon the most emotional and most human creation of ancient art.

Compared with the Laocoon, the Torso del Belvedere (Fig. 50) is an image of calm. Though it is undoubtedly the work of some master's chisel, the history of the work is enveloped in the greatest uncertainty. It is doubtful whether the artist Apollonius, son of an Athenian named Nestor, is the original creator of this work which bears his signature, or a mere copyist. We cannot say to what exact period of Hellenism it belongs; how the movements of the head, arms and legs should be reconstructed; or whom it represents—Polyphemus or Prometheus, Mars or Hercules. But, neglecting the aureole of mystery which surrounds it, we must admire the figure above all as an image of powerful youth. Only a sculptor who was at once a profound student of anatomy and an artist of sublime conception could create so calm and so well linked a composition of muscles and bones.

From what we have already said it will be recognized that, even in the Hellenistic period, the nude always remained the central problem of Greek art, and was still conceived ideally. In the fifth century, when strength and firmness were adopted as the ideal of the nude, and art aimed at the expression of these bodily qualities rather than of the qualities of the soul, the head was also characteristic of strength and firmness rather than expressive of mental qualities. In the fourth century, on the other hand, the ideal of the nude was grace and delicacy, and in harmony with this conception are the gentleness and benevo-

Bas-relief from the Ara Pacis Augustæ (Fig. 77)
(Græco-Roman Period)

lence of the face. During the Hellenistic period, however, since the
ideal of the nude was energy or relaxation as an effect of a physical or
psychological condition, the body became subservient to the head, in
which was concentrated all the expression of the soul. Consequently it
was not a pathological preference for ugliness, but a passionate search
for a more eloquent language of forms which spurred Greek sculpture
to abandon the palæstra—the hothouse of beautiful but odorless flowers—and to seek in the streets of the Hellenistic cities for individuals
on whose bodies ethnic origin or the practice of certain trades had imprinted a condition of the soul.

Thus, if Hellenism derived pleasure from the creation of the figure
of the Fisherman (Fig. 51), it was attracted, not by his trade, but by this
body, which, seasoned and warped, is a commentary on the brutishness
of the face. In the Laocoon every muscle has been rendered taut by
the internal shudder which the desire for liberation sends through the
limbs; in the Fisherman, every muscle is relaxed as the result of the
atony and colorlessness of his wretched life. This is evidently the body
of an old man—but of an old man in whom none of his spiritual energy
survives, as is shown especially by his glassy eye and trembling mouth.

Even in portraiture the body is now treated as the mirror of the soul.

We parted with Greek portraiture in the fifth century when it was engaged with the nobility and dignity of Pericles; we meet it once more in the Hellenistic period, engaged with the melancholy brooding of Demosthenes (Fig. 52). Polyeuctus, an artist of the third century, created the original of this statue, which was erected a little later than forty years after the orator's death. Owing to the mistaken restoration of the forearms with the rotula, this copy represents Demosthenes as a thoughtful reader; his attitude in the original, wherein his hands were linked, represented him as the devoted son of Athens, mourning for the lost liberty of his city. At first sight, all the expression seems concentrated in the lean and deeply furrowed face and in the small fixed eyes; but expressive also are the lean breast, the thin arms, the crossed fingers and the carelessness with which the himation is flung around the body. The hatred of Demosthenes for Philip of Macedon is an affection of the mind, and thus does not directly concern the body and dress. The body and dress are therefore used to reflect his sorrow.

THE GRÆCO-ROMAN OR IMPERIAL PERIOD.—This wonderful patrimony of works, accumulated in the course of the six centuries intervening between the Archaistic and the Hellenistic period, was inherited from the Greeks by Roman civilization. The attraction which the Romans at first found in these works was an esthetic one: for their esthetic pleasure they had copies made of the Greek masterpieces, and it is mostly these copies which we have here used in tracing the course of the development of Greek art. Later, when the Romans availed themselves of this artistic patrimony for their religious and social needs, they did not copy the Greek originals, but readapted them.

An archaic type of Apollo, dating from the end of the sixth or the beginning of the fifth century B.C., was transformed by the Romans into their own "Semo Sancus Deus Fidius" (Fig. 53). Roman art of the period of the Antonines (130–180 A.D.) has softened the nude and given more freedom to the hair, but has preserved the posture of the Greek original. This posture has also been correctly interpreted by the restorer in remaking the right forearm with the bow, but the addition of the left hand with the bird is arbitrary. It is noteworthy that, in an age when deities were represented even in the immodest position of the Aphrodite of Dædalus, this rigid figure could still awaken some sense of mysterious religiosity.

A face with features reminiscent of Polycletus, or at least of the art of the second half of the fifth century B.C., is united with a Hellenistic body in the Juno Sospes Lanuvina (Fig. 54). The arms with the spear and shield, the feet and the serpent are restorations. Covered with a goatskin, the goddess stands in a menacing attitude; but the spectator

Honorary High Relief showing the Figure of Rome (Fig. 78)
(Græco-Roman Period)

feels not so much the religious power of this figure as an artistic irritation, for under the dignified head of a Greek Hera he recognizes through the transparent chiton the agile limbs of a Mænad. This work must also be credited to the superficial religiosity of the age of the Antonines.

And, when Rome had to create figures, not of her own indigenous gods, but for the new Oriental cults which were spreading throughout the Empire, she had recourse always to the Greek tradition. In the Sacrifice of Mithra (Fig. 55)—that is, the Persian Sun-God overtaking and stabbing the bull, while a dog and serpent lap its blood— Roman art has reproduced the scheme of a group which perhaps dated

back as far as the fifth century B.C., and represented Victory hurling a
bull to the ground.   The Classic spirit is also reflected in the idealized
face of Mithra.

The relief showing an Isiac procession (Fig. 56) is Classicistic, rather
than Classic. Priests and priestesses with solemn and rigid gait carry
the symbols of the goddess, and the coldness of their regular features
extends also to the channelled and parallel folds of their garments.
Compared, however, with this procession, that to the figure of Artemis

Sarcophagus depicting the Triumph of some General (Fig. 79)
(Græco-Roman Period)

(Fig. 57) seems ridiculous—in fact, an infantile masquerade. Artemis
has the Greek aspect, but in the exaggerated gravity of the children the
artist vainly tries to conceal how lacking in sincerity is Roman religiosity.

Even when Roman art descended from the realms of the gods to
mingle with men, and desired to honor the latter not for their bodily
forms, but for the victories they had won in contests with other mortals; even when, in distant imitation of the athletes of the fifth century,
it created the figure of the Charioteer (Fig. 58), that vulgar type of
imperial athlete who alone continued able to awaken the enthusiasm

Painting from the Tomb of Farnaces (Fig. 80)
(Græco-Roman Period)

of the cosmopolitan crowds of the Empire—even then it could not forget the Polycletus tradition. We certainly have in this figure the powerful thorax of the Doryphorus enveloped in the corset of straps which forms the most interesting part of the work. Moreover, the head, which perhaps belongs to the figure, and the arms and the legs, which are correctly restored, remind one of the Greek athlete.

But the greatest obsession of Roman art was the Greek myth. Excluded from the decorations of the temples, it invaded the homes and the sarcophagi—the homes in the guise of paintings, and the sarcophagi in the guise of reliefs. To a cycle of paintings which represented the celebrated sinners of antiquity belongs the figure of Pasiphaë (Fig. 59). This cycle decorated the walls of a villa and illustrated the fatal consequences of guilty love. Pasiphaë seems to be disturbed by a presentiment of the opprobrium which her guiltiness will bring down on her: she hesitates, and in this hesitation is again seen the strength of Greek art, which aims at expressing sentiment in bodily forms.

Not mythic, but full of religious gravity, is the most beautiful ancient painting that the Vatican possesses, the Nozze Aldobrandini (Figs. 60, 61, 62 and 63). From criminal love this painting takes us to the chaste apartment of the bride, who, however, also seems perturbed and trembling. Hymen, the god of marriage, crowned with ivy and flowers, sits impatiently on the floor near the couch. Near the bride is seated Aphrodite, who calms and encourages her, while the friends and servants of the bride, confident of the efficacy of Aphrodite's eloquence, proceed undisturbed with their preparations for the nuptial ceremonies, music and lustrations. We believe that an Hellenistic artist would have conceived in no different spirit the scene in which the hesitating Helen is persuaded to follow Paris, for the figure of Hymen might also be that of the waiting bridegroom or lover.

In the Roman homes the myths extended from the paintings on the walls to the mosaics on the floor. All gracefulness of forms and all expression of sentiment are lost in these crude works, wherein the myths are reduced to a purely ornamental element. Even the head of the stern Athena may be trampled on in a mosaic (Fig. 64); and while the artist, preoccupied with the decoration, has surrounded it with an ægis resembling the calyx of a flower, he has not been able to rid it of that pathetic expression which Hellenism finally gave to all her figures, whether heroic or divine.

But departing from the Roman home, resounding with life, let us approach the solemn peace of the tomb, and there again we shall find the spiritual Greek ideal triumphant in its myths. On one of the sarcophagi we are once more confronted with the terrible scene of the Niobids (Fig. 65). Apollo and Artemis hurl their arrows from either side of the group, while, supported and sheltered by their mother, nurse and pedagogue, the innocent children vainly strive to escape the divine vengeance. But the Roman who ordered the reliefs for sarcophagi of this character felt in his soul a sensation entirely different from that which he experienced when he contemplated the statues of the Hellenistic group gathered on the rocky wall of a public garden. In the group in the garden he admired only the strong expression of sorrow; in the relief of the sarcophagus he saw foreshadowed the fatality of death which must sooner or later overtake every man.

Leaving the gloomy atmosphere of Greek fatalism, let us now breathe for a while the vital air of the Roman hills. Here is an atmosphere of honor and imperial power, for the people who dominated the world in politics could not be mere slaves in art. They have certainly copied and readapted, but they have also created the two genres most intimately related with their life—the honorary portrait and the commemorative relief.

Both genres are found united in one figure in the Vatican—the Augustus found at Prima Porta in the Villa of Livia (Fig. 66). This statue, which is intact except for some insignificant elements, presents the emperor as a general haranguing his soldiers, but in his left hand Augustus must have held a spear rather than a sceptre. The Cupid with the dolphin at the foot of the statue may refer to the origin of the Gens Julia, which claimed descent from Venus. This statue does not offer any original element in its posture to distinguish it from Greek figures, nor is there anything particularly Roman in the mantle, the rich folds

Sarcophagus of St. Helena (Fig. 81)
(Græco-Roman Period)

of which envelop the emperor's thighs.   The real artistic value of the
work lies in the face of the emperor and in the cuirass.   The face expresses the tranquil majesty of the man accustomed to command, while
the regular hair, the broad forehead, the round eyes and the delicate
mouth seem almost to idealize his expression.   The sculptor portrays
Augustus in the fifth decade of his life, but idealizes rather than exactly
copies nature.   In the cuirass the great deeds of the emperor are lauded
in commemorative reliefs.   Below is the earth, happy under the rule

of Augustus; the two children, the horn of abundance, and the tympan of Cybele attest to its fertility. Above are Apollo with the gryphon and Artemis with the stag, the two divinities beloved of Augustus and conceded so important a part by him in the *Ludi Sæculares.* And on this happy earth, under the mighty arch of the sky, a new day is about to dawn, for we see the chariot of the sun advancing, preceded by the personifications of Aurora. This is the new day on which the Roman army recovered from the Parthians the military insignia taken from the legions of Crassus at the battle of Cære. The return of these insignia is represented in the two central figures of the cuirass. To the right of this group sits Gallia, defeated in her Aquitani, and to the left Hispania, tamed in her Celtiberi—two other exploits of the reign of Augustus. If Phidias gathered together the myths of remote ages on the shield, the sandals and the pedestal of his Athena Parthenos, the Roman sculptor summarizes recent glories in a few figures on one lorica.

After the statue of Augustus, which is in itself a synopsis of imperial art, we shall examine separately the two genres of Roman art—the portrait and the honorary relief. In the supposed Caius (Fig. 67), nephew of Augustus, we have a delightful childish head, to which the large skull and the conspicuous ears lend individuality, while the almond-shaped eyes, the mouth, and the small chin lend an ideal grace.

Wearing the civic crown of oak and bearing the attributes of Jupiter, Claudius presents himself for the adoration of his subjects (Fig. 68). The restorer has appropriately placed the sceptre in his left hand; his right hand, however, should rather have held the thunderbolt. But let us forget this most unrealistic figure of Jupiter and examine the face of the emperor. The artist was certainly no flatterer, for we seem to discern in the features the narrow intelligence of him who devoted so much attention to erudite studies concerning the Etruscan Sphinx.

And here before us is the benevolent, though sensual and almost embarrassed face of Titus (Fig. 69). His bulky frame is buried under the immense folds of his toga, and his square face corresponds to the shape of his body. Near him we see that intellectual and bold portrait of a matron of his period, perhaps that of his own daughter Julia (Fig. 70). The head has been placed on a greatly restored body belonging to Classical Attic art. Coming to the second century, we recognize in the head of Hadrian (Fig. 71) a mobile, intelligent and open spirit, while in the image of Faustina the Elder, wife of Antoninus Pius (Fig. 72), we have the most authentic type of the woman of ancient Rome—a type at once energetic and sensual. To a still later period belongs the statue of the Venus Empress (Fig. 73), to which reference has been already made at the beginning of this chapter.

But Roman portraiture does not restrict itself to imperial figures: in the statues of Antinous, beloved of and deified by Hadrian, it strove to create an ideal of melancholy and dreamy beauty. In the Antinous Braschi (Fig. 74), the young Bithynian is represented as Dionysus, but only the nude parts of the figure are original. He leans his head towards his strong and square shoulder—not out of benevolence towards his adorers, as a Greek god might do, but because he is oppressed by his inner sorrow and by the mental obsession which will drive him to suicide. In the head and features of the noble chieftain prisoner Dacus

Sarcophagus of St. Constantia (Fig. 82)
(Græco-Roman Period)

(Fig. 75), Roman art has expressed his ethnic characteristics and the sorrows of defeat and slavery.

If we are tempted to believe that Roman portraiture owed all its expressive strength to the inspiration which it drew from the imperial dignity, or from subjects (like Antinous or Dacus) in which such dignity was reflected, the sepulchral tablet of L. Vibius and his wife and son (Fig. 76) will help to modify somewhat this view. Though the work of a modest marble-worker, it shows the scope of this art. We read vulgarity, old age and ugliness in the irregular lines of the faces of the couple; and, if their child in the middle has a more delicate expression, his large sail-like ears prove clearly that he is his father's son, and that at some future day the flower will develop from the bud!

Turning now to the votive reliefs, we find that the Vatican possesses a slab from the Ara Pacis Augustæ (Fig. 77), that monument which Augustus erected in the Campus Martius on his return from Gaul and Spain (13 A.D.). In the reliefs was represented the imperial procession which went to assist at the sacrifice. The slab in the Vatican preserves that part of the cortège which walked towards the right: some lictors, a veiled priest and men wearing the toga form the group. Our thoughts turn instinctively to a similar scene—the cortège of the Parthenon. And if here we do not find the grace and nobility of the figures of Phidias, if we miss the harmonious rhythm of his cavalcade, we behold all the sober dignity of the Romans and the compact mass of the imperial crowd. In the frieze of the Parthenon we witness the advance to the conquest of the ideal; in the frieze of the Ara Pacis we witness the advance to the conquest of the real world. Posture, drapery, and the expression of the faces—all in the Ara Pacis seems to personify the solid strength of Rome.

Rome herself, bearing a banner in her left hand and mingling with the crowd, precedes the chariot of the triumpher in an honorary high relief (Fig. 78). We do not know to what public monument it belonged, but it too is certainly a work of the first century after Christ. Although the work is much restored—the head of Rome being one of the more important restorations—this scene of the Empress City opening her way through the crowd remains one of the best expressions that art has given of the imperial idea.

The glory of the Roman army and the apotheosis of the emperor are celebrated on the pedestal of the honorary column of Antoninus and Faustina, which M. Aurelius and L. Verus erected not far from the Obelisk of Augustus. This pedestal is now in the Cortile della Pigna. Two of the sides contain a scene showing a review of the army, perhaps in honor of the emperor (see page 28): horsemen with their banners ride in a circle around the legionaries carrying the ensigns. On the main face of the pedestal, in the presence of the imperial figure of Rome, Antoninus Pius and Faustina are borne aloft from the Campus Martius (personified as a youth lying on the ground and holding in his left hand the Obelisk of Augustus) to Olympus, seated on the wings of a genius and accompanied by two eagles (see page 29). In these eagles, in the figure of the celestial globe which the genius holds in his left hand, and in some other elements, there might be traced the influence of the Mithraic cult and of the religious spirit of the Orient; but in the general conception of the scene, in this Rome which salutes her own deified emperors, we can recognize only the imperial sense which dominated Roman art.

That this imperial sense was shared by the generals and magistrates who upheld the Roman ideal in remote provinces among uncivilized nations, we see from the slab of a sarcophagus celebrating their deeds (Fig. 79). Some prisoners are seated under the trophies of victory, while a genius bearing a palm branch places a crown on the head of the general, before whom the conquered enemy kneels imploringly.

And if the emperor had his apotheosis, if the general recorded his victories in stone, why should not the modest boatman perpetuate on his tomb in a still more modest manner the field of action of his daily life? In one ancient painting (Fig. 80) we see "Magister Farnaces," the pilot, superintending the loading of his boat. The idea of representing so insignificant and banal an incident, and in such poor forms, would never have occurred to a Greek of the Classical period; it occurred to a Roman because his little freight-boat was to the modest boatman what the ship of state was to the emperor. And we notice that Farnaces is given the same dominating position at the poop of his tub as Antoninus and Faustina occupy on the wings of the genius between two eagles.

But an art which was born and triumphed together with a political ideal was doomed to decay as this ideal faded; and the fascination of the imperial idea waned long before the actual fall of the Roman Empire. That art alone is vital and lasting whose roots reach deep into the heart of man; and such art is, above all, the religious. Though the imperial art of Rome had also clothed itself in a vague religiosity; though sometimes, in figure and posture, it had made of the emperor a god, it never ceased to be an art which, instead of rising from the hearts of the people, was imposed upon the people by the state. And, since the beauty and idealism of a conception are dependent on the suggestive capacity of the subject, the figures in imperial art grew poor and graceless as the attraction of imperialism declined. Of this growing poverty we have already seen an indication on the pedestal of the column of Antoninus and Faustina: not on the side where the artist availed himself of Greek models for Rome, the Campus Martius and the genius, but on the two sides containing the review. What a decay there has been in both composition and forms from the dignified cortège of the Ara Pacis to this childish carrousel!

But poverty of forms is not so fatal for art as poverty of inspiration or subject. If the inspiring idea be rich, some day forms also will flourish. That this is true, has been proved by an art which appeared in the midst of this very civilization at the moment when the imperial idea began to wane. This art is the Christian. Its first figures have an aspect similar to, where not uglier than, the figures of contemporary Roman art. In the Catacomb paintings of the third and fourth centuries, Moses resembles our "Magister Farnaces." But this new art sprang from a religion which had won the whole heart of man; and the Bible and the Gospel of Christ had an inspiring force altogether different from that exerted by the imperial idea. Consequently, some day this Moses will become the Moses of Michelangelo.

And the Vatican Museum possesses two works which, while characterized by an equal poverty of forms, seem to forecast the different destinies which awaited the Empire and Christianity. These works are the sarcophagi of St. Helena (Fig. 81) and St. Constantia (Fig. 82). In the former we have the notes of imperial war and glory: horsemen pass in triumph above, while barbarians are dragged into captivity below. The second sarcophagus is filled with an atmosphere of natural peace and glory: some Cupids gather and press the grapes, and in this scene the Christian saw symbolized the good work which the faithful perform in the vineyard of the Lord, while in the lamb and the peacock below he saw the symbols of the Good Shepherd and immortality. And if there is still imperial buoyancy in the sarcophagus of St. Helena and Christian humility in that of St. Constantia, the day is not far distant when the buoyancy and the humility will be reversed. The barbarians who now bend their captive heads under the hoofs of the Roman horses will soon raise them menacingly and will overthrow the Empire, while the humble Faith which masks itself under the symbols of the peacock, the Cupid and the lamb, will victoriously extend its dominion throughout the earth.

THE GALLERY OF INSCRIPTIONS

HE Gallery of Inscriptions is situated along the corridor built by Bramante to link the old palace of Nicholas V and Alexander VI (the Borgia Tower and Appartamento) with the smaller palace built by Innocent VIII in the Belvedere. The collection of ancient inscriptions was begun under Clement XIV, the real founder of the Vatican Museum, and was enriched by Pius VI, the slabs being set in the walls of the Bramante Corridor near the Pio-Clementino Museum. But at a later date Pius VII, anxious to place his Chiaramonti Museum here, had the slabs taken to the other end of the corridor, which is adjacent to the lowest tier of the Loggie, near the Appartamento Borgia. This collection of inscriptions comprises those formerly assembled in the Vatican, together with those which were brought together from various quarters by Cardinals Zelada, Galletti, Di Pietro and Capponi, and many inscriptions discovered by that famous epigraphist, Gaetano Marini, not to mention the many marbles found in the excavations made by the papal authorities at Rome and Ostia or bought from various dealers in antiquities. Many new additions were made to the collection under Leo XIII and Pius X.

Altogether these inscriptions number more than 3000, and thus form the greatest collection of ancient writings on stone in the world. While this gallery appeals in a special manner to the student of ancient epigraphy, who will here find the richest materials for his researches, it also holds a wonderful interest for every visitor who has some knowledge of history and classical antiquity. Gaetano Marini classified the collection in accordance with the critical archæological ideas of his time, and although, had the work to be done anew, a different arrangement would be followed to-day, yet, out of respect for the great archæologist who planned it, it has been thought fit not to make any change. There is another reason for retaining the present arrangement, namely, the fact that many of the inscriptions have been described in various works (for example, the "Corpus Inscriptionum Latinarum"), wherein their position in the Vatican Gallery is indicated.

Persons who wish to examine the collection properly should begin at the gate leading to the gallery from the lowest tier of the Loggie, near the Appartamento Borgia, and follow the line of the walls, on which, as we go along, we shall point out the most important inscriptions. Having reached the Chiaramonti Museum at the end of the gallery, we shall pass through that museum, and pay a visit to the first two rooms of the Pio-Clementino Museum, where recently, through the munificence of Pius X, three remarkable groups of inscriptions have been set up as a fine complement to the Gallery of Inscriptions.

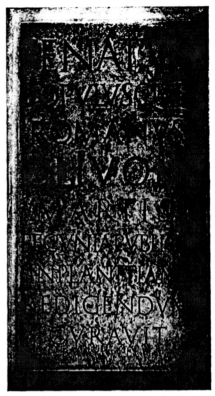

Inscription found near the Site of the ancient Temple of Mars

On the left as you enter, between the two screens, is a large inscription, found near the door of St. Sebastian's on the Appian Way, where the Temple of Mars Outside the Walls once stood. This temple was dedicated in 368 A.U.C. (386 B.C.), after the Gallic War, and is famous in Roman history. The inscription, which belongs to the later days of the Republic, records the work of levelling the slope that led from the Appian Way to the temple, and which was carried out by the Senate at public expense.

In the vestibule which leads to the gallery a few inscriptions have recently been placed. They were brought here from a hall near the sacristy of St. Peter's, where they had been set up in the days of Pius VI because some of them had been found during the work connected with that building. The most important among them are: on the left, that relating to Ursus Togatus, a ball-player whose victories in the Baths of Nero, Titus and Trajan are recorded; on the right, the record of a charioteer in Nero's time, containing the names of his winning horses and enumerating his victories. Below the latter is a small inscription relating to a circus charioteer named Scirtus, again giving the names of his horses and the number of his victories.

Wall 1 contains, on the right, an advertisement or announcement concerning a bathing establishment in the country, which tells that the latest improvements have been made and that all the city comforts will be found there (*more urbico omnis humanitas præstatur*). Noteworthy also are the inscriptions concerning a woman's association (*collegium mulierum*), and an association of wine-merchants who lived in taverns or huts (*collegium vinariorum in canabis consistentium*).

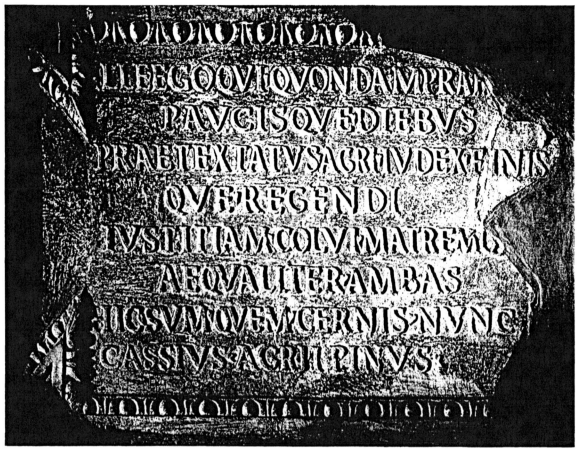

Inscription in Hexameter Verse with Letters in Relief

Wall 3 shows, on the right, a votive relief with an inscription concerning Marcus Quartinius Remus, a Sabine soldier of the Seventh Prætorian Cohort, called the Antonine Cohort in the days of Caracalla. It relates how, in answer to a vision, he dedicated this monument to five divinities who are carved on it, with their names above—Saturn, Mars, Jupiter, Mercury and Hercules. There is a curiosity among inscriptions on this very wall, namely, an inscription, with the letters in relief and in hexameter verse, relating to the tomb of a Roman judge named Cassius Agrippinus.

On Wall 7, to the right, we see a sepulchral marble slab on which are sculptured in relief two raised arms with the hands opened. The inscription records the protest of a young woman named Procope against the deity who caused her to die so young: PROCOPE MANVS LEBO [LEVO] CONTRA DEVM QVI ME INNOCENTEM SVSTVLIT. It is not improbable that Procope died a violent death. Here also is a small sepulchral bust of a woman bearing an inscription threatening that whosoever should profane this tomb would die the last of his race—that is, that he would see all whom he loved die before he did: QVISQVIS HOC SVSTVLERIT AVT JVSSERIT VLTIMVS SVORVM MORIATVR.

On Wall 8, to the left, is a fragment of a list containing the names of the *Kalatores pontificum et flaminum* (Ushers of the Pontifical College). This important inscription was found during the old excavations of the Roman Forum near the house known as the Regia, which was the residence of the Pontifical College. Here may be also seen one of the *cippi* which marked off the zone that was to remain free near the banks of the Tiber. The inscription tells us it was set up during the consulship of Censorinus and Gallus in the year 8 B.C. Another inscription refers to a freedman of the Emperor Hadrian who is called Archimagyrus (or chief cook), and also mentions a cooks' club which met in the imperial palace (*collegium cocorum quod consistit in palatio*).

Wall 9 contains, on the right, an inscription from the sepulchral monument of the Roman matron Claudia Semne, found on the Appian Way near the Basilica of St. Sebastian. The inscription describes the various parts of that most noble monument, and we are told that her perfections, to be properly treated, should be represented by statues after the likeness of various deities (*in forma omnium Deorum*).

On Wall 10, which lies on the left, we see a truly remarkable inscription relating to Lucius Balerius, and ending in a formula which maybe Christian, since the reader is warned that God will be witness if he has not prayed: TV QVI LEGES ET NON ORAVERIS ERIT TIBI DEVS TESTIMONIO. The meaning of this phrase is hard to explain in a pagan sense, but it may be that the inscription belonged to some one who, while not a Christian, professed doctrines analogous to the teachings of Christianity.

Procope's Protest against her
Early Death

On Wall 12, to the left, is a large pedestal with an honorary inscription dedicated to Emperor Constantius, son of Constantine, by Memmius Vitrasius Orfitus, Prefect of Rome. This pedestal once held the statue of Constantius and stood in the Roman Forum.

On Wall 14, to the left, begins the series of Christian inscriptions, found for the most part in the Roman Catacombs, and nearly all dating from the third, or especially from the fourth and fifth centuries. While this series would be of immense importance in any other city, it is rather overshadowed in Rome by the unrivalled collection of Christian inscriptions in the Lateran Christian Museum and by the wealth of important inscriptions that are to be found in the Catacombs themselves. Nevertheless, this collection is of high importance, not alone in itself but also in view of the ease with which one may here compare the Christian and pagan epigraphy. For instance, we may notice that the Christian inscriptions, which are generally of a later date, are also more careless both in expression and in palæography. Moreover, it will be noticed that set formulæ were used in the Christian inscriptions: for example, *in pace* and *depositus* (an obvious reference to the resurrection), expressions never found in pagan inscriptions. Then, too, the early emblems of the Christians are scratched on

Fragment of Column giving the Names and Numbers of Roman Legions

their sepulchral monuments: the anchor, the dove, the fish, and more often the combination of the first two letters of the Greek name of Christ (Χριστός). This last symbol is generally known as the Constantine monogram (☧), because it was used particularly in the days of Constantine, and came into common use afterwards. This series of Christian inscriptions is continued along all the walls on the left of the gallery, until we come to the screen which separates this gallery from the Chiaramonti Museum. We return now to the pagan inscriptions.

On Wall 15, to the right, is an altar (No. 63) dedicated to the Sun—*Soli Invicto*—that is, to the Sun as conceived in the Persian religion. The altar was dedicated by a college or society which practised a special cult of the Sun under this title; and in the inscription the name of Marcus Aurelius Cripanto, the president (*magister*) of the association, is mentioned.

On Wall 17, to the right, is a large pedestal (No. 73) which at different times served two distinct purposes. It supported originally a statue of Gallus, as we learn from a relief carved on the right side; later it was the base for an honorary statue of Furteius Tertullus, a consular dignitary of the fourth century of the Christian era, as we may learn

from the later inscription carved on the front of the marble block. On
this wall there is also a fine sepulchral inscription in cursive script,
which tells us of two children named Pupus Torquatianus and Pupus
Lætianus. The slab was erected by their parents, Cajanus and Eucha-
ris, who sing their children's praises, and declare that they will grow
old before their time because of the death of their dear children.

On Wall 21, to the right, is No. 91. Over a miniature temple is set the
top of another temple of an apparently different size. From the inscription carved on the top we learn that the monument was dedicated
to the protecting genius of a Prætorian century in the time of the Emperor Commodus, or, more precisely, in the year 181 A.D.

In this same wall there is another noteworthy inscription, namely,

Inscription giving the Names and Birthplaces of Soldiers and the
Corps to which they belonged

that of Claudius Narcissianus, wherein we are told that the sepulchral
monument was surrounded by a wall, and contained a garden, a stable
and other outhouses.

No. 93 is seen on the left; this is an unusual sepulchral group representing a bearded man seated on a high chair between two figures, a
boy portrayed as Harpocrates and a girl carrying flowers in the folds
of her mantle. The inscription gives us the name of the individual as
Cornutus, and tells us that he was buried there together with his eight
children. Very probably the figures of the boy and girl represent two
of his children.

On Wall 25, to the right, are arranged many inscriptions concerning
offices in the imperial household or referring to various workmen. For
instance, there is an inscription dealing with a hairdresser (*ornatrix*)

and a nurse, and another telling of an imperial servant employed in the Servilian Gardens, which lay between the Via Appia and the Via Ostiensis. Another inscription refers to a private road which ran from the highway through a garden and belonged to a sepulchre (*iter privatum a via publica per hortum pertinens ad monumentum sive sepulchrum*). Still another inscription, dedicated to a goldsmith named Ilarus, is of some importance since it shows that there was a college or association that met in the house of a noble lady named Sergia Paulina (*collegium quod est in domo Sergiæ Paulinæ*).

On Wall 26, to the left, is the sepulchral cippus of Gavius Musicus and his wife, Volumnia Januaria, who lived at the end of the first century. This noteworthy slab has characteristic figures of these two persons.

On Wall 29, to the left, we find many inscriptions recording military events, and concerning soldiers of the legions and urban cohorts as well as of the prætorian cohorts and cohorts of the watch. There is one in particular dealing with Thysdrus, a soldier of the sixth cohort of the watch, on which is carved his portrait with the outfit proper to his calling. Important, too, are the fragments of a column in cippolino marble, on which, under the heading NOMINA LEG[IONVM], are inscribed the names and numbers of many Roman legions. Herewith also we give an example of the many lists of soldiers (*latercoli militari*), showing their names, the corps they belonged to, and their native towns. Alongside is a brick inscription, containing the name of a Roman legion that was stationed near the Danube in ancient Mœsia (now Bulgaria), where this brick was recently found.

On Wall 30, to the left, is a travertine altar (No. 132), with an inscription telling that it was dedicated to the goddess Juturna. This is one of the very rare monuments to this Goddess of the Waters, whose sanctuary has been recently discovered in the Roman Forum near the foot of the Palatine.

Wall 31 contains on the right a large cippus (No. 138), that served a double purpose. First of all, it has a second-century inscription dedicated by Claudia Quinta to her *pædagogus,* or tutor, Caius Julius Hymetus, who was also custodian of the Temple of Diana Planciana. Later the cippus was used to support the honorary statue of Lucius Turcius Secundus, a famous personage of the fourth century of the Christian era, and the list of his honors (*cursus honorum*) is given in an inscription thereon. On the plinth his surname, Asterius, has been added as an afterthought. There are also on this wall several sepulchral pillars containing inscriptions dealing with the *equites singulares,* that is, with the knights who made up the horse-guard of the

Roman emperors, and who were chosen from the various countries in the empire. They generally give a portrait of the knight reclining on a banquet couch, and below one sees his orderly holding one or two horses by the reins. These inscriptions are valuable since they show the native countries of these knights, most of whom came from the northern provinces of the empire. A stele which we have here reproduced belongs to one Titus Flavius Julius, a native of Noricum, who served as a soldier for thirteen years, and was thirty years old at his death. The monument was erected by his heirs, Titus Aurelius Victorinus, a standard-bearer, and Titus Flavius Flo-

Stele of Titus Flavius Julius (*Eques Singularis*)

rentinus, a soldier of the eleventh urban cohort, "to their best friend."

To the left, on Wall 32, is a votive pedestal (No. 142), dedicated to Hercules Victor by Caius Julius Rufus, military tribune, curator of the Temple of Hercules and attached to the Treasury of Saturn. The abbreviations to be seen on the upper part of the pedestal, H. V. V. S., must be interpreted *Herculi Victori votum solvit*.

On Wall 33, to the right, is a sacred well-top (No. 144), dedicated in 197 A.D. to Ceres and to the Nymphs by two patrons of an association in Ostia, from which city this monument comes. No. 147 is the sepulchral cippus of a cutler named Lucius Cornelius Atimetus, and is noteworthy on account of the scenes carved on the two sides. To the left of the onlooker is represented the workroom of Atimetus, whose assistants are intent on their work; to the right is seen the shop in which Atimetus is showing his goods to a customer. In this same wall are set several inscriptions which were found during the excavations carried out by

Pius VII in the old city of Ostia. Remarkable among them are an inscription in honor of the Emperor Vespasian and a list giving the names of the members of a college who had contributed to a certain work. Another inscription refers to an association of wood-workers (*fabri lignarii*). Of importance, also, are some inscriptions dealing with the Mithraic cult, accompanied by effigies of the god Mithra Tauroctonus (Bull-slayer). There is, moreover, a noteworthy inscription which was set up by the priests of Cybele (*dendrofori*) at Ostia.

On Wall 34, to the left, is a marble stele (No. 152) with an inscription to Zeus Optimus Maximus Heliopolitanus, calling on him to protect the Emperor Gordian. This was erected by a citizen of Heliopolis who had once been a centurion in the Third Legion, known as the Flavia Gordiana.

Wall 35 contains, on the right, a remarkable monument relating to the triumphal column erected in honor of Marcus Aurelius near the Via Flaminia (on the modern Piazza Colonna). The fragment, No. 153, contains part of a petition addressed by Adrastus, an imperial freedman, to the Emperor Septimius Severus for permission to build himself a house near the said column, of which he was custodian. On the long stele, No. 154, three letters have been transcribed. Two are from the procurator of the imperial patrimony of Septimius Severus: the first is addressed to Epaphroditus, asking him to give Adrastus, the imperial freedman and custodian of the column of the divine Aurelius, materials for the building of a house near by; the other is addressed to Adrastus, and authorizes him to use the materials for the construction of a house destined for a habitation and the better custody of the column. The third letter is from the administrators of the imperial patrimony, granting Adrastus a plot of ground for his house near the column. There are also on this wall a few inscriptions relating to ancient municipalities outside Rome. Among these is a cippus with an inscription relating to Valerius Frumentius, patron and defender of the town of Laurentum; another inscription records the building of a flight of steps in Laurentum, and a third gives the names of the soldiers who, in the year 168 A.D., erected a building with a tribunal there, probably something along the lines of a basilica.

Wall 37 contains inscriptions dealing with various magistrates and civic dignitaries. Among these may be mentioned: a *terminus,* or landmark, from the banks of the Tiber, set up by the consuls Censorinus and Gallus in the days of Augustus; an inscription recording a legacy left to the College of the Augustales of Laurentum and Ostia by one Rusticelius so that the college might erect him a statue and celebrate his birthday every year; a fragment of the records of the *Ludi sœculares,*

which were cele-
brated in Rome in
the days of Augus-
tus, and at which the
famous "Carmen Sæ-
culare" of Horace
was sung.

There are also a
number of small in-
scriptions bearing
the names of per-
sonages of various
times and once
placed underneath
their statues. One
of these statues, we
learn, was dedicated
to Titus Cornasidius
Sabinus and his son
by the College of
Dendrofori at La-
vinium.   Another

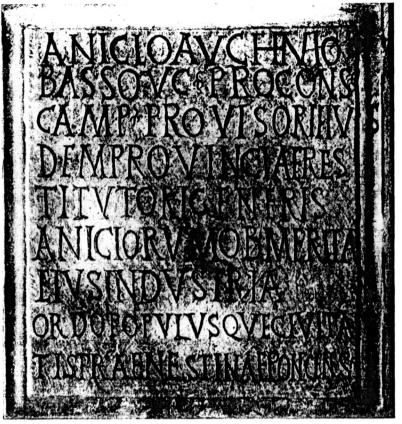

Tablet erected in Honor of Anicius Auchenius Bassus

was dedicated to Marcus Cesonius Saturninus and his brother Clavius
Martinus, who lived in the fourth century A.D. and were patrons in Ocri-
coli, for their munificence to that municipality and also for having
restored the Juvernal Baths to the south of the city. An important and
fairly old inscription, dating from the seventh century A.U.C., has been
recently set up here. It records the building of the walls around Ecla-
num, near Beneventum, by the quadrumvirate of that city and by C.
Quintius Valgus, patron of the municipality. The gates and towers of
the town are there mentioned. On this same wall there is a curious
honorary tablet set up by the city of Præneste to the most noble Anicius
Auchenius Bassus, Proconsul of Campania, who is styled the *restitutor
generis Aniciorum.*

On Wall 38, to the left, is a cippus (No. 163) bearing in bas-relief
the effigy of a centurion of a Roman legion in the time of Septimius
Severus.

Wall 39 contains a large marble pedestal (No. 165) which once supported the statue of Postumius Julianus, a noble citizen of ancient
Præneste who lived at the end of the fourth century. The inscription
was set up in the year 385 of the Christian era in the forum of Præneste,
in accordance with a will which left several farms to the town on con-

dition that his statue be set up in the forum and an anniversary celebrated each year in his memory.

There are a few inscriptions from imperial days on these walls. One tells how Trajan restored certain buildings in his sixth consulate; another relates that some works were done by the Emperor Antoninus Pius. The pedestal which supported the statue of Aurelian was voted him, we are told, by the citizens of Castronovum. Lastly, there is an inscription erected in honor of the Emperor Constantius by Memmius Vitrasius Orfitus.

On Wall 40, to the left, we see a large cippus (No. 170 B) with an inscription which gives the names of Cornelius Atimetus and refers to a farm belonging to the Gens Bruttia in Sabinum, known as the Villa Bruttiana.

On Wall 41, to the right, is a cippus (No. 173) from the city walls, telling that the *pomœrium,* or city boundary, was extended in the time of Emperor Claudius. It has the usual formula: AVCTIS POPVLI ROMANI FINIBVS POMERIVM AMPLIAVIT TERMINAVITQVE.

On this wall there are several imperial inscriptions. The carved lettering of one large inscription bears traces of having been filled with bronze. Only the central portion remains, but the whole can easily be reconstructed: it was dedicated to the divine Trajan and his spouse Plotina, and stood on the Temple of Trajan built at the end of his splendid forum. Here also are two other cippi from the pomœrium of Claudius, like that already referred to (No. 173), and dating from the year 43 of the Christian era. There is also an inscription dedicated to Caracalla by the Association of Divers (*stricatores*).

No. 173 B is a slab dating from the time of Antoninus Pius; it was dedicated to Fortuna Primigenia by Lucius Sariolenus, a citizen of Præneste. The inscription says that Sariolenus adorned with statues the temple of that divinity and another building known as the Junonarium. The inscription is very noteworthy in view of the information it gives concerning the topography of ancient Præneste, and also because it mentions the goddess Isityches (Isis-Fortuna).

Some other inscriptions from imperial times follow on Wall 43: for instance, the monumental inscription in which are recorded the works done by Antoninus Pius in the Ostian Baths, which had been begun by the Emperor Hadrian; the inscription dedicated to Diocletian and Maximian by Acilius Balbus, curator of the Tiber banks and the Roman *cloacæ* (sewers); an important municipal inscription from which we learn that in the third consulship of Emperor Hadrian (119 A.D.) a new street was run through the forum as far as the capitol of the town, which was built in imitation of the Capitol in Rome; an inscription on a large pedestal bearing witness to some monumental work done by Nerva; a cippus from the Aqua Vergine aqueduct, erected in the fifth consulship of Emperor Tiberius (31 A.D.).

On Wall 45 are many inscriptions relating to the gods and their ministers. The principal are as follows: (1) an inscription of Scurreius Fontinalis, a priest of Fortuna Primigenia; (2) a cippus, beginning with the words *Locus sacer* and relating to the College of Silvanus and its buildings on the Via Appia between the second and third milestones from Rome, on the plot of one Julia Monime in the Ager Curtianus Talarchianus (*i.e.,* near the Catacomb of St. Calixtus). The inscription contains notices concerning right of way and the custom of funeral banquets; (3) a fragment of a calendar, remarkable because it points out the festivals kept in honor of Aunia Regilla, sister of Queen Dido, at the first milestone on the Via Flaminia.

High up near the window is a broken architrave found at Ostia, bearing an inscription of Acilius Ægrilius Plavianus, prefect of the military treasury, pontifex of Vulcan, and religious head of the colony at Ostia, who dedicated to Vulcan a statue of gold and a silver shield. On the lower part of this wall was recently placed an important inscription from the second century of the Christian era, containing the *lex,* or rules and statutes, of the Association of Æsculapius and Hygeia. We are told that a lady named Salvia Marcellina, in memory of her husband, Flavius Apollonius, had given this association a meeting-place near the Temple of Mars on the Appian Way between the first and second milestones. Added to this inscription is a list of the festivals kept by the association. This inscription was a gift from Prince Louis Barberini, in whose palace it had been preserved.

Wall 47 contains many inscriptions concerning divinities and sacred ministers. The principal are: (1) a cippus dedicated to Mars Gradivus, with an inscription sacred to the Sabine god Semo Sancus, found on the Island of the Tiber. It is thought by many critics that the Christian apologist Justin was misled by this inscription into thinking that there had been a statue to Simon Magus on the Island of the Tiber; (2) a few fragments of the records (*fasti*) of the priestly college of the Salii Palatini, giving the names of the newly elected and those whose places they filled. These records date from the time of Marcus Aurelius; (3) an altar dedicated to the Sun, and another to Sol Invictus and Luna Æterna; (4) an important fragment alluding to the ancient tradition that the Vestal virgins were brought from the city of Cære to Rome in the early days of its history; (5) an inscription dedicated to Hercules for the health of Emperor Pertinax.

On Wall 48, to the left, are many Christian inscriptions, some of

Pedestal of Statue of Postumius Julianus

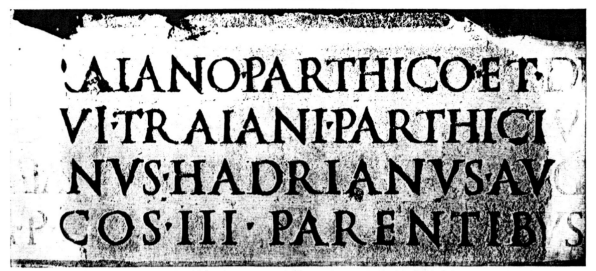

Fragment of Inscription from the Temple of Trajan

which have a special importance on account of the fact that they bear the names of the consuls in office, and we can thus fix their dates in every case. The dates run from the fourth to the sixth century of our era, the earliest being the year 363 and the latest the year 530. The best and largest collection of Christian consular inscriptions, however, is in the Lateran Christian Museum.

ADDITIONS TO THE GALLERY OF INSCRIPTIONS.—In 1912 the Directors of the Papal Museums gathered together three groups of most important ancient inscriptions, which form a worthy complement to those collected in the gallery proper. These groups are known as: (1) the Inscriptions of the Scipios; (2) the Triumphal Inscriptions; (3) the Inscriptions of the Fratres Arvales. The first two groups were placed in the small hall of the Pio-Clementino Museum, where the statue of Meleager originally stood, and the third group has been placed in the square recess opening on the Hall of the Torso Belvedere.

Inscriptions of the Scipios.—These most important inscriptions came from the underground tomb of the famous Scipio family on the Via Appia near St. Sebastian's Gate, where they were discovered in 1780. In the middle of the room is the sarcophagus of Lucius Cornelius Scipio Barbatus, consul 456 A.U.C. (298 B.C.), great-grandfather of Scipio Africanus. The inscription carved on the front of the monument is in ancient Saturnian verses, praises the strength, wisdom and beauty of the deceased, tells that he was consul, censor and ædile, captured Taurasia and Cisauna in Samnium, overcame all Lucania, and brought back hostages to Rome. The architectonic decoration on the sarcophagus consists of a Doric frieze with roses and triglyphs and a cornice with dentils. This is of great importance, as it shows us that Greek art had already penetrated into Rome in the third century B.C.

The lid has cushion-shaped ornaments, but the portion to the left of the spectator is a modern restoration. On the original part to the right remain some traces of the original inscription in red letters, which must have read as follows: L. CorneliO CN. F. S C I P I O

In the wall to the left have been added other inscriptions of the Scipio family, found in the tomb, and all having great importance on account of their antiquity. No. 2 is the inscription of Lucius Cornelius Scipio, son of Barbatus, who was consul in 495 A.U.C. and censor in 496. The text tells us that he was by common consent the best of the good, that he was consul, censor and ædile, that he conquered Corsica and dedicated a temple to the Winds, which stood near the Porta Capena and is referred to by Ovid in the sixth book of his "Fasti," where he writes:

"Te quoque, Tempestas, meritam delubra fatemur
    Cum pæne est Corsis obruta classis aquis."

The inscription is placed on the front of the sarcophagus, while on the lid was painted in red letters the name of the individual to whom it belonged.

No. 3 is the inscription of Publius Scipio, son of P. Cornelius Scipio Africanus Major, the conqueror of Hannibal. This man, having no heirs of his body, adopted the son of Lucius Æmilius Paulus, later known as Scipio Æmilianus or Africanus Minor, the famous conqueror of Carthage. The inscription deplores the brevity of his life and declares that had he lived longer his glory would have outshone that of his ancestors. On the same wall is No. 5, an inscription of Lucius Cornelius Scipio, son of Asiaticus, which tells us that he was quæstor (587 A.U.C.) and military tribune, that he lived thirty-three years, and that his father, who was dead at the time when the inscription was set up, had conquered Antiochus, King of Syria: *Mortuos* [*mortuus*] *pater regem antioco*[*m*] *subegit*. This victory took place after that of Consul Glabrio at Thermopylæ in 564 A.U.C. No. 6 is the inscription of Scipio Comatus, son of the preceding, who died, at the age of sixteen, in 600 A.U.C.; No. 7, the inscription of Cn. Cornelius Scipio Hispanicus, son of Cn. Cornelius Scipio, consul in 578 A.U.C. We are told that the deceased was prætor, curule ædile, quæstor, military tribune, legal decemvir, and sacred decemvir. Some archaic verses are added praising the dead man as one who emulated the glory of his sires and the nobility of his lineage. No. 8 is a panegyric of Lucius Cornelius Scipio, son of the preceding, which tells us that the defunct, though still a young man, had attained to great wisdom and knowledge and lived little over twenty years. On the wall at the back of the sarcophagus of Barbatus there is a broken travertine architrave with an inscription of one Paula

imp. Caes. M. Antonio Gordiano pio felice Aug.
et Manio Acilio Aviola   cos.   (a. 239)

III. *non*   I A N ·

*Fratres Arvales in Capitolio a*NTE CELLAM IVNONIS REGINAE CONVEN*erunt ad vota annua*
*solvenda et vota decen*NALIA NVNCVPANDA PRO SALVTE IMP CAES · M · A*ntonii Gordiani Pii*
Felicis Aug. P*o*NTIF · MAX · TRIB · POT · II · COS · P · P · TOTIQ · DOMVI · DI*vinae eorum* . . . . .
promagister . . . . . *no*MIN · M ANTONI GORDIANI · AVG · MAG · PRIMI · *collegii fratrum arvalium*
hoc die immolavit I · O · M · B · M · A · IVNONI REG · B · F · A · MINERVA*e b(ovem) f(eminam) a(uratam)*
adfuerunt . . . . · ET · IMP · CAES · M · ANTONIVS · GORDIANVS · PIVS · FE*lix Augustus magister* . . .
. . . . *Caesonius Lu*CILLVS T · FL · ARCHESILAVS M SAENIVS DONA*tus* . . .
. . . . VS · C · ANNIVS · PERCENNIANVS · SOLITO · MOR*e* ? . . .
. . . . *in crebras* VOCES ADCLAMAVERVNT

isdem consulibus . . . . . *idu* S · I A N ·

*Fratres Arvales in aede Co*ncor*DIAE CONVENERVNT AD INDI*
cendum sacrificium Deae DIAE IN XVI · XIIII · XIII · K · IVN
adfuerunt Imp. Caes. M. Antonius Gordianus pius FELIX · AVG · MAG · COLL · FRATR
Arvalium . . . . P. *Aelius Co*ERANVS T · CAESONIVS LV
cillus . . . *L. Fabius Fo*RTVNATVS VICTORINVS
. . . . . *in cre*BRAS VOCES · ADCLAMAV ·

ON
VVL
BILI
RIC ? ·
. . . . ·

*pro magister Iure et vino sacrificium Deae Diae con*CEPIT PRIMO MANE
. . . .

Arvalian Fragment, with Restorations (239 A.D.)

Cornelia, wife of Cn. Cornelius Scipio Hispallus, who died when he was consul in the year 578 A.U.C.

Triumphal Inscriptions (on the wall to the right as you enter).— These most important inscriptions were discovered in Rome in the days of Urban VIII (1623–1644) in the neighborhood of the Roman Forum. They were, therefore, taken at first to the Barberini Palace, and thence derived the name "Barberini Tables." They remained in that palace until 1910, when they were acquired by the Vatican Museum. They are included in the famous collection of "Corpus Inscriptionum Latinarum" (Vol. I, pp. 477 *sq.*). The triumphs recorded in this group of inscriptions all belong to the eighth century of Rome; that is, to the last years of the Roman Republic. The first dates from 711 A.U.C., the year following the death of Julius Cæsar, and the last has the date of 733 A.U.C., or the twenty-first year before the Christian era. Of note in these inscriptions are the phrases "Triumphavit," "palmam dedit," which have reference to the ceremonies of a Roman triumph. These precious inscriptions were placed on the wall in the order they must have had originally, and as they appear in the "Corpus Inscriptionum." They all relate to triumphs won by generals of the republic in Spain, Africa, Illyria, the Alps, Macedonia and Sicily.

High up on the wall is placed the most famous inscription, dedicated to Jupiter Victor by Lucius Mummius, consul in 609 A.U.C. It tells how, having destroyed Corinth and conquered Greece, which became the

Roman province of Achaia (608 A.U.C.; 146 B.C.), he returned to Rome in triumph and dedicated a temple and a statue to Jupiter Victor in fulfilment of a vow made during the war. This celebrated monument was found in 1786 within the wall near the hospital of St. John Lateran.

Inscriptions of the Fratres Arvales.—The Fratres Arvales were a priestly college of very ancient origin and great importance, charged with the solemn sacrifices in honor of Dea Dia for the fertility of the fields (*arva*), whence came their name *Arvales.* They met in a sacred wood at the sixth milestone on the Via Portuensis, and it was their custom to carve on marble the accounts of their meetings, describing in detail their ceremonies. These marble tablets were set up near the Temple of Dea Dia in the above-mentioned wood, and there many fragments of them have been found. The most important collection of these records is that in the National Museum delle Terme in Rome, but the Vatican collection is older, and extends from the time of Nero to that of Gordian.

The most noteworthy among the inscriptions in this collection were kept for a long time in a room near the sacristy of St. Peter's, and have only recently been set up in their present position. Taking them successively as we go along, we see: (1) an inscription from the time of Nero, giving the date 58–59 of the Christian era; (2) fragments from the time of Nero, belonging to the years 59–60 of the Christian era; (3) an inscription dating from Domitian's reign and bearing date of the year 91 of our era. It records the sacrifice announced by the Fratres Arvales in the pronaos of the Temple of Concord; (4) fragments belonging to the period of Antoninus Pius, with the date 145 of our era; (5) an Arvalian inscription from the time of Elagabalus (218 A.D.). This last inscription is most important as it has preserved for us the ancient Arvalian hymn, or poem, composed in the primitive and rough language of Latium, which was recited by the Fratres Arvales in some of their ceremonies. A few lines or sentences of this curious text may be of interest:

> "Enos Lases juvate [thrice repeated]
> Neve luerve marma
> sini incurrere in pleores [thrice repeated]."

("Be propitious to us, O Lares, and do not allow the crops of the fields to be spoiled.")

This Arvalian hymn is one of the oldest documents in the Latin tongue, and is thus of great philological importance.

The remaining inscriptions are: (5 A) a tablet (the back of the preceding one, the slab having been sawed in two). The text dates from the days of Elagabalus; (6) another inscription from the days of Elagabalus and dating from the year 221 of our era; (7) an Arvalian fragment from the time of Gordian (239 A.D.). It was found in February, 1911, when some excavations were being made in a field near the sacred wood of the Fratres Arvales on the Via Portuensis, and was immediately bought for the Vatican Collection. We give elsewhere a facsimile of this inscription (with restorations), which was published at the time by the present writer ("Bulletino della Commissione archeologica comunale di Roma," 1911, pp. 2–3).

The above description of the Vatican Gallery of Inscriptions, if very curtailed, will nevertheless show that it is the richest in the world, and that it deserves not only a visit, but the patient study of every educated person who has the opportunity and the time to examine its treasures.

THE CHRISTIAN MUSEUM

THE Sacred or Christian Museum was founded in 1756 by order of Pope Benedict XIV, who desired to collect in one place the various small objects connected with Christian worship which had previously been more or less neglected, and were scattered here and there as mere curiosities. To understand the reason of this neglect, we must remember that after the Renaissance period everything connected with the Middle Ages was commonly considered a relic of a barbarous era; thus, in calling the ogival style of architecture "Gothic," the intention was to declare it barbaric. It was only in the seventeenth century that a few enlightened minds began to realize the importance of these relics of the Middle Ages, and to appreciate the artistic beauty of the precious works of earlier piety which had previously been so unjustly despised and ignored. Private collections of a more or less specialized and restricted character then began to be made, and, as time went on, men began to collect glassware with gold-leaf insertions, inscribed or carved gems, medallions, seals, ivories in bas-relief and alto-relief, and other pious objects of various materials.

But Pope Benedict's idea was far more comprehensive when he aimed at uniting in one hall of the Vatican Library the various private collections that had any important bearing on the history of the Primitive Church. As a first step he bought the three most famous collections then existing—that of Cavaliere Filippo Buonarroti of Florence; that of Cardinal Gaspare dei Conti Carpegna of Rome, and that of Commendatore Francesco Vettori, of the illustrious Roman patrician family—besides some minor collections. This action on the part of the Lambertini Pope is recorded in an inscription over the entrance-door of the Museum.

Before entering on a description of the priceless treasures here collected, it may not be amiss to say a word concerning each of the three collections which formed the main portion of the Museum at the time of its institution, and which form even to-day an important part of the exhibits. The most noteworthy of these collections was that made by the discriminating and industrious Cardinal Carpegna (1626–1714). This great patron of archæological studies, after filling various important ecclesiastical offices, was created Cardinal by Pope Clement X on

December 22, 1670, and appointed Cardinal Vicar. In this capacity he had under his jurisdiction the Roman Catacombs, which in those days were chiefly regarded as the precious receptacles of the bodies of the early martyrs. But the Cardinal was anxious likewise to save from dispersion whatever other objects might be found in the excavations that took place there, and particularly the ivories. It was the custom of the early Christians, when closing the *loculus,* or tomb, to insert in the fresh mortar some article which, in the absence of an inscription,

Entrance to the Christian Museum

would enable the friends and relatives of the deceased to recognize their last resting-places. His precious collection was purchased from the heirs of the Cardinal, and was catalogued by order of Cardinal Passionei. Owing to various circumstances, however, the transfer of the collection to the Vatican was delayed until the time of Clement XIII, when, there being no further room for the whole collection in the cases of the Sacred Museum, part of it had to be accommodated at the other end of the Library, in a room which, in contradistinction to the Sacred Museum, is known as the Profane Museum.

The collection of the Florentine Filippo Buonarroti, senator and member of the Academy of the Crusca, constitutes a highly important part of the glasses which, from the place of their discovery, are known as cemetery glasses. They are the bottoms of cups, to the lower surface of which a leaf of gold was attached by means of an acid, another layer of glass being then added. When fused, the two layers of glass enclosed the gold leaf, out of which certain symbols or ornaments were formed; the figures were left in the gold leaf, the remainder of which

Interior of the Christian Museum

was removed with some pointed implement, thus leaving a background which was transparent or azure according to the texture of the glass.

The Vettori Collection was offered to Pope Benedict XIV by its owner through Cardinal Giovanni Antonio Guadagni, and probably it was this very gift that suggested to the Pope the plan of founding a museum by the purchase of the above-mentioned collections. The Pope named Vettori custodian of the Museum at a monthly salary of one hundred scudi. The Vettori Collection was not limited to one class of objects like the two others, but contained relics of various centuries

French Cross of Silver Gilt
(Fourteenth and Fifteenth Centuries)

French Cross of Silver Gilt (Back)
(Fourteenth and Fifteenth Centuries)

Italian Cross of Bronze Gilt
(Fifteenth Century)

Crosses of Wood, Metal and Enamel
(Sixteenth Century?)

Enamel Triptych from Limoges, with Scenes from the Passion
(Jean Penicaud, Sixteenth Century)

Byzantine Triptych with Christ, the Virgin and Saints
(*Circa* 1000)

and of different materials, all, however, connected in one way or another with Christian history and worship. Later, in the pontificate of Pius VII, the collection made and owned by Don Agostino Mariotti, a lawyer, was acquired, and of this we still have the old and most accurate manuscript catalogue of Abbate Francesco Cancellieri (Codex Vaticanus 9189).

The Museum was greatly enlarged and enriched by Pope Gregory XVI, who devoted special attention to the collecting of the small painted Greek tablets and the small panels painted by the Primitives of the thirteenth, fourteenth and fifteenth centuries, which are now in the New Picture Gallery. While he was Prefect of the Library, Monsignor Laureani bought many valuable enamels and objects of all kinds, thereby greatly increasing the importance of the Museum. His work, however, had disastrous results in some cases; for, not satisfied with collecting, he unfortunately also wanted to restore and regild the bottom of the tablets, and to arrange symmetrically with in rich golden frames things entirely unrelated both as to age and character period of devel ter. A new peopment arrived with the reign of Pius IX. Having founded in 1852 the Commission of Sacred Archæology for the purpose of undertaking

Bronze Medallion with Portraits of Sts. Peter and Paul
(Third Century)

scientifically planned excavations in the Catacombs, this Pontiff directed that all objects found during the progress of these works should be arranged systematically in the Museum. In 1855 the Hall of the Museum was restored, and Commendatore Giovanni Battista de Rossi, who had been named Prefect of the Christian Museum, had six horizontal cases made to receive the abundant new material. His system of arranging objects relating to the early centuries of Christianity has been followed ever since, and in 1913 the Museum was enriched by new additions—glasses, lamps, phials, earthenware and bronzes. The history of these collections has been fully treated by the present writer ("Gli avori dei Musei profano e sacro della Biblioteca Vaticana," Rome, Danesi, 1903).

Having thus taken a hurried survey of the history of the Museum,

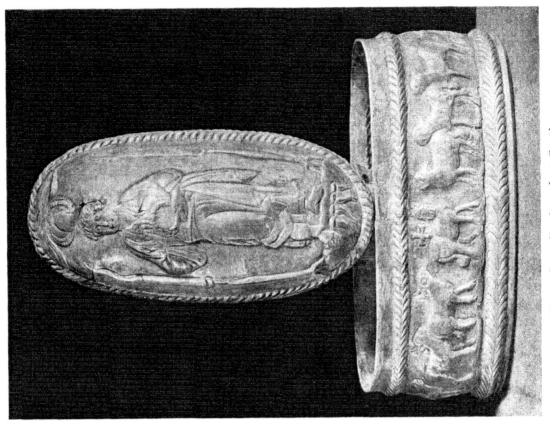

Silver Capsella found at Carthage
(Sixth Century)

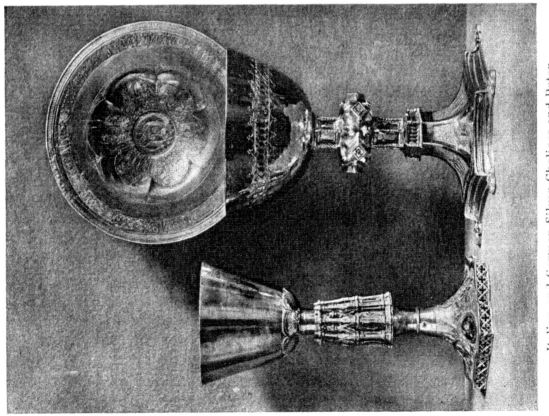

Italian and German Silver Chalices and Paten
(Fifteenth Century)

we shall now pass quickly over the various groups of archæological treasures which it contains, dwelling on the most important, which lend the Museum its great value and celebrity. With the idea of preserving the atmosphere of an old collection, the directors have not tried to bring the arrangement of the Museum into exact accord with the methods followed in modern museums. De Rossi tried to attain both ends by grouping objects according to the material of which they were made, or according to the place of origin. The presses are divided into twenty compartments or cases, in eight groups of two or three; there are, besides, the six horizontal glass cases added by de Rossi himself in 1855.

Polychrome Greek Triptych, with Madonna and Child and Scenes from the Life of the Virgin

To the left as you enter there is an important collection of crosses and crucifixes. In Case I are gathered especially bronzes representing Christ on the Cross; generally the figure is robed in the *colobium* (a long, sleeveless tunic), and each foot is nailed separately. Such crucifixes antedate the thirteenth century, when it became customary to represent the Saviour on the cross with an expression of physical pain. Previously the cross had been merely a support for the figure of the Crucified; Christ was represented as triumphant and glorious, all signs of suffering being absent. In the upper part of the case there is a bell of many chimes hung on two straps joined by a bronze clasp, which, when held in the hand and shaken, causes the bells to ring out a carillon. Peret says that this bell dates from the Catacombs, and Esperandieu has recently written in support of this view. However, in view of the shape of the bells and the incised cross, this object is probably not earlier than the eighth century.

Among the crosses in Case II may be mentioned a Greek sepulchral cross in bronze and one intended to be worn round the neck (an *encolpion*), on which is represented a figure of the Saviour wearing the *colobium*. Noteworthy also are a number of Italian processional crosses of the fourteenth and fifteenth centuries, one of the most remarkable of which shows a Calvary with small figures of the Virgin

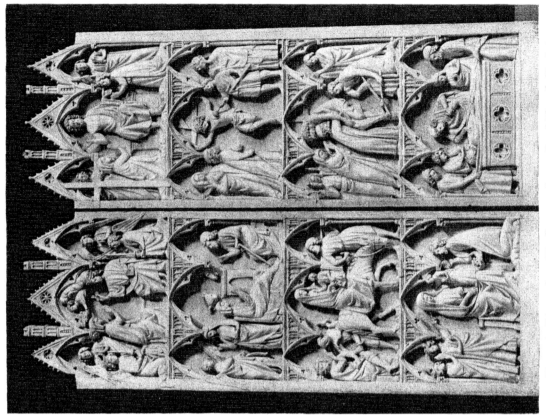

French Diptych with Scenes from the Life of Christ
(Fourteenth Century)

Enamelled Gold Cross with Scenes from the Life of Christ
(Sixth or Seventh Century)

and St. John, ornamented with enamel and little crystal spheres. Particularly admirable is a beautiful cross set with precious stones; this is of French origin and dates from the fourteenth century. The figure of the Crucified is a fifteenth-century work, and was added later to the older cross.

The horizontal glass case next to the case containing the crosses has some of a series of eighteen small enamel panels dating from the sixteenth century, which depict the Passion of the Saviour. But the most precious object in this collection is undoubtedly an enamel triptych from Limoges, showing the Crucifixion in the central panel, the Scourging on the left and the Crowning with Thorns on the right. This glorious treasure is by Jean Penicaud, who was born in the fifteenth century, and worked in the first thirty years of the sixteenth.

Cemetery Glass, representing St. Peter as Moses
Striking the Rock
(Fourth Century)

In Case III are to be found all the most important bronzes dating from the first centuries of Christianity: hanging lamps with the Constantine monogram, two bronze lamps in the form of a dove, a baptismal ewer with graffito figures on it, a slave's collar with the inscription "servus Dei fugitivus," and finally several medallions in relief, of which the chief is undoubtedly the well-known and frequently reproduced medallion showing the heads of the Apostles Peter and Paul turned towards each other. The last-mentioned probably dates as far back as the third century, and was found in the Catacomb of St. Domitilla. It deserves special attention in view of the iconographic characteristics which have been perpetuated unaltered down to our own day.

Case IV is given over to objects in silver and niello. Only two specially important articles will be mentioned: the first is a votive chalice with an inscription, which was found in a garden near St. Gregory's on the Cœlian Hill and dates from about the eighth century; the second is a beautiful pastoral staff in silver-gilt and niello which belonged to Pope John XXII and was found in his tomb at Avignon. This same Pope's mitre is in the Museum; it is in an excellent state of preservation, and is a most important specimen of fourteenth-century white damask.

Bronze Reliquary, showing the Crucifixion
(Eleventh Century)

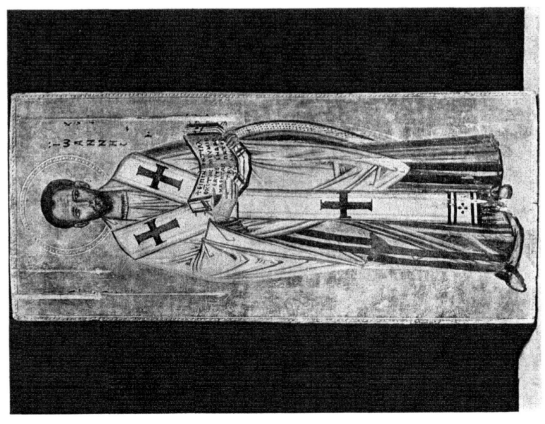

Reliquary Casket with Painted Figure of St. John Chrysostom
(Eleventh Century)

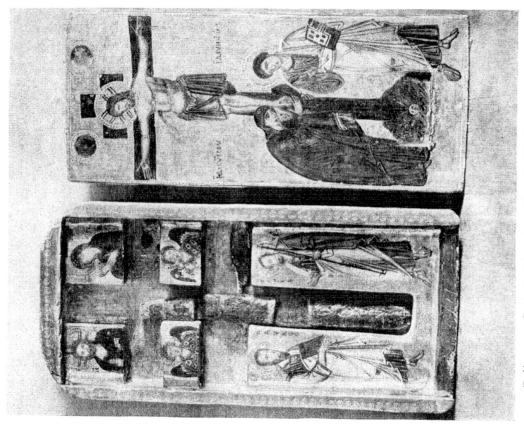

Reliquary Casket (showing Christ, Virgin and Saints)
and Cover (showing the Crucifixion)
(Eleventh Century)

Silver Reliquary, with Enamelled Medallions, in which the
Head of St. Praxedes was preserved
(Tenth Century)

Case V contains a collection of chalices dating from the fourteenth to the seventeenth century, the majority being Italian works of the fifteenth century. One of the latter is remarkable for the small figures of the Apostles made of translucent enamel, which are inserted in as many Gothic niches; these niches, bounded with toothed cusps, form the knob of the chalice. Another very beautiful chalice is of German origin, an unusual feature being the figure of the Redeemer in relief on the bottom of the paten.

The horizontal glass case which follows Case V contains objects of a very varied nature and of more recent acquisition. The first object worthy of note is a large silver plaque which for a long time was thought to be the work of Benvenuto Cellini, but which is now held, with greater reason, to be by Leone Leoni. It depicts the apotheosis of

Reliquary Capsellæ
(Sixth and Eleventh Centuries)

Charles Quint: the Emperor, dressed in ancient attire, is seated on a throne holding in his hands a globe and a sword; above his head planes an eagle holding in its beak a chain to which are attached warriors symbolizing the lands conquered by the Emperor. In this same glass case, among other relics, is a silver eucharistic capsella, or reliquary, found in the excavations at Carthage and dating from the sixth century. There are also some interesting crosses in intagliated wood, metal, and enamel, wrought by the monks of Mount Athos and dating probably from the sixteenth century; but it is by no means easy to fix the date of the works of these monks, whose iconographic style is so conservative and traditional that it is difficult to distinguish the output of centuries far removed from one another. We must also mention two small bells, one in gold and the other in silver, found in the tomb of a child: it was customary among the ancients to wear these bells to ward off ill-luck. Here are also a ring belonging to the Anti-Pope Clement VII, several episcopal rings of the fifteenth century, various little bronze plaques by Visentino and others, and many bronze Christian medals which were used as *encolpia* and hung around the neck by a small chain or string.

In the vertical case that comes next we find many gilt glasses similar to

Fragment of Cloth dating from the Pre-Carolingian Epoch

those of which we have already spoken. These constitute one of the most precious collections in the whole Museum, and whereas all other museums, even in Italy, contain only a very few of them, the Vatican has more than one hundred and fifty. We have already spoken of their origin and manufacture; it only remains to speak of the most characteristic types found in this collection, which may without any exaggeration be described as unique. The bottoms of the cups very often have a portrait of the owner, or a portrait between two saints, or simply the heads of the Apostles Peter and Paul. A few represent St. Agnes, who always wears a veil over her shoulders, fastened with a little brooch set with six gems like that of the Vestals, thus signifying that the Saint died a virgin. Others have a mystic meaning, as for instance that showing Moses causing water to flow from a rock and inscribed with the name Petrus. This scene, which recurs several times, agrees very well with the idea of the Fathers, who styled Peter the Moses of the New Testament and likened the spring of water to the source of grace. From an artistic point of view, the finest object in the collection is the picture with the inscription, "Eusebi anima dulcis." It was found in the Cemetery of St. Agnes, and its workmanship is so Classical and accurate that it cannot be referred to a later date than the third century. The figure is shown robed in a chlamys

Silver Reliquary with Engraved Figures

Ivory Cover of the Lorsch Evangeliary
(Ninth Century)

The Codex is in the Vatican Library
(Cod. Vat. Palat. Lat. 50)

The Rambona Diptych
(Eighth Century)

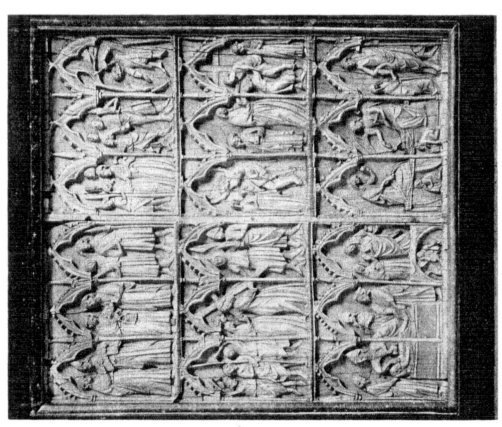

French Diptych with Scenes from the New Testament
(Fourteenth Century)

fastened on the shoulder with a round brooch.

The collection extends through the next vertical case and the horizontal glass case on the floor, in which are also contained many fine fragments of vases and beautiful samples of phials of various shapes, bearing palm leaves in relief. In the vertical glass case, besides the cemetery or gilt glasses, are a collection of fine fragments of Roman enamel-ware and a small collection of carved Christian gems. Especially noteworthy among the latter is a beautiful golden ring found in 1912 during the excavations in the Cemetery of St. Domitilla; in the ring is set a hard carved stone, on the left of which is represented a

Fragment of Silk Material
(Seventh Century)

dolphin entwined round a trident (a well-known symbol of Christ on the cross), and on the right the Good Shepherd seated among his sheep in the shade of an olive-tree on which is perched a dove holding in her beak a branch of the same olive-tree.

Cases VIII, IX and X contain a collection of enamels, some important small reliquary urns from Limoges, two beautiful episcopal rochets, and a number of small Greek, Italian and German plaques; but, except for the triptych by Penicaud and the Passion scenes above referred to, there is nothing here to compare with the exhibits in the Louvre and other French collections.

The fourth horizontal glass case contains a number of very small objects from the Catacombs, but, many as are those that are shown here, a large number of others of recent acquisition are possessed by the Museum, but cannot be shown for lack of space. These range from objects in ivory and bone to bronzes, enamels, hard stones, nard boxes, solar pocket clocks, sword-hilts, balance weights, scourges, medallions, bone dolls with jointed legs and arms, leaden toys, and so forth. It is unnecessary to describe these objects in detail, but it is well to remind the reader that all of them were found in the Catacombs, fixed in the mortar used to close the *loculi,* or tombs.

In Cases XIII and XIV are exhibited a few fragments of Coptic cloths found in the tombs of Upper Egypt and donated to the Museum by the

Armor of Pope Julius II, which he is said
to have worn at the Capture of Bologna in 1506

Armor of the Connétable de Bourbon, who
fell during the Siege of Rome in 1525

Committee of the Exposition of Sacred Art, which met at Turin in 1898. The finest specimen is that hanging on the end wall of Case XIV; this was found in a tomb at Akmim, and was given to the Museum by Monsignor Sogaro. In the lower part of these same cases are a number of silver, bronze and terra-cotta objects found in the excavation of the Xenodochium of Pammachius at Porto. Very beautiful silver-rimmed shells bear on the inside surface the cross in niello. Here also are bronze tubes with palms and inscriptions, magnificent terra-cotta lamps with important symbols, and a whole series of fragments of glass bowls bearing images of saints and Christian symbols put on by the potter's wheel. These are, for the most part, works of the fourth century and are very well preserved. In one of these cases is also to be seen a singularly beautiful reliquary in the shape of a bowl, with a silver lid with niello decorations; this was intended as a reliquary for the head of St. Sebastian. On its foot is the dedicatory inscription of Gregory IV, and on the inside a beautiful monogram about whose meaning there is still much discussion. It was taken from its case, where it had lain hidden since the seventeenth century in the Church of the Four Crowned Martyrs, and was brought to the Museum in March, 1913.

The next case and the fifth horizontal glass case contain the highly

Tablet showing the Man Born Blind and Capsella
with Bacchic Scene
(Sixth and Third Centuries)

Upper Surface of Engraved
Silver Reliquary Casket
(Ninth Century)

Tablet showing the Madonna and Saints
(Sixteenth Century)

Side View of Engraved Silver Reliquary Casket
(Ninth Century)

Byzantine Triptych with Cross, Ornaments and Saints
(Tenth Century)

important collection of ivories. The glass case also contains a wooden comb with Christian symbols, which is referred to the fifth or sixth century and was found in the bottom of a well at Chiusi. Most of the ivories are of French origin and date from the fourteenth and fifteenth centuries, and among them are some remarkable triptychs. But the objects which particularly deserve our attention are a diptych of Rambona, the cover of an evangeliary of Lorsch, and a large Byzantine triptych dating from the eleventh century. The Rambona diptych is an eighth-century work, and shows to the left a Calvary in which the cross rests on the she-wolf that fed Romulus and Remus. To the right, above, the Madonna is seated, holding on her knees the Infant, who is attended by two seraphim; below three nimbused saints are shown, their names (St. Gregory, St. Sylvester, St. Flavian) being given in the inscription separating the two panels. Below all, in the centre of another inscription, is a figure having a nimbus and bearing a palm branch. The cover of the evangeliary, the codex of which is in the Vatican Library (Cod. Vat. Palat. Lat. 50), is from the Abbey of St. Nazarius at Lorsch. It is divided into five panels, showing the Saviour, some Angels, and the Adoration of the Magi. For a long time it was thought that the ivory was a sixth-century work, but as the result of recent studies we cannot refer it to an earlier date than the ninth century. The Byzantine triptych is an example of that renaissance of art which flourished in Byzantium about the year 1000, and of which this relic is a glorious specimen. It consists of three ivory tablets on which is carved the Redeemer on a throne, with St. Joseph and the Madonna on either side. In three zones, one above the other, we see many saints whose names are written near them.

The case following and the last horizontal glass case contain the treasures of the Sancta Sanctorum. In the middle altar of the chapel of the Sancta Sanctorum near the Lateran many precious relics were enclosed in very ancient and valuable reliquaries that had not been opened for five centuries. In 1903, while seeking for the head of St. Agnes, the Church authorities not only succeeded in finding it, but were led by their search to the discovery of many other relics of inestimable value. When the slab that enclosed the altar was opened there were found, under a layer of dust, some small bags of ancient Sassanide and Carolingian cloth, within which were preserved many reliquaries of rare beauty. Lack of space prevents our giving a description of even the most important things in this collection, but we must call attention to an enamelled gold cross of sixth- or seventh-century workmanship, and a magnificent tenth-century silver reliquary with enamelled medallions, in which the head of St. Praxedes was preserved. Most remarkable too is the well-preserved state of the cord which fastened the bags and the seal of Nicholas III. Other features of interest are a seventh-century ivory bas-relief depicting the healing of the man born blind, a splendid Greek *crux gammata* enclosed in a silver case decorated with bas-reliefs, and, finally, precious pieces of cloth which were used as bags to contain reliquaries, and which, now unfolded and displayed, constitute the most beautiful and rare specimens of cloth-weaving prior to the time of Charlemagne. For a more discursive treatment of a collection which, for adequate appreciation, would require careful and extensive description, the reader may be referred to the works of Philippe Lauer ("Le trésor du Sancta Sanctorum," Paris, Leroux, 1906) and H. Grisar ("Il Sancta Sanctorum ed il suo tesoro sacro," Rome, Civiltà Cattolica, 1907), published since the discovery of these treasures. These works reproduce photographs of the most interesting among the exhibits.

The last two cases contain medieval woodwork and the "steatites," which include some unusually interesting specimens of Greek medieval art. In the lower part of the cases is the most important existing collection of Christian earthenware lamps, richly decorated with monograms, crosses and symbols of every shape. Although this collection is not at present on exhibition, it is placed at the disposal of any student desirous of examining it.

The Christian Museum is being constantly enriched by new objects from the excavations of the Catacombs or donated by friends.

THE NUMISMATIC COLLECTION

T̲HE Vatican Numismatic Collection began very modestly about the middle of the sixteenth century, when a few coins and leaden pontifical seals were donated to the Popes by private individuals to form a Cabinet of Coins in the Papal Library. So far as is known, however, the Vatican did not possess an important collection of coins and medals until the middle of the eighteenth century. This is all the more surprising as many cardinals are known to have had splendid collections as early as the end of the fifteenth century. It will be sufficient to cite here that which Cardinal Barbo, afterwards Paul II, had formed in his glorious Palazzo Venezia.

About 1738 Clement XII took the first step towards making an important collection, when he bought the celebrated Roman medallions belonging to Cardinal Albani. Benedict XIV added to these the ancient coins and medals of every age and country which had been sedulously collected by Cardinal Carpegna. Later were acquired the Papal coins which belonged to the famous numismatist Saverio Scilla, and which had formed the basis for his fundamental work on Papal numismatics. Subsequent Popes acquired minor collections, and strove in every way to extend the existing series of coins, so that, when Pius VI secured the celebrated collection of Queen Christina of Sweden, which had passed into the hands of Prince Livio Odescalchi, the Vatican collection became one of the richest and most famous of the age.

One result of the French occupation of Rome in 1798 was the complete dispersal of this numismatic collection, for such of the coins as were not stolen or lost were sent to France and incorporated in the collection in the Bibliothèque Nationale at Paris. Only the less important part of the collection was given back after the Treaty of 1815, the unique collection of Roman coins, as well as all the coins of which the French museum did not possess duplicates, being retained. Pius VII immediately set about the formation of a new collection, and succeeding Popes followed his example by adding to it all coins found during the excavations around Rome, and after 1870 by acquiring private collections which extended the series of special importance for the history of the Holy See. Particular mention must be made of Cardinal Lorenzo Randi's collection of pontifical coins, upon which he spent fifty years, and which was bought by Leo XIII. These accessions rendered the collection one of the richest in Italy, and for some special series the richest in Europe.

The Numismatic Collection possesses at present about 80,000 coins, medals, seals, tesseræ, bullæ and incised stones of every age and country.

The series of Papal coins is undoubtedly the largest and most important; it comprises about 15,000 specimens, of which about 1100 are in gold, 8000 in silver, and the rest in alloy or copper. This collection, which has been recently described in three large volumes with over one hundred and eighty plates, is rightly considered the most important medieval and modern series in existence, and has always enjoyed the high appreciation of students of art. The collection contains an almost unbroken series of Papal coins from the eighth century to the year 1870, and, together with the splendid series of Papal medals, bullæ and leaden seals, furnishes a history of Italian engraving art from the fall of the Roman Empire through the Middle Ages and Renaissance period down to our own time. Guazzalotti, Cristoforo di Geremia, Camelio, Grechetto, Leone Leoni, Sperandio, Francia, Benvenuto Cellini and many other celebrated artists worked in the Papal mint during the fifteenth and sixteenth centuries; the Hamerani family, which came from Germany to Rome in the early part of the seventeenth century, furnished a large number of excellent artists, who in the nineteenth century had equally famous successors, such as Girometti and Cerbara. The specimens in this department are so excellent and numerous that they need not fear comparison with any other collection.

The collection of ancient coins dating from Republican and Imperial Rome is not inferior in number, rarity or state of preservation. As this series is continued by the Papal coins of the first part of the eighth century, the two collections give a faithful reflection of the artistic history of the Eternal City for twenty-four centuries, and thus form the noblest series of coins in the world. Selected from numerous collections, the series of Republican coins is unsurpassed, whether in the number, rarity or excellence of its specimens. It contains more than 7000 coins, including the heavy bronze ones of the primitive age, and its historical interest is universally recognized, since it furnishes authentic information of an epoch which has left but few contemporaneous records. Portraits of heroes, both legendary and historic, are combined in these small coins with notices of the most celebrated events in the history of Rome, furnishing us with almost contemporary

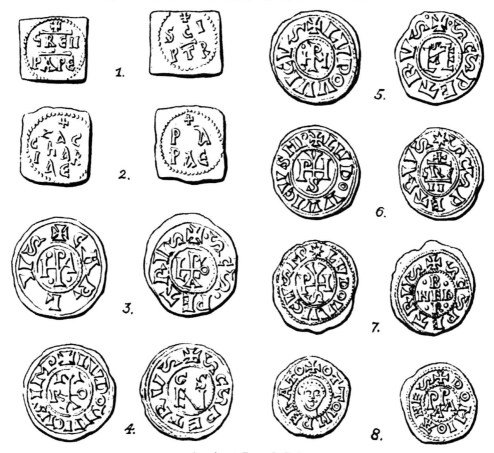

Ancient Papal Coins

(1) Gregory III, 731–741. (2) Zacharias, 741–752. (3) Leo III, 795–816. (4) Eugene II, 824–827.
(5) Valentine, 827. (6) Gregory IV, 827–844. (7) Benedict III, 855–858. (8) Marinus II, 942–946.

comment. With this rare collection are linked the names of many famous numismatists, such as Borghesi, Garrucci, Tessieri and Baron d'Ailly, either because they collaborated in its development or because it furnished them with material for their profound studies.

Of all the numismatic series, however, that of Imperial Rome has received the most attention from students. This starts with Julius Cæsar and ends with Romulus Augustulus, and, if it cannot be compared with the original collection taken to Paris (particularly in the number and value of its medallions), it still retains a high place among Italian collections. It contains no less than 12,000 coins, of which about 500 are of gold, and has besides over 100 bronze medallions. Most rare and unique specimens are not lacking, or specimens of an exquisite art in a marvellous state of preservation. These products of the mint of Rome, which worked longer than that of any other city, form a collection of artistic monuments and historical documents of the highest value for the multiform researches which have been instituted into the historical development of this extraordinary city.

Less numerous and important, if considered separately, is the collection of Greek, Græco-Roman and colonial coins, although it is ample for the study of those unsurpassed and insurpassable products of the great engravers of Tarentum and Syracuse, and allows us to follow the artistic development of Greek numismatics from its beginnings down to the Roman conquest. This event marks the sudden and pronounced decadence of the technical and plastic arts in the land of every beauty, for thenceforth to Rome, as the centre of all activity, turned the best artists, deserting a province which no longer favored the development of genius.

The other series are also representative collections. For example, the series of Italian coins and medals contains all that is necessary to complete the study of Italian art in modern times. Gifts from missionaries have enriched the gallery with series of coins from India, China, Japan and other Asiatic lands, and there have been some donations of American coins, especially from South America.

At the present time the directors of all numismatic collections aim at limiting their scope to the completion of those series that are of most interest to the institute of which the collection is a part, or to the city or country in which the collection is situated. Thus it has been the chief care of the Popes to increase the series of pontifical and Roman coins so as to make this collection ever more worthy of the artistic traditions of the Vatican.

THE HALL OF THE GEOGRAPHICAL CHARTS

The Loggia delle Carte Geografiche, or Hall of the Geographical Charts, occupies portion of the site of the former Cortile del Bramante. It is a large vaulted hall adorned with arabesques and painted figures, and takes its name from the number of charts, or maps, painted on its walls. The historian Giovanni Baglioni says its first architect was Girolamo Muzzani of Brescia, and in the large inscription over the entrance door we read that the gallery was begun and completed, maps and all, under Gregory XIII, in the year 1581. Pius VII placed in this gallery as ornaments some marble seats and numerous pieces of sculpture, the most valuable of which are a double hermes of Bacchus, an Epicurus, a Pythagoras, and an Aristotle. Other alterations and repairs were made by Urban VIII, as the arms of that Pope suggest and an inscription dated 1631 informs us.

The first two maps we meet on entering show us Genoa and Venice face to face. Under the former is written: "Genua, maritimæ Liguriæ caput, navalis militiæ studio et civium virtute atque opulentia inclyta, minutissimis nuper ædificatis mœnibus, tutam clarissimæ Reipublicæ sedem præbet." Under the other we read: "Venetiæ civitas admirabilis post eversam ab Attila Hunnorum Rege Aquileiam, condita anno a salute hominibus restituta CCCCLIV."

Next to the map of Genoa we find Civitavecchia, the ancient name of which (Portus Trajanus ad Centumcellas) is used. Facing it we see Ancona—Civitas Dorica, as the legend runs. The decorations on the ceiling corresponding with these maps show us the Baptistery of the Lateran with the Baptism of Constantine, the building of old St. Peter's, and the building of St. Paul's with figures painted by Antonio Tempesta, a Florentine artist known as Il Tempestino. He was a pupil first of Giovanni Strada and later of Santi di Tito, died at Rome in 1630 at the age of seventy-five, and was buried in S. Rocco alla Ripetta.

Near these paintings are the portraits of two famous geographers, Flavio Biondo and Raffaele Volterrano; between them is a representation of New Italy, while on the opposite side is Ancient Italy between the figures of Strabo and Ptolemy. After these on the roof are painted

St. Sylvester on horseback while Constantine holds his stirrup, and the Apparition of the Cross to Constantine. On the side walls we next see two large maps, one of Liguria and the other of Piedmont and Monferrato; the corresponding decorations on the ceiling are the scene showing the Translation of the Remains of St. John the Baptist in the harbor of Genoa, and the Exposition of the Holy Shroud at Turin. In the centre is St. Ambrose forbidding Emperor Theodosius to enter his church.

Maps of Tuscany and the Duchy of Milan come next in order on opposite walls; on the ceiling above we see the hermitage of Camalduli, where St. Romuald founded his order, St. Francis receiving the sacred stigmata on Mount Alvernia, and St. Ambrose driving away the enemies of the Church from the gates of Milan.

The map of Perugia faces that of the territory of Venice beyond the Po. On the roof we are shown Bishop St. Constantius healing a large crowd of the infirm from his prison window; two scenes from the life of Jacob stand on either side of this picture. The central panel shows us the Venetian Ducal Palace, where Pope Alexander III is in the act of receiving the homage of the Emperor Frederick Barbarossa, who kneels before him. This scene is flanked by pictures of the Bolsena miracle and of St. Anthony of Padua preaching.

Next follow the map of the Papal Estates in Tuscany and the map of Friuli. In the central panel of the ceiling we are shown Pope Gregory VII on his throne, while Countess Matilda offers him all her possessions.

Maps of Umbria and the Duchy of Parma and Piacenza follow, and on the ceiling we see the meeting of Pope Leo IV and Attila, King of the Huns; over the window on one side is St. Clare freeing the town of Assisi from the invasion of the Saracens, and above the opposite window Pope Innocent IV frees the town of Parma from the siege of Frederick II.

The map of Latium and the Sabine country faces that of the Duchy of Mantua. In the centre of the ceiling above, Christ is represented preventing St. Peter from leaving Rome, while on either side are painted Moses and Jacob. Another scene shows the Fall of Simon Magus. Over one window we are shown the City of Naples and the miracle of the blood of St. Januarius, and on the opposite side the town of Modena is freed through the intercession of this Saint.

We now come to a map of the Terra di Lavoro, the Campagna Felice, which has the following inscription: "Campania ea est amœnitate, ea utitur cœli benignitate, ea terrarum fœcunditate . . . " Facing this map is that of the Duchy of Ferrara. On the roof St. Benedict is seen

The Hall of the Geographical Charts

discovering Totila in disguise, and in the following panel Christ is
represented among the Apostles entrusting to St. Peter the supreme
care of the Church. This last painting, with its life-size figures, is the
work of Romanelli. Above and below this scene are a view of the
Monastery of St. Michael in Bosco, outside Bologna, and a scene show-

ing the transfer of the miraculous image of the Madonna to Monte della Guardia, also at Bologna. These paintings are thought to be the work of Giovannangelo Canini, a pupil of Domenichino. Beside the window we have the miracle of St. Petronius bringing back to life a laborer who has been crushed under a column, and St. Dominic at table with his companions in the refectory of his monastery, while angels wait on them with bread.

The two maps that follow show the Principality of Salerno and the City of Bologna. The central painting depicts the miracle of the manna rising from the body of St. Andrew and its distribution among the people by the deacons. Here also are paintings of Sts. Bernard and Rainulf, St. Liberius driving out demons from the possessed, and St. Anthony of Padua preaching to the fishes on the sea-shore. After the tenth window we come to the map of Lucania, which faces that of the Romagna. Scenes on the roof show us the election of St. Severus as Bishop of Ravenna, and St. Peter Damian in cardinalitial robes dictating the rules of a hermit's life to a group of solitaries. Over one window we see St. Francis of Paula crossing the sea on his cloak, and over the other St. Ubaldo liberating Gubbio from a siege.

We come next to the maps of Calabria Citerior and the Duchy of Urbino. The ceiling shows us the miracle of St. Francis of Paula in the fiery furnace. Then follow maps of Calabria Ulterior and the March of Ancona. The miracle of the translation of the Holy House of Loretto is shown on the roof. In the panel over the window to the right the Pope gives Communion to the Emperor Henry, while to the left we see St. Marcellinus miraculously saving the City of Ancona from fire. Next we have maps of Corsica and the territory of Ancona. The scene on the roof shows the cavalcade which went to seek for Pietro Celestino on the Majella Mountains when he was elected Pope; beside this painting are Pope Symmachus and St. Bernardine. The map of Sardinia faces that of the Abruzzi. On the roof above, Pope John I and Boetius consign King Theodoric to destruction.

Maps of Sicily and Apulia come next. On the roof are shown Mount Garganus and the apparition of St. Michael the Archangel. The next map shows the County of Venaissin, that is, the territory around Avignon formerly possessed by the Popes. Opposite this map is that of the Salentine Peninsula. Beside this is a small tablet with an inscription telling us that he who carefully and accurately drew these maps was Padre Ignatio Danti, a native of Perugia and a Friar Preacher. On the ceiling above, the Emperor Valentinian receives St. Martin, St. Paul heals the father of Publius, who was ill at Malta, and St. Paul is seen setting out from Malta for Rome.

At the end of this hall we are shown the old harbor at the mouth of the Tiber as it existed in the time of the Emperor Claudius, and on the opposite wall the same harbor as it was in the time of Gregory XIII. Near the exit, where the arms of Pope Gregory are seen, we have a view of the Island of Malta and a scene showing Malta freed from the Turks.

It is no easy task to determine the artists who painted the pictures in this Gallery. We have already given the names of the designer of the maps and of some of the artists who painted the frescoes on the ceiling. But so many artists have worked in this gallery that it is impossible to identify each individual artist and his work. We know that Antonio Danti (brother of the geographer), Muziano, Raffaellino da Reggio, Paris Nogari, Pasquale Cati, Ottaviano Mascherini, Marco da Faenza, Giovanni da Modena, Girolamo Massei, Giacomo Sementa, and Lorenzino da Bologna were employed here. The names of very many others have escaped the historian of art, but this fact is not so very regrettable since the pictures, with few exceptions, have little artistic merit and serve merely as a pleasing decoration of the gallery. The maps, however, are precious, not from the point of view of art but of culture. They are most valuable for the history of geography, and also, where they represent the various cities, for the study of topography. Here lies the real value of the Gallery, and the reason why it deserves mention among the great halls of the Vatican, although to remarkable artistic grandeur it can make no claim. Besides the maps, but in no way connected with them, this Gallery contains seven large cartoons executed by the German painter, J. F. Overbeck, between 1857 and 1862.

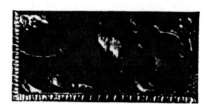

THE VATICAN LIBRARY

HE collection of books has always been pursued by persons of wealth who occupied a position of prominence among their fellow-men. The earlier the age, the more difficult, of course, was this collection, and the rarer were the libraries; for in olden times even a library of moderate dimensions, consisting as it did exclusively of manuscript materials, represented a fortune.

In Christian antiquity the active scientific studies pursued in the great monasteries necessitated a collection of books. This need was met by procuring a loan of the books and having them copied by learned monks in the different monasteries. In the Scriptoria (or copying-rooms) of their monasteries the monks prepared not alone the books for their own use, but executed also the commissions of outsiders.

The writing material used for extensive works was generally parchment. In the early Middle Ages the use of papyrus was practically confined to documents prepared for the state chanceries, and paper had still to be invented. Parchment, however, was very dear. Consequently, when one wished to have an important new work copied and could not afford or did not wish to incur the expense of new parchment, it was not unusual to take another book from one's library, efface the writing from the parchment, smoothen the surface, and use the parchment for the new manuscript. In such a case a book was usually chosen of which there were several copies, or of which its owner did not recognize the value. For example, the choice often fell on a manuscript because its language was antiquated and thus difficult or impossible to decipher, or because its text possessed no special interest for its owner. Parchments which were thus utilized a second time are known as palimpsests, or *Codices rescripti.* They may be recognized from the fact that here and there traces of the first manuscript, or at least perforations made by compasses and unconnected with the second manuscript, are still visible. The custom of using parchment a second time is very ancient, since the early Greek and Roman writers speak of palimpsests, and was especially common in the seventh and eighth centuries of the Christian era. Until recent times a gall-nut mixture or Gioberti tincture was very successfully employed to render the first manuscript again visible. At present, however, much better results are attained by a special photographic process, without the use of corrosive inks. Later on in this chapter we shall have to speak of one of the most successful and renowned discoverers of palimpsests, Cardinal Mai.

It is a well-known fact that, generally speaking, important collections of books were confined during the Middle Ages to churches, monasteries, and the libraries of high ecclesiastics; and among these libraries that of the Popes in Rome was always especially prominent. Often depleted and destroyed by war and revolution, no library, however, could hope to enjoy unarrested development. Beginning from the earliest days, the Popes labored tirelessly to provide in the greatest possible completeness the literary materials necessary for the proper discharge of their exalted office, and strove to preserve for future generations the civilization of Classical antiquity. But, as the result of the never-ending troubles of the early and later Middle Ages, their library had all but disappeared by the end of the thirteenth century.

At Avignon, in the fourteenth century, the Popes again applied themselves with zeal to the collection of books. John XXII (1316–1334) made a beginning by purchasing books and having manuscripts copied at Avignon. Presents of manuscripts arrived from all sides, and a very important source of increase lay in the exercise of the papal right to the inheritance of prelates—the *ius spolii,* which declared that all the possessions of a deceased member of the Curia fell to the Apostolic Camera—that is, the Papal Exchequer. The glorious pontificate of Clement VI (1342–1352) raised the Papal Library to a position of great splendor. The management, or prefecture, of the Library was then entrusted to the Sacristan of the Apostolic Palaces. Until 1411 the Avignon Library was located in the Turris Angelorum (Tower of the Angels), which had been erected by Benedict XII (1334–1342).

In so far as juridical literature was concerned, the Papal Library at Avignon surpassed even that of the Sorbonne in Paris, although, generally speaking, the latter was without a rival in the fourteenth century. The Papal Library, unfortunately, did not escape the common misfortunes of that age, and was so scattered that scarcely any of the books there collected were brought to Rome when the Popes returned to their residence beside the Tiber after the Council of Constance. A large number of the Avignon manuscripts did not find their way back to the Papal Library at the Vatican until our own day, when Leo XIII purchased the library of the Borghese family, which had secured a large portion of the stolen treasures of the Avignon Library.

The Vatican Library
(D. Fontana, Architect)

Left Wing of the Vatican Library

Martin V (1417–1431) and Eugene IV (1431–1447) resumed in Rome the collection of books, although these were now intended only for the private use of the Pope and the Curia. The idea of founding a public library occurred first to Nicholas V (1447–1455), when he made the fourth effort to establish a great papal library. Eugene IV had bequeathed him three hundred and forty manuscripts, and, by adding these to his private library, he formed the first important division of the new collection. In systematic fashion he increased his collection by employing copyists at a fixed salary to copy those originals which could not be bought from their owners. His passion for books induced him to send experienced men to Germany, England, and even Denmark to search for and purchase manuscripts. At the fall of Constantinople the Turks had scattered the extremely valuable Imperial Library. Papal agents were commissioned to acquire for the Pope all valuable manuscripts which had belonged to the Imperial Library and were for sale. At the same time the Pope invited all the exiled Byzantine and also competent Italian scholars to Rome and commissioned them to translate the Greek classics into Latin for his library. Before this inde-

Another View of the Vatican Library

fatigable collector died in 1455, he had assembled twelve hundred manuscripts—an extraordinary number for that time. And the high importance and value of his additions increased the worth of the Library as a whole far beyond anything that the mere numerical increase would indicate.

The collection of Nicholas V had not as yet any special, fixed, and public habitation, nor was there any special librarian. These developments were reserved for Sixtus IV (1471–1484), who determined to house the Library in the Vatican Palace. The Papal Library thus became the Palatine Library, in which originated the Vaticana, as the collection is now commonly known. That Sixtus IV should have accommodated these precious treasures in the rather dark and damp rooms comprising the ground floor of the Cortile del Papagallo is a little surprising. But it should be remembered that, in the first place, the palace was not then so extensive that one could choose at pleasure, and in the second place experience had not yet discovered the proper arrangement and requirements of a public library. These rooms now serve as store-rooms for the Floreria, and those who view these quarters to-day cannot suppress their surprise that for so many decades they were the scene of brisk scientific activity.

The Pope had the two large halls painted by Domenico and David Ghirlandaio, and the other two rooms by Melozzo da Forlì and Antoniazzo. Many traces of these glorious paintings are still visible, although the mosaic floor of this period has entirely disappeared. Nor has any trace remained of the stained glass windows made by the German artists Herrmann, Georg, and Konrad. The gloominess of the rooms was, of course, still further aggravated by these windows. Sixtus IV named Giovanni Tortelli director of the Library of Nicholas V, and the renowned Platina librarian. The latter prepared a catalogue of the collection. In one of his mighty paintings Melozzo da Forlì has immortalized the moment when Sixtus IV, with his two nephews beside him and surrounded by his Court, received Platina and entrusted to him the management of the Library. This fresco has since been removed from the old library, and is now one of the treasures of the Vatican Picture Gallery. The library halls were then well equipped with shelves, desks, benches, and presses. Many of these pieces of furniture have been preserved, and serve their purpose even to-day. Under Julius II (1503–1513) the halls were still further decorated; but while the collections continued to grow, the rooms were not increased, and the majority and most important of the manuscripts were still fastened with chains, as was usual in those days. In exceptional cases, however, but only as a favor to specially prominent scholars, individual manuscripts were lent out. As we turn over the extant lists of those who used the Codices, we are met by the name of every one who was then prominent in learned circles in Rome.

The officials of the Library were known as the Custodians. Beginning from the time of Paul III (1534–1549), we find mention of the purely scientific officials known as the Scriptores and Correctores. Finally, in 1548, the Library was entrusted to the care of a Cardinal Librarian, an office and title which stood in the highest repute during the Middle Ages. This first Cardinal Librarian of the Holy Roman Church, Marcello Cervini, succeeded in 1555 to the papal throne as Marcellus II, but enjoyed a pontificate of only twenty-two days. During his term of office as librarian, Cardinal Cervini presented two hundred and forty manuscripts and many books to the Library. It need scarcely be said that, with the invention of printing, a collection of printed books was immediately begun, the development of which department will be dealt with in detail below.

After this fundamental reorganization of the Palatine Library and the assembling of its treasures in one place, a new period of internal development began. Externally also an extremely important change took place, when Sixtus V (1585–1590) carried into execution the plan already conceived by Gregory XIII (1572–1585), and provided a new and magnificent home for the Palatine Library. Among the numberless undertakings upon which Sixtus V engaged during his short pontificate, one of the most famous is the erection of the huge hall of the new library. In so far as one may judge from bills of cost, this gigantic hall was begun and completed in about thirteen months by Domenico Fontana, at a cost of $25,850, which sum was paid him by Sixtus V on September 16, 1588. This building divided the huge Cortile di Belvedere into two portions, and before it was provided with bookshelves, furniture, and other accessories the expenditure amounted to $42,075. It should be remembered that, inasmuch as the purchasing power of money was then about four times as great as now, the cost would be equivalent to about $170,000 at the present day. The painters Cesare Nebbio and Giovanni Guerra, who were also given various other commissions by Sixtus V, were entrusted with the great task of decorating with frescoes the Sistine Hall (Il Salone Sistino), as the library hall was named. These frescoes represent the most famous libraries, the councils, the discoverers of the

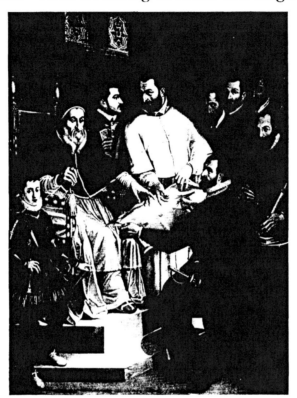

Pope Sixtus V (1585-1590) approving the plan of the new library (in Sistine Hall). Beside the Pope are his two nephews; the prelate in a mozetta is Cardinal Librarian Carafa; Fontana kneels before the Pope

arts, and the chief events of the pontificate of Sixtus V. The last-named paintings are of great importance for a knowledge of Rome as it was at that time, since they show us how many of the chief monuments, which were later surrounded with buildings or otherwise altered, then looked.

Into this hall were transferred all the treasures of the old library, a task which the great Pope did not live to see completed. With the change of location the name of the Library was also altered, being henceforth known as the Vatican Library. Adjacent to this depository for manuscripts, with its princely equipment, Sixtus V erected a large Reading-room, and had there carved in marble regulations for readers drawn up by himself. The whole glorious work was in every way worthy of the exalted conception which Sixtus entertained of the offices of the Papacy, and it alone would be sufficient to immortalize the fame of this most industrious and resolute Pontiff. Marco da Faenza painted the pictures of the Sibyls in the Reading-room, and Paul Brill decorated the walls with landscapes. The wood panels from the Library of Sixtus IV and the benches made by Giovannino de' Dolci were removed to the new library, as already stated. To-day these highly remarkable pieces of woodwork have almost all been assigned to the Appartamento Borgia, for which place they seem preëminently suitable.

In the course of time the rooms of Pope Sixtus V proved too small for the ever-growing Library, and it was decided to devote gradually to the collection the long, narrow wing which is adjacent to the Gardens and stands at right angles to the Sistine Hall. It has thus come to pass that the whole wing of the palace, running from the Chapel of Pius V to the entrance to the Museum, has been given over to the treasures of the Library and kindred collections. The old reading-room of Sixtus V was very poorly lighted, since there was but a single window on one of the narrow sides. Yet for three hundred years the leading scholars of all nations here carried on their scientific borings into the inexhaustible mines of the Vaticana—a fact which in itself shows how glad men were to gain admission to the Library under any terms. Leo XIII built the new reading-room immediately adjacent to the old and extending to the Cortile della Stamperia. The lofty windows on the left side of this room give excellent light to every worker.

But whereas at first the rooms for the manuscripts and books had offered more than ample accommodation, the Library again outgrew its quarters. A very large number of the printed books were accessible only with the greatest difficulty, since they had to be accommodated in one of the halls of the Appartamento Borgia, which was not yet restored. When Leo XIII decided to have these glorious state-rooms restored to their former splendor, the books had to be removed. He therefore directed that the armory situated under the Sistine Hall should be cleared and that a consulting library of printed books should be here established, with the proper conveniences for scholars. The old armory (Armeria pontificia), which is the same size as the Sistine Hall, was beautifully decorated, and in it were set up a life-size figure of St. Thomas and a marble bust of the founder of the Consultation Library to perpetuate his memory.

But, even with these extensive and beautiful additions, the demand for space was only temporarily satisfied, and it was reserved for Pius X to cope with the situation in comprehensive fashion. Under the old

Codex Vaticanus Græcus 1209 (Codex B)
The most famous of all Greek MSS. of the Bible. (Fourth Century)

and the new reading-rooms lay the Vatican Press, and adjacent to this a lofty and very long hall situated under the Gallery of Inscriptions. Pius X first assigned this hall for the accommodation of the books and numerous manuscripts of the Barberini Library and Archives. Then, when the Polyglot Press of the Propaganda was suppressed, a new home was found elsewhere for the reorganized Vatican Press. The rooms formerly belonging to the Vatican Press were then redecorated and assigned to the administration of the Library. These changes made it possible to change the Reading-room from the first to the ground floor, where it was immediately adjacent to the Consulting Library. For readers this innovation meant an extraordinary facilitation of their work, since a few steps now bring them to the printed books in the Consulting Library. The new reading-room lies exactly under the second Sistine reading-room, while under the first lies the Biblical Library of Printed Books. A number of adjacent rooms, which, together with the second reading-room, are still unoccupied, are to be taken over by the Library administration or utilized in connection with the fundamental rearrangement of the manuscripts. What considerations led to the undertaking of so important and extensive an enterprise may be here briefly explained. The manuscripts were preserved, according to collections, in the low, beautifully painted wooden presses of the state rooms of the Sistine Hall and of the wing of the palace, several hundred yards long, which borders on the Gardens. Consequently, when a scholar desired certain manuscripts, the attendants of the Library had a very long distance to go from the Reading-room to execute his wishes. Thus, when the attendance at the Library was large, the attendants had frequently to walk many miles in the forenoon, carrying the often very massive volumes. This condition of affairs made serious demands on the strength of the attendants, and was a cause of considerable delay for the readers. Furthermore, the state rooms of the Library are accessible to strangers. Experience otherwise gained had revealed to the authorities the danger that at any time an attempt might be made to steal some of the manuscripts, if one of the presses were left open and careful watch were not kept by the attendants. The safety of the manuscripts was thus not so well assured as the administration desired. The fact that no manuscripts had been previously stolen from the presses was no guarantee for the future. Finally, there was the danger of fire, however remote it might be: should some evil-minded visitor enkindle a smouldering fire in one of the presses, and should the fire break out during the afternoon or night, priceless treasures might be lost. Since the Library halls are vaulted and rest on arches, all other danger of fire, except from lightning, was practically eliminated. Some persons may think the caution of the Library authorities excessive. But inasmuch as the Vatican officials have such a tremendous responsibility and are answerable to the whole educated world, they cannot be too careful. The instalment of automatic fire-alarms may bring quick

ITIAM·SVMMATROCVLVILLARVMCVLMINATVMANT
MAIORESQVECADVNTALTISDEMONTIBVSVMBRAE A

POETA   CORYDON
FORMOSVMCORYDONTASTORARDEBATALEXIN
DELICIA·DOMININICONTDSPERARETHABEBAT
TANTVMINTERDENSASVMBROSACACVMINAFAGOS
ADSIDVAEVENIEBAT·HIS·HAECINCONDITASOLVS

Codex Vaticanus Latinus 3867
Fifth-century MS. of Virgil in rustic capitals, showing the poet
with book-stand and book-case

help in the case of a fire, but can never prevent one. It was thus resolved
to remove all the manuscripts from the state rooms and lodge them in
adjoining fire-proof compartments in the immediate vicinity of the
Reading-room. Thus all the above fears and difficulties were removed
in so far as human efforts could remove them.

Before this task was accomplished, great difficulties had to be overcome. After extensive rebuilding and alterations, roomy quarters were
provided immediately above the Reading-room and fitted with iron
presses. Here all the collections of manuscripts in the Vaticana could
be preserved, while ample room was left for future additions. Thus
the endless journeys of the library attendants were brought to an end:
a few steps and the manuscript is now found, and a pressure of the
hand brings the elevator down to the Reading-room. The manuscripts

are now safe from every attempt at theft, and the security against fire is greatly increased, since all means at the disposal of modern technic have been employed to attain these ends. This reorganization of conditions is an accomplishment for which the gratitude of the educated world is due to Father Franz Ehrle, S. J., the indefatigable Prefect of the Vaticana. The presses in the state rooms which formerly contained the manuscripts are now filled with printed books, of whose number and importance we shall speak below. Although these also receive the greatest care, their preservation is not a matter of the same supreme importance as the preservation of the manuscripts.

The huge extent of the halls of the Library is all the more astonishing when we consider that the Vaticana has ever been, and is still, an exclusively manuscript library—not a library of printed books or even a mixed library, in which one may study equally books and manuscripts. Only readers who have declared their desire to study manuscripts are admitted to the Vaticana, for both elsewhere in Rome and in other cities throughout the world there are so many places where one may study printed books that no one need come to the Vaticana for this purpose. The Vaticana will thus always preserve the character which it has always possessed—namely, that of a purely manuscript library. To this character it owes its importance and its fame.

Some readers may believe that, inasmuch as Leo XIII established a general Consulting Library, the above statement needs at least some qualification. The Consulting Library, however, was never established as an independent institution, but to facilitate the work of the scholars engaged in the study of manuscripts. All the literature which is required for the proper study of the manuscripts may be already found in this Consulting Library, or will be added later. Printed literature which is valueless as sources of information on manuscripts is excluded. Admission is thus absolutely denied to persons who desire to work exclusively in the Consulting Library of printed books. If the Library authorities aimed at collecting printed literature in the same way as has been found useful and necessary in general libraries, they would very soon find themselves at the end of their moderate funds and their available space. The firmness with which all proposals to change the Vaticana from its historical position as an exclusively manuscript library have been rejected will be thus better understood and appreciated.

ADMINISTRATION.—The Papal Library collected in Rome in the fifteenth century was entrusted to the care of a Bibliothecarius or Custos, subordinate to whom were, as already said, the Scriptores and later also the Correctores. It was only after the first collections of manuscripts

Codex Palimpsestus Vaticanus 5757

Page of Cicero's *De republica*, in uncial script of the fourth century, over which is written, in the uncial script of the seventh or eighth century, St Augustine's tract, *Supra Psalmos*

Codex Barberini Latinus 570, fol. 51 r

Evangeliary in large folio with glorious miniatures, written in the insular script of the seventh or eighth century. At the end of the MS., which is one of the most famous of its kind, is written: *Ora pro Muibaldo* (Pray for Muibald)

began to assume importance that the ancient office of Cardinal Librarian of the Holy Roman Church was revived in 1548. Since that time, however, the care of the Vatican Library has always been entrusted to a Cardinal, who was in later days given the title of Protector of the Library. The subordinate officials of the Library have always performed the same duties, although their names and the distribution of duties among them have changed from time to time. It will be unnecessary in the present work to give a detailed history of these changes. It will be more to the purpose to inquire more fully into the present organization and the various activities of the staff employed in the Library.

Codex Palatinus Latinus 65, fol. 137 r

Psalter with glosses, liturgical prayers and a tract of Boetius, written in the peculiar insular script of the ninth or tenth century

The office of Cardinal Protector was recently left vacant by the death of Cardinal Rampolla, whose numerous learned works and treatises established his claim to be numbered among the great scholars of his time. Even while he had to bear the enormous burden of the Secretariate of State during the reign of Leo XIII, he managed to find some leisure to devote to works which awakened the admiration of scholars. The most conspicuous of his predecessors in office during the nineteenth century was Cardinal Angelo Mai, who was equally famous in two fields. In the first place, he was the discoverer of a practically endless number of previously unknown texts of high importance for both religious and secular science as well as for Latin and Greek literature; these texts fill fifty stout volumes. In the second place, he was so fortunate as to discover a remarkable number of palimpsests, and succeeded in restoring and deciphering the effaced writing—a task that was attended with enormous difficulties. The most important of these discoveries was Cicero's lost work "De republica," of which one page is here reproduced. After Cardinal Mai, special mention must be made of Cardinal Mezzofanti, a life-sized oil painting of whom hangs in the line of Cardinal Librarians, although he never occupied this office, but only the more modest post of Prefect. It was believed, however, that an exception should be made in the case of this Cardinal in view of his extraordinary celebrity. Before being called to Rome in 1831, he was professor of Oriental languages in Bologna. Two years later he was appointed Custodian or Prefect of the Vatican Library.

Codex Vaticanus Latinus 3868
MS. of Terence's Comedies, written in the Carolingian script of the tenth century

In 1838 he was raised to the Cardinalate, and later filled a great number of important offices. He was chiefly famous for his extraordinary knowledge of languages, in which he was without a rival. He spoke and wrote about fifty languages and dialects perfectly, and understood some twenty more. He was thus regarded as one of the wonders of the world; and when he visited the College of the Propaganda, where theologians from the five continents and from every nation were educated, he could converse with each individual in his mother tongue.

While the Cardinal Librarian exercises supreme supervision over the Library, and all special and important regulations must have his express approval, the real burden of the administration of the Vaticana is borne by the Prefect. The present incumbent of the Prefecture of the Vaticana is the above-mentioned Jesuit Father, Franz Ehrle. When he entered into office, the old traditional methods prevailed in very many details of administration, insufficient consideration being paid to the altered conditions of modern times. The whole administration was of a more or less patriarchal character, and certainly no undue importance was attached to the punctilious performance of duties or to the exact observance of the appointed working hours. To abolish these and other defects in the administration of the Library; to initiate and carry to a successful conclusion the fundamental revision of the general regulations; to rearrange and make easily accessible the printed books, and find proper accommodations for the library thus reorganized; to install a department which would undertake the enormously important task of restoring and preserving the damaged manuscripts in accordance with the latest discoveries of science; to bring about the transfer of smaller collections of manuscripts and archives from the possession of religious bodies to the safer custody of the Vaticana, where their perfect preservation would be assured; to cultivate intimate technical and scientific relations with the other great manuscript libraries of the world, and to extend the usefulness of the Vaticana in every possible way—these were the gigantic tasks for which Father Ehrle was summoned, and to assist him to execute them he was given the most binding assurances that in every instance he might count on the firm support of the Cardinal Librarian, the Secretary of State, and above all of the Holy Father himself.

The success of this mighty undertaking required tact, patience, unbending energy, wide scientific and technical knowledge, and especially a perfect knowledge of the new surroundings in which the Prefect found himself. During his first months of office Father Ehrle had to contend with all manner of obstacles, and only little by little did he succeed in winning first the respect, and afterwards the veneration, of his subordinate officials. Notwithstanding their absolute necessity, his innovations encountered in many instances a passive resistance which it appeared scarcely possible to overcome. Thanks, however, to his wonderful patience and exemplary firmness, he finally carried the day. It was only when it became clear to every class of the officials that Father Ehrle's system aimed solely and directly at extending the fame and importance of the venerable Library of the Popes, that the true spirit of coöperation began to inspire every member of the Library administration, which thenceforth became a body striving for one object and animated by one ideal. This happy outcome redounds to the credit of all parties, and has made it possible to carry the Vaticana to its present pitch of development.

After Father Ehrle had borne the burden of the administration for many years unassisted, he desired to be relieved of some portion of his duties so that he might have leisure for scientific work. At his suggestion, the Prefect of the Ambrosian Library in Milan, the celebrated Mgr. Ratti, was appointed Vice-Prefect of the Vaticana with right of succession. Consequently, the Vaticana has now at its head two scholars in whom the educated world places unbounded confidence on

Eleventh-century Silver Binding of the Evangeliary of S. Maria in Via Lata

account of their learning and ripe experience in all questions of modern library administration. The wide knowledge of languages which distinguishes both these scholars was not possessed by some of their predecessors, whose intercourse with foreign scholars was for this reason often carried on under the greatest difficulties. Furthermore, some of the former Prefects of the Vaticana were not completely versed in the details of library administration, and this led to all kinds of misunderstandings and difficulties. At present conditions could not possibly be more favorable, since an experienced specialist is given time and leisure to make himself thoroughly conversant with the peculiarities of the institution whose administration he will later have, in all probability, to undertake alone. This wise provision to secure continuity in the administration cannot be rated too highly, and all persons who have contributed towards bringing about this condition may well feel proud at the results of the very difficult negotiations which had to be undertaken to attain their goal. A special secretary is entrusted with the official correspondence pertaining to the Prefecture.

The staff of the Vatican Library may be divided into two classes—the scientific staff and the attendants. In the former class are included, besides the regular officers, those who have received their appointment as an honorary distinction. They are known by the collective title of Scrittori (Scriptores), a modest and indefinite term which, however, assumes great importance when we add the words "della Biblioteca Vaticana" (of the Vatican Library). The well-informed person knows that this title guarantees its possessor to be an able librarian and scholar. The number of regular Scrittori is seven; there are besides three emerited Scrittori and one assistant Scrittore (Scrittore aggiunto), two honorary Scrittori, and some honorary assistants. To these officials, who are also known as interpreters of manuscripts, are assigned as their special tasks the investigation, arrangement, and description of the Codices, the preparation of the catalogues of manuscripts for printing, and the supervision of the printing. Besides these scientific officials, whose work is confined to the manuscripts, there are a large number of subordinate officials who are entrusted with the care of the printed books, the books of plates, and the illustrated works. The attendants perform the manual labor, but even for this duty only very experienced and trustworthy men are appointed. A number of bookbinders are engaged in manufacturing new bindings or repairing the old. It may be mentioned here that the leather covers of manuscripts are provided with the coat of arms of the Pope during whose reign the Codex was added to the Library. The bindings of the printed books do not contain this imprint.

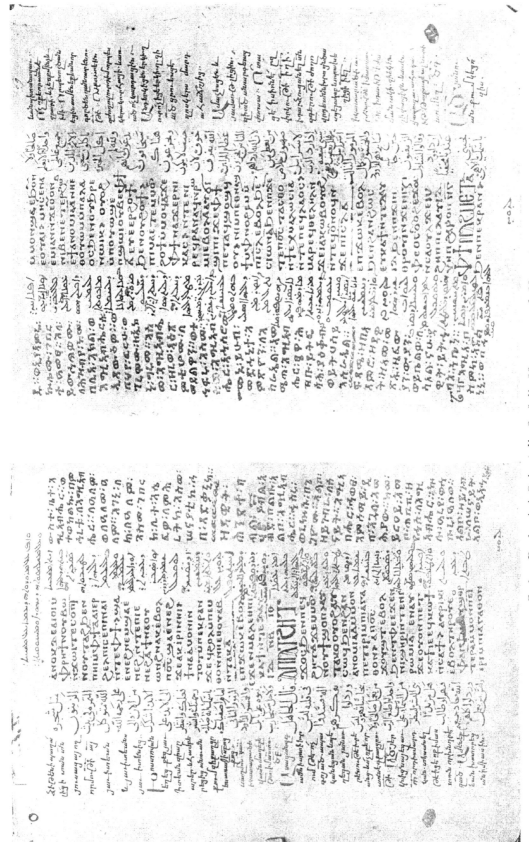

Codex Barberini Orientalis 2, foll. 68 verso and 69 recto

Famous Polyglot Psalter dating from the thirteenth century. Beginning from the middle, and proceeding to the right and left respectively, we have the following languages: Ethiopian, Syrian, Coptic, Arabic and Armenian

The Manuscript Clinic, or the department devoted to the repairing of damaged manuscripts, occupies a very important place in the Library organization. Many Codices of the sixteenth and seventeenth centuries, for example, were written with a broad pen, and thus reveal a quantity of ink on the paper. In very many instances this ink contains strongly corrosive elements which destroy the paper and cause letters, syllables, and words to fall away. When the paper is written only on one side, the damage thus done is serious enough, although many of the missing portions may be deciphered from the silhouettes which have been left behind. But when both sides of the paper have been written on, whole pages may

Codex Urbinas Latinus 112
Breviary of King Matthias Corvinus of Hungary, painted about 1487

be irretrievably lost. How is a halt to be put to this progressive decay? Or suppose that the Vatican Library has acquired a parchment manuscript which has suffered greatly from damp, the ravages of time, mould, or bad treatment; while in such a condition it cannot be placed at the disposal of scholars, since use would only cause it still more serious damage; and besides, many pages and lines have become absolutely indecipherable. Or suppose again that a parchment manuscript has fallen into water, and half of its pages have become so tightly stuck together that to open them is now scarcely, if at all, possible. Are such manuscripts to be lost to science, or can any remedy be devised to save them from their present wretched condition? Or, finally, let us suppose that a number of parchment leaves and remnants of Codices are found in some corner, where they have lain in utter neglect for long centuries and been exposed to all the indirect influences of the weather. Perhaps it may not be possible even to determine what text stands on the pages, to such an extent has it been erased by the tooth of time. Is it possible in such a case for the careful and skilled hand of the restorer of manuscripts to unveil the mystery shrouded in these written lines? Such are a few of the problems which the Manuscript Clinic of the Vatican Library has to solve. Nothing further need be said of the importance of this department, since it is evident that an institution that could solve these problems in a satisfactory way would be sure of the commendation of all educated people.

In the Vaticana, and indeed to a certain extent in all important libraries, great importance was attached from the very beginning to the repairing of manuscripts. In earlier times this was, of course, a more or less summary business which was confined to the binding, a general cleaning of the manuscript, the adding of lost corners, and so forth. No attempt was ever made to institute a scientific inquiry to discover some means of removing the cause of the progressive decay. This task was reserved for our own times, and the Prefect of the Vatican Library, Father

Codex Urbinas Latinus 112
Another page of the Breviary of King Matthias
Corvinus of Hungary

Ehrle, was the inspiring spirit of all the investigations which had for their object the general prevention of damage to manuscripts. From the year 1896 onwards, all new processes were tested in the Manuscript Clinic of the Vatican Library, and special processes further developed. At the instance of Father Ehrle, an international congress assembled in the summer of 1898 at the celebrated Monastery of St. Gall in Switzerland for the purpose of enabling the directors of the leading libraries to exchange views and experiences. It was there decided to place a large sum at the disposal of the Manuscript Clinic in the Vatican Library to be applied to extensive researches in the domain of manuscript preservation. These researches were attended with very favorable results, and have given rise to a comparatively extensive literature on the subject, to which persons interested in the matter may be referred for detailed information.

Not alone has the Vaticana undertaken a number of extraordinarily tedious and difficult works of repair in connection with its own manuscripts, but it has also restored in exemplary fashion celebrated Codices belonging to religious bodies of various countries. One of the most famous cases of this kind was its work in assuring the preservation of the Vercelli manuscript of the Bible, which had fallen into utter decay. This manuscript dates from the fifth century. Some years ago the Morgan Collection sent fifty damaged Coptic manuscripts to the Vatican, accompanied merely by a short note requesting that the Manuscript Clinic undertake the task of repairing them. Father Ehrle was unable to take up the matter at the time, but later answered that he would not be in a position to grant the request until it had been established that the Codices were really valuable. The mere fact that some three hundred thousand scudi had been paid for the manuscripts was in itself no guarantee of their scientific value. After an unbiassed opinion of experts had been secured, with a view to determining that the manuscripts were really worth the expenditure of money and labor necessary for their repair, the Prefect answered that he was willing to undertake the task on the understanding that the work was to be done as opportunity offered, since of course the current repairs for the Vatican Library could not be interrupted and preference given to manuscripts belonging to outside parties. The owners of the manuscripts agreed to this condition, but several years must still elapse before the extensive repairs can be executed in this incidental manner. The cost of the repairs is naturally defrayed by the Morgan Collection.

A few years ago, late in the evening, a fire broke out in this Manuscript Clinic as the result of the spontaneous ignition of some chemicals. These were very anxious hours for the Library administration, but fortunately the fire was finally extinguished without any serious damage being done. The roof, which had been burned, was quickly restored, but the fire was the occasion of more elaborate precautionary regulations than had previously prevailed.

The salaries enjoyed by the officials of the Vatican Library are more than modest. Not one of them—not even the Prefect himself—receives more than fifty dollars a month. For supplies, and so forth, the Library has at its disposal only the insignificant sum of six thousand dollars, as, in view of the present financial position of the Holy See, the Pope is unable to assign more to the Library. Thus, if the Prefect did not succeed in securing from private sources large sums for the needs of the Library, even the most urgent purchases would be often neglected. The great expense entailed by the rebuilding of the hall for the manuscripts and the various works connected therewith was gladly met by the Pope because these changes were absolutely necessary. In financial matters the Library is subject to the Prefect of the Apostolic Palaces, who, although forced at times to postpone necessary appropriations, always ends by making them.

The Library Archives, in which the administrative acts are preserved,

have been recently put in order. Unfortunately, they do not extend
back beyond the time of the first Cardinal Librarian, Marcello Cervini
(1548). By far the most interesting of the old papers are the loan

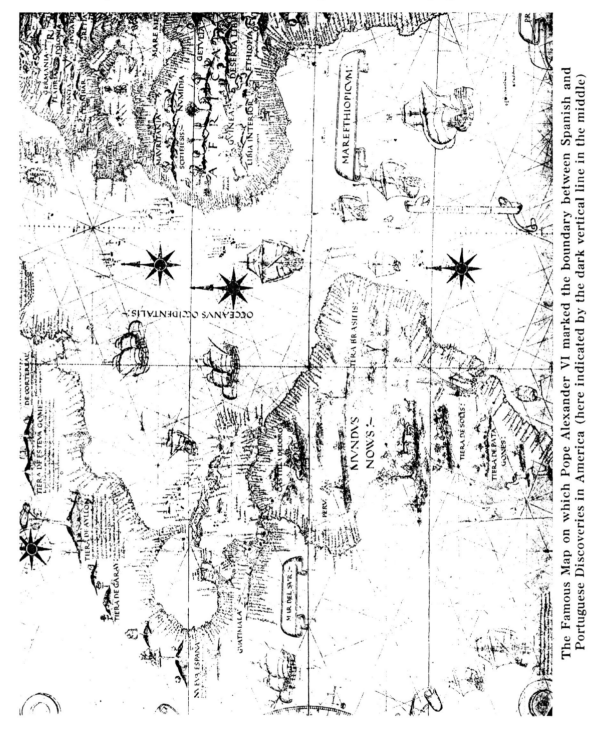

The Famous Map on which Pope Alexander VI marked the boundary between Spanish and Portuguese Discoveries in America (here indicated by the dark vertical line in the middle)

registers. One of the illustrations shows a loan certificate signed by
the Pope himself. Besides its inherent interest, this certificate is also
important as a specimen of papal documents.

Map of Europe of the year 1506

Containing so many details that it is very difficult to read them all, even in the original. The figure
of the Madonna, between two angels, and the figures typical of the various races are of great beauty.
It will be noticed that the north of the map is to the right

Admission to the Reading-room of the Library was formerly given on practically the same conditions as prevailed in other places. All that is required at present is that the request for admission be signed by a scholar known to the Library authorities. No other formalities of any kind are required, the reader being immediately admitted. It will thus be seen that there are very few important manuscript libraries to which admission can be obtained so promptly and easily as the Vaticana.

In former times it was customary to mark a small black cross on the back of all manuscripts which, because of their contents, it was not deemed advisable to place at the disposal of all scholars indiscriminately. When such a Codex was asked for, the attendants had to refer to the Prefect, who decided in each instance whether the Codex might be delivered to the reader or not. This custom of regarding certain materials as semi-secret was very common at the time, and found a much wider application elsewhere than in the Vatican. Father Ehrle has entirely suspended this old custom, and to-day every scholar, without exception, is entitled to examine any manuscript. Of course, in delivering extremely rare documents and highly important works of art to readers, all the precautions are taken for their safety which the special regulations of the Library require. It was formerly a rule that two copies of all photographs of manuscripts should be given to the Library. This regulation, which seemed to serve no intelligible need and only multiplied unnecessarily the quantity of materials to be preserved, was summarily abolished by Father Ehrle, although it still prevails in the Secret Archives.

The regulations, dating from the time of Sixtus V and defining the conditions under which the Library may be used, may, as remarked above, be seen chiselled in marble in the old reading-room. In the course of time these regulations were altered by the Chirographa ("Manuscripts," a special kind of Curial document) of Clement XII (1730–1740), Benedict XIV (1740–1758), and Clement XIII (1758–1769). By the Decree "Ex audientia Sanctissimi" Pius IX abolished some holidays which were especially irksome for foreign scholars. In his "Motu proprio" of September 9, 1878, Leo XIII introduced other alterations, all these changes being included in the Decree of March 21, 1885, which supplied a new "Regolamento della Biblioteca Vaticana." Appended thereto was a "Calendario per l'apertura e per lo studio e servizio della Biblioteca Vaticana." After three years' trial this new ordinance was carefully revised, was declared a permanent law by the "Motu proprio" of October 1, 1888, and still determines the administration of the Library.

The number of Italian and foreign scholars attracted to the Vaticana grows unceasingly. The importance and number of the manuscripts, the ease with which they may be consulted, the favorable conditions for working, attract all these scholars to Rome. While it is indeed true that the working hours might be increased, at least the complaints which were formerly entered concerning the number of holidays are no longer valid to-day. In winter the working-room is open from 9 to 1; at other times from 8 to 12. The working year extends from October 1 to June 27. The Library is closed on all Thursdays and also on certain memorial days, the Feriæ of Christmas, the Carnival season and Easter, and certain ecclesiastical feasts. Since Father Ehrle became Prefect, many scholars have been admitted to work during the afternoon, on Thursdays and on many holidays, when they could show satisfactory reasons for this preferential treatment. The liberality of the present administration in this respect is gladly recognized by every reader.

GROWTH OF THE LIBRARY.—To trace the growth of the Vatican Library is an inspiring task, and a list of the most important acquisitions will clearly reveal that the Popes of every century have shown true zeal and inspiration in their labors for the development of the Vaticana. Every favorable opportunity was embraced, and no sacrifice shirked, to foster in every possible way this centre of scientific activity and scholarly research.

In the Fondo antico Vaticana may be still found traces of the 340 manuscripts of Eugene IV, which were mentioned at the introduction of this chapter. Before the death of Nicholas V the number of Codices had greatly increased. Under Sixtus IV, 770 Greek and 1757 Latin manuscripts were purchased. The pontificate of the next Pontiff, Innocent VIII (1484–1492), fell in the period when printed books began to be widely disseminated. During this reign many printed books found their way to the Vaticana, so that the collection now numbered 3650 manuscripts and books. Among the purchases of Alexander VI (1492–1503) were 40 famous Codices from the old Abbey of Bobbio; these were bought from Tommaso Inghiranni. The four halls of the Library of Sixtus IV were enlarged by Julius II (1503–1513), since the rooms had become inadequate to receive the numerous acquisitions to the Library. After Leo X (1513–1521) had presented to the Vaticana his own Greek Codices, the Library possessed 4070 books and manuscripts. There was at this period no collection in the world which contained so many manuscripts.

In addition to the princely gift of 240 Codices, Marcello Cervini, the first Cardinal Librarian, presented many printed books to the Library.

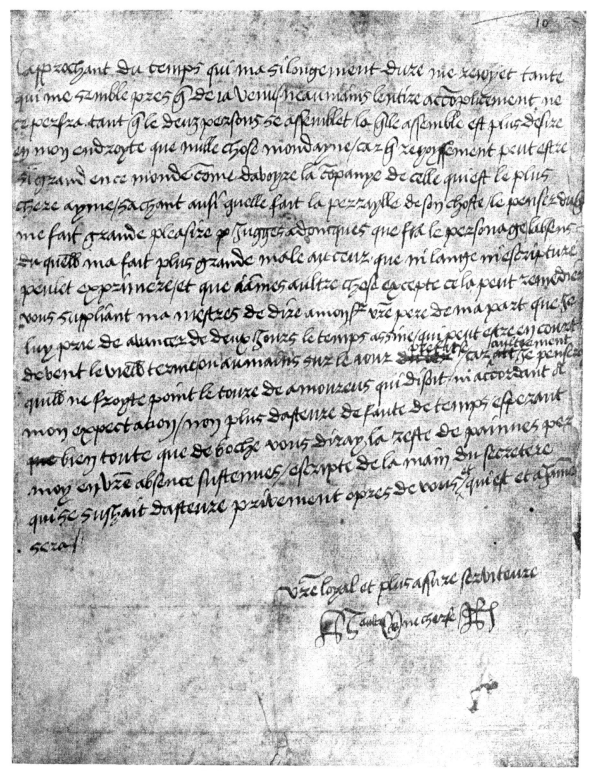

Codex Vaticanus Latinus 3731 A
Manuscript Letter of King Henry VIII of England to Anne Boleyn,
written in French and signed "H. R."

These additions and the 250 manuscripts acquired under Gregory XIII (1572–1585) filled the last available nook in the old library, the rebuilding of which under Sixtus V thus became an absolute necessity. A contemporary informs us that this last Pontiff sent forth emissaries in every direction in search of manuscripts that were purchasable. At the end of the sixteenth and at the beginning of the seventeenth century we find a glorious interest displayed in the Vaticana. The celebrated brothers Guglielmo and Tommaso Sirleto, the scholarly Antonio Carafa, and Marcantonio Colonna, known equally for his political influence and his knowledge of languages, bequeathed their great collections of

Library Archives, Tomus XXVI, fol. 38 r

Cardinal Carafa's petition to Gregory XIII for the loan of some MSS. from the Library. The Pope grants the request by adding: *Placet et Ita mandamus. V.* As signature he thus appends the first letter of his baptismal name (Ugo), as was prescribed in the case of such documents. The Pope has also added to the text the words: *e ne pigli quietanzo*

manuscripts and printed books to the Vatican Library. Fulvio Orsini, who united a wide scholarship with an extraordinary zeal for collecting manuscripts, was appointed Corrector græcus to the Vaticana, and on his death bequeathed it no less than 413 manuscripts and a very extensive collection of printed books. The manuscripts comprised 30 Italian, 270 Latin, and 113 Greek Codices. Thanks to this addition, the Greek manuscripts, which were highly prized, mounted from 1287 to 1400.

Pope Paul V (1605–1621) proved himself a true Mæcenas. He presented the Library with 212 Greek and Latin manuscripts, and during his reign Silvarezza contributed 30 Codices from the Abbey of Bobbio to the collection. From the library of the princely house of Altemps

(Altaems) came 100 manuscripts. In 1616 the same Pope purchased 83 Codices from the estate of Prospero Podiani for 1974 scudi ($1914); he had previously acquired 25 Coptic manuscripts from the estate of Raimondo. All the manuscripts and books which formed part of the estate of Cardinal Pole found their way to the Vaticana, so that the reign of the Borghese Pope must be reckoned one of the most important eras in the life of the Vatican Library. When, besides these services, mention is also made of the fact that on July 1, 1607, Paul V issued his Brief "ad perpetuam rei memoriam," "Alias felicis recordationis," containing detailed instructions concerning the management

De Luxe Binding from the Bibliotheca Palatina (1577)

of the Library, the sketch of his activity is complete. This document is carved in marble on the narrow wall of the Sistine Hall.

Pope Urban VIII (1623–1644) purchased a large number of manuscripts and many books. He had 39 parchment Codices and many books transferred from the Ethiopian Hospice behind St. Peter's to the Vaticana, which then contained 6026 Latin and 1566 Greek manuscripts. At the same time Urban added a new hall to the Library, and separated the office of Custodian from that of Prefect of Archives. But one of the most important of all the Vatican acquisitions was obtained in the transference of the Heidelberg Library to Rome. At the foundation of the University of Heidelberg, this collection was started with the private libraries of Marsilius von Inghen and Konrad von Gelnhausen. Constantly increasing in size, it received valuable additions through the confiscation of the library of the Monastery of Lorsch, in the manuscripts of the Cathedral of Mainz, the Arabian manuscripts of the great Orientalist Postel, and in the extensive library of Ulrich Fugger of Augsburg, acquired in 1584. In the union of all these glorious treasures and the library of the Count Palatine Ottheinrich the Bibliotheca Palatina had its origin. This contained about 3500 manuscripts and a large number of printed books when Elector Maximilian of Bavaria, after capturing Heidelberg in 1623, confiscated it and presented it to Pope Gregory XV (1621–1623). This Pontiff sent his librarian, Leo Allatius, to Heidelberg to receive the present and bring it to Rome. It was only during the reign of Urban VIII, however, that the Codices and books came into the actual possession of the Vaticana. Through the Treaty of Paris (1815) 38 manuscripts from the Palatina at Rome were restored to Heidelberg, and 852 followed as a gift from Pius VII in 1816. This great increase in manuscripts and books maintained the Vatican Library in its old position as the leading library in the world. At this period the Heidelberg Library in Rome was called the Gregoriana, because it had been presented to Gregory XV, but it later resumed its old name, the Palatina.

A little later the Vaticana made a second great acquisition, when Alexander VII (1655–1667) brought the renowned library of the Dukes of Urbino to the Vatican. This included 1767 Latin and Italian, 165 Greek, and 128 Hebrew and Arabian manuscripts. The printed books of the Urbinatic Collection were separated from the above, and served as the nucleus for the library of the Roman University, which is known even to-day as the Alessandrina, after its true founder. Another very large library, that of Queen Christina Alexandra of Sweden, the well-known convert, passed from her heir, Cardinal Decio Azzolini, to his nephew, Pompeo Azzolini. Alexander VIII (1689–1691) purchased it from the last-mentioned and assigned it to the Vaticana. After the duplicates had been presented to Cardinal Ottoboni, the Pope's nephew, and much archival material had been assigned to the Secret Archives, the additions to the Vaticana from the Queen's library consisted of 2102 Latin and 119 Greek manuscripts. To this division were added 1754 Latin and 45 Greek Codices of Pope Pius II (1458–1464).

From the information given above it will be seen that there were already a fair number of Oriental manuscripts in the Vaticana. Clement XI (1700–1721), however, must be regarded as the real founder of the Oriental section. According to Carini, he dispatched a number of scholars into all parts of the Orient to purchase manuscripts, and thus succeeded in adding to his library several hundred Orientalia of very high value. Clement XIII (1758–1769) added the collection of manuscripts from the private library of the brothers Assemani, which consisted of 202 Syro-Chaldæan, 180 Arabian, and 6 Turkish Codices. Including several small purchases, the already notable collection of Oriental manuscripts was increased by about 500 during this reign. Benedict XIV (1740–1758) secured the Fondo Capponiano, consisting of 288 Codices, and in 1748 purchased for 5500 golden thalers the whole collection of Cardinal Pietro Ottoboni, which contained the libraries of Altemps and Sforza, and the duplicates from the library of the

Procession of Pope Sixtus V (1585–1590) to take formal possession of
St. John Lateran, the episcopal church of the Bishop of Rome

In the procession are the Japanese ambassadors who were sent with letters from their Emperor to the Pope
This fresco is in the Sistine Hall

Fresco in the Sistine Hall, showing the plan for the rebuilding of a large
portion of Rome begun by Pope Sixtus V (1585–1590)

Queen of Sweden (see above). The total number of manuscripts was 3300. To this collection additions were later made, and it now contains 3394 Latin and 472 Greek manuscripts.

During the last century also the Vaticana made some extremely important acquisitions. The papers of Angelo Mai, Gaetano Marini, Eneo Quirino Visconti, Mazzucchelli, and Giovanni Battista de Rossi, together with a portion of the Maurist correspondence, were all acquired by or presented to the Library. These were put in order and arranged into volumes, and now form a goodly series of important manuscripts. Leo XIII purchased for $4500 the manuscripts of the Borghese family, which contained 300 Codices from the old papal library of Avignon. These came to the Borghese through the Aldobrandini family. The Borghese themselves purchased 100 Codices, which were thus really Borghesiana. The extensive archives of the Borghese Collection were assigned to the Secret Archives. More extensive and more costly were the collections of the Barberini family, purchased by Leo XIII in 1902. All the manuscripts of this collection, among which were many of the highest value, a vast number of printed books, and all the archival materials were incorporated in the Vaticana.

In recent times the Codices Borgiani (not to be confounded with the Burghesiani) were transferred from the Propaganda to the Vaticana. These are mostly Oriental manuscripts, although there are many Latin and Greek manuscripts among them.

In the above enumeration only the larger acquisitions have been mentioned. It would be quite impossible to mention in detail the extraordinarily large number of small purchases, presents of a few manuscripts, or the less important collections acquired by inheritance. Sufficient, however, has been said to show that the Popes, mindful of their position and their obligations towards the civilized world, have developed in a lavish manner this nursery of science.

De Luxe Binding, showing the arms of Pope Clement VIII Aldobrandini (1592–1605)

MANUSCRIPTS.—From the account given above it will be seen that a large number of closed collections have found their way into the Vaticana. These collections are not divided, but are administered as separate and absolutely distinct divisions, or *fondi,* provided that they are large enough to merit this treatment. All other acquisitions are united in one large collection. Accordingly, we have closed, or historic, and open fondi. The open fondi form really only a single division, that of the Codices Vaticani. These Codices are, however, divided according to languages, and thus form sixteen open fondi. The historical, or closed, divisions, if we divide them according to language, form 34 fondi, as enumerated below.

The Open Fondi are as follows: Codices Vaticani Latini, 11,150; Græci, 2330; Hebraici, 599; Arabici, 935; Syriaci, 472; Turcici, 80; Persiani, 83; Coptici, 93; Æthiopici, 77; Slavi, 23; Rumanici, 1; Georgiani, 2; Armeni, 14; Indiani, 39; Sinici, 20; Samaritani, 3.

The Closed, or Historical, Fondi are: Burghesiani, 381; Notarii Aurasiacenses, 377; Palatini Latini, 2017; Palatini Græci, 432; Urbinates Latini, 1767; Urbinates Græci, 165; Urbinates Hebraici, 128; Reginæ Latini, 2103; Reginæ Græci, 190; Reginæ Pii II Græci, 55; Ottoboniani Latini, 3394; Ottoboniani Græci, 472; Capponiani, 288; Barberini Latini,

Codex Mexicanus Vaticanus 3738, fol. 66 verso
Mexican figures with explanatory inscriptions and comments

10,000; Barberini Græci, 590; Barberini Orientales, 160; and the following Codices Borgiani: Latini, 760; Græci, 26; Syriaci, 169; Coptici, 132;
Hebraici, 18; Arabici, 276; Persiani, 21; Turcici, 77; Armeni, 90; Indiani,
31; Tonsinici, 22; Sinici, 521; Illyrici, 22; Æthiopici, 33; Georgiani, 16;
Hibernici, 2; Islandici, 1; Slavi, 1.

The total of the above manuscripts amounts to 40,658. In addition
to these, the Vaticana possesses all the Codices of the Barberini Archives, which still await proper arrangement and accurate computation. As these probably number from 8000 to 10,000, the collection of
manuscripts in the Vatican Library amounts, in round numbers, to
50,000. The Library formerly possessed, in addition, a number of
manuscripts from the Fondo Zelada; these, however, were restored to
Toledo, while the printed books of this collection remained in the
Vatican. All new acquisitions of a minor nature were, and are still,
added to the Codices Vaticani. This collection contains all the manuscripts which were acquired by the Library since its restoration in the
fifteenth century, and will also serve in future as the depository for all
new purchases, presents, and so forth, one or more new sections being
opened as circumstances require.

Inasmuch as the world-famous manuscript treasures of the Vatican

Library are distributed among the different fondi, it cannot be said that this or that division is the most important. So many personal views and interests must influence one in passing judgment on the relative importance of manuscripts of different natures that an objective answer to this question is quite impossible. All these treasures are, as already stated, preserved in the new compartments which are situated in the immediate vicinity of the Reading-room.

BOOKS.—Readers who have followed closely our description so far will not expect to learn that the collection of printed books is an enormous one. The Vatican Library contains more than 350,-

De Luxe Binding, showing the arms of Paul V Borghese (1605–1621)

000 printed books. There are, of course, a large number of libraries which can show much larger figures, but such libraries place at the disposal of their readers all the books contained in their collections. This is not the policy of the Vatican Library. As already stated, it places at the disposal of readers only those works which are of value for the study of the manuscripts. All other printed books are, generally speaking, reserved for the use of the officials of the Vaticana. The reason for this regulation has been already mentioned.

The two open fondi of books are the Raccolta Generale and the Consulting Library. All new acquisitions are assigned to the first division, unless their subject matter renders them suitable for the second—that is, unless they are immediately connected with the study of manuscripts. The closed fondi of printed books are the Biblioteca Barberini, Palatina, Zeladiana, and the Prima Raccolta. This last division contains all the books which were acquired by the Vaticana before the year 1620 or 1630, approximately. About this date a new division was formed, the Raccolta Generale, to receive all future acquisitions. The names of the other divisions will be easily understood from what has been already said.

An exact computation of the books in these collections has hitherto been impossible, nor is such of any special value in the case of the Vaticana. The following is a fairly accurate estimate of the various collections: Prima Raccolta, 10,000 to 11,000; Raccolta Generale, 200,-000; Biblioteca Palatina, 25,000 to 30,000; Biblioteca Zeladiana, 4000 to 5000; Biblioteca Barberini, 25,-000 to 30,000; Biblioteca Leonina (Consulting Library), 60,000 to 70,000.

While this collection of printed books is not especially remarkable for mere numbers, the percentage of rare and valuable works is much greater than is found in any other library of such proportions. And if readers desire to use any of the books in the closed fondi, they will find no serious obstacle in their way. They need only apply to the official in charge, who will see that the works are delivered to them. They themselves cannot take a work from its place; this is permitted only in the case of books standing in the Consultation Library, all of which may be taken down by any reader. The arrangement of the printed books

Codex Urbinas Latinus 365 (Ferrarese School) From the "Purgatorio" of Dante. The text is a paraphrase of the Lord's Prayer. In the upper part of the picture is the "Pardon of Trajan"

has undergone a complete change in the last two years, owing on the one hand to the great increase in the room available and on the other to the removal of the manuscripts from the state rooms of the Library. As more detailed information concerning the position of the various divisions would serve no useful purpose here, it may be passed over.

DUTIES AND PUBLICATIONS OF THE LIBRARY STAFF.—Although naturally the officials must in the first instance fulfil their duties in maintaining order in the Library, the administration provides that a fair amount of leisure be left them for independent scientific studies. Furthermore, they are encouraged in such studies and the printing of their works is greatly facilitated.

The most important official work of the Scriptores is the arrangement, description, and cataloguing of the manuscripts with a view to making the whole collection more readily accessible as soon as possible by printed inventories. There are 170 volumes of manuscript catalogues dating from olden or recent times; these may be found in the working-room and are conveniently accessible to every one. Leo XIII issued directions for the printing of these catalogues; but, inasmuch as they had to be revised and modified according to modern principles and in accordance with recent research work on the manuscripts, an almost completely new and independent work has resulted. The detail work on these inventories and catalogues is very tedious, but it is being promoted vigorously, and twenty-two volumes have been already issued.

Bronze Bust of Emperor John VIII Palæologus (1421–1448), ascribed to Philaretes (Antonio Averlino)

These volumes are distributed over the various collections, so that all divisions are being dealt with simultaneously. They are of extraordinary value to those engaged in research work, since they enable a scholar to determine quietly at home what is of value to him; then only, after he has provided himself with all the references, he undertakes the journey to Rome. The books of the Palatina have been brought within the scope of this cataloguing because, in view of their origin in the Heidelberg Library, they possess a special interest.

At the command of the Pope, the administration of the Vaticana entered some time ago upon a gigantic undertaking which is of the greatest possible value for the educated world. This undertaking consisted in the publication of a de luxe phototypical full-size reproduction of the most important Codices of the Vaticana, together with a description and analysis. These publications form a series bearing the following title: "Codices e Vaticanis selecti phototypice expressi iussu Pii Papæ X consilio et opera procuratorum Bibliothecæ Vaticanæ." In this series there is a major and a minor division. Those manuscripts are chosen for reproduction which are especially important on account of their venerable age, the importance of their text, or their artistic form. As may be easily understood, the cost of these works is very great, since every page of the manuscripts has to be reproduced by phototypical processes. As a rule, only between one hundred and two hundred copies are published, but this number seems to meet completely the demand for the works.

The most important of these publications is the reproduction of the "Codex Vaticanus" (to give the manuscript its distinctive title). By this title is understood in learned circles the fourth century Codex containing the Greek text of the Old Testament according to the work of the seventy translators who rendered the Hebrew Old Testament into the popular Greek of their day in the third century before Christ. Such, at least, is the tradition which has come down to us, but with this tradition the critics find themselves at variance. Avoiding controversial questions, we may say here that the Codex Vaticanus at least represents the purest tradition of this old Judaic Greek translation. In the scientific system of abbreviations, it is known as "Codex B." This greatest treasure of the Vaticana, which has been often edited, has been perfectly reproduced by photomechanical processes in three volumes. The first volume contains pages 1–394, and costs 230 lire; the second volume includes pages 395 to 944, and costs 320 lire; the third volume contains pages 945–1234, and costs 150 lire. The total cost of the edition is thus 700 lire. In the Vatican Library this manuscript is known as "Codex Vaticanus græcus 1209." The Greek New Testament forms a separate volume, and costs 170 lire. Of the major series thirteen works have been already published in seventeen volumes, and of these the first is out of print. Two volumes of the minor series have already appeared.

A second collection of works has been begun in the "Collezione Paleografica Vaticana," of which two parts have been issued. In collaboration with the administration of the Museums and Galleries, the Library has also undertaken a grand descriptive series on the art treasures, which is appearing under the title: "Collezioni Archeologiche, Artistiche e Numismatiche dei Palazzi Apostolici pubblicate per ordine di Sua Santità a cura della Biblioteca Vaticana, dei Musei e delle Galerie Pontificie." The Numismatic Collection (Medagliere Vaticano), attached to the Library, is described in three illustrated volumes. The rich ivory carvings included in the antiquities of the Vaticana are illustrated, explained, and catalogued in one volume, the edition of which has been already exhausted. The old pagan frescoes exhibited in the Library, and known by the name of the Aldobrandini Marriage and Scenes from the Odyssey, have been beautifully reproduced in a huge volume. All these, with numerous works which cannot be mentioned here, show the great activity of the officials of the Vatican Library.

Besides the above-mentioned publications, mention must also be

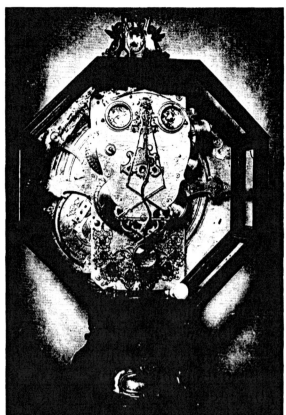

The famous Farnese Clock, presented to Leo XIII on the occasion of one
of his Jubilees, and now exhibited in the Sistine Hall

made of a fourth series of works, published by the Prefect of the Vaticana himself. The title of this series is: "Le piante maggiori di Roma del Secolo XVI e XVII riprodotte in fototipia a cura della Biblioteca Vaticana con introduzione di Francesco Ehrle, S.J." This contains the important plans of the City of Rome, dating from the sixteenth and seventeenth centuries. Among these, some of the greatest rarities are reproduced, their value investigated, and the fate of the originals established.

Finally, we have the last series of the publications of the Vaticana, entitled "Studi e Testi pubblicati dagli scrittori della Biblioteca Vaticana." Altogether twenty-five volumes have been printed, and five more are in preparation. This series was instituted by Father Ehrle, and in it we find the Scriptores of the Vaticana represented by an immense number of researches and scientific treatises of the most varied kind. Hagiography, the culture of the Renaissance, nunciature reports, Italian philology, Biblical science, patrology, religious drama, history of literature, Oriental science, chronicles, art—in short, every imaginable subject is treated, according as inclination, a fortunate discovery, or other circumstance suggested it. This series shows what incentives come to those engaged in the tiresome work of cataloguing.

From this very summary survey of the scientific work of the officials of the Vatican Library it will be seen that under the management of Father Ehrle there has developed a brisk spirit of literary activity unrivalled in earlier times. There is probably no library in the world whose officials have produced in so comparatively short a period such a tremendous amount of scientific work of the highest quality. That this claim can be made for the Vatican shows that in the Pope's palace true Science has found a sanctuary, and nowhere does she find more reverence. It is, indeed, the greatest pleasure of the Pope when, as happens almost daily, some new works of the officials of his Library are laid before him.

HALLS OF THE LIBRARY.—The stranger who visits the Vatican Library enters at its extreme end, where the entrance to the Museums also is. The first room contains pagan antiquities of great value, which are referred to elsewhere.

Then begins the suite of Library rooms proper, in which we see the low wooden presses with richly painted doors referred to above. In this second room is an inscription, stating that in 1818 Pius VII had this hall painted with events from his life. A marble inscription recalls the fact that Pius VI had the pillars which separated the halls removed and replaced by dividing walls (1794).

In the seventh hall are scenes from the life of Pius VI, while over the two doors are two large frescoes. The plan of the city of Ferrara and a rather schematic picture of the port of Civitavecchia fill the panels over the doors of the eighth hall; the walls to the left commemorate the zealous activity of Paul V for the Library, while the wall to the right is decorated with scenes from the history of the Library. Two other paintings dealing with Paul V, and three paintings of Pius V, Sixtus IV, and Nicholas V respectively, proclaim in the ninth hall the care of these Pontiffs for the Library; over the doors are represented the canonizations of Charles Borromeo, Archbishop of Milan, and Frances of Rome, foundress of the Oblates of Tor di Specchio.

The antechambers of the Sistine Hall, which we now enter, are decorated with historical paintings and pictures dealing with local Rome. Descending a few steps by the left, we enter the celebrated Library of Sixtus V. Numerous mural paintings proclaim the achievements of this great Pontiff, who performed more in a short pontificate of only five years than the majority have performed in double that period. Here may be seen the show-cases of the Library, containing the most celebrated and glorious Codices to which the Vatican Library can lay claim. As a number of these treasures have been reproduced in our illustrations, the reader will be able to form his own idea of the precious heirlooms here shown. In this hall are exhibited no less than twenty-eight works of art, which were presented to the Popes in the last century by Napoleon I, Charles XII of France, Napoleon III, Presidents MacMahon, Grévy, and Carnot, Emperors Nicholas I and Alexander III of Russia, King Frederick William IV of Prussia, Emperors William I and William II of Germany, Prince Regent Leopold of Bavaria, Emperor Francis Joseph I of Austria, the City of Vienna, the Count of Caserta, Mehemet Ali, Viceroy of Egypt, Prince Demidoff of Russia, the Republic of Ecuador, the dioceses of Rheims and Clermont, Cardinal Antonelli, and the Catholic Associations of the City of Venice. It may be here mentioned that the other halls also contain a vast number of presents which Leo XIII had here exhibited when, on the occasion of his various Jubilees, artistic gifts were presented to him by the whole world.

If we leave the Sistine Hall and return to the long wing of the palace which we left a short while before, we enter the twelfth hall, wherein are exhibited two great frescoes representing the Proclamation of St. Bonaventure as a Doctor of the Church and the Canonization of St. Diego (1588). Over the windows are small pictures dealing with the life of Sixtus V. The mural pictures of the thirteenth hall are extraordinarily interesting and important. One of them shows how the obelisk was erected in the Piazza di S. Pietro, while the other represents St. Peter's as Michelangelo had conceived the building. Over the windows is the continuation of the pictures of the preceding hall. An inscription over the doors of the fourteenth hall states that Pope Pius VII made alterations here in 1818. The simple ornamentation of the walls and ceiling offers nothing of special interest. In the middle of the hall, however, stand two gigantic iron cases with large glass plates under which may be seen seven manuscript maps on huge sheets of parchment. These maps show the state of geographical knowledge in the fifteenth and sixteenth centuries, the most important being that on which Alexander VI marked the dividing line between the Spanish and Portuguese possessions in America. Benedict XIV's inscription over the lower door, which leads to the Christian Museum, commemorates the founding in 1756 of this collection of archæological treasures. We then pass through the fifteenth hall, which contains these treasures, and find ourselves in the sixteenth hall, devoted to papyrus documents; these were formerly immured in the walls behind glass, but are at present in the Manuscript Clinic awaiting repairs. In the middle stands a glorious mosaic table, and about the walls are golden pieces of furniture covered with green silk. The cupola is decorated with the famous frescoes of Raphael Mengs. The stained glass windows are no particular ornament to this inspiring hall, since their coloring is not at all in harmony with the general scheme. An inscription records that Clement XIV (1769–1774) began the decoration of the room in the year of his death, and that the decoration was completed under Pius VI (1775–1799). Finally we reach the seventeenth hall, which formerly contained the Byzantine and other paintings, but whose shelves are now filled with books. To the right is a smaller room, in which the precious Old Roman frescoes from Ostia (see pp. 373–374) are preserved. At the very end of the long gallery which we have just passed through lies the Chapel of Pius V, which is not open to visitors.

This short description gives only a very rapid survey of the most important features of the Apostolic Library of the Vatican. Sufficient has, however, been said to show what a tribute of gratitude is due to the Pontiffs for having, by their zeal in fostering and managing this great Library, contributed so greatly to the advancement of culture and of science.

THE VATICAN SECRET ARCHIVES

ROM very early times the recognized importance of a knowledge of the past led men to perpetuate current events in one form or another. The events of to-day belong, to-morrow, to the past, and the systematic collection of memorials of the present best ensures for the future a knowledge of the past. Regardless of the persons by whom it may be practised, this preservation of current information was and is equivalent to the formation of archives—that is, collecting-places for documents of any kind which have a bearing on the making of history.

All bodies that must render an account of their activities are compelled to preserve official documents. State authorities and rulers, in so far as they desire to ensure a well-ordered administration, must duly record the progress of official business, and must so regulate their books, registers, correspondence, and all other records of importance that they can be referred to at any time. This practice was followed even in gray antiquity. And, with the progress of the centuries, the method of preserving archives was constantly improved, until finally the present scientifically arranged archives were developed out of the clumsy methods of the past.

At various periods extremely valuable reminiscences of the past were destroyed by fire, war, water, pure vandalism, or gross neglect. And the further we seek to penetrate back into the past, the scarcer are the testimonies which inform us how men then lived and suffered, thought and acted. If we were still in possession of the most important archives of Christian civilization in their original completeness and uninterrupted sequence of documents, the writing of history to-day would present an altogether different aspect. Unfortunately, however, the original documents pertaining to the ages antecedent to the tenth century of the Christian era have been preserved only in rare cases where the conditions were especially favorable. Copies of a large number of important documents have, of course, been preserved, and these are of high value for history.

In view of the peculiar nature of the documents and registers preserved in the Archives of the Roman Curia, and in view of the extensive correspondence which the Popes, in virtue of their office, had to maintain with every part of the civilized world and even beyond its borders, the Archives of the Holy See were from the very beginning among the most important known to history. From the first they were administered with the greatest care, since their contents were liable to be required at any time in connection with negotiations of the most diverse nature. But, just as the Popes themselves underwent extraordinary vicissitudes in the early centuries, the fate of the Papal Archives was likewise eventful. Robbery, fire, destruction, pilfering, and every other imaginable misfortune diminished the collections to such an extent that finally only the documents and acts from Innocent III (1198–1216) onwards were saved and preserved to our day. Furthermore, there are serious gaps in the sequence of the documents and registers which have come down to us, especially in the case of those referring to the thirteenth, fourteenth, and fifteenth centuries.

The Vatican Secret Archives may thus be regarded as a collection of the documents and papers concerned with the Papacy which have been accumulated during a period of something over seven hundred years. The collection as it stands to-day does not represent a unit, but consists of many parts united at various times and under different circumstances. The Vatican Secret Archives are not a "closed" archive in the sense that no additional materials will be added to the collection in the future. Every year new acts are committed to these Archives in the regular way, and from time to time the collection is further increased by purchases, presents, and legacies. In another sense, however, the Vatican Secret Archives were formerly a closed archive, since they were not accessible for purposes of study and historical research. It was reserved for Leo XIII to accede to the wishes of all students of historical science by opening unconditionally to the whole world the doors of this most important of all central Archives. "The Church fears nothing from the publication of these documents," said Leo when, on June 20, 1879, he made the announcement that he had raised to the cardinalate Hergenröther, the Würzburg historian, appointed him Archivist of the Holy Roman Church, and opened the Vatican Secret Archives to the public. Not without serious misgivings was this decision received in many ecclesiastical circles in Rome, where all kinds of undesirable consequences were anticipated as the result of the Pope's action. Leo XIII, however, remained firm in his determination, and refused to be influenced by any representations of the timid. All preparations were completed by the beginning of 1881, a suitable working-room prepared, and the necessary staff appointed. The doors were then thrown open, and the scholars of the whole world might enter.

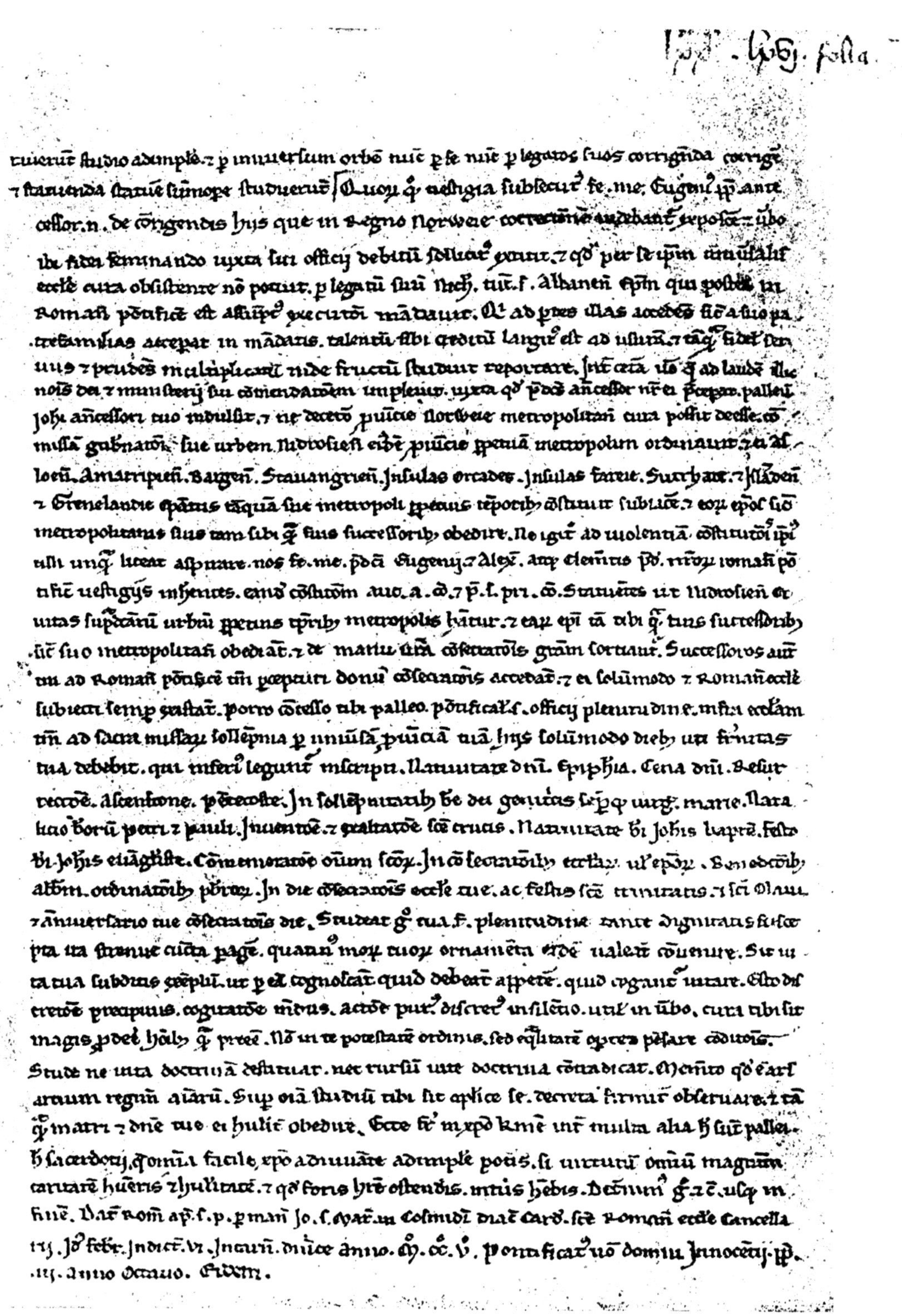

Reg. Vat. (Innocentii papæ III), Vol. VII, fol. lxvi recto, cap. 214, containing the first mention of Greenland in the Papal Registers (February 13, 1206)

The thirteenth line from the top begins, "Grenelandie episcopatus." That this is a Solemn Bull, signed by the Pope and Cardinals, is shown by the date given at the end of the page, where the Chancellor of the Holy Roman Church is mentioned (cf. Potthast, "Regesta Pontificum Romanorum," cap. 2686)

For some years previously individual historians had been admitted, but only by special permission of the Pope in each instance. On May 1, 1884, a regulation (*regolamento*) was issued, making the new conditions permanent. A short time before, on August 18, 1883, Leo had given noteworthy expression to his appreciation of the value and importance of historical studies in a letter addressed to Cardinals Pitra, De Luca, and Hergenröther.

It must not be supposed that the almost inexhaustible treasures of the Vatican Secret Archives were never placed at the disposal of historical science until the time of Pius IX. It is true that the ecclesiastical authorities regarded the Archives as primarily a source of information in connection with their official business, and the staff of the Archives had to answer in the most exact and prompt manner all questions relating to this official business of the Papal Court. Even in the volumes of registers dating from the thirteenth century we find occasional references to documents which then lay in the Archives but are now lost. In later centuries these references to the ancient collections in the Secret Archives increased whenever earlier documents, decisions, evidence, etc., were used in deciding legal disputes and other questions referred to the Curia. Requests were also addressed to the Curia, asking for copies of certain documents or at least an assurance that these documents were really in existence. Such a request was made very recently by Lord Rothschild when he addressed himself to the Cardinal Secretary of State in connection with the trial of a Jew for ritual murder in Russia. The Cardinal was asked to certify that two papal decrees in favor of the Jews, issued in the thirteenth century, were authentic. Cardinal Merry del Val commissioned the officials of the Secret Archives to undertake the necessary investigations, and to lay before him the result of their researches. Having found that the decrees were actually contained in the papal registers, and examined them personally, the Cardinal addressed a short letter to Lord Rothschild, answering his question in the affirmative. That this recent case is but a single example of what took place commonly in earlier centuries, there is an abundance of evidence to prove.

Consequently, although the Vatican Secret Archives were founded and administered as the official archives of the Roman authorities, their contents were even in earlier times utilized for scientific purposes. Towards the close of the Middle Ages, when the interest in the writing of history was awakened, and about the middle of the sixteenth century, when heated theological and historical polemics broke out between Catholics and Protestants, Catholic apologists could scarcely dispense with the infinitely rich materials contained in the Secret

Archives. Nor were the Curial bodies oblivious of the necessity of drawing upon the historical treasures there collected.

We thus see that in the most celebrated work of this period, a work which enjoys high consideration even to-day, the treasures of the Archives were turned to excellent account. This work is the "Annales Ecclesiastici" ("Ecclesiastical Annals") of the unassuming Oratorian, Cæsar Baronius, who afterwards became Cardinal, and would have become Pope had he not energetically declined the honor. The twelve folio volumes of his epoch-making work appeared between 1588 and 1607. In 1596 he was named Cardinal, and in the following year was appointed Librarian of the Holy Roman Church. Thanks to Baronius

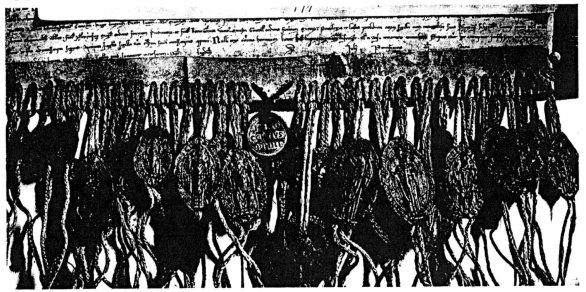

Arch. Arcis Armar. I, caps. 10, cap. 6

Lower part of one of the Rouleaux of Cluny, in which the most important privileges of the Roman Church were recapitulated, and to which the Pope and forty of the Prelates present attached their seals at the Council of Lyons. The small bulla of Innocent IV is seen in the middle, while to the left and right are the large wax seals of the Prelates. The document was executed on July 13, 1245

and the work of the authors who continued his "Annals," the scientific world was for the first time made fully acquainted with the great importance of the materials of the Vatican Archives. The desire for fuller information concerning the collections in these central Archives was thereby increased, and from every quarter were addressed questions to the officials, requests for copies of documents, and petitions for admission to the collections. An almost endless list of writings of the seventeenth and eighteenth centuries proves how comparatively rich was the harvest reaped from the collections. The Archives, however, were not yet placed unconditionally at the service of scholars, but still remained a business department of the Vatican administration.

DIVISIONS OF THE ARCHIVES.—In the preceding paragraphs, the term "Secret Archives" has been used in speaking of times when the Secret

Archives of to-day were not yet founded. The term offers, however, a convenient method of describing the materials which were later to comprise these Secret Archives. In earlier times, for example, many of the most important volumes of papal registers were preserved in the old library of Sixtus IV in the Cortile del Papagallo; other volumes were not yet in Rome, but in Avignon, while the rest of the materials were preserved in various places in Rome.

The first step towards the foundation of the present Vatican Archives, topographically speaking, was taken by Paul V when he directed the Cardinal Librarian Cesi to prepare a number of rooms in 1611–1613, and in these gave accommodation to a large quantity of archival materials. This Pope also expended large sums in arranging the collections and repairing damaged documents. The quarters of the Archives were constantly extended, and other independent Archives added: the Archives of the Secretariate of State in 1660; the extensive collections from the Papal Archives at Avignon, where the Curia resided in the fourteenth century, at various periods (the final portion in 1783); the Archives of the Castle of S. Angelo in 1798; the Archives of the Buon Governo in 1870; the Archives of the Dataria in 1892; the Borghese Archives in 1893; the Archives of the Congregazione dei Memoriali in 1905; the Archives dell'Uditore Santissimo in 1906; the Archives of the Consistorial Congregation in 1907, and the Archives of Briefs in 1909.

The oldest collection in the Archives was and is still called the Archivio Segreto (Secret Archives), and its name has been extended to the whole department. Its materials are distributed in seventy-four *armari* or presses, as follows: the series of the Vatican Volumes of Registers, *armari* 1–28; the Diversa Cameralia, or Financial Acts, 29–30; the Collectoria Cameræ Apostolicæ, or Series of Registers of Donations, 57; the Series of Transcripts, 31–37, 46–49, 52–54, 59–61; the Registers of Briefs, 38–45; the Indices, 50–51, 56, 58; the Acts of the Council of Trent and various Acts relating to German Affairs, 62–64; the Registers of Receipts and Expenses of the Apostolic Chamber (Introitus et Exitus Cameræ Apostolicæ), 65–74; and the valuable Series of Miscellaneous Documents (*Instrumenta Miscellanea*).

All the archival materials collected by the Popes from 1305 to 1387 and by the Anti-Popes from 1387 to 1417 at their seat in Avignon, as well as the records kept by the secular and spiritual administrations of the County of Venaissin (then belonging to the Curia), were finally added to the Secret Archives in 1783. Whatever financial acts were to be found in this collection and in the above-mentioned Archivio Segreto (or oldest part of the Archives)—for example, the Introitus et Exitus, the Diversa Cameralia, the Obligationes or Payments and Obligations of Prelates, and Collectoriæ—were recently united into one collection, the systematically arranged Archives of the Apostolic Chamber.

The Castle of S. Angelo, which was occupied by the Popes until recent times, was the strongest fortress of the Papal States. It was therefore a prudent decision of Popes Sixtus IV (1471–1484), Leo X (1513–1521), and Clement VIII (1592–1605) to deposit in this fortress for surer protection all the most important privileges and titles of the Roman Church. It was only in the year 1798 that these Archives were transferred to the Vatican Secret Archives. They were not, however, simply added to the other collections, but formed a special department and were placed under a special management. These collections, known as the Archives of the Castle of S. Angelo, are of the highest value.

The Archives of the Dataria include: (1) the great series of Registers of Petitions (*Registra Supplicationum*), beginning from the year 1342; (2) the Series of the Lateran Registers of Bulls, extending from 1398 to 1823; and (3) the Registers of Briefs of the Dataria, which Briefs are different from those just mentioned. Many parts of the Consistorial Archives are now in the Vatican Library, but the remainder of the collection is to be found in the Secret Archives.

It is easy to understand the very great value of the Registers of Briefs of the Secretariate of State for the political, ecclesiastico-political, and purely ecclesiastical history of modern times. In these registers we may find the legates' and nuncios' reports from Germany (1515–1809), France (1517–1809), Spain (1563–1796), Poland (1567–1783), England (1565–1689), Cologne (1575–1799), Bavaria (1786–1808), and other lands, with the corresponding answers. These reports of the legates and nuncios were often accompanied by other valuable documents and rare printed papers, which add in no small measure to the value of the Registers. This separate Archive also contains several series of Letters and Petitions, Memorials, and Reports from Cardinals, Princes, Bishops, and prominent laymen, which are of great historical value. Finally, a special section contains the letters written by the field-marshals, condottieri, generals, and other officers in the pay of the Curia. In this collection of letters is assembled everything concerned with the part played by the Curia in the wars waged between 1572 and 1713. All these and other divisions of the Archives have been zealously investigated and have afforded entirely new side-lights especially on the history of the sixteenth and seventeenth centuries.

In the collection known as the Varia Miscellanea are found, first, all the material which could not very well be included in any of the other divisions, and also a large number of small collections, most of which were purchased or presented to the Archives.

Papal Bullæ of the Thirteenth, Fourteenth and Fifteenth Centuries
From right to left the Pontiffs and dates are as follows: Gregory X, April 1, 1275; John XXII, February 22, 1329; Pius II, October 18, 1458; Clement IV, July 27, 1267; Clement IV, April 23, 1265

The Congregation which had charge of the financial administration of the Papal States until 1870 was known as the Congregazione del Buon Governo. The gigantic Archives of this Congregation, which filled sixteen rooms, were added to the Secret Archives in 1870, as already stated. Of the other divisions, the Archives of the Borghese family, purchased by Leo XIII, deserve particular mention. This is really an integral portion of the Archives of the Secretariate of State for the pontificates of Clement VIII (1592–1605) Aldobrandini, Leo XI (1605) Medici, and Paul V (1605–1621) Borghese, because under these Popes the "Cardinal nephews," or Secretaries of State, appropriated to themselves the entire official correspondence and bequeathed it to their families. It was only after this purchase by Leo XIII that the Holy See recovered possession of its property. This evil practice was followed not merely by these three Cardinal nephews, but was likewise practised by others at this same period. Even nuncios and legates purloined their official correspondence, so that in the publication of nuncios' reports extensive recourse has to be had to private archives.

The Varia Diplomata, or Sundry Archives of Deeds (derived mostly from monasteries), contain valuable material for investigators of documents in general and for students of diplomacy in particular. These special Archives are not yet completely arranged, so that only in exceptional cases is knowledge concerning them available.

The bare statement of the various divisions of the Secret Archives, however, gives the reader no real idea of their full extent; and even the description of the collection as "the most important of central Archives" conveys only a remote suggestion of the vast quantity of materials assembled there. Some few statistics are necessary if the reader is to carry away a conception that is at once accurate and clear. It must be stated beforehand that a number of the collections cannot be included in these statistics; for, inasmuch as no attempt has been made

Reverse of the Papal Bullæ of the Thirteenth, Fourteenth and Fifteenth Centuries,
given on opposite page

The bulla of April 23, 1265, is weather-worn, and shows how the string was passed through

to put them in order as yet, no figures can be given indicative of their extent. Although the work of classification is being pursued steadily and zealously, in view of the limited staff employed in the Archives it will require several decades before all the assembled materials will be ready for research work. The greatest of the still uncounted collections is that of the Buon Governo, incorporated in the Archives in 1870.

The chief collections preserved in the Archives are the following: the Vatican Series of Registers, 2048 volumes; Volumes of Briefs, 7654; Petitions (*Supplicationes*), 7011; Lateran Series of Registers, 2161; Varia Miscellanea, 2051; Borghese Archives, 2000. Total, 22,925. To this total must be added 48 smaller divisions, ranging from 6 to 968 volumes and containing in all over 12,000 volumes. There are thus, in round numbers, 35,000 volumes in the collections already accessible for research work. It must be remembered that many thousands of these are large imperial folio volumes, which contain often several thousand documents, and are thus extraordinarily fertile fields for historical investigation. These volumes are of a colossal size seldom to be seen in any other Archives. Some of them are so heavy, thick, and large that it requires a strong porter to carry one on his shoulder to the student. Turning to the contents of the volumes, we find that the transactions dealt with extend to the whole of the then known world. Side by side with matters of a purely local interest are documents of the highest importance, which concern perhaps a large empire, if not, indeed, all Christendom. It is quite impossible to form even an approximate idea of the number of documents contained in these volumes. Any attempt at an estimate might easily be millions wide of the mark.

In the document cases and rolls, which contain loose papers and parchment documents, there may be about 120,000 pieces. The writer has had the great majority of the parchment documents in his hands and examined them, and is thus in a position to state from personal knowledge that many are of the highest possible value.

INDICES AND INVENTORIES.—In view of the numerous subdivisions of each collection, how were the scholars, admitted into the Archives in 1881, able to find their way in the midst of such vast collections of materials? It is quite certain that for the first few years many scholars were haunted by purely fantastic ideas of the contents of the Archives, and imagined that the materials were much more extensive than they actually were. Gradually, however, a more correct estimate prevailed, thanks principally to the progressive study of the Indices. At first these Indices were only rarely and reluctantly placed at the service of students. But in the last fifteen years their use by readers has been unrestricted. It will be necessary to inquire a little more closely into these scientific instruments to understand of what great value they are, and will always be, for bringing to the light the treasures stored away in the Archives.

In the office of the Assistant Archivist stands a large library of folio volumes, six hundred and eighty-one in number, all of which have been compiled in manuscript by the staff of the Archives in the last three hundred years. To give a rapid sketch of even one of the great series of Registers and Acts, the indexer had to take cognizance of the entire contents. The contents had then to be linked according to certain aspects, so that all matters of the same nature could be included under the same heading. After a searching investigation, for example, all the proper names of persons and places were taken from many hundreds of volumes; with these names were given the volume and document in which they occurred, and also the date of the document in every case. These entries were written on tickets, and the tickets arranged alphabetically (see below), so that one can in a very short time discover every recorded event, say, in the life of a certain Bishop of Verona in the thirteenth century. These numerous Indices are worked out in the most various ways—some in detail, some along synoptical lines, some according to the chief divisions of a subject, and some according to the detailed contents of the separate documents. To save scholars the necessity of continually repeating the same questions to the officials, an Index to the Indices was compiled in 1901 under the title, "Inventarium indicum in secretiori Archivo Vaticano unica serie existentium." With the assistance of this guide, the reader may always find his bearings pretty well in the labyrinth of the Indices.

In the preparation of these numerous Indices many persons have naturally participated. Among the most industrious of these workers was Johannes de Pretis (1712–1727), his brother Petrus Donninus de

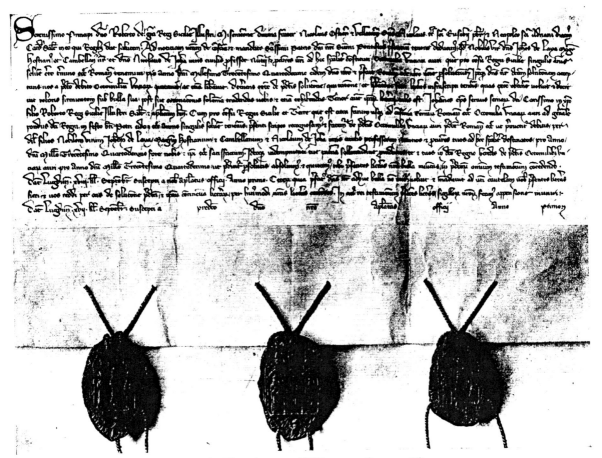

Arch. Vat. Armar. XIV, caps. 8, cap. 50

Letter of three Cardinals to King Charles of Sicily, dated August 16, 1316. In the letter is inserted a Bull of Pope John XXII of August 15, 1316, which was, however, not executed on that date because the Pope-elect refused to attach his seal to any document before his coronation. The three wax seals of the Cardinals hang on red silken strings

Pretis (1727–1740), and Josephus Garampi (1749–1772). The million and a half tickets which Garampi prepared with his assistants are an inexhaustible mine for students whose researches are concerned with the period covered by these workers. These tickets are pasted in one hundred and twenty-four large folio volumes and follow a strictly alphabetical order. Before the magnitude of this huge work one stands astonished, nor can one quite understand how, within the brief span of one human life, such a work could have been accomplished, even with some assistants. Felix Contelori (1626–1644) also worked very industriously on the Inventories and Indices, and copied numerous documents which threatened to become illegible owing to water-rot, mold, decomposition, or fading. But for this work of Contelori's, many extant texts would have been irretrievably lost to science. Dom Gregorio Palmieri, O. S. B., Assistant Archivist of the Holy See, printed a "Manuductio ad Vaticani Archivi Regesta," the value of which was so evident that the edition of the guide was quickly exhausted.

It must be emphasized here that the Indices written in manuscript were intended, not to assist scientific researches in the Archives, but simply and solely as administrative conveniences to facilitate as much as possible the work of the Roman officials. We thus see how unreasonable it would be to turn up our noses at the gigantic achievements of the assistant archivists, and seek to deny their work its special scientific value. For their period all these Inventories were works of the highest rank, and in the seventeenth and eighteenth centuries no other Archives could offer anything that compared even distantly with them. The modern card index which is being at present prepared for the Instrumenta Miscellanea will be, from every standpoint, a model for difficult works of this class.

ADMINISTRATION.—The administration of the Vatican Secret Archives was determined by Leo XIII. A Cardinal Archivist of the Holy Roman Church, with the title of Prefect, stands at its head and exercises supreme supervision. He settles all questions of general administration, determines the duties of the various officials, and decides upon the order to be followed in making the Inventories. In all extraordinary questions connected with the service in the Archives his opinion must be sought, and in all questions of discipline his decision is final. In individual instances he modifies, in favor of scholars, the rules laid down by the Regolamento. He discusses the purely economic questions of his department with the Prefect of the Apostolic Palaces, and sees that their joint decisions are executed. He submits in person to the Holy Father recommendations for the purchase of archival materials, and receives his decision.

The Assistant Archivist attends to the routine management, and acts as the representative of the Archives in all dealings with readers. It is his duty to be present daily in the Archives from 8.30 to 12 o'clock for the purpose of giving information and answering questions. The other officials receive their orders from him as to their duties and activities. Two Custodians are in charge of the Reading-room, and, in so far as they are qualified to do so, answer all inquiries of the readers on scientific questions. The first Custodian is a distinguished palæographer, and is head of the School of Palæography, instituted by Leo XIII in the Secret Archives. Many very able palæographers have graduated from this school. Of all the officials, the Secretary of the Assistant Archivist, whose office is of recent origin, possesses the most extensive knowledge of the Indices and Collections. Too high a value can scarcely be set upon the information which he can give to readers.

Four ordinary and one honorary Scrittori fill a double function. They are, on the one hand, engaged on work connected with the Indices, and, on the other, prepare copies of documents for all who apply for them. They are also given special charge of certain divisions of the Archives, with which they are thoroughly conversant. The Archivio del Buon Governo, as it was formerly known, has its own Custodian, but concerning his activity no detailed information is procurable. The attendants are engaged partly in the Reading-room, where they learn the wishes of readers, and partly in the rooms containing the Archives, where they find the documents or manuscripts asked for.

The working year extends from October 1 to June 27, and the working hours are from 8.30 to 12 o'clock on five days of the week, Thursday being a holiday. The same feriæ are observed in the Secret Archives as in the Vatican Library (see page 456). During the summer holidays the great annual cleaning of the halls takes place, and an inventory is taken with a view to determining whether any manuscripts are misplaced or missing.

An extraordinarily large number of historians throng from practically all civilized countries to the Secret Archives. On the basis of his knowledge of all the great central archives of Europe, the writer can declare that in none will so vast a crowd of scholars be met as in the Secret Archives of the Vatican. The reason for this lies in the universality of the materials collected in the latter place, which have an interest for every historian. The halls of the Archives are reached by the door on the ground floor of the Tower of the Four Winds. The visitor enters immediately the Reading-room, adjoining which along the court lie the old reading-room and the office of the Assistant Archivist. Besides the extensive rooms on this ground floor devoted to the collections, a large number of rooms on the three higher stories are given over to the same purpose, while the rooms high above in the Torre dei Quattro Venti, where the old observatory was situated, have lately been occupied by the Archives Administration. It was in these last-mentioned halls that Gregory XIII had the preparations made for his reform of the calendar. The spatial increase of the Vatican Archives would appear to have reached its limit with the incorporation of these rooms. Should still more halls prove necessary, the already mooted proposal to transfer the Archives elsewhere must be adopted, unless it is decided to separate the collections. Since, however, the Holy See has not the funds at its disposal to undertake great changes, things will probably be allowed to remain as they are for the present. The inadequacy of the rooms, however, is already beginning to make itself felt.

The reader is now entitled to some details as to how research work is carried on in the Vatican Secret Archives. A view of the workshop of the historian engaged in researches has always a special interest, especially when that workshop is located in a palace so celebrated as the Vatican.

WORK IN THE ARCHIVES.—Let us suppose that we are studying the history of the College of Cardinals during the fourteenth century. We have consulted all the literature on our subject, but have been unable to discover any precise information as to the sources from which the Cardinals composing the Curia procured the funds to support themselves and keep up an appearance in accordance with their station. To ignore so important a question is impossible; the only alternative is to have recourse to the sources to find whether they contain any exact information concerning this financial question. An inquiry addressed to the officials of the Archives brings us the welcome answer that a small collection of manuscripts deal exclusively with this matter. We thereupon pack our trunks, proceed to Rome, a brief and simple request to the Holy Father secures us entry to the Archives, and we may begin our researches at once. Extraordinarily valuable materials here await us, and in a short time we are assured of being able to treat this part of our work on the fourteenth century with the greatest completeness.

In distant Japan Dr. Murakami is engaged on the history of the Christian Missions in his fatherland. Although he has at home a vast number of accounts and reports, laws, decrees and decisions, traditions, letters and chronicles on his subject, he finds that the compilation of these materials would give only a one-sided picture of his theme. Until he has established organic connections with European, and especially with Roman, sources his work will be but half accomplished. Undeterred by the long journey, he sets out for Rome, and begins his investigations in the Secret Archives and in the Archives of the Propaganda. Here he finds all suggestions and instructions sent to the missionaries, the reports of the latter, the correspondence of the Curia with the colonial powers, and much additional information, which gradually corrects the partiality of his earlier views.

To attempt to write the history of the Jews in the Middle Ages, or even in modern times, without considering the attitude of the Popes and the Church towards the Jewish question in general and towards the Jewish settlers in the different lands, would be to condemn beforehand one's work to incompleteness. The Vatican Secret Archives contain very important documents on this question, and Moritz Stern, Felix Vernet, and others have attached special importance to the thorough investigation of these documents.

A large number of American scholars, among whom Professor Charles Homer Haskins is especially prominent, have often availed themselves of the hospitality of the Holy See in connection with their

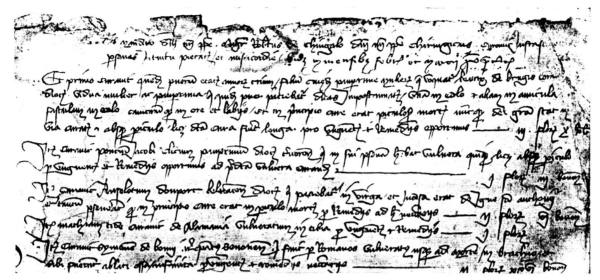

Arch. Vat. Instrum. Miscellanea ad annum 1369, cap. 7

Cedula of the Papal Surgeon, Magister Robertus de Chingalo, for his expenses in caring for the needy sick.
The cedula was forwarded to the Camera Apostolica, and was there paid (April, 1369)

investigations for American history in particular and historical questions in general. The searching report of Professor Haskins, published in the "Catholic University Bulletin" in 1897, is an important historical contribution.

Besides investigations arising from personal initiative, there are others which are inaugurated by a government, an historical society, a diocese, and so forth. Such investigations have usually a well-defined object, and their prosecution is entrusted to some historian. The latter travels to Rome with his plans already made, and strives by every means in his power to become acquainted with the materials in the Archives which are connected with his work. If he has friends or acquaintances in Rome, these initiate him into the ways of the Archives in so far as their knowledge extends. With the assistance of the Secretary, he becomes acquainted with the Indices, and, being led from one collection to another, is soon able to declare with more or less certainty what divisions of the Archives contain matter pertinent to his studies. His further progress then depends on his industry and patience in discovering what documents in the volumes are of value to him. In the course of a few months he will have acquired a sufficient survey of the materials to reckon with a fair amount of accuracy how much time will be required for the completion of his task. If the time and funds at his disposal are not sufficient to enable him to complete his work, he will at least be able to make some progress with it, and will have amassed exact information which will be of great value for the guidance of subsequent investigators.

A third method of pursuing historical investigations at the Vatican

Archives is by collaboration. This work may be temporary or permanent. We say the work is temporary when a commission of scholars is dispatched to Rome, under a single director, for one or several years, to perform definite work in the Secret Archives. There have been many commissions of this kind—for example, that which the Academy of Sciences of Cracow sent to Rome to investigate some special problems of Polish history. That these studies undertaken by collaborators should prove much more successful than those undertaken by individuals is only to be expected. Permanent work by collaborators is, of course, the ideal method of research work. According to this

Leaden Bulla of Pope Paul II Barbo (1464–1471), carved like the bullæ of the Doges of Venice as the Pope belonged to a Venetian family

method, every discovery made by each collaborator is contributed to the common fund, and new members of the circle derive full advantage from all the facts established by their predecessors and colleagues.

This permanent collaboration is carried on by the various historical societies which have been founded for research work in the Vatican Secret Archives. These institutes constitute a phenomenon which can be duplicated in no other archives in the world. While the foundation deeds of the institutes refer only to the Vatican Archives, it is only natural that the holidays, during which the Vatican Archives are closed, should be devoted to other scientific investigations in Rome and Italy. Such investigations are, however, only a subsidiary object, the pursuit of which in no way alters the fact that these societies are *Vatican* institutes for historical research. By this last method of investigation much time and money can be saved, and historical undertakings planned of such an extent as could not be dreamed of by individual scholars. A short survey of the historical institutes and other bodies of a similar character will show what astonishing work is performed in the Vatican Archives.

The effect of the opening of the Archives upon Catholic science was immediately seen when the Rector of the German National Institute of S. Maria del Campo Santo Teutonico near St. Peter's urged the German bishops to send young priests to his college so that they might begin investigations in the Secret Archives. He founded a number of chaplaincies at Campo Santo, which are always filled. The foundation of the "Römische Quartalschrift für Archäologie und Kirchengeschichte" placed an organ at the service of these young historians. This plan of utilizing the German National College showed a fine appreciation of the needs of the day. The judicious extension of the Library admirably fostered the work which was undertaken there. While the researches inaugurated do not follow any uniform plan, most of the publications are devoted to the Middle Ages and the sixteenth century.

Reverse of the Leaden Bulla of Pope Paul II, with the figures of the Apostles Peter and Paul

It was only after a long and careful study of the question from every standpoint that the Görresgesellschaft finally decided to establish a special historical institute in the Vatican Archives. The moderate means then at the disposal of the society rendered this caution intelligible. But before the close of the eighties it decided to take this bold step, and since that time its historical institute has been represented at all times by able scholars. With the Austrian and Prussian Institutes, it has undertaken the editing of the Nunciature Reports from Germany. The Görres Institute has engaged on a gigantic task of the highest importance in its edition of all the Acts of the Council of Trent. Twelve unusually stout quarto volumes have been planned, of which four have already appeared and met with a most flattering reception. Many years, however, must elapse before the huge task can be completed. Not less in scope is another work which has for its object the publication of the Financial Acts of the fourteenth century. The two very large volumes which have been already printed cast an entirely new light on the Avignon Papacy, and have finally discredited the old, deep-rooted fables which were copied by historians in general from the Florentine Villani. The second volume treats with admirable clearness and fullness of court life at the papal palace in Avignon. These contributions to the social history of the fourteenth century in general, and to the history of the Papacy in particular, cannot be prized too highly. Besides the volumes dealing with the Nunciature Reports from Germany, the Görresgesellschaft has published a large number of volumes of its "Quellen und Forschungen," each of which is independent of the others and has no connection with the more extensive undertakings of this society. It has recently published a series of volumes dealing with the intervention of the Teutonic Order in the Italian wars of the fourteenth century. No other private society has displayed an activity at all comparable to that of the Görresgesellschaft, whose success is universally recognized.

The Austrian Leogesellschaft lends its collaboration in the publication of the Financial Acts of the fourteenth century, to which reference has been made above. But, although it frequently appoints individual scholars to work for a few years in Rome, it maintains no regular institute in that city.

The same remark holds true of the English Government, in so far as the maintenance of a state-aided institute for research work in the Archives is concerned. England has not established any regular historical institute, apparently because broadly planned historical researches and treatises find less favor in that country than in any other country of Europe. For the most part, English investigations are undertaken merely to supplement the native sources and only with a view to delineating historical characters as clearly as possible. Documents, as such, have no interest for the Governors of the Public Record Office, who use only short excerpts in English to suit the convenience of a public interested in genealogy. The tasks entrusted to the English scholars are, from the scientific standpoint, of so exceedingly modest a nature that many of these workers have bitterly complained of this kind of hod-carrying. They would gladly have joined in the scientific rivalry of the nations, but they might not. Owing to the cramping commission given them by the English Government, they play a very subordinate rôle in the investigation of those problems of medieval ecclesiastical and civil life which possess such an absorbing interest for all who work in the Secret Archives.

Through the special favor of Pius IX, Rev. Joseph Stephenson, a High Anglican commissioned by the English Government, was allowed to make copies of documents in the Archives which were connected with the relations of England with the Curia. After this scholar had become a Catholic and was appointed Scrittore in the Vaticana, he laid his resignation in the hands of Sir Thomas Hardy, who, at the suggestion of Cardinal Manning, appointed William H. Bliss, an Oxford convert, to succeed him. The latter continued his work until 1909, but,

Reg. Alex. VI, Tom. 775, fol. 43 recto

First mention of the Discovery of America in the Papal Registers (June 25, 1493). In the eleventh line from the top we read: "Crhistoforum Colon"—*Crh* being a mistake for *Chr*

even though he was given younger men to assist him in completing his task more quickly, there was no question of founding a regular historical institute. Any scientific treatment of the material, even in the most modest way, was expressly forbidden, and was thus not attempted. The large volumes, consisting of excerpts from documents, are provided with a brief introduction in London, and then published absolutely without comment. From time to time the London Board, in its "Annual Reports of the Deputy Keeper of the Public Records," gives information of the progress of the researches in Rome. From this source we learn that Acts of the sixteenth and seventeenth centuries were also copied at Rome, and were published in the Calendars of State Papers. While it is to be regretted that the English Government has not instituted investigations on a broader and more scientific scale in the Secret Archives, we may be thankful that so much material has been made accessible to investigators in English, if not in the original Latin.

The Ecole Française de Rome was founded in 1873 in connection with the French Archæological Institute in Athens, and soon extended its activities also to Naples, where the study of the registers of the Angevin dynasty was undertaken. A member of the Ecole Française may perhaps have worked in the Secret Archives before they were opened to the public, and begun the glorious undertaking which is not yet completed—namely, the editing of the volumes of Papal Registers of the thirteenth century, beginning from 1216. The mode of publishing the extant registers is as follows: the most important documents are published complete, but only excerpts of the less important are given, the original Latin being employed in both cases. This method naturally leaves much to the discretion—often to the arbitrariness—of the individual. Documents dealing with French matters are given a marked preference, even when no real, intrinsic reason for this is apparent. No rigid, uniform treatment of the volumes is in evidence, one editor adhering to one plan and a second to another. The standpoints of various editors are often quite different, and even the typographical arrangement varies greatly. The delay between the appearance of successive parts is a great trial for both individual subscribers and libraries, a large number of works having been begun which, failing an index, are of real value only to very few. Those persons alone who are thoroughly conversant with the original registers can turn these fragments to account, and those only with great loss of time. When all the pontificates are finally completed, the question may perhaps be seriously raised whether the whole work should not be begun all over again on a different basis and with a fixed and uni-

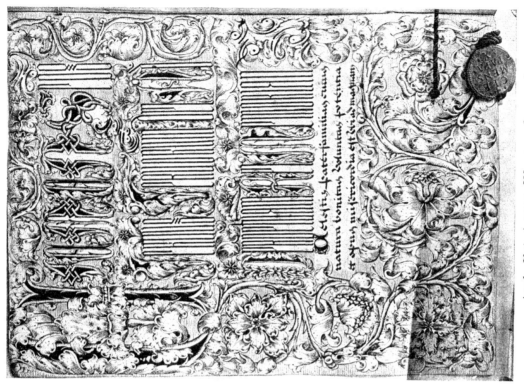

Arch. Vat. Armar. IV, caps. 3, cap. 3

First page of the Bull of Canonization of St. Rose of Lima, April 12, 1671. It owes the elaborate ornateness of its form to the fact that it is a Solemn Bull. The first three lines read: "Clemens Episcopus | servus servorum Dei Ad | perpetuam rei memoriam." The lead seal hangs on a red and yellow silken string

Arch. Vat. Armar. VIII, caps. 11, cap. 3

Conclusion of the renowned Bull of Gregory XV (November 15, 1621), dealing with the manner in which the papal election was to be held thenceforth. Under the five lines of text stands the manuscript signature of the Pope: *Ego Gregorius Catholicæ Ecclesiæ Episcopus.* Then follow the round ornament, called the *Rota*, with the motto of the Pope, and finally the signatures of the six Cardinal Bishops, who add after their names the formula, *promitto, voveo et iuro* (I promise, I vow and I swear)

form plan. However, in spite of their undeniable defects, the volumes already issued have done much to elucidate the history of the thirteenth century. The gigantic undertaking of the Ecole Française will be given for all future time a place of honor among the sources of the thirteenth century.

The social conditions during the Renaissance era have received special attention from the young scholars of the French Institute, as their published works prove. Special mention must be made of a monumental work published by Monsignor Duchesne during his early years in the Ecole Française, when he was Director of the Institute. This work is the celebrated "Liber Pontificalis," the authentic source for the history of the Popes in Christian antiquity and in the early Middle Ages. Mention must also be made of the "Liber Censuum," the great rent-book of the Roman Church, which received its definitive form at the end of the twelfth and the beginning of the thirteenth century. Paul Fabre had prepared this for press and was engaged on its publication when death overtook him. His friend Duchesne then continued the task and completed it.

In the periodical of the French Institute, entitled "Mélanges d'archéologie et d'histoire," are published all the lesser works of its members, including many treatises on archæology and the history of art. The seat of the Ecole is in the ambassadorial palace, the Palazzo Farnese, which has been for some time the property of the French nation. Its library is very extensive and well arranged.

In speaking of the societies formed to turn to advantage the treasures of the Secret Archives, we should have mentioned also the Chaplains of St-Louis-des-Français. The reason for our failure to mention them above was because their activity is more appropriately treated in connection with the Ecole Française, with which they have become in a certain manner affiliated. They have undertaken a comprehensive and highly important work, with which they have already made very gratifying progress, namely, the editing of excerpts from all the fourteenth-century documents contained in the volumes of Avignon Registers. This series appears in connection with the editions of the Registers published by the Ecole Française, and the editing of the documents of John XXII (1316–1334) is already far advanced. Unfortunately, the special periodical of the French Institute, "Annales de St-Louis-des-Français," has been discontinued. Many of the works of the Chaplains, based upon Vatican materials, are of a high importance for the history of the Avignon Papacy. With the further development of scientific studies, it may perhaps be possible to revive their special periodical. Another plan has been promoted by private persons to afford Catholic

Arch. Vat. Instrum. Miscell. ad annos 1466 sqq.

Bull of Pope Clement XI of September 17, 1707, in the not yet exaggerated script called "Scrittura Bollatica."
The leaden seal hangs on a yellowish white silken string. The document is addressed to
Magister Franciscus Columna, jurist of the two Signaturæ

French scholars an opportunity to study in the Secret Archives, but it has not yet been sufficiently developed to merit mention here.

From small and modest beginnings the Prussian Historical Institute has now reached such a stage of development that it can compete successfully with any other. The plan to found this institution was first conceived in 1883, but it was only in 1888 that the first Prussian "Station," as it was then called, could be opened. In the following year the writer became one of the collaborators of this Station, and he remembers well how exceedingly modest were its pretensions in its infancy. Since that time the Station has grown into the Prussian Institute, which was fundamentally reorganized in 1902 and thereafter showed constant development. Its most important undertakings are the series of Nunciature Reports from Germany, the elucidation of Prussian relations with the Curia in a series of works dealing with Curial administration and kindred subjects, and the collection of German sources in the "Repertorium Germanicum." From the Institute have also issued individual works of importance which cannot be included in any of the above-mentioned series. In Rome, or even in all Italy, there is no library which can compare with that of the Prussian Institute as a complete collection of all works dealing with a special department. Absolute completeness is aimed at for all the important territories investigated by the Institute, and, in consequence of the liberal funds at its disposal, it may well happen that within ten years it will be the most important and best special library in the world.

The organ of the Institute is entitled "Quellen und Forschungen aus italienischen Archiven," and contains once annually a highly valued bibliographical survey of all pertinent literature which has appeared in book form or in periodicals during the year. In recent times the Institute has extended its studies to Naples and Simancas (Spain), just as it had previously extended its investigations to central and northern Italy. In collaboration with the Istituto Storico Italiano it publishes the "Registrum Chartarum Italiæ," of which eight volumes have already appeared. Only the briefest mention can be made of the extensive department of the Institute which is devoted to art researches, and which possesses a splendid equipment of photographs, plates, and editions de luxe, besides a valuable library.

Since 1904 Belgium also has had an historical institute in Rome—the Institut Historique Belge à Rome. According to its charter, the Institute is to devote itself, first, to the study of all materials connected with Belgium in the Vatican Secret Archives, and, secondly, to materials elsewhere in Rome and in Italy in general. The Institute is also to serve as the centre for all historians coming to Rome, to whom it is to extend assistance, both actively and by its advice. Since its activity is confined strictly to the history of Belgium, the formation of a library is easier, inasmuch as it is necessary to collect only those works on Belgian history which are not to be found elsewhere in Rome. Needless to say, the library also contains those works of a general character which are the daily tools of the historian. If, sometime in the future, the additional plan should be realized of developing the Institute into an Ecole des Hautes Etudes, in which secular and ecclesiastical history, classical philology, archæology, and art history would be studied, the library would naturally have to be put on an entirely different footing. Of the "Analecta Vaticano-Belgica," in which the Institute publishes the results of its studies, many fine volumes have been already issued, and others are in the press.

Of similar character to the above is the Dutch Historical Institute, founded in 1906 and devoted exclusively to the investigation of materials dealing with Holland. This Institute is not immediately concerned with the publication of documents, but with researches to determine exactly what documents pertaining to Holland are in existence. Three great catalogues of Dutch materials have been already issued, and these publications will be continued until an exhaustive list has been completed. On the basis of these extraordinarily careful surveys, it will then be easy to decide what materials should be edited and published. The same work has been undertaken in connection with Dutch art, of which so many roots extend into Italy. This programme of the Dutch Institute is an unusually practical one, although it is not concerned immediately with the publication of documents.

The liberality of the Hungarian Canon, Monsignor Fraknói, made it possible to found in 1892 the Hungaricorum Historicorum Collegium Romanum. Although this college was discontinued some years ago, it has left behind important traces of its existence in the "Monumenta Vaticana historiam regni Hungariæ illustrantia," of which ten folio volumes were issued.

The Austrian Historical Institute had for its founder no less a personage than Theodor von Sickel. It was founded in 1883, and its chief object is to enable a larger number of young historians to study for a short term in Rome. A number of the members have, however, dwelt some years in Rome, performing the Institute's share in the preparation of the Nunciature Reports from Germany, of which a large number of volumes are already available. Sickel's studies on the "Privilegium Ottonianum," his edition of the "Liber Diurnus," which created a sensation in historical circles, and his important Roman Reports, together with the works of Tangl, Ottenthal, and others, won for the Institute a high position among the historical bodies of Rome. The Bohemian historical commissions, which often visit Rome, always receive efficient support from the Austrian Institute.

In the preceding sketch only a very hurried consideration could be given to the chief points which must be reviewed in appraising the importance of the Vatican Archives. Sufficient has been said, however, to give the reader an idea of the importance of Leo XIII's ever-memorable act in opening these Archives to the public. The scientific harvest of thirty-three years' researches in the Archives has been glorious, and, now that an exact knowledge of the collections has been secured, the future harvests will be still richer.

THE MOSAIC FACTORY

HE word "mosaic" is derived from the Greek word Μοῦσα, as it was said that the Muses were the inventors of the mosaic art. Mosaic-making is undoubtedly a very ancient art, and was practised in the Orient and among the Egyptians, who employed it in the decoration of their mummies. The Greeks also used mosaics in their temples, while Demetrius Falerius and Hieron II were the first to adorn their palaces in Athens and Syracuse with mosaics. Mosaics were used also on the floors of the houses in Greece, for which purpose, on account of their solidity, they were well suited. Among the Romans the mosaic art was a comparatively late development, since they borrowed the fine arts from Greece. Sulla introduced mosaic work into Rome to adorn the Temple of Fortune at Præneste, and it was not long before the art became particularly popular in Rome, where it found such favor that the military commanders, including Cæsar, had portable mosaics to serve as floors for their tents while on their campaigns. Among the most beautiful mosaics of ancient times may be mentioned the Greek Cross mosaic of the Pio-Clementino Museum, and the Doves of the Capitol, generally known as Pliny's Mosaic, because Pliny, in his "Historia Naturalis" (l. XXXVI, c. lx), speaks of such a mosaic as having been executed at Pergamos. Thus, the Capitoline treasure, found at Hadrian's Villa near Tivoli, is perhaps a copy of the Pergamos mosaic. Famous also are the mosaic of Palestrina and, finally, the most beautiful specimen found in the Casa del Fauno at Pompeii, showing a battle scene with fifteen horsemen, twenty-six warriors, and a chariot bearing a figure said by some to be that of Darius. So much did the Romans love mosaics that they used them to adorn not only their floors but also the vaults of their banquet-halls and the external walls of their dwellings. The scenes in these mosaics were taken from real life, and were generally framed by an arabesque or Greek scroll.

In the Christian era mosaics were employed to represent sacred images. The most beautiful ancient specimens are found in Rome and at Ravenna in the Mausoleum of Galla Placidia and S. Apollinare Nuovo, an Arian temple changed by Archbishop Agnellus into a Chris-

The Entrance to the Mosaic Factory   The Sample Room where the Enamels are kept

tian church. Mosaic ornaments were used in the Catacombs also: in the Chigi Gallery is preserved a portrait found in the Catacomb of Cyriacus, which De Rossi declared to be a fourth-century work. In the Mausoleum of S. Costanza are some mosaics dating from the Constantinian era, while that in the apse of S. Pudenziano is said by De Rossi to date also from the fourth century. Following the Byzantine custom, these mosaics often have a gold background and a blue tint; sometimes the figures themselves are laden with gilding. While the mosaics were inspired by the Christian faith, both their art and technique were decadent. Instead of studying true proportions, the mosaic workers endeavored to compensate with an abundance of gold for errors of drawing. Among the first cultivators of the mosaic art, which together with painting began about this period to undergo a favorable change, we may mention the Florentine Andrea Tafi, who in 1200 devoted himself to the study of the composition of the enamels used in mosaic work, and adorned with his mosaics the Church of S. Giovanni at Florence. Thanks to Florentine artists, the mosaic art now took on a new life. Cimabue practised it in the apse of the Cathedral at Pisa, for which he made a mosaic of the Saviour against a background of gold. Giotto, his pupil, busied himself greatly with this art: of his many works it will be sufficient to mention here his famous Bark of St. Peter, made for the Vatican Basilica. Encouraged by the wealthy, and especially by the Popes, workers then began to copy pictures, and we find the Venetian painters executing their very best works to be copied in mosaic. And so, with increasing perfection, the mosaic workers reached a state of development where their works may compare with the masterpieces of painting.

In 1586 Pope Sixtus V founded the mosaic factory of the Vatican, and set its artists to prepare mosaics for the walls and ceiling of St. Peter's. The original site of the factory was near St. Martha's, beside St. Peter's, where the street is still known as the Via del Musaico. Exi-

The Collection of Mosaic Works

A Mosaic Artist at Work

gencies of space necessitated successive changes of location, and the factory was removed first to rooms in the Palace of the Holy Office, and then to the Palazzo Giraud (now the Torlonia) in the Piazza Scossa-cavalli. Finally, in 1825, worthy quarters were found for it in the Vatican itself by Pope Leo XII.

Persons who have never seen a mosaic made find it difficult to imagine how with small bits of colored enamel the most valuable paintings may be exactly copied. The mosaic worker, who decorates tabernacles and niches with his composition, does an accurate and patient work, which attains the level of an art, because he uses his enamels just as the painter does his brush. Mosaic work is of two kinds: (1) work executed with enamel cubes, which are used in the case of all large decorative work; and (2) work executed with enamel threads, which are used for finer work. With these threads the most beautiful and modern works may be executed. How different are these works from the work of the Quattrocentesti, admirable as that work was! If you look around in the factory, you see works representing garlands of flowers in which every shade of color is caught, together with the vivacity, grace and softness of flowers fresh from the garden. You see hunting scenes with animals represented to perfection; the mosaics lend themselves to every shape and movement in the scene, imitating the mottled coat of a hound and the bristles of a boar. Besides scenes such as these, which are fit to adorn the drawing-room of the most exacting connoisseur, there are copies of the most famous paintings, each of which represents the work, not of months, but of many years.

On entering the factory, the visitor first meets the sample-room, where the number of tints will undoubtedly awaken his astonishment. As many as twenty-eight thousand gradations of color are here to be found, and each sample has a number corresponding to a shelf where the worker can immediately find a supply of the particular shade he seeks.

The second room contains all the best mosaics in enamel cubes re-

The Furnace for the Fusion of the Enamels   The Manufacture of Enamel Threads

cently made, as well as painted copies of all other mosaic works heretofore executed. This well-arranged collection is well worth seeing. It contains, for instance, a copy of Il Guercino's Ecce Homo and Guido Reni's St. Peter; these are the artistic gems of the collection, and are so perfect that they can hardly be distinguished from the originals. There are, besides, very fine portraits of the Popes, images of saints, Madonnas, and artistic works of every kind, from sacred subjects to reproductions of flowers and fruits.

From the second gallery the visitor enters the workroom where the artists are busy. Around the walls are the shelves containing the enamels. Each worker has his original before him, and he builds up his picture piece by piece, chipping the enamel to the proper size and then passing it over a lathe to bring it to the desired shape. First of all a bed of plaster is prepared and put in an iron frame. The outlines of the picture are then drawn on this plaster. Piece by piece the plaster is removed and replaced by a layer of stucco (a mixture of lime, marble dust and the dregs of flaxseed oil). The worker next breaks the enamel with a tiny hammer, reduces it to the proper shape on the lathe, and fixes it in its place in the stucco, which, drying rapidly, holds the enamel firmly in its place. Only then is another piece of the plaster removed, because the stucco must be always fresh to receive and hold the enamel.

The furnace for the fusion of the cut enamels is shown in one of our illustrations. In 1856, under Pius IX, Monsignor Giraud, Administrator of St. Peter's (Economo della R. Fabrica di S. Pietro), was ordered to build this furnace for the preparation of the enamels for the workers who were to undertake the great task of making the mosaics for the chronology of the Popes, the façade of the Basilica of St. Paul, and the apse of the Lateran. These enamels were made under the direction of a chemist named Raffaelli, and the result was a great success. The enamels are made of glass and minerals. When the glass has reached the necessary degree of heat the minerals are mixed with it; the mixture is then poured into small round moulds, and, once it has cooled, is ready for use. In the case of the gilt enamels, the procedure is as follows: The workman takes a disc of colored enamel, covers it with a small leaf of gold, places above this a layer of glass, and puts

The Office of the Director of the Mosaic Factory

back the disc in the furnace. On melting, the glass forms an amalgam with the enamel and the gold, which, when cool, is ready for use. The room leading to the furnace-room contains a stock of the enamel threads, which are used in a different way. The mosaic workers, with the help of a lamp flame, mould them to the shape desired. Of the coloring material used in these enamel threads there is also an ample supply, for, like the cut enamels, new threads have to be made daily to meet the demands of the workmen. The man who has charge of the composition of the tints must have long experience in his work. Notwithstanding the fact that theory furnishes him with the required formulæ for the various combinations of the "mother tints" which blend to produce certain colors, experience always teaches him new combinations. After being scrupulously weighed, the mother colors are put in a large crucible over a strong gas-jet, the flame being augmented by the pressure of a bellows. When the enamel has become red-hot the worker kneads the fiery mass thoroughly with an iron, and then draws the enamel into long threads with a pliers. He must often make many trials before getting the right tint, but success is finally attained with patience, which is the chief gift of a good mosaic worker and artist.

The mosaic artist who has to copy exactly a certain work must proceed very slowly, because the shades, which are obtained rapidly with the brush, need careful study before they can be rendered in mosaic. Looking at the finished work, it is difficult to realize the time and patience it requires. But the result is worth all the trouble, because, while the picture may deteriorate, the mosaic lasts throughout the ages with its beauty unimpaired.

The mosaic factory really forms a part of the building department of St. Peter's, and is thus under the charge of Monsignor Giuseppe De Bisogno, Administrator of the Vatican Basilica. Its immediate management is in the hands of Professor Salvatore Nobili, who has now guided its fortunes for twenty-six years.

PART FOUR

—

THE VATICAN ADMINISTRATION

THE VATICAN ADMINISTRATION

CONCLAVE.—It is a matter of universal knowledge that the chief advisers of the Popes form a special college, and are known by the name of Cardinals. Their office is, first, to assist the Pope in the government of the Universal Church, and, secondly, when the Pope dies, to elect a successor from their number. To describe the manner in which the Cardinals fulfil the former function would be out of place here, since that would necessitate a treatise on the central administration of the Church. But since the elections of the last three Popes took place in the Vatican Palace, and since in all probability future elections will also be held there, some information concerning this important event seems to be called for.

Canon law prescribes that, on the death of a Pope, the Cardinals shall assemble as soon as possible at the place of his death for the election of his successor; for it is reasonable to suppose that a large number of Cardinals will be already assembled at this place. At the end of the nine days which are prescribed for the burial ceremonies, and which are also used for the preparation of the assembly hall, the Cardinals meet to elect the new Pope. This elective assembly is called the Conclave. Strict precepts require that the Conclave be held in rooms which are completely secluded by the stopping up of all entrances and windows that might make possible any communication with the outer world. Each accompanied by one priest (called a Conclavist) and one servant, the Cardinals are here immured until they have elected some one of their body by a two-thirds majority. The votes are cast each forenoon and afternoon by ballot in the Sistine Chapel. If the necessary majority has not been secured, the Master of Ceremonies burns the ballot papers, together with damp hay, in a small stove specially set up for this purpose in the Sistine Chapel. The stove-pipe extends over the gable of the chapel facing towards the Piazza di S. Pietro, where thousands assemble at the appointed hour in the morning and afternoon to obtain the latest news from this little chimney-flue. The thick, bluish-gray smoke, caused by the moist hay, indicates to the populace that the voting has been held without result. When, however, a Cardinal has been chosen by a two-thirds majority of the electors present, the ballot papers alone (without the hay) are burned, the consequence being that only a light and almost invisible smoke issues from the chimney. A feverish excitement then seizes all the assembled crowd, and on every side the discussion rages as to the identity of the Pope-Elect. Meanwhile the elected candidate is clothed with the white papal soutane in the sacristy of the Sistine Chapel, where three such soutanes of various sizes are always held in readiness. The Cardinals then pay him solemn homage for the first time, and the oldest of the Cardinal Deacons later announces the result of the election from the Loggia of St. Peter's. With lightning rapidity the news spreads throughout Rome, and every one hurries to St. Peter's to receive the first blessing which the new Pope gives from the above-mentioned Loggia.

The method of voting is as follows: Each Cardinal first signs his name at the top of the ballot paper (*e.g.,* Ego *Thomas* Card. *Riarius*); he then inserts in the middle (after the words Eligo . . . D. Card.) the name of the candidate for whom he wishes to vote, and finally writes at the bottom of the paper the numeral indicating his order of precedence in the Sacred College and also some motto which has been chosen especially for this occasion and does not in any way suggest his identity (see illustration on page 513). The upper and lower parts of the ballot are then folded (see No. 3) and secured with three seals to the left and right of the printed words *Nomen* (name) and *Signa* (motto). Should no candidate secure the prescribed two-thirds majority, the ballots are burned unopened. When a candidate has received the necessary majority, he must reveal his motto, whereupon the bottom folds only of all the ballots are opened until that containing this motto is discovered. The upper fold of this ballot is then opened to ensure that the candidate has not voted for himself. After this formality all the voting ballots are burned as before. To bring to an end a deadlock, or for various other reasons, the Cardinals are always at liberty to transfer their votes. They are then said to "vote by *accedo*," since the word *Accedo* (I go over to) occurs in the special ballot paper (No. 2) used in such an instance.

One of the illustrations shows the Sistine Chapel prepared for the Conclave. The seat of each Cardinal is surmounted by a canopy, which is violet in color for all the Cardinals created by the deceased Pontiff, and green for those created before his pontificate. Immediately after the election, all the canopies are turned down except that under which the new Pope is seated; this remains open, and is the first indirect homage shown to the new Pontiff. It has been remarked that a

Cardinal may never cast his ballot for himself, and that after the voting a careful investigation is always made to discover if this has been the case. If it should really prove to be the case, the election would be invalid.

POPE'S DAILY ROUTINE.—A few general remarks concerning the business dispatched by the Pope may not be out of place.

The personal affairs of the Holy Father, and of those dependent on him, are entrusted to the Papal Private Chancery. This department is under the care of the senior of the two private secretaries, and claims

Cortile del Maresciallo

It is the duty of Prince Chigi, as Hereditary Marshal of the Conclave, to guard the doorway here shown (which is the only entrance to the Conclave during the Papal Election)

the attention of four persons. It is not an ecclesiastical department, but is an entirely personal affair of the Pope. It occupies a mezzanine within his suite, being situated over the Privy Antechamber and the three adjoining rooms beyond his private library.

The business of the Universal Church and also the affairs of his own diocese (Rome and its precincts) are laid before the Pope by the Cardinals and prelates who preside over the various congregations and boards created in the course of time to attend to the endless business details which are referred to Rome. This does not mean that the Pope does not receive direct information—that is, without the mediation of the high church officials. This immediate information is obtained partly in audiences, and partly in letters opened by the Pope person-

ally.   The most important information is secured in the audiences
given to the bishops of the whole world, when they make their regular
visits to the Tombs of the Apostles to give an account of their administration.   With other members both of the clergy and of the laity the
Pope discusses special affairs.   As the result of more than twenty-six
years' observation, the writer is in a position to declare that there is
probably no ruler in the world who is kept so perfectly informed as to
everything of interest to his office as the Pope.   Through the medium

Crowd in the Piazza di S. Pietro awaiting the result of the Papal Election

of correspondence, a mine of highly valuable and confidential information reaches the Holy Father, and often leads to his direct intervention.

Should a person desire a letter to reach the Pope's hands, he need
only place it in an envelope, address it "Alla Santità di Nostro Signore
Pio Papa Decimo," and write in the lower corner on the left "Riservato
al sacro tavolino."   This letter should be then placed in a second envelope and sealed; and, after the above address has been again written,
with the additional words "Rome, Palazzo Apostolico Vaticano," the
letter should be registered.   The writer may then be certain that his
letter will be opened by the Pope himself.   Needless to say, this method
should be adopted only by a person who has a really important com-

munication to make, which is of immediate interest to the Holy Father, and is of such a nature that it cannot well be conveyed through the medium of the ecclesiastical officials. To burden him with unimportant trifles would be a gross offence to the Pope.

Five or six times a week the Cardinal Secretary of State has the first audience with the Pope. He lays before him all business which calls for his attention, hears his decisions, and also receives commands concerning new regulations emanating from the Holy Father. The

The Sistine Chapel Prepared for a Conclave

prefects or secretaries of the Congregations of Cardinals have, according to the extent and importance of the business on which they are engaged, one audience weekly or one or two audiences a month at specially appointed hours on special days. According to the nature of the business to be discussed, these audiences last one or two hours. It is thus seen that the Pope not only hears reports and confirms decisions, but in specially difficult cases he also takes cognizance of the documents, and gives his decision only after a searching investigation of the question with his official advisers.

After the reform of the Curial administration a change was made in the regulations for antecameral audiences. The order of these official audiences is now as follows:

On the first Monday of each month, the President of the Accademia dei Nobili Ecclesiastici and the Grand Almoner; on the second and fourth Mondays, the Cardinal Datarius, the Assistant Datarius, and the General Secretary of the Congregation of the Propaganda.

On the first and third Tuesdays of each month, the Cardinal Prefect of the Congregation of the Council.

On the first Wednesday of each month, the Cardinal Prefect of the Apostolic Signatura; on the fourth Wednesday, the Secretaries of the Biblical Commission; on the second and fourth Wednesdays, the Secretary of the Propaganda for Oriental Affairs.

On every Thursday, the Assessor of the Congregation of the Holy Office; on the second Thursday of each month, the Cardinal Prefect of the Congregation of the Index; on the first and third Thursdays, the Cardinal Prefect of the Propaganda.

On every Friday, the Cardinal Secretary of the Congregation of the Consistory; on the first and fourth Fridays, the Cardinal Grand Penitentiary.

On the second Saturday of each month, the Cardinal Chancellor of the Holy Roman Church; on the third Saturday, the Cardinal Prefect of the Congregation of Studies; on the fourth Saturday, the Dean of the Court of the Holy Roman Rota and the Master of the Apostolic Palace; on the first and third Saturdays, the Cardinal Vicar for the administration of the Diocese of Rome.

On the first and third Sundays of the month, the Cardinal Prefect of the Congregation for the Discipline of the Sacraments.

When these regular audiences will be omitted owing to special functions, and in what weeks audiences will be held, is announced each year by the Maestro di Camera.

SECRETARIATE OF STATE.—The suite of the Cardinal Secretary of State lies on the first floor near the Appartamento Borgia. In these rooms is dispatched all business between him and the diplomats accredited to the Holy See. All bishops and archbishops coming to Rome here visit the Cardinal Secretary; innumerable persons of every rank and station call here with information on the most diverse things, and numerous petitioners of every kind crowd the antechamber of the Pope's most important assistant. The extent of the business here discharged is, as regards both its variety and its extent, literally astounding.

Immediately after the audience of the Secretary of State with the Holy Father, the Assistant Secretary waits on the former and together they distribute the daily business among the various officials. The offices of the Secretariate of State lie on the third floor behind the Gallery of Geographical Charts, and almost completely surround the Cor-

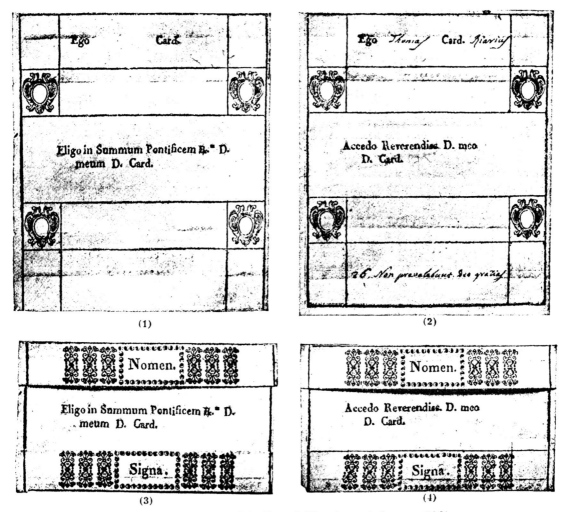

Voting Ballots used in Papal Elections (cf. page 508)

tile del Papagallo and the Cortile del Maresciallo. The extremely important and extensive Archives of the Secretariate are also located here. A special feature of these Archives is the ease and dispatch with which every document in the collection can be found by means of the special filing system, which is attended to daily.

Since its amalgamation with the Secretariate of State, the Secretariate of Briefs has been accommodated in the rooms on the third floor left free by the removal of the old Pinacoteca. The business of this department of briefs is very extensive and important. Apart from the special questions of church administration, the briefs for all kinds of ecclesiastical privileges are prepared here (*e.g.*, for the maintaining of private oratories, for the reservation of the Blessed Sacrament, and so on).

PAPAL ORDERS AND DECORATIONS.—It may interest wider circles to know that all Papal Decorations and Orders are conferred by a brief. And since in such cases the matters arise from no immediate necessity, but are undertaken merely to give pleasure and satisfaction to indi-

The Interior of the Sistine Chapel after the Election of Pius X
All the canopies are turned down except that of the Patriarch of Venice

viduals, it is entirely proper and reasonable that the chancery fees for the preparation of the briefs for decorations conferred on private persons should be comparatively high. The different classes of an Order call for the payment of fees of varying amounts when the Order is conferred. The Grand Cross is the highest taxed, the Commander's Cross the next highest, and the Knight's Cross the lowest. There is also a difference of rank among the Orders themselves, and this difference is reflected in the fees, since the Orders standing highest call also for relatively higher taxes. The foolish calumny formerly so often heard, that the Papal Orders were purchasable, is now discredited—at least among intelligent people. Such a thing is absolutely impossible, since the same principles are observed in granting these Orders as are observed in every other responsible state.

The Holy Father confers the following Orders and Decorations:

(1) The Order of Christ. This highest of all Orders was founded by Pope John XXII on March 14, 1319. It has only one class, and is also known as the "Militia of Our Lord Jesus Christ." The Order is worn on a ribbon around the neck.

(2) The Order of the Golden Spur. This also has but a single class, and was founded at some very ancient date which can no longer be exactly determined. It is known in history as the "Militia Aurata," and was reorganized by Pius X in 1905.

(3) The Order of Pius, named after its founder, Pope Pius IX, who erected it by Bull of June 17, 1847. This possesses four classes: (a)

Knights of the Grand Cross; (b) Knights of the Commander's Cross with the Plaque; (c) Knights of the Commander's Cross; (d) Knights of the Simple Cross. The main reason for the founding of this Order was to provide a decoration which did not bear the name of a saint, and with which non-Catholics might be honored.

(4) The Order of St. Gregory the Great, founded by Gregory XVI on September 1, 1831, in honor of his patron saint. This comprises both a civil and a military class, each possessing four degrees like the Pius Order.

(5) The Order of Pope St. Sylvester. This also was founded by Gregory XVI on October 31, 1841. It was reformed by Pius X in 1905, when its insignia were somewhat altered. It has the usual four degrees.

(6) The Order of the Holy Sepulchre. This Order was founded by the Apostolic Brief "Cum multa" of January 24, 1868, and was reformed by Pius X in 1907. The Order is conferred in the name of the Pope by the Latin Patriarch of Jerusalem, and the Pope himself is its Grand Master. The Order has the same four degrees as above, and may be conferred on women.

(7) The decoration of the Cross, "Pro Ecclesia et Pontifice," which formerly had four classes, has now only one. It was founded by Leo XIII.

(8) The Service Medal, "Bene merenti," which was formerly so frequently conferred, was revived by Pius X.

In our illustration on page 517, the following decorations have been reproduced: (1) Plaque (Badge) of the Order of Christ, worn at the breast. (2) The Order of Christ. (3) Knight's Cross of the Order of St. Sylvester. (4) Count's Cross of the Order of St. Sylvester. (5) Grand Cross of the Order of Pius. (6) Plaque of the Grand Cross of the Order of Pius. (7) Count's Cross of the Order of Pius. (8) Knight's Cross of the Order of Pius. (9) Grand Cross of the Second Class of the Order of St. Gregory for Civilians. (10) Knight's Cross of the Order of St. Gregory. (11) Grand Cross of the Second Class of the Order of St. Gregory for Officers. (12) Grand Cross of the First Class of the Order of St. Gregory for Civilians. (13) Plaque of the Grand Cross of the First and Second Classes of the Order of St. Gregory. (14) Grand Cross of the First Class of the Order of St. Gregory for Officers.

The external form of the Solemn Briefs, as they are called, is wonderfully impressive. The ancient tradition of the Church has in this connection supplied a type which other state chanceries might well envy. These documents, which are written on vellum, display a perfect simplicity of form, while in the distribution of space and the styles of penmanship the highest degree of perfection has been attained. The ordinary briefs, used for the transaction of current business, are naturally of an essentially simpler character.

THE PAPAL FAMILY.—Almost without exception, the Popes have chosen, after their election, a new Secretary of State. In view of the extreme importance and confidential nature of this position, it is quite natural that the new Pope should select for it the man in whom he personally reposes the greatest confidence. The Secretary of State and the Datarius are now the only Palace Cardinals. These were formerly four in number, but the Secretariate of Briefs and the Secretariate of Memorials, offices formerly held by Palace Cardinals, are no longer separate departments. The above-mentioned two Palace Cardinals are the highest members of the "Papal Family"—that is, of the circle of persons who, in virtue of their office or position of honor, belong to the immediate household of the Pope. To this household naturally belong in a special manner the high court officials, who render constant service to the Pope and are in constant contact with him. These all are included under the general title of the Nobile Anticamera Segreta (Noble Privy Antechamber).

At the head of this Antechamber stand the four Palatine Prelates, all of whom have the right to free quarters in the Vatican Palace. The first of these is the Majordomo (Præfectus Palatii Apostolici), or Chief Governor of His Holiness the Pope. It should be noted that, during the vacancy of the Papal See, this official continues in office as Governor of the Conclave until the new Pope has been elected. When the Pope takes his place on the throne, it is the right and duty of the Majordomo, as the highest of the prelates, to stand immediately to the right of the throne. He exercises supreme supervision over all religious functions at which the Pope and his court assist. The Chief Master of Ceremonies is thus under obligation to discuss such functions with the Majordomo beforehand. The drawing up of all nominations to court offices or posts of honor is also the task of the Majordomo, and he is an ex-officio member of the Palatine Commission entrusted with the administration of the Apostolic Palaces. Formerly the Majordomo was also the chief director of the Papal Choir (also known as the Cappella Sistina), which he directed in accordance with the special Apostolic Constitutions and Statutes governing this body. The Majordomo enjoys many other rights and privileges, which however may be passed over here.

The second Palatine Prelate is the Maestro di Camera (Præfectus Cubiculi Secreti), or High Chamberlain. His authority extends mainly to those persons and things connected with the daily service of His Holiness. He thus enjoys, in the first place, jurisdiction over all papal

Papal Decorations (see page 515)

The Order of the Holy Sepulchre
(1) Commander's Cross. (2) Knight's Cross. (3) Plaque of the Grand Cross
(4) Commander's Plaque. (5) Grand Cross

chamberlains, both ecclesiastical and lay, and regulates their duties in the Antechamber. He informs the Commanders of the Noble, Swiss, and Palatine Guards of their hours of service, controls all proceedings in the Antechamber, and dismisses the Gentlemen-in-waiting at the close of the audiences. Since all requests for an audience pass through his hands, he is by far the best known of all the court officials, and every morning and afternoon his antechamber is besieged by a crowd of persons of all nations and classes, all giving expression to a single wish—namely, their desire to see the Holy Father. Day after day the routine continues, so that this office demands an extraordinary patience and absence of nerves in its occupant, who must always give a friendly hearing to the never-changing request of endless thousands.

While, as was already stated, official ecclesiastical functions are under the supervision of the Majordomo, the Maestro di Camera arranges all receptions that are not directly official and fixed, such as audiences given to pilgrimages, musical and other performances in the presence of the Holy Father, and so forth. From the fact that the Maestro di Camera receives daily the orders of the Pope for the service of the following day, the confidential nature and special importance of his position will be immediately recognized. In processions he takes precedence of the numberless Prothonotaries Apostolic, entirely regardless of the date of his appointment. Naturally, this rule is not intended to apply when, as happens in exceptional cases, the Maestro di Camera is a titular bishop or archbishop, the ordinary rules of precedence being followed in such instances. It is also worthy of mention that, in the absence of the Majordomo, most of his duties are performed by the Maestro di Camera.

Decoration of the Vexillifer or Standard-bearer

Inasmuch as the third place among the palace prelates has not been occupied for a long time, and there is little prospect of a future appointment, it calls for little mention here. The occupant bore the title of Auditor of the Pope, and was a kind of theological and legal counsellor, especially in questions connected with appointments to vacant sees.

According to tradition, the office of the fourth palace prelate extends back to St. Dominic. However this may be, it is certain that the Magistro del Sacro Palazzo (Magister Sacri Palatii), the Master or Teacher of the Sacred Palace, is always a Dominican. And as a natural result of his office of counsellor to the Curia, this prelate is to-day the special theologian of the Pope. In this capacity he has, for example, to examine carefully beforehand all sermons and religious discourses which are to be delivered in the presence of the Pope. During such addresses he sits near the preacher with the manuscript in hand, and carefully notes whether the sermon is delivered verbatim as it was written. The reason for this procedure is, first, to ensure that the theological contents shall not suffer any alteration, and, secondly, to prevent the preacher from drifting away from his subject in pursuit of some new line of thought which may suddenly suggest itself. Such improvisations, if tolerated in the presence of the Pope, might possibly have undesirable results. The Magistro also exercises the censorship over the manuscripts of all books appearing in Rome, and

Service Medal of Pius IX

grants the Imprimatur. As a palace prelate, he occupies a prominent place in all religious functions at which the Pope assists. He is an ex-officio member (Consultor) of several Congregations which discharge business closely allied with his office. Like the Majordomo and the Maestro di Camera, he resides in the Vatican Palace, but, although he belongs to the prelature, he has no external badge of his office. Many in the long line of clerics who have held this office have passed from it to the cardinalate, but the custom has not been sufficiently regular to amount to a prescriptive right.

It has been said above that the prelate who associates most intimately with the Holy Father is the Maestro di Camera, since it is he who

arranges daily the whole order of
the audiences, and daily receives
the Pope's commands for the following day. In these duties he is
assisted by four Chamberlains in
the religious state, who, either individually or in pairs, render
weekly service in the Antechamber. In all things they are subject
to the Maestro di Camera, who, at
regular intervals, fixes their hours
of service. Even when there are
no audiences or receptions, these
chamberlains must be ready to
wait on the Pope—for example,
to accompany him on his walk or
drive in the Gardens, to execute
commissions in the city, and so on.
They all reside in the Vatican
Palace, and are, as a rule, of different nationalities, since service in

Privy Chamberlain in Spanish Costume
(Cameriere di spada e cappa)

the Antechamber requires the occasional use of many languages.
French and Italian are of course the staple medium of conversation.

Since the service which the Privy Chamberlains render to the Pope
is purely personal, their period of office ends with his death. Although
it commonly occurs that the new Pope appoints to important positions
men whom from personal experience he knows to be worthy of his
confidence, he almost always retains temporarily in office the Chamberlains of his predecessor, so that the service in the Antechamber may
continue efficient and uninterrupted.

Besides these four Privy Chamberlains proper (the number actually
holding office varies at different times), mention must be made of five
other prelates who hold important offices in the court and the church
administration. These are the Assistant Datarius (Sotto Datario), the
Secretary of Briefs to Princes (Segretario dei Brevi ai Principi), the
Secretary of Latin Briefs (Segretario delle Lettere Latine), the Under-
Secretary of State and Director of Ciphers (Segretario della Cifra), and
the Privy or Grand Almoner (Elemosiniere Segreto). The last-mentioned, who administers all the funds assigned to him by the Pope for
charitable purposes in accordance with special rules drawn up for his
guidance, deserves special notice. The extent of his duties may be
gathered from the fact that he is assisted by one secretary, two book-

keepers, one cashier, and two clerks. Besides the large sums given to him for current demands, the Holy Father assigns to him special sums on great feasts and extraordinary occasions (*e.g.*, a Jubilee), to be distributed, either personally or through the medium of the pastors, among the poor and needy. The Privy Almoner is customarily a Titular Bishop and an Assistant at the Throne, and has his official residence and offices in the Vatican Palace. His offices are reached through the door behind the Colonnade which also gives access to the quarters of the Swiss Guard. The Almoner has regular audiences with the Holy Father, in which he submits petitions to His Holiness, discusses all matters connected with his office, and receives the commands of the Pope. His office is *ad vitam Pontificis*—that is, it is terminable with the life of the Pope.

Privy Chamberlain in Service Uniform

The office of the Prefect of the Apostolic Chapel (also called the Sacristan of the Pope) is for life. From the very earliest times a cleric was assigned to the service of the Papal Chapel—that is, to exercise the care of souls at the Papal Court. In the course of time this office became of great importance, and great privileges were associated with it. In 1497 Alexander VI (1492–1503) decreed that the Sacristan should be always chosen from the Augustinian Order, and this practice continues to the present day. The Sacristan is always the Titular Bishop of Porphyreon and an Assistant at the Throne. He is an ex-officio Consultor of a number of Congregations and Commissions, and in his official capacity has participated in the Conclave since the reign of Pius IV (1559–1565). Besides supervising the Papal Chapels and administering the treasures of the Sistine Chapel and of the Vatican Chamber of Relics, the Sacristan is pastor of the Apostolic Palaces. In connection with this last duty he is aided by the Assistant Sacristan, who is also an Augustinian. Before the Pope pontificates, the Sacristan must test the host and the wine and water which are to be used in the Mass. On fixed occasions he assists the Pope at the altar, and then wears the mantelletta and mozetta without rochet. The rite of blessing the Papal

Apartments on Holy Saturday, in connection with the general blessing of houses which takes place on that day, pertains to him. When he reaches the room occupied by the Pope he removes his stole and presents the aspersorium to the Holy Father, who blesses this room. It is from the hands of the Sacristan that the dying Pope receives Extreme Unction.

A very important rôle at the Papal Court is filled by the Masters of Ceremonies. Their office is confined to ecclesiastical functions, while questions of ceremonial in general (for example, questions of precedence among the Cardinals and diplomats) are decided by the Congregation of Ceremonial. The Magistri Cæremoniarum Apostolicarum were not formed into a college until the close of the fifteenth century. The Prefect, or Antistes Cæremoniarum, has a most responsible task, because he has complete charge of the very complicated ceremonies at all great ecclesiastical functions—for example, at the death of the Pope, during the Conclave, at the proclamation of the election, and especially in connection with the coronation of the new Pope.

The source of the general ceremonies for the coronation is probably to be sought in the Byzantine court ceremonial. The details thence derived were further developed and completed. In the course of time new elements were added when deemed necessary, and thus was evolved the ceremonial as it stands to-day. Those who judge this gigantic ceremony in its entirety must admit that, individual details aside, its progress is one of glorious solemnity and majesty. The special ecclesiastical ceremonies which emphasize the absence of the Pope are inspired by the thought that for him, as Christ's Vicar, a central position must be prepared. This is effected with such unostentatious precision, with so refined a moderation in all details, that every spectator must concede that no more solemn and worthy development of a religious service could be imagined. The profane ceremonies in connection with the receptions, audiences, and so forth, differ only in a few details from those customary in secular courts.

The development of divine worship into an act of the highest solemnity is a requirement of human nature, and the Church satisfies this craving by giving a sublime aim to customs and ceremonies common among men. And the highest and most solemn expression of those ceremonies is found in the regulations which have been gradually elaborated for divine service celebrated by the Pope or in his presence. Tradition, which always, when possible, harks back to earlier occurrences, exercises here her full power, and cares for the homogeneity of the development of papal ceremonial. New cases, seldom as they occur, are always decided according to the analogy of similar cases in

Consecration of Hungarian Bishops in the Sistine Chapel

Mass according to the Greek Rite in the Aula delle Beatificazioni

the past, and the rich archives of the College of the Masters of Ceremonies always offer an inexhaustible mine of information to the prelates in office.

Besides the above-mentioned active Chamberlains, there is a large number of honorary Privy Chamberlains, who enjoy merely the title and the right to wear the distinctive dress. Corresponding with this class is the large body of lay Chamberlains who are called upon to render service only at very rare intervals. But, just as there are four ecclesiastical Privy Chamberlains in the strict sense who are court officials, there are also four lay Chamberlains. The first of these is the Maestro del

The Tiara or Triple Crown

Sacro Ospizio (the Master of the Sacred Hospice), whose office is for life and is hereditary in his family. Pope Martin V (1417–1431) vested the Conti family with this honorable office, but as their property was inherited by the Ruspoli family, the latter now enjoy this office also. The Maestro del Sacro Ospizio had formerly an extensive sphere of activity in all questions relating to the reception and accommodation of kings and princes, members of the Curia, and other distinguished personages who visited the Pope; but under existing conditions his duties are greatly modified. He greets sovereigns and princes and princesses of the royal blood at the foot of the Scala Nobile in the Cortile di S. Damaso when they come to visit the Pope. Presenting his arm to the ladies, he escorts them up the staircase to the Throne Room or the Antechamber, and also acts as their escort when, at the close of the audience, they wish to pay a visit to the Vatican Collections. He must appear at all functions attended by the Pope, and must always receive a special invitation from the head of the Apostolic Ministry. In processions he takes precedence of the Judges of the Rota, and follows immediately the Ministers General of the Mendicant Orders. He is also known as the Custos Sacri Sacelli (Custodian of the Sacred Chapel) or Custos Interior Augusti Consessus Cardinalium (Custodian of the Sacred College), because he guards the entrance to the quadrangle in the Sistine Chapel which the Cardinals occupy on solemn occasions.

The Singers of the Sistine Choir, with Maestro Perosi

Besides the above-mentioned official Privy Chamberlains, there are five Privy Chamberlains who do not lose their honorary title at the death of the Pope. These are known as Chamberlains *di numero,* in contradistinction to the Supernumerary Chamberlains. Lifelong is also the title enjoyed by the laymen who form the second class of honorary chamberlains. This small body of privileged Chamberlains of both classes is usually recruited from those longest in office, and was founded so that there might be some Chamberlains available during the papal election for service in the Antechamber. While all the other Chamberlains lose their title and office at the death of the Pope, since their relations with the Holy Father are of a purely personal nature, the senior Chamberlains of both classes continue in office permanently for the above reason, and become Chamberlains for life. As all lay Chamberlains wear with their full-dress uniform a sword and mantle, they are known as Camerieri di spada e cappa (Cubicularii ab ense et lucerna).

Every Chamberlain, whether privileged or supernumerary, is a member of the papal family, and enjoys free access to all papal functions, provided that he appears in his official dress. Every week one Privy and one Honorary Chamberlain are summoned for service in the Antechamber, and on festival occasions the attendance of a larger number is required to see that the order prescribed by the Majordomo or Maestro di Camera is observed on the platforms. Their dress uniform, which is in the style of the sixteenth century, with ruff and large golden chain, is very picturesque. The number of lay Chamberlains throughout the world, who have received this distinction on the recommendation of their bishops, is very large.

There are at present four Private Chaplains of the Pope, and these also hold purely personal offices at the Court. The number of these chaplains has varied greatly at different times. Two of them perform special offices in liturgical functions as bearer of the pontifical cross and train-bearer. There are a large number of honorary Papal Chaplains throughout the world, who enjoy the title without the duties.

PAPAL FUNCTIONS.—From the above information concerning the most important court officials, the reader can form a fair idea of how rich is the development of ceremonies when the Pope celebrates a great festival. All these various classes of court officials, members of the Papal Household, are represented on such occasions, and in the pontifical procession the place of each is exactly determined. The variety of the dress worn by the court officials excites great curiosity among the beholders, and the brilliant uniforms of the laity give additional life to a picture already glowing with color.

On the anniversary of his coronation and on a few other special occasions the Pope wears the tiara, or triple crown (triregnum), instead of the episcopal mitre. In its present form, with three crowns, the head-dress dates from the fourteenth century. Formerly it tapered to a point, but during the eighteenth century it assumed the shape of a beehive, thus developing into one of the most unbecoming head-dresses in the world. Lately the old graceful pointed Phrygian head-dress with three crowns seems to be returning into favor, a change for which we may feel grateful. There are many tiaras in the treasury of the Sistine Chapel, but among them there is only one whose lines can be described as beautiful. This was presented to Leo XIII by the Catholics of Paris.

Among the honorary offices of the Vatican must be mentioned also that of Custodian of the Triple Crown (Custode dei Sacri Triregni). In the later Middle Ages we find the papal Master of the Treasury mentioned by this title. As he had in his charge most valuable jewels (chalices, rings, pectoral crosses, mitres, etc.), he was often entrusted with the very costly tiaras, which were encrusted with precious stones. When these were to be used he demanded a receipt before allowing them out of his possession. This arrangement continued for a long period, but in recent times the Sacristan has been the real custodian of these precious objects, although he is not given the title. When a tiara is to be worn in pontifical processions, it is borne by a papal chaplain in black soutane. Beside the chaplain walks the Jeweler of the Apostolic Palaces in black uniform and wearing a sword. The latter guards the tiara from the time it leaves the Sistine Treasury until it is returned to the Assistant Sacristan. During the function, therefore, he is the real Custodian of the Triple Crown, although he has nothing to do with its guardianship.

On these and other solemn occasions the celebrations are heightened by the presence of the Sistine Choir. This bore from the beginning the title of Schola Cantorum Domini Papæ, because even in ancient times it was already formed into a college. As might be supposed, this college was composed exclusively of clerics in the early Middle Ages and even later, since these alone possessed the necessary training to qualify them to fill the office. Consequently, when in recent centuries the laity also

Papal Processional Cross

were admitted to the Choir, it was made a condition of their service that they should always wear the clerical dress. The Schola was extended greatly, especially in the thirteenth and fourteenth centuries, and was fostered with great privileges and large endowments. In times still more recent the repute of the Choir has been firmly established, owing partly to its famous conductors and partly to its own splendid performances.

Since the Sistine Choir sings only *a cappella*—that is, unaccompanied by the organ or other musical instrument—in the presence of the Pope, it has developed the custom of singing only *a cappella* on all occasions. Apart from papal functions, the Choir sings only at Requiem Masses for the high court officials, and on other occasions for which the special permission of the Holy Father has been secured.

Until a few years ago a director was chosen annually from the ranks of the singers, but this did not tend to raise the efficiency of the Choir. At present Maestro Perosi, the celebrated composer, is permanent director, and is assisted by a permanent Vice-maestro. Perosi has attained a lifelong wish in the establishment of a boys' school for sopranos and altos, in which able singers are developed. To the college proper twenty-two virtuosi belong, and of these nine are emerited. Besides the boys, the service of a large number of other singers is requisitioned for all performances of the Choir, so that its singing strength is about one hundred

Pontifical Mazziere or Mace-bearer

voices. The rich archives of the college contain a large number of valuable musical works by the most famous masters, still in manuscript. After long neglect, these have been now put in proper order.

Whenever the Pope takes part in any liturgical celebration, whether he himself pontificates or (for example, in connection with a Solemn Requiem) undertakes the Absolution of the Tumba, it is the right and duty of the prelates entitled to sit in the Court of the Signatura to serve as acolytes and candle-bearers. They also present the censer and incense to the Pope in connection with the incensing. The Auditors of the Court of the Rota, on the other hand, discharge the office of Apostolic Deacons. Two Clerics of the Chapel, as they are known officially, act as the clerics on such occasions, and are then called *clerici in posto*. Their duties extend to the indirect service at the altar, as they have to see that all things necessary for the altar are prepared. In the fourteenth century they were named *clerici campanarum*, because they had charge of the bells of the Apostolic Palace.

The papal processional cross has been represented from ancient times as one possessing three cross-bars of diminishing size towards the top. A papal cross of this fantastic character has never existed; it is a pure fiction. The processional cross consists in reality of a plain crucifix attached to a staff. There is a special college of clerics, five in number, who fetch the cross from the Throne Room when it is required, and guard it until it is returned after the service. These clerics are known as the Doorkeepers with the Red Rod (Magistri Ostiarii a Virga Rubea). As their name indicates, they formerly discharged other duties. The officiating Master of Ceremonies always gives them the signal for handing the cross to the appointed Auditor of the Rota to carry, and later for receiving it back again.

Only in connection with solemn functions undertaken by the Pope or performed in his presence, and with the ceremonies of the Sacred College during a vacancy of the Holy See, does a college of lay functionaries participate in the services. These carry silver-

Prince Orsini
Assistant at the Papal Throne

mounted maces, and are thus known as Mazzieri (*Mazerii Papæ*). Their origin dates back probably to the Servientes Armorum (henchmen or body-guard), who were well-known figures in the Papal Court during the Middle Ages. This body was responsible for the safety of the Pope and of the Apostolic Palaces. To-day the Mazzieri are entrusted with the duty of guarding the entrance to the quadrangle in the Sistine Chapel occupied by the Sacred College during solemn services at which the Pope is present. They have also to escort all persons who proceed from the credence-table near the altar to the papal throne. Two Mazzieri are also sent to episcopal consecrations in Rome to clear a path for the new bishop through the crowd during the singing of the Te Deum, and thus lend a special dignity to the occasion. In so far as the duties of their office are concerned, the Mazzieri are subject to the papal masters of ceremonies; in all other things they are subject to the Majordomo.

In the long list of personages who act as assistants to the Pope during solemn services, the Prince Assistant at the Throne occupies an office of an entirely exceptional nature. His official title is Stator Proximus a Solio Pontificis Maximi. He stands on the highest step of the throne, to the right of the First Deacon, and ranks immediately after the Vice-Chamberlain of the Roman Church, but before the prelates. He is incensed during the incensing of the choir, and receives the Kiss of

Peace. When the papal or annual medals are distributed, the Prince Assistant receives his immediately after the Cardinals and before the ambassadors. He also has the right to pour water over the Pope's fingers at the washing of the hands. On the Feast of the Purification two large candles are prepared, one for the Pope and the other for the Prince Assistant. He attends functions in the traditional dress of the old Roman princes, and is accompanied by his Gentiluomo, his Maestro di Camera, and other servants of his household. From the above remarks it will be seen that there is but one Prince Assistant at any function. But since this dignity is hereditary in both the Colonna and the Orsini families since the sixteenth century, the heads of these families have to perform alternately this service at the throne—when they can arrive at some common understanding on this matter, which has not always been the case.

TEMPORAL ADMINISTRATION.—Enough has been said above to enable the reader to comprehend how unusually great and diversified is the administration of the Vatican Palaces. A few words may be said concerning the origin and development of this administration. On November 1 of the stormy year 1848 the Pro-Secretary of State, Cardinal Antonelli, was given by Pius IX the supreme supervision of the Apostolic Palaces under the title of Prefect, and continued to fill this office until his death. When Leo XIII a little later succeeded to the Fisherman's throne, he issued, under date of December 11, 1880, two "Motus Proprii" in which he first separated the Prefecture of the Apostolic Palaces from the administration of the goods of the Holy See, and secondly issued exact instructions regarding the duties of the Prefect. The Secretary of State is now Prefect of the Apostolic Palaces, and a prelate is Sub-Prefect. With the exception of the few administrative matters for which the Majordomo is personally responsible, the whole administration is now discharged by the Prefecture. At regular intervals the heads of all the administrative departments assemble in congress under the presidency of the Sub-Prefect, and then all matters of importance are discussed. In questions of special importance the decision is given by the Cardinal Prefect.

The most important person in the household administration of the Vatican Palaces is undoubtedly the Maestro di Casa (Magister Domus). His social position is shown by the fact that he is the first of the honorary Chamberlains *di numero*. The staff of household employes are subject to him, and he is responsible for the execution of all orders connected with household affairs. As in innumerable cases he comes into contact with the Italian authorities, he possesses their *procura* (power of attorney) for the signing of written documents. For example, when a present is sent by parcel post to the Pope from Germany or France, it is delivered free of duty at the palace after the Maestro di Casa has signed the postal receipt. Again, when the palace administration places large orders for building materials with foreign firms, these are delivered free of duty to the Maestro di Casa. Should it be decided later not to use some of this material for the palace, the Italian Board of Finance is informed of the fact and the duty paid before the material is sold; for only those things which are used by the Pope are duty free. In the Italian Parliament it has been sometimes insinuated that the Vatican abuses

Marchese Clemente Sacchetti
Foriere Maggiore

this right to the detriment of the Italian exchequer. The libel was as often sharply stigmatized by the Italian ministry as pure imagination; the character of the Maestro di Casa was so completely above all suspicion that such an insinuation could not be entertained for a moment. The above regulation is rigidly observed on the part of the Vatican authorities. During the Conclave the Maestro di Casa, besides superintending the material administration, must provide for the comfort of the assembled Cardinals. This is a very responsible task, since many of the Cardinals are so advanced in years and delicate that they need special care and attention. While in earlier times this office was mostly held by clerics, it is now filled by a layman.

In so far as the household administration of the Vatican is concerned, the Foriere Maggiore dei Sacri Palazzi Apostolici (Quartermaster-Major of the Apostolic Palaces) is the next official after the Maestro di Casa. He performs a number of the latter's duties during his absence. This very ancient office was reorganized by Sixtus V (1585–1590), was made lifelong, and was given its present name. The special duty of the Foriere Maggiore is to superintend the buildings, gardens, water supply, furniture, magazines, and so forth, and from him the architect and the Sotto-Foriere take their instructions.

When the Pope uses the portable throne (*sedia gestatoria*), this official gives the order for its raising and lowering, and is responsible for its being borne quietly and securely. The servants, who are assigned to this duty only after long training, have to exercise the greatest care lest the throne should sway in the crowd which frequently presses around it when the procession turns a corner, or at other places where progress is difficult. As any rocking of the throne might easily give the Pope a feeling of vertigo or be the cause of some other indisposition, this duty of the Quartermaster-Major is an extraordinarily responsible one. Inasmuch as the Holy Father is invariably a man of advanced years, the greatest precaution and care are necessary. When we stand among the spectators and watch the Pope borne past us, it is only with great difficulty that we can realize how little enviable is his position—no more enviable, in fact, than that of his bearers. Immediately before him the Pope beholds the advancing line of the pontifical procession; to the left and right crowd excited throngs who can with great difficulty restrain themselves from greeting the beloved Father with loud exclamations. A mere trifle under some exciting circumstance may cause a venerable, white-haired priest uneasiness or even illness. We thus see that this side of the Pope's public life, at first sight so glorious and inspiring, is associated with no little anxiety. In contrast to Leo XIII, Pope Pius X avoided the *sedia gestatoria* whenever possible, since he always felt a predisposition towards vertigo when borne along above the heads of the crowd.

The papal stables and everything connected therewith are under the charge of the Chief Equerry (Cavallerizzo Maggiore), whose period of office closes with the death of the Pope. The succeeding Pope, however, almost invariably reappoints the old equerry. As the third of the Privy Chamberlains *di numero,* the Chief Equerry is one of the highest officers of the household. Since the time of Leo XII (1823–1829) he has been a member of the Administrative Commission of the Apostolic Palaces. As the number of horses kept for the Noble Guard and the higher court officials has been greatly reduced by Pius X, the duties of the Chief Equerry are no longer very extensive. The Pope's coachman and also his postillion and the grooms receive their orders from the Chief Equerry. The state coaches of earlier times were formerly kept where the new Picture Gallery now stands. They were then transferred to a large vault in the Cortile di Belvedere, where they can now be viewed by visitors. Since the automobile has already gained entrance into the Vatican, the number of horses is destined to decline still lower. When the Pope rides in a closed carriage, the latter is provided with a hammer-cloth and footman's step; both of the latter are omitted when he rides in an open carriage. A number of the higher officials have a carriage at their disposal when they wish to drive out on official business. A papal carriage fetches all Chamberlains when their services are required, and conveys them home again at the end of the functions. On the occasion of great festivities, when the services of thirty or forty ecclesiastical and lay Chamberlains are needed, the problem of providing sufficient equipages is solved by hiring public vehicles. All night long a papal carriage is at the disposal of the confraternity which undertakes the vigil during the night hours of the Forty Hours' Devotion.

The Portantina of Pope Leo XIII

The Marshal of Papal Journeys has for his official title Sopraintendente Generale alle Poste—which literally means General Superintendent of the Posts. This title has often given rise to misunderstanding, as some believed this official to be a kind of postmaster-general. This is, of course, quite erroneous. The Princes Massimo, in whose family this office is hereditary, have never had anything to do with the letter post; their office was to attend to the "posts" in the old meaning of the word—that is, to provide the things necessary for the continuation of a journey. Before the building of railroads, this official performed a most important function when the Pope undertook a journey. From its very nature, it is evident that the office must have been in existence from the very earliest time, since provision had

always to be made for the performance of the duties connected
with it. For when the Curia proceeded from one place to another,
there was always, as it were, a
small "migration of nations." The
account-books in our possession,
dating from the reign of Clement
V downwards, give us an accurate
idea of the extent and importance
of the preparations which were
necessary when the Pope, the Cardinals, the Court and Church officials, the Curial tribunals, and all
the other persons in the papal
retinue decided to move to another city. All necessity for such
preparations has now ceased. The
Pope is a prisoner in the Vatican,
and all thought of travelling is

Marchese Serlupi
Cavallerizzo Maggiore

past. But the Marshal of Papal Journeys is still entered in the calendars
of the Curia, because in Rome important offices of the past are still held
in honor. The successive Princes of the Massimo family attend all
court festivals and all religious functions, clad in their beautiful uniform, and thus impart additional color to the picture of the Papal Court.

What has been just said applies also to the Marchese Naro Patrizi
Montoro, the hereditary Gonfalonier (Banner-bearer) of the Holy
Roman Church. He enjoys the rank of lieutenant-general and wears
the uniform of the Noble Guard. The origin of this purely military
office must be traced to the Crusades of the thirteenth century. According to the exigencies of the time, first this and then that prince was
named banner-bearer until Pope Urban VIII (1623–1644) appointed the
Marchese Naro to the office. Even after this family merged with the
Patrizi, the honorable distinction descended from father to son, and
has now become a vested right.

FINANCIAL POSITION OF THE VATICAN.—The writer has received many
dozens of letters from friends and acquaintances, asking him to secure
early for them a place in the Sistine Chapel for the ceremonies of Holy
Week. To all these letters only one answer could be given, namely,
that the world-famous functions in the Sistine Chapel have ceased to
be held since 1870. This fact should be generally known, but as a
matter of fact such is not the case. Since the incorporation of the

Papal States in the Kingdom of Italy, everything has been discontinued except the absolutely indispensable. The feasts which were celebrated in regular succession by the Pope in the churches of Rome could, in view of the existing circumstances, no longer be thus celebrated. And the other celebrations also were either abolished or essentially simplified. These regulations were partly the expression of public mourning

Papal State Coach

at the persecution of the Church, and were partly necessitated by changed financial conditions which demanded simplification.

Since the Popes have never accepted the annual allowance of 3,225,-000 lire made by the Italian Government, although the revenue from the Papal States was irretrievably lost, they have been compelled to rely exclusively on the generosity of the faithful. Under the venerable name of Peter's Pence, pious offerings are collected throughout the Catholic world to enable the Pope to meet the cost of the central government of the Church. Since its resources are thus entirely dependent on voluntary offerings, the Holy See can never know what the morrow may bring, or whether a certain large expenditure, if made, will be covered by the receipts from Peter's Pence. The collections, especially in France, produced sufficient funds to enable the Holy See, by economical management in every department, to meet all its most important needs; but, after the separation of Church and State had compelled French Catholics to provide personally for all the ecclesiastical needs of their own country, the Peter's Pence collection naturally declined in France. To compensate for this loss, Germany especially, and also other countries, made special and very acceptable efforts to come to the assistance of the Holy Father. In the United States, also, this voluntary self-taxation of Catholics is extending each year.

The Popes practise the strictest economy in their own household, in their appropriations for the multiform objects of the Holy See, and, in short, in everything where economy is possible. When, however, important religious issues are at stake, they know no parsimony, but give freely to the fullest extent necessary. The artistic and scientific inheritance of the past, into which they have entered, is administered by them with such loving zeal, and they have been so successful in finding the necessary means for fostering modern development in the same fields, that even their critics must admit that, in the fulfilment of this important cultural duty, they have never been found wanting. In the chapters of this work which deal with the Vatican Library, the Picture Gallery, the Observatory, the Museums, and so forth, every reader will find the proof of this statement. Even in their poverty, the Popes have ever been the fosterers of art and science. And in this matter, just as when in the face of a great calamity (e. g., the earthquake in Sicily and Calabria) they have thrown all dictates of thrift to the winds and come forward with an immense contribution for the relief of the sufferers, they show only their implicit confidence in the Catholic spirit of sacrifice, which will never fail them in time of need.

A special Commission of Cardinals administers the Peter's Pence and the goods of the Holy See. This commission consists of seven Cardinals with a prelate as secretary. The bookkeepers, cashiers, and other employes are laymen. The offices are situated on the third floor on the Cortile di S. Damaso. For the material side of the administration of the ecclesiastical bodies of Rome there is another Commission, which has a Cardinal for president and a prelate for vice-president. This department, which is an innovation of Pius X, is also located in the Vatican Palace, and has proved very successful. It was characteristic of all the activities of Pius X that he finally replaced antiquated by modern and efficient administrative methods. The progress made during his reign, compared with that of preceding decades, was so striking that it is very easy to see how much more economical and efficient was his administration.

PAPAL ARMY.—The Swiss Guard is by far the most important military body in the service of the Pope. Besides guarding the exterior entrances to the palace, the Swiss Guard is entrusted with the honorable duty of guarding the immediate entrance to the papal chambers in the Sala Clementina. Furthermore, members of the Guard are posted in various parts of the palace, day and night, all serving immediately or remotely for the same purpose of guarding the Pope. The special work of the Swiss Guard is thus to guard the sacred person of the Pontiff and also to keep watch over the Apostolic Palaces. In accordance with an old tradition, they participate in all pontifical functions at which His Holiness is present, but at the order of the Prefect of the Palace, the Majordomo, or the

Prince Massimo
Grand Master of the Posts

Maestro di Camera, have also to appear on other occasions. In public processions they take their place immediately behind the Noble Guard, as directed by the official regulations. When the Holy Father is borne in the portable throne (*sedia gestatoria*), the latter is surrounded by six Swiss Guards carrying their large two-handed swords. We may thus see the extraordinary honors enjoyed by the Swiss Guard, as well as the great responsibility of their duties.

The origin of the Papal Swiss Guard extends back to the fifteenth century. Their position was secured by treaty under Julius II (1503–1513), who, at the instigation of the Swiss Cardinal Schinner, entered into an agreement with the Cantons of Zurich and Lucerne, in accordance with which these cantons undertook to supply two hundred and fifty men as a body-guard for the Pope. Since then the Pope has always had around him a corps of Swiss Guards, although in the course of time their number has been reduced and the conditions of their service have changed.

When the corps is at full strength it has the following officers, all of whom rank three degrees higher than their titles indicate: one captain, one lieutenant, one second lieutenant, one chaplain, one quartermaster, one judge, one *esente,* four sergeants, seven corporals, two turnkeys, and two drummers.

The members of the Swiss Guard are called halberdiers, because they carry halberds on solemn occasions. Their number exceeds half a hundred, but varies considerably at times owing to retirements and recruiting. The general qualifications demanded in recruits are that they be Swiss citizens, Catholics, born in wedlock, unmarried, under twenty-five years, 1.74 metres tall in their stockings, healthy and free from bodily defects. Men unfit for military service in Switzerland are ineligible for the Swiss Guard. Any member may leave the Swiss Guard at pleasure, after giving two months' notice to the commander. After eighteen years' service each member is entitled to a pension for life amounting to half his pay; after twenty years this pension amounts to two-thirds; after twenty-five years to five-sixths, and after thirty years to his full pay.

The chaplain of the Swiss Guard has to celebrate the usual services in the little Church of S. Martino, which has been assigned to the Guard and lies near their quarters. It is also his duty to assist the members of the corps in all their needs and troubles, and to take a fatherly interest in their welfare. In a special audience granted to the chaplain each year, the Pope renews the great spiritual privileges granted to the Guard.

If on solemn occasions the Swiss Guard, who surround the *sedia gestatoria* on which His Holiness is borne, awaken our interest with their full harness and huge two-handed swords, that interest is greatly increased by the scarlet uniforms of the Noble Guard, their white leather breeches, top-boots, long white gloves, shoulder-belts, and helmets with plumes and horsetails. The Noble Guard follow the Pope when he appears in public, and later withdraw with him, since they are specially summoned for the protection of his sacred person.

The Noble Guard of to-day trace their origin from the Cavalleggieri, a kind of body-guard which was reorganized by Benedict XIV in 1744, and received new regulations as to service and rank from Leo XIII. With the exception of the quartermaster, the equerry, the four trumpeters, and the master-at-arms, all the members of the Guard must be of noble birth. Their captain, who is always a Roman prince, holds the rank of lieutenant-general, and the other officers rank correspondingly. The privates in this Guard hold the rank of captain. A detail of the Guard render service daily in the Antechamber, where they stand sentry at the door leading to the Privy Antechamber. Taking the place of the earlier cabinet couriers, they enjoy the right of carrying the news of their elevation to the cardinalate to prelates residing outside Italy, and of delivering to the latter, at their residence, the red skull-cap (*pileolus, zucchetto*). The captain, whose appointment depends, not on length of service, but on the free choice of the Pope (whether the person favored has previously belonged to the Noble Guard or not), receives on his appointment the highest papal decoration—the Order of Christ. Besides evidence of nobility, the applicant for admission to the Noble Guard must submit proof of his good conduct through testimonials from his pastor and bishop; he must not be over twenty-five or under twenty-one years of age, and must be at least 1.72 metres in height. The acceptance or refusal of an applicant is decided by a mixed commission. A Guard must procure the consent of the commander before marrying, and produce evidence that his proposed bride

Platoon of the Swiss Guard in Old Uniform

possesses an adequate dowry. During a vacancy of the Papal See the Noble Guard is subject to the College of Cardinals, which communicates its instructions to the captain through the Cardinal Camerlengo. The custom of having a picket of the Noble Guard escort the papal carriage on horseback has been discontinued for the time, but not abolished. Since under present conditions the service rendered by the Noble Guard is almost exclusively honorary, their purely military training is no longer so strictly insisted on.

When the pontifical procession of the Pope descends to St. Peter's for a canonization, we may see a third division of the papal military lining the entire path traversed. This is the Palace or Palatine Guard. Pius IX united the forces of the *civici scelti* and the *capotori* into one corps, to which he gave the name Guardia Palatina d'Onore (Palatine

Guard of Honor). The ordinances of December 14, 1850, declared expressly that no new institution was contemplated, but merely a reorganization of existing conditions. From the regiments recruited in 1860, four companies of eighty men each were formed in 1870, after the fall of the Papal States. Inasmuch as they belong to a corps of Guards, the officers enjoy a rank one grade higher than their name indicates. The lieutenant-colonel in command thus has the rank of colonel, and the other officers rank accordingly. While the Swiss Guard has for its task the guarding of the Pope's person, the Palatine Guard is devoted to the service of the

Colonel Commander Repond
of the Swiss Guard

Pope. In so far as their duties are concerned, they are subject to the Prefect of the Apostolic Palaces and the Majordomo. Again, while the Noble and Swiss Guards are soldiers by profession, the Palatine Guards are recruited from the Roman burgesses, and are summoned in turn to render service in the Antechamber and in connection with the more important festivals. Furthermore, unlike the other corps, the Palatine Guards receive no pay other than a yearly allowance for the maintenance of their uniform. The Palatine Guard guards the Conclave during its sessions, and then takes its orders from the hereditary Marshal of the Conclave, Prince Chigi. While performing this duty, a company of Guards occupies the Cortile del Maresciallo, being thus stationed where the Marshal has his headquarters.

We have seen that the Noble Guard renders service in the immediate vicinity of the Holy Father, that the Swiss Guard is entrusted with the guardianship of the person and dwelling of the Pope, and that the Palatine Guard is a guard of honor in the papal service. When we remember that the interior of the Vatican Palace, with its huge dimensions and numerous inmates, and the Vatican Gardens cannot be left unguarded, the necessity of a police force sufficiently numerous to undertake this responsible duty becomes evident. The official title of this body is Gendarmeria Pontificia addetta ai Sacri Palazzi Apostolici (Papal Gendarmes assigned to the Sacred Apostolic Palaces).

Shortly after his triumphant return from imprisonment in France, Pope Pius VII (1800–1823) organized a select body of police under the name of Carabinieri Pontifici (Papal Carbineers). By decree of February 16, 1850, their name was changed to Veliti. After retaining this title for only two years, they were given their present title of Papal Gendarmes. They discharge the duties of both court attendants and police. As court attendants the Gendarmes render the service proper to their position in the Antechamber. One of the papal reception rooms is named after them, as already stated, because a small body of Gendarmes in full-dress uniform

Captain of the Swiss Guard

with high busbies are stationed there on solemn occasions. As a police corps, the Gendarmes are entrusted with the guarding of the palace and the patrolling of the Vatican Gardens, a duty which they perform day and night. One division of Gendarmes is accommodated in the quarters of the Swiss Guard in the Torrione di Niccolò V, but the remainder dwell in their own barracks in the Vatican Gardens. They are all upright men of good bearing. They must have had an untarnished record in the Italian cavalry, and must produce unexceptionable testimonials from the spiritual and secular authorities of their native town. Like the Swiss Guard, they also have a band, which frequently gives a concert in the Cortile di S. Damaso. The strict discipline maintained in the corps insures the conscientious fulfilment of its duties.

Every forenoon a division of the Gendarmes, under the command of an officer, is stationed in service uniform in the Cortile di S. Damaso. These inquire into the business and identity of every visitor and give him whatever directions are necessary to reach his destination. Should his answers be unsatisfactory, a Gendarme is assigned to escort the visitor, and accompanies him until convinced of the truth of his statements. The duties of the Gendarmes do not bring them into contact with the outside world, since the Swiss Guards, as already explained, guard all doors and gates leading to the city.

It will thus be seen that, of the four military corps which render service in the Vatican, the Swiss Guard would have to bear the first shock of an attack on the Palace, since to them is entrusted the defence of the entrances. The Gendarmes, all of whom are quartered in the palace or the Gardens, would be the second line of defence. It is unlikely that the Palatine Guard, consisting of Roman burgesses who dwell in the city, could arrive in time to render much assistance. Of the Noble Guard, also, probably only a very few would be found in their quarters on the Cortile del Maresciallo, unless they had been summoned beforehand.

In view of the possibility of a sudden attack on the Vatican by the

Sergeant Banner-bearer
of the Swiss Guard

anti-clerical factions, the commander of the Swiss Guard has provided his men with the most modern weapons, and the necessary ammunition has been procured. Hand-grenades have also been prepared. An exhaustive study of the strategical possibilities of the palace has resulted in a plan according to which certain portions, which could not be held with the forces at the disposal of the Vatican officers, would be evacuated immediately. The other portions could be successfully defended for a long period until help would arrive from the Italian Government or the better-disposed citizens. It is certain that before an enemy could cross the threshold of the Bronze Gate or of any other entrance included in the plan of defence, the last member of the Swiss Guard would shed his blood in defence of the Pope, and sell his life dearly. The reorganization of the Swiss Guard has made it a highly capable military corps, every member of which is fully conscious both of the honor of his position and of the accompanying responsibility. With the active support of the other corps, in so far as they can be mustered in case of a sudden attack, it will always be able to withstand successfully the first onset of any fanatical mob. It should be here remarked that various uprisings against the Vatican have been attempted in the past, but the authorities have hitherto succeeded in nipping all such attempts in the bud, so that nothing serious resulted.

Any person, therefore, who entertains the idea that the Vatican soldiery are a body of no importance, labors under a serious mistake. In the first place, he completely loses sight of the above-mentioned possibility of an anti-clerical assault on the Vatican, and, in the second place, forgets that so huge a palace needs careful guarding, both within and without, if disorder or happenings still more serious are to be avoided. Undoubtedly, the Pope would not bear the heavy cost of maintaining this armed force if he were not quite convinced of its expediency, and even its absolute necessity. The ecclesiastical, scientific, and artistic interests of the Vatican, of which the Pope is the guardian, are of such world-wide importance that

Sergeant of the Swiss Guard

he may neglect no precaution in taking measures for their protection.

LEGAL POSITION OF THE VATICAN.—The above remarks may lead many readers to ask the question: What is the exact legal position of the Vatican at present, surrounded as it is by Italian territory and possessing no free outlet to other countries?

The answer to this question is furnished by the Law of Guarantees of May 13, 1871. When the Piedmontese entered Rome through the breach in the Porta Pia on September 20, 1870, they seized immediately all the possessions of the Papal States, whereupon the independent existence of these States came to an end. Pius IX, who had resided earlier in the Quirinal Palace, then occupied the Vatican. Halting before the Vatican, and abstaining also from occupying the Lateran, the victors proceeded to study the question of the legal position of the Pope under the new conditions. Although the Franco-Prussian War then held the world in suspense, the new masters of Rome fully realized how deep and wide-spread a commotion their step had caused both among the Catholics of the world and among the Powers. Prompt action was therefore indispensable before concerted steps could be taken to give expression to the general feeling of disapprobation. After long negotiations, the Italian authorities decided upon the draft of a law which was to guarantee the position of the Pope as the supreme head of the Catholic Church. In the extended discussions in the Italian Chambers the intentions of the Government were fully explained by its representatives, so that the character of the law executed by Victor Emmanuel on May 13 was established beyond possible doubt: (1) The law had for its basis, not Italian, but international law; (2) consequently, all alteration of this law at any future date by the Italian legislature, without consulting the Vatican, was excluded; (3) the law thus became binding for the Italian Government, regardless of the fact whether it was recognized or not by the other party as of valid origin; (4) the Italian State bound itself so completely that only by an act of violence, in violation of an international public obligation voluntarily undertaken, can it alter any portion or the whole of this law.

Swiss Guard

This interpretation, the correctness of which has been so often demonstrated in long legal argumentations, is accepted by all responsible Italian statesmen. This, however, does not deter the anti-clericals from incessantly demanding the abrogation of the law, and from making it the chief issue of their programme to bring the Pope under the Italian law. But so long as a government which appreciates its responsibilities stands at the wheel of state in Italy, there can be no fear that their demand will be given serious consideration. Under present political conditions it is evident that, to avoid foreign complications, the Italian Minister for Foreign Affairs would be the first to offer the most strenuous opposition to any measure aimed at making a prejudicial alteration in the legal position of the Pope. Thus, despite the hubbub raised by the Socialists, Italian statesmen are convinced that in this matter it is wisest to pay heed to the principle: *Quieta non movere* (Let well enough alone).

It may be asked what are the special provisions of the Law of Guarantees. In the first place, the Italian State undertakes to pay to the Pope a yearly sum of 3,225,000 lire ($650,000). Should no claim be entered for this sum, it is allowed to accumulate for five years and then reverts to the Italian exchequer. Although the sum has never been claimed by the Pope, it is still included without debate in each annual

Budget. Supposing a claim should now be entered for the payment of this money, would the Italian State b^ obliged to pay all the arrears s: ice 1871? It appears that it would undoubtedly have to do so, since the ordinance providing that the sum voted should revert to the Treasury each five years is merely a matter of financial expediency which cannot affect the legal claim of the Pope to the money guaranteed him.

In the second place, the Law of Guarantees provides that the palaces of the Vatican and the Lateran, and also the summer residence of Castel Gandolfo, shall be extra-territorial. This means that the Italian Government may exer-

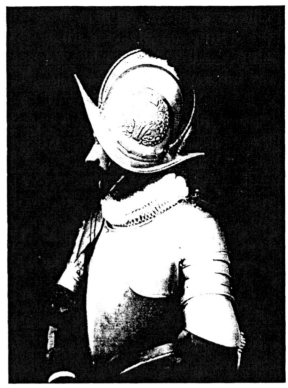

Swiss Guard in Old Uniform

cise no authority whatever in these places; its powers end at the gates of these buildings. They cannot subpœna or tax any person in the papal service. In these palaces the Pope rules as an independent sovereign.

In the third place, the Law of Guarantees gives the Pope the right to receive accredited ambassadors and envoys from all powers with which he desires to cultivate diplomatic relations. Of this right he has always availed himself, so that there are in Rome two diplomatic corps —one accredited to the Quirinal (where the King lives), and the other to the Vatican. As a consequence, the Italian Government must concede to these Vatican diplomats and their residences all the privileges granted to the persons and residences of diplomats throughout the entire civilized world. Again, the Italian Government can never prevent the Pope from accrediting at pleasure his diplomats—for example, his nuncios of the first and second classes, his internuncios, apostolic delegates, and resident ministers. From these facts and considerations it is beyond denial that, now as earlier, the Pope is a sovereign in the strict sense of the word. When Bismarck addressed his famous letter to Leo XIII, referring to him the settlement of the dispute between Germany and Spain over the Caroline Islands, he addressed the Pope as "Sire"—a term which is used only when addressing sovereigns.

In the fourth place, the Italian State is bound to send free to every part of the world all official telegrams of the Pope and the Holy See, whenever these are provided with the stamp of the Secretariate of State. All letters posted in Italy are delivered free to the Pope.

The other less important provisions of the law may be passed over here, inasmuch as the Pope has never recognized the law as of valid origin. The Italian Government, however, has repeatedly declared that it regards itself bound by every provision of the Law of Guarantees.

In the seventies of the last century there was no recognition between the Italian and Vatican authorities. The wound was too fresh to permit of any *rapprochement,* even in an entirely unofficial way. The most illuminating

Noble Guard of His Holiness

evidence as to the position at that time is afforded by the refusal of the Italian Government to guard the remains of Pius IX when they were brought from St. Peter's to their last resting-place in San Lorenzo. The coffin of the great Pontiff very narrowly escaped being thrown into the Tiber by an irresponsible rabble. A change has since taken place, for time has shown that an interchange of information between the Quirinal and the Vatican authorities is of advantage to both. All communications, however, are carried on through non-official agencies, and both parties, while preserving unaltered their fundamental attitude, aim at being good neighbors, inasmuch as circumstances forbid them to be close friends.

In maintaining his claim to the temporal power, Pius X took exactly the same position as Pius IX and Leo XIII. The passing of the years has not altered this claim. The negotiations for a reconciliation, twice inaugurated under Leo XIII, came to naught, and no attempt to renew them was made by Pius X.

Throughout the world the Pope is known as the "Prisoner of the Vatican." In what sense is this term to be interpreted? The actual foundation for the expression rests on the fact that Pius IX, Leo XIII, Pius X and Benedict XV have never set foot outside the Vatican and its gardens. As Popes, they have never stood on Italian soil. There exists thus in reality a "Vatican Captivity"; of that there can be no doubt.

But what is the legal significance of this attitude? It means that the entering into Italian territory could scarcely take place without the recognition of some of the conditions created on September 20, 1870, and this recognition has been withheld by each successive Pope.

It must not be imagined that the three Popes since 1870, who, having once entered the Vatican, never afterwards left it, have found life in this rich and glorious palace uniformly agreeable and pleasant. Even the most beautiful palace loses its charm when it serves as a setting for a lifelong imprisonment. Pius IX, Leo XIII, and Pius X discovered how bitter it was to have one's freedom straitly limited, to be for ever debarred from beholding *de visu* many places and objects which hold for one a special interest. As they have stood at the window of their apartments, and allowed their gaze to sweep over Rome, a regretful yearning must have often risen within their breasts, to be smothered only by a prayer of resignation.

LAW COURTS.—In the extensive dealings which the household administration of the Apostolic Palaces necessarily has with contractors and purveyors, and upon numerous questions of equity and law, some differences of opinion and disputes cannot but arise. Since the Vatican boards cannot be cited before the Italian courts, some provision had to be made so that outside parties might seek and find justice in the Vatican. Under the name of Commissions of Prelates, courts of law have been established "to settle all disputes with, and claims against, the Palatine Administration." The Commission of the first instance and of the second instance (court of appeals) consists of three judges; in extraordinary cases, both commissions sit together under the presidency of a seventh prelate and with the assistance of a secretary. In all questions of law the Prefecture of the Palace has a special counsel as its legal representative. Although this board no longer has a special court, it still retains a special inquisitor, who practically takes the place of the Court of the Prefecture. In criminal cases, provided that the criminal action occurred within the limits of the palace, this official conducts the investigation, establishes the facts, and then hands the accused, together with the official report of the case, over to the Italian authorities, which continue the criminal proceedings in the usual way.

In civil disputes the procedure is as follows: The case is begun by lodging written complaints with the Court; within an appointed period the defendant answers, also in writing. Further replies from each side are then permissible. On the conclusion of these written explanations, or after the lapse of the appointed interval, which has come to an end without the lodgment of further papers, the decision is given and is, according to the ancient custom of the Curia, announced on placards hung in the official chamber. A six months' interval from the date of the decision is allowed for an appeal. These Courts or Commissions are empowered to employ every means of arriving at a knowledge of the facts, such as the summoning of witnesses, the administering of oaths, the taking of corroborative or supplementary evidence on oath, the consulting of experts, and so on. The legal fees are regulated according to the provisions of the laws of the Papal States in 1870. The small recourse had to these Commissions shows that the palace boards

Officers of the Palatine Guard

make it a rule to arrange disputed points with the other party in a friendly way. As years often elapse without any resort being had to them, these Commissions lead a very quiet existence.

MEDICAL AND HYGIENIC BOARDS.—In so far as the medical, sanitary, and hygienic service of the Vatican is concerned, the following details may be given. Under Leo XIII there were already a papal physician and surgeon in ordinary. Pius X placed things on a somewhat different footing by appointing an acting and a consulting physician. The reader will remember what unselfish devotion was shown by both these physicians when the Pope was desperately ill in 1912. While nothing could be more honorable than this attendance on Christ's Vicegerent, the duty is also a very responsible one. And it is doubly responsible when the patient can be persuaded only with the greatest difficulty to obey the orders of his physicians and to abstain entirely from work. Tact, care, and energy are as important in such cases as medical skill.

The general sanitary corps of the Apostolic Palaces was reorganized in 1893 and placed on an entirely modern footing. This corps consists of a director, five physicians, and a number of assistant physicians. Two of the physicians are assigned to day and two to night duty. The Swiss Guards are attended by a special physician, and when they are so sick as to require nursing they are brought to the Hospital of the Swiss Sisters of the Cross in the Via S. Basilio. The assistant physicians take the place of the regular physicians when some obstacle prevents the attendance of the latter. Both classes of physicians have to appear at all great functions, when they occupy, with two Sisters of Mercy, a specially erected ambulance station, and are thus on the spot to render medical aid if an accident of any kind should occur among the vast throng of persons assembled.

This College of Physicians is assisted by two apothecaries, who must have always in readiness, especially on great festivals, the necessary materials to render relief. These apothecaries conduct a public pharmacy, which was formerly situated in the Cortile di S. Damaso, but is now located more favorably for general purposes in the Torrione di Niccolò V. Since the Vatican pharmacy distributes medicines to every one at the prices fixed by the Italian Government for the poor, it is extensively availed of. The apothecaries belong to the order of the Brothers of Mercy, which has its mother-house in Rome on the Island of the Tiber. The apothecaries proper are assisted by some of their brothers in religion, since the business of the pharmacy is extraordinarily heavy. When the Pope is sick one of these brothers takes full charge of the nursing of the patient, and is responsible for the execution of the physician's orders. In the pharmacy hangs a list of the residents of the palace, who are entitled to free medicines. The sanitary corps and the pharmacy are under the immediate supervision of the Prefect of the Apostolic Palaces. The supervision of the hygienic equipment of the palace is in the hands of the director of the College of Physicians, who is assisted in the matter by the technical boards of the Prefecture. When an infectious disease breaks out in Rome, detailed instructions are prepared for the administration of the palace, with a view to obviating as far as possible all danger of the disease being brought within its precincts. The plentiful water supply and the excellent drainage system of the Vatican have rendered this danger very remote.

DEPARTMENT OF REPAIRS.—The architectural repairing of this huge mass of buildings is under the general supervision of the Prefect of

Officer of the Papal Gendarmes

Marshal of the Papal Gendarmes

the Apostolic Palaces, and under the special supervision of the Foriere Maggiore, to whom reference has been already made. The office of Architect of the Apostolic Palaces is committed to a prominent member of the profession, whose assistant, known as the Sotto-Foriere, is also a trained architect. It will be easily understood that where there are so many roofs and walls, only the most careful attention can guard against serious damage. Throughout the year this department is busily engaged keeping everything in repair, and when extensive repairs are undertaken in regular succession the assistance of outside workers has to be requisitioned.

Naturally, one of the duties of the architectural department has been to prepare various plans of the Vatican Palace, and its officers feel always incited to inquire further into the mysteries of the buildings. But, notwithstanding all their past inquiries, it still happens that whenever extensive alterations or repairs are undertaken they stumble across some stairway of whose existence no one had been aware. Consequently, however exact they may be for the main divisions of the palace, none of the plans remains for long entirely reliable in all its details regarding the portions which have been used perhaps for centuries as living-rooms or magazines, or perhaps left entirely unoccupied.

It is evident that the architectural care of the Vatican Palace is a very difficult task. The fact that not a single serious accident has resulted from the numberless water-pipes, the more recently installed hot-water pipes, the great sewerage system, or the conduits for gas and electricity is sufficient proof of excellent supervision. In a modern palace these works present scarcely any difficulty; but in an ancient palace like the Vatican, planned without the least regard for these modern requirements, their installation and maintenance present inconceivable difficulties.

FIRE BRIGADE.—Naturally, the Vatican possesses its own fire-brigade,

Papal Gendarmes in Service Uniform

called the Guardia del Fuoco, although a fire is one of the rarest occurrences in the palace. When, a few years ago, a fire broke out in the Manuscript Clinic of the Vatican Library as a result of the spontaneous ignition of some acids and other chemicals, the chief danger was that which threatened the valuable manuscripts. With a great effort, however, the Guardia del Fuoco succeeded in extinguishing the fire after two hours. Had an equally extensive fire broke out in any other part of the palace, the same trouble would of course have been taken to extinguish it, but it would not have caused so much anxiety as was felt by the Pope, the Cardinal Secretary of State, and the Librarian during this short interval on account of the unique treasures of the Library. Since the Guardia del Fuoco has little or nothing to do at its proper calling, the members of the brigade are called upon to discharge other duties; but the fire-brigade station on the Cortile di S. Damaso is, of course, never completely depleted of its staff.

HEATING SYSTEM.—The present writer remembers well the time when a huge copper receptacle, filled with blazing coals, stood in the Sala Clementina. Night and day during the winter, the heat which radiated from this stove had to suffice for the picket of Guards stationed there, for there was then no other source of heat. Conditions were the same in the Anticamera Bassa and the most important of the reception rooms. The halls were not arranged for any well-ordered system of heating. Often has the writer warmed his stiffened fingers at the stove in the Secret Archives before he could resume his writing. Throughout the palace ruled the ancient and primitive methods of heating. Foul gases were frequently generated, causing a dizziness, if not a violent headache, to every one present.

That some method of heating was extensively used by the Curia in the earlier centuries is clear from the account-books of the Apostolic Chamber. But at that period the windows were constructed, not of panes of glass, but of waxed white linen. With the introduction of glass, which afforded an infinitely better protection against the inclemencies of the weather, the use of the huge fireplaces seems to have ceased.

However that may be, it is certain that the problem of heating the Vatican Palace according to modern methods offered unusual difficulties. Under Leo XIII the question was first considered, and was then made the subject of long and careful study. Every one knows that when a system of central heating is installed, the heat as it radiates upwards is very liable to produce in the course of a few years black stripes on the walls, which are very objectionable. Again, since the walls of the reception rooms are hung to three-fourths of their height with damask, while the other fourth is covered with frescoes, the problem of installing the system became doubly difficult. In the living-rooms of the Pope, occupied by the late Cardinal Rampolla when he was Secretary of State to Leo XIII, the task was far easier.

A very important matter connected with this heating problem was the inquiry into the possible benefit or injury to the paintings in the Sistine Chapel if this were heated. With the use of the earlier heating methods it was possible to raise only very slightly the winter temperature of the Chapel. The Chapel, however, was greatly heated during important functions, when it was filled with a great crowd of persons and a huge number of candles were lighted, as was the case in connection with comparatively many functions before 1870. This sudden raising of the temperature of the Chapel made the walls sweat, and the fine dust raised by the crowd of persons present and the smoke from the candles settled on the sweating walls. In the course of the centuries a crust was thus formed on the mural and ceiling paintings, which, while it could not destroy, greatly impaired their unrivalled beauty. If by skilful, regular, and uninterrupted heating one could succeed in

Residence Erected by Pope Pius X for the Vatican Servants and Employes

warming the walls in such a fashion that the temperature of the Chapel would penetrate deeper and arrest the cold coming from outside, it might then be hoped that the sweating of the walls would be reduced to a minimum on occasions when a great throng of people assembled in the Chapel.

These considerations led to a decision of great importance in the history of art—namely, to include the Sistine Chapel within the circuit of the first central heating system installed in the Vatican Palace. And experience has shown that the good effects that were hoped for have been attained. It must not be imagined, however, that the same demands are made on the heating plant in the Vatican as are made on heating plants in more northern climes. Such is far from being the case. It is quite sufficient—and an Italian would find anything more very unpleasant—if the ordinary winter temperature of the rooms is raised a few degrees. The inconveniences and damage usually caused by central heating are thus reduced to the minimum.

After the installation of the first heating plant, the system was extended in the following years to other portions of the palace. The Vatican Library and the Secret Archives were given their own plant, and the innovation proved especially agreeable in the Leonine Hall of the Library, since in winter this huge room was always swept by an icy draft. The working conditions of these two departments are now very much better than formerly, for which readers cannot feel too grateful.

LIGHTING AND ELEVATOR SERVICE.—As there was in the Vatican Gardens great water-power to be harnessed, the Prefecture of the Apostolic Palaces had an electric power-house installed to provide light for the whole palace. The new passenger elevator is also worked by electricity, although the old elevator in the Cortile di S. Damaso is still worked by water-power. It is worthy of remark that Pius X was the first Pontiff to use a modern elevator as Pope. On August 5, 1903, when he was returning from receiving the homage of the Roman prelates in the Sistine Chapel immediately after his election, he waved aside the papal chair which was waiting for him at the door of the Chapel, and proceeded on foot through the Sala Regia, the Sala Ducale, and the Loggie of Giovanni da Udine. On reaching the entrance of the elevator, he directed that he be taken up from the ground floor. His whole escort stood speechless; such a thing could not have happened under Leo XIII, who could never have pictured a Pope using an elevator to overcome differences in altitude.

It has just been said that Pius X is the first Pope who used a *modern* elevator. More than three hundred years ago, however, there was a passenger elevator for the Popes—not, indeed, in the Vatican Palace, but in the Castel S. Angelo. When the Popes were compelled to fly for safety to the strong fortress of S. Angelo, as was frequently the case at the end of the fifteenth and at the beginning of the sixteenth century, they used this elevator. It was very small and narrow, uncomfortable in the highest degree, and was naturally worked by hand. Times have certainly changed greatly since the days of Alexander VI and Clement VII.

DOMESTIC AND CLERICAL STAFFS.—There is a vast number of servants and clerks engaged in the Vatican Palace. This can occasion no surprise when we remember all that is collected together into a comparatively small place. Especially worthy of mention are the servants of the Pope, known as the Palafrenieri. These are occupied in the inner corridor which connects the working-room of the Pope with the staircase leading to the story above. The visitor coming to an audience also sees them in the Anticamera Bassa, where they maintain order, receive the invitations, and give the necessary directions. They wear a dark-red

Spanish garb with knee-breeches. On the uniform may be seen the arms of the reigning Pope in brocaded velvet. Lace jabot, red silk stockings, and buckled shoes complete the handsome uniform.

Besides their private staff of servants, the Cardinal Secretary of State, the Maestro di Camera, and the Assistant Prefect of the Apostolic Palaces have also clerks and servants to assist them in their official capac-

Cortile della Stamperia Nuova

ity. The official apartments of the Secretariate of State are divided into three sections: (1) that for extraordinary and (2) that for ordinary ecclesiastical affairs, and finally (3) that for Apostolic Briefs. As may be easily imagined, a large number of persons are employed in this department. The household administration of the Apostolic Palaces also demands a whole staff of servants, each class of whom is recognized by a special badge. Again, the Picture Gallery, Museum, Appartamento Borgia, Stanze and Loggie of Raphael, Library, Secret Archives, and all the other dicasteries of the Vatican Palace, need, of course, minor functionaries and a reasonable number of servants.

As a result of the accumulation of the official, court, scientific, and artistic interests in this one palace, which make it absolutely unique in the world, the crowd of servants is much greater than is usual in other great palaces of like dimensions. Those of the servants who are entitled to free lodging in the palace and who form the smaller part of the staff, were long given temporary accommodation of some kind or another, with the promise of better quarters in the future. And there still remained, after the hurried evacuation of the Quirinal Palace in 1870, the large number of servants who had resided there, and for whom quarters had to be found in the Vatican Palace.

In the matter of accommodation which it could offer to families, the Vatican Palace was very deficient. With this dearth of quarters Pius X dealt on a magnificent scale. After thoroughly considering the matter, and a searching investigation into the question of expense, he gave orders for a huge building to be erected beside the new Printing Offices. This building has been already referred to. Simple but solidly constructed, and fitted with every modern hygienic equipment, it will remain a glorious memorial to the solicitude of Pius X for the social welfare of the servants and employes of the Vatican.

The erection of the building enabled the Pope to attain another object. Since the large majority of his servants are married, and their quarters were formerly distributed over various portions of the palace, all the staircases of the palace were crowded during the forenoon with women taking their children to school, girls going shopping, and so on. This crowding of the staircases, which was then unavoidable, was regarded by the Pope as most unbecoming. He therefore chose the site for the new building in such a position that under no circumstances would it be necessary for the inmates to pass through the palace to communicate with the city. Intercourse with the town is now effected in the simplest manner through the door on the Torrione di Niccolò V, and all trooping along the staircases of the palace has come to an end.

It may be added here that the removal of the Picture Gallery from the rooms on the third floor in the Cortile di S. Damaso has freed the uppermost Loggia of the unceasing stream of visitors which used to extend to the immediate vicinity of the entrance to the living-rooms of the Pope. Furthermore, the scholars who work in the Vatican Library are no longer compelled to pass through the Appartamento Borgia and the Gallery of Inscriptions, but have now a more convenient entrance to the Library from the Stradone dei Musei, on a level with the street.

The whole Sistine portion of the palace and the stairways leading to it are now freed of an extensive traffic that had no business there. This object was steadily pursued by Pius X until he finally attained it—not, however, without great difficulties and expenses.

THE VATICAN PRESS.—A splendid example of the business insight and foresight of Pius X is afforded by a consideration of the reorganization of the Vatican Press and Private Press. For the full appreciation of this reorganization, it will be necessary to delve a little into the past.

The Sacred Congregation for the Propagation of the Faith (S. Congregatio de Propaganda Fide, known briefly as the Propaganda) had from the year 1626 a special printing-office in which were gradually manufactured the alphabets of all the most important Asiatic languages, which were then exceedingly rare and thus most valuable. For a long period the Polyglot Press of the Propaganda was the most re-

The New Vatican Press

nowned of its kind in the world. Although looted under Napoleon I, it soon recovered, and in the time of Gregory XVI (1831–1846) could still print in fifty-five languages—twenty-seven European, twenty-two Asiatic, and six other languages. And even though the high tide of the Polyglot Press had then passed, it could still lay before the Fathers of the Vatican Council in 1870 the Pater Noster in two hundred and fifty languages and dialects, printed with the use of one hundred and eighty different alphabets. From the commercial standpoint, this press is to-day of scarcely any importance, having grown to be almost a burden to the Propaganda. This fact should be kept in mind while we consider the history of the Vatican Press.

Pope Sixtus V (1585–1590), at the beginning of his reign, established at great expense a printing-office that was for that period entirely unique. This press was to print his revised edition of the Latin Bible. Sixtus entrusted its direction to the Venetian, Domenico Pasa, and appointed a special commission of Cardinals to supervise the printing.

In 1590 his "Biblia Sacra Vulgatæ Editionis" appeared in three sumptuous volumes, which were for various reasons withdrawn immediately after his death. In 1592, 1593, and 1598 appeared three editions of the "Vulgata Clementina," which is used even to-day. Since that time an exceedingly large number of works of the most varied character have issued from the Vatican Press. In the course of time the most important Oriental alphabets were manufactured to meet the needs of the pagan missions and for the promotion of linguistic studies, although the Typographia Medicæa (founded by the Florentine ruler of the house of Medici) already existed in Rome. Inasmuch as the Oriental alphabets were more urgently needed by the later instituted Propaganda than by the Vatican Press, the Holy See assigned these alphabets to the former.

In connection with the Vatican Press, which at first served for purely scientific and literary purposes, there soon developed a Private Press, in which were printed the acts, decrees, instructions, formularies, and so on, used by the Curia in the discharge of its official business. Though there was no well-marked division at first, a special department gradually developed, with strict secrecy and special precautions and a staff selected only from employes who had been found entirely trustworthy.

It has been already seen that the small court situated between the Cortile di Belvedere and the Cortile della Pigna is known as the Cortile della Stamperia (Court of the Printing-press). For a long period the Vatican printing office adjoined this court and there pursued its work peacefully and undisturbed. So long as all work was done by hand-presses and the business continued to be of a more or less patriarchal character this condition obtained. But when, at the opening of the last century, the modern presses began to find wider adoption daily; and when, later, the firm of König and Bauer of Würzburg introduced one innovation after another; and, lastly, when American inventors began to construct huge machines which could do in one hour more than the old presses could do in a week, the Vatican Press had to keep pace with these advances or to resign all claim to importance. Why reorganization was not begun immediately, need not be dwelt on here. It is sufficient to say that the lack of buildings adapted for a modern Press presented one great difficulty, and that an incomplete appreciation of the importance of the matter left the Press in the position of a stepchild. Nothing was done except what was absolutely necessary to enable the Press to cope with current demands.

The first impulse towards the reorganization of the Press was an indirect one, being given by the Prefect of the Vatican Library, Rev. Franz Ehrle, S. J. As the result of many petitions, the rooms adjoining the Library and previously occupied by the Vatican Press were placed at his disposal, since for a long period it had been impossible to find space sufficient for the needs of the ever-growing Library. But before the Prefect of the Vatican Library could enter into possession of his new rooms, another location had to be found for the Vatican Press. And since his inquiries in connection with the reform of the central administration in Rome had revealed to Pius X the sorry state into which the Polyglot Press of the Propaganda had fallen, he resolved

Cortile della Stamperia Vecchia

to cope energetically with the matter once and for all, and to organize a Press which, properly equipped, would be thoroughly efficient and, under capable management, might even become a source of revenue to the Holy See. With this correct appreciation of the situation, he decreed as follows: (1) The Vatican Press was to consist of a general and a private section; (2) the former riding-school of the Noble Guard (Cavallerizza) in the Torrione di Niccolò V was to be reconstructed in such a manner as to afford ample and proper accommodation for an entirely modern printing-plant; (3) the equipment of presses and type was to be completed so that the Press would be in a position to meet even the greatest demands; (4) the Propaganda Press was abolished;

(5) its whole stock of type (including the Oriental alphabets) was assigned to the Vatican Press; (6) in view of the amalgamation of the Vatican and Propaganda Presses, the Press was to be known thenceforth as the Tipografia Poliglotta Vaticana (Vatican Polyglot Press). These instructions were executed without delay, and thus, thanks to Pius X, a new, efficient, and well-conducted Press has been formed from two printing-plants handicapped by antiquated equipment and other defects.

In connection with the reform of the Curia, the Pope established an official law journal for the whole Church—the "Acta Apostolicæ Sedis." Almost from its very institution more than ten thousand subscribers have taken this periodical, which appears in stout numbers twice a month. A periodical of this nature is of great value to a large printing establishment, because it affords something to engage the staff steadily, and is also remunerative on account of the great number of subscribers. The great printing orders of the Roman Congregations (formularies and so forth), which were formerly placed anywhere by the separate bodies, are now all met by the Vatican Press, and are charged by the general administration to the separate Congregations. This task also adds greatly to the current business of the Vatican Press, and contributes very greatly to the consolidation of the internal affairs of the palace.

It is not possible here to give in detail the various activities of the Vatican Press; it may, however, be mentioned that a large number of works—some of them very costly, but from which only in rare cases do the returns correspond with the expenditure—must be undertaken to meet the official needs of the Curia. The printing of the new Psalter will serve as an example. Before the Holy Father and the Commission appointed by him for the rearrangement of the Psalter gave their final Imprimatur to the director of the Vatican Press, "proofs" of the text had to be so often printed, and the pages rearranged so many times, that the cost of this comparatively small booklet reached a huge figure. Since, however, it was desired to attain a result that would be satisfactory from every standpoint, it was not possible to avoid this heavy expense. The great sale of the Vatican edition, which still continues undiminished, may perhaps one day recoup the Vatican Press for this outlay.

From the general publishing department, which was always connected with the Vatican Press, have issued a large number of works, which are listed together with all new works in a recently published catalogue. No accurate list of all the books issued by the Vatican Press since 1587 has been yet published. Were such a catalogue in existence, it would serve as an extraordinarily valuable contribution to the history of culture. From the inventory of books for sale given in the above-named catalogue, we may choose the most important works to give the reader an idea of the style of publications issued.

That this list should contain a large number of official editions of the Acts and Decrees of General, National, and Provincial Councils was only to be expected. The first great plan of Pius X, the reform of Church music, finds clear expression in the "Graduale Sacrosanctæ Romanæ Ecclesiæ De Tempore et De Sanctis," published in 1908, and in the long and anxiously expected "Antiphonale Sacrosanctæ Romanæ Ecclesiæ pro diurnis horis," which was published in large octavo in 1912, and costs unbound eight lire. Among the large number of publications dealing with the history of Rome and of the Church, special mention may be made of a highly important work by Armellini, "Le Chiese di Roma dal Secolo IV al XIX," the only useful history yet published on the churches of the city of Rome. Mention may also be made of Calenzio's great work, "La Vita e gli Scritti del Cardinale Cesare Baronio," the very famous "Nova Patrum Bibliotheca" of Cardinal Angelo Mai, Cristofori's "Storia della Marina Pontificia," the folio edition of the Registers of Popes Honorius III and Clement V, and finally Denifle's celebrated specimen plates of the Registers of the Popes of the thirteenth century—"Specimina Palæographica Regestorum Romanorum Pontificum ab Innocentio III ad Urbanum V." In addition to editions of the Martyrology, there are works on Canon Law by famous authors, the Acta of Leo XIII and Pius X, the well-known Gandé edition of the "Theologia Moralis" of St. Alphonsus Liguori, the complete set of the highly important series of "Dissertazioni della Pontificia Accademia Romana di Archeologia," the three series of the "Pubblicazioni della Specola Vaticana," and the whole series of the "Studi e Documenti di Storia e Diritto," which offers a rich mine of information for the history of Rome. After mentioning the Catalogues of the Vatican Library, of which eighteen volumes have been printed and four are still in the press, we believe that we have given a sufficiently extensive survey of the wide publishing activity of the Vatican Press to enable the reader to complete the picture.

The Vatican Polyglot Press issues annually a stout volume under the title "Annuario Pontificio." It is described as an official publication, and is published by the Secretariate of State. This volume may be regarded as the directory of the Roman Curia. Annual publications of various kinds, giving more or less reliable information concerning the Curia and Church States, were issued for four centuries under different names and partly with official assistance and support. The little booklets of the sixteenth and seventeenth centuries, now yellow with age, are of great value to investigators into the personnel of the Curial administration at that period.

In the nineteenth century appeared an official publication called the "Annuario Pontificio." This, however, ceased in the year 1870, after which year a similar but more private publication was issued, entitled "La Gerarchia Cattolica, la Cappella e la Famiglia Pontificie per l'anno —— con appendice di altre notizie riguardanti la Santa Sede." In 1899 the title was somewhat altered, and the words "Edizione ufficiale" added, but these were omitted in 1905. The title continued to vary until 1912, when the old title "Annuario Pontificio" was resumed and the information given in the volume was much better arranged and greatly increased. This annual publication supplies the reader with information concerning the Papal Court and the central administration of the Church. Here will be found all pertinent information concerning the personnel of the Vatican and a good quantity of facts, which, however, might be very profitably increased. As is the case with all manuals of this kind, this publication is of most value to persons who, through other sources, already possess a knowledge of the organization with which it deals. For information concerning those priests who have received an honorary title from the Holy See this manual is important, since their names must be entered therein. No list is given of persons on whom an order or other decoration has been conferred.

The long-standing desire that this official directory should be published in Latin, which would best meet general needs, has not yet been realized. The publication of the Congregation of the Propaganda, the "Missiones Catholicæ," is issued in Latin; and what is possible in its case, appealing as it does to a much smaller circle of readers, is surely possible in the case of an annual of a much more general appeal. Since the new Editorial Board are very open to reasonable suggestions, we may hope that the decision to publish the "Annuario" in Latin will be soon reached.

Printed in the United Kingdom
by Lightning Source UK Ltd.
123083UK00001B/1/A

9 780766 139411